Public Relations and Communications for Natural Resource Managers

Second Edition

James R. Fazio
Associate Dean for Academics,
College of Forestry, Wildlife and Range Sciences,
University of Idaho

Douglas L. Gilbert
Late Professor of Wildlife Biology and
Head, Department of Fishery and Wildlife Biology,
College of Forestry and Natural Resources,
Colorado State University

KENDALL/HUNT PUBLISHING COMPANY
2460 Kerper Boulevard P.O. Box 539 Dubuque, Iowa 52004-0539

Copyright © 1981, 1986 by Kendall/Hunt Publishing Company

Library of Congress Catalog Card Number: 86–80172

ISBN 0–8403–3882–1

Printed in the United States of America
10   9   8   7   6   5   4

In memorial to
Douglas L. Gilbert

and dedicated to our students.

Contents

Foreword

Since the first edition of *Public Relations and Communications for Natural Resource Managers* was published in 1981, public scrutiny of natural resource management decisions, philosophies, and actions has intensified. It is increasingly important for today's natural resource managers to be skilled in presenting, explaining, and defending decisions involving natural resource stewardship. Not only must the explanations be in terms that the public understands but they must also be delivered effectively and efficiently.

Public relations and communications can no longer afford to be the stepchild of the decision-making process. The public is intensely and legitimately concerned about actions that affect our natural resources. Natural resource managers must recognize and respect that concern in order to establish and maintain credibility and keep the public trust. The process of communication, explanation, and evaluation is an ongoing one, and the success of public and private natural resource management efforts depends very much on its effectiveness.

Obviously, a clear understanding of how public relations and communications works is essential for students and professionals in all natural resource fields. *Public Relations and Communications for Natural Resource Managers* has become both an accepted text and a popular reference. It can be found in forestry offices worldwide and in classrooms in the United States and Canada.

The late Dr. Douglas L. Gilbert, regarded as one of the outstanding advisors on natural resource management public relations, wrote his first book on the subject in 1962 and followed it with a second in 1971. The first edition of this book, also coauthored by Dr. James R. Fazio, built on those two works while expanding the concepts to more disciplines and introducing new theories and techniques.

This edition represents a further refinement, expansion, and provides updated statistics and information including new material such as the use of computer technology in public relations. It is another step in the authors' long-time goal to stimulate the study and practice of public relations within the natural resource disciplines.

Clearly, this book has become and will continue to be a valuable text and reference. It is an outstanding guide to the understanding and practice of public relations and communications and should be read by all students and practitioners of natural resource management.

William H. Banzhaf
Executive Vice President
Society of American Foresters, 1988

ix

About the Society

The Society of American Foresters, with about 21,000 members, is the national organization representing all segments of the forestry profession of the United States including public and private practitioners, researchers, administrators, educators, and forestry students.

Objectives of the Society are to advance the science, technology, teaching, and practice of professional forestry in America, and to use the knowledge and skills of the profession to benefit society.

Gifford Pinchot and six other pioneer foresters established the Society in 1900.

Members subscribe to a code of professional ethics. The Society is the accreditation authority for professional forestry education in the United States. Its periodicals are the *Journal of Forestry, Forest Science, Southern Journal of Applied Forestry, Western Journal of Applied Forestry, Northern Journal of Applied Forestry,* and *Proceedings* of the SAF national conventions.

SOCIETY OF AMERICAN FORESTERS
5400 Grosvenor Lane
Bethesda, MD 20814

About the Authors

James Fazio was born in Pittsburgh, Pennsylvania and was raised in an urban environment. This helped provide an understanding of the human element in natural resource management that he could apply after graduating from West Virginia University with a degree in forest management. After working for the USDA Forest Service in three western states, and as associate editor of *The Northern Logger and Timber Processer,* he received a master's degree in conservation and communication at Cornell University while employed there in Cooperative Extension. He then received the Ph.D. in recreation resource management at Colorado State University while working part time in law enforcement and pursuing a research project on the use of communication to increase low impact camping knowledge among wilderness users in Rocky Mountain National Park.

Dr. Fazio has been active in The Nature Conservancy and was presented their Stewardship Award for management of a natural area preserve near Moscow, Idaho. He is also past president of the Idaho Trails Council, chairman of the governor's Lewis and Clark Trail Committee, and a member of the Society of American Foresters. He was the recipient of the Inland Empire SAF's Forester of the Year Award in 1983, and is the author of another book, *The Woodland Steward— A Practical Guide to the Management of Small, Private Forests,* and contributor to numerous books and periodicals.

A native of Colorado, Douglas Gilbert's roots were in the natural resource management professions. He worked with several state and federal natural resource management agencies and taught at Colorado State and Cornell Universities and the University of Montana. Bachelor's and master's degrees were earned at Colorado State University while his Ph.D. was from the University of Michigan. He belonged to many honorary and professional organizations and wrote for popular and scientific publication in numerous magazines and journals.

Although his major efforts were in wildlife science, and his degrees were in that field, he had a very strong interest in the people problems of natural resource management. His first book on *Public Relations in Natural Resources Management* won The Wildlife Society award for Conservation Education in 1964. In 1971 he published his second book, *Natural Resources and Public Relations,* and won the American Motors Conservation Award in 1972 for his many endeavors to improve public understanding of natural resources and their management. A book of which he was especially proud is *Big Game of North America—Ecology and Management* which he co-edited with John L. Schmidt for publication by the Wildlife Management Institute in 1978.

Dr. Gilbert passed away August 8, 1980 after a long struggle with cancer.

Preface

It has been said that a true professional is not only good at what he does, but he knows why he is good and is always trying to get better. This book is intended to help natural resource managers and students appreciate and get better at what we believe is the most important, yet most neglected, part of our profession. Effective public relations, and its principal component—communication—are integral to the successful stewardship of natural resources. We have attempted to show this relationship, emphasize its importance and provide the tools to transfer concept into practice.

The book before you expands on Gilbert's earlier book, *Natural Resources and Public Relations*. It, in turn, had grown out of a volume titled *Public Relations in Natural Resources Management* which was based largely on his doctoral work at the University of Michigan. *Public Relations and Communications for Natural Resource Managers* is, admittedly, a long and somewhat awkward title. It does, however, better portray the contents than the earlier titles. Still, the title is less than descriptive because the book can be applied by individuals other than managers. In short courses based on the same material, we have seen secretaries, technicians, administrators, dispatchers, consultants, extension specialists, recreation managers, information specialists and scientists benefit from learning the tenets and practices of public relations and communications. It is for convenience only that we use the term natural resource managers. The book is really intended for *anyone* with a professional interest in the management of any or all of our great natural resources.

All books have limitations and this one is no exception. This book will *not* produce public relations specialists. Like any other calling, public relations is too complex and intellectually demanding to allow comprehensive treatment in a single volume. But the essence is here. From this foundation the reader may want to delve more deeply into one subject or another, or to pursue a variety of the areas necessary to truly master public relations on a professional basis. This is not an apology. We have no desire to produce public relations professionals, cinematographers, television specialists or related professionals. Instead we have tried primarily to acquaint natural resource and recreation specialists with the basics, the theories, the pros and the cons of using the many tools of public relations to achieve management goals. We hope we also excite some interest in trying new approaches or polishing skills already possessed. But, in the end, most of us are specialists in *natural resources*. We can go only so far on our own, then we must recognize the need to work in concert with professional communicators.

On the other hand, none of what is presented is the exclusive province of information specialists, journalists or other professional communicators. This may be one of the problems facing the natural resource professions. It is analogous to a high school that sets up a new course in "Environmental Education 101." It is a sterile exercise if taught by one teacher and confined to a single classroom, for it will only be useful if integrated into all subjects and all facets of a student's life. By comparison, public relations and public information functions cannot be delegated to one person only. We likewise miss the point of public involvement if we assign it to a single specialist. Developing good public relations will only be possible if *every* employee of an organization understands its role and practices its tenets. This requires assistance from communication specialists—but *not* delegation to them.

We need to point out two features of this book that could cause misunderstanding if not explained in the beginning. One is our use of the masculine pronoun, he or him, and the possessive form, his. In the first draft we attempted to use more accurate combinations such as "he or she" and "his/hers". It was so awkward and difficult to read that we returned to the more traditional style. However, we wish to make it very clear that we intend the masculine word to reflect neutrality. We trust that any reader today realizes that what is true of men in any professional sense is equally true of women, *et vice versa.*

The other point is that the suggested references at the end of each chapter are by no means all inclusive. They are simply publications we have found especially helpful and want to recommend for anyone seeking more depth in the subject.

Preparation of this book has truly been a labor of love. We recognize the special qualities of natural resource management that make it a profession of individuals deeply devoted to stewardship. We recognize, too, that most are highly competent in their knowledge of wildlife and forests and of minerals, fish and livestock. They practice their profession not for personal gain or out of mercenary interest, but because of a desire to protect our quality of life and to pass on our natural assets to unborn generations. This is our professional tradition. But, we also recognize that certain forces have changed the nature of challenges faced by resource managers. As never before, we have the problem of increasing demands as a result of increased population, energy needs, leisure time, mobility, income, and the increased diversity and sophisticated organization of special interest groups. In many cases the demands confront a diminishing supply brought on by the competition of other land uses, excessive use or harvest, water pollution, drainage, improper highway or other construction and general ecological disturbances. And on top of all else has come renewed political interest as elected officials increasingly intervene in resource policy direction.

In short, natural resource management today operates in a highly charged political and social milieu. More than ever before the actions of managers are dependent upon the efforts of sympathetic individuals and groups. All professionals in the natural resources arena require a working knowledge of public relations if they are to develop and maintain the necessary support to meet today's challenges. Providing this knowledge and alerting professionals to its importance were central missions in the career of Doug Gilbert. His guidance and encouragement were badly missed in the preparation of this second edition and during the latter stages of the first. But the results— especially the thousands of students who have a better education because of his efforts—are the most appropriate memorial to my mentor and friend. I hope this book helps meet that purpose.

James R. Fazio
August, 1985

Acknowledgments

During the several years of preparing the first edition, then this updated second edition, it has been extremely gratifying to have the enthusiastic assistance of so many. I believe this reflects the growing recognition of the need for public relations in natural resource management, and for this, too, I am grateful.

I wish to acknowledge the following individuals and organizations for their assistance, and to extend sincere thanks to the many others who have made this possible.

For criticism of *Natural Resources and Public Relations,* a forerunner of this book, and for helpful comments about the first edition, I am indebted to students in my classes, photographer *par excellence* John F. Marshall, and former Humboldt State University student David Klippert. Helpful comments were also received from George Cheek and Richard Lewis then of the American Forest Institute, Eugene Decker of Colorado State University, and Dr. W. Leslie Pengelly of the University of Montana. Kathy Pendegraft, University of Idaho, served as typist and research assistant for the second edition.

Assistance from the Society of American Foresters helped make this project possible, and financial support for obtaining baseline data on information and education activities in natural resource agencies was provided by The National Wildlife Federation. University of Idaho graduate student Robert Mindick was the recipient of a NWF award and his research provided much of the 1979 information that was used in the first edition. The College of Forestry, Wildlife and Range Sciences at the University of Idaho provided support for a follow-up study in 1985. The aid of hundreds of employees in the agencies must also be acknowledged, for without their laboring through the questionnaires of both surveys it would not have been possible to obtain state-of-the-art data. Many agency personnel also generously assisted in providing photographs. Our thanks to these individuals although only their agencies are acknowledged with the photos.

I am especially grateful to those who spent untold hours reviewing, correcting, criticizing and otherwise helping to improve the manuscript of the first edition. These reviewers were: Dr. Ernest Ables, Head, Department of Fishery and Wildlife Resources, College of Forestry, Wildlife and Range Sciences, University of Idaho; Jack Cawthon, Associate Editor, Agricultural and Forestry Experiment Station, West Virginia University; Dr. David Cockrell, Assistant Professor of Outdoor Recreation, Division of Health, Physical Education and Recreation, Virginia Polytechnic Institute and State University; Dr. Paul Dalke, Professor Emeritus of Wildlife Resources, College of Forestry, Wildlife and Range Sciences, University of Idaho; Dr. Alex Dickson, Coordinator of Continuing Education in Forestry, University of New Brunswick; Dr. H. Sydney Duncombe, Professor of Political Science, University of Idaho; Dr. Jo Ellen Force, Associate Professor of Forest Resources and Forest Products, College of Forestry, Wildlife and Range Sciences, University of Idaho; Richard Guth, Leader, Information Group, Northern Rocky Mountain Region of the USDA Forest Service; Sam H. Ham, Associate Professor, Department of Wildland Recreation Management, University of Idaho; Dr. David L. Hanselman, Professor of Environmental Education/Communications, State University of New York, College of Environmental Science and Forestry; Donald

Hansen, former Program Manager, Cooperative Forest Fire Prevention Campaign, USDA Forest Service, Washington, D.C.; Richard Johnson, Public Relations Consultant, RFJ Associates, Oceanside, California; John Madson, Assistant Director of Conservation, Olin Corporation, East Alton, Illinois; John Marker, National Fire Prevention Officer, USDA Forest Service, Washington, D.C.; Ken Myers, Staff Assistant (Legislative Affairs), USDA Forest Service, Washington, D.C.; Dr. Lewis Nelson, Professor of Wildlife Resources, College of Forestry, Wildlife and Range Sciences, University of Idaho; Dr. James Peek, Professor of Wildlife Resources, Department of Wildlife Resources, University of Idaho; Philip V. Petersen, former Director of Information, Society of American Foresters; Dr. Jack Ward Thomas, Chief Research Wildlife Biologist, USDA Forest Service Range and Wildlife Habitat Laboratory, La Grande, Oregon; Fred E. Winch, Jr., Cornell University Professor Emeritus and Consulting Forester, Bradford, New Hampshire; and Dr. Alan Woolf, Assistant Director, Cooperative Wildlife Research Laboratory, Southern Illinois University.

Additional reviewers of parts of the second edition were Harvey Hughett, Director of the Instructional Media Center at the University of Idaho, and Michelle D. Crawforth, Senior Editor for Marketing Communications Practices, Eastman Kodak Company.

Douglas Gilbert expressed many times his special gratitude for having such a supportive family—his parents, brothers and sisters for being ever-encouraging and helpful in all ways, and his wife, Dorothy, who he said provided encouragement and was the impetus behind the original project.

I also am grateful to my family, including Walter and Ann Chapman for their encouragement and for providing shelter from my other responsibilities during the summer of 1979, a critical period in bringing the first edition to life. Finally, to my wife, Dawn, I say thanks for so many helpful suggestions, the many tedious reviews of manuscripts and proofs, and especially for patience during the countless weekends and evenings devoted to the preparation of this book.

JRF

An Introduction
to Public Relations

Chapters 1 through 3 provide the essential background necessary for understanding the substance, history and basic principles of public relations. Part I is the conceptual foundation upon which we can build using the techniques of following sections.

1

Introduction

Natural Resource Management is 90 percent managing the public and 10 percent managing the resource.

It was not too many years ago that young men and the occasional woman who entered the study of natural resource management did so almost entirely because of a love for the outdoor life. In most cases, the motivation was almost anti-social; a desire to escape urban life and live in the forest as stewards of the land and its wild inhabitants. The image was one of living somewhere in a pleasant log cabin, hunting and fishing and driving about in a pickup to oversee the land. It was a heroic image, too, with the rest of society seen as looking on with envy and admiration. It was indeed, the good life at its outdoor best. Today anyone entering forestry, wildlife or any of the other natural resource disciplines for those reasons is in for a rude awakening.

College students now have a better opportunity to learn what old timers in the field have come to find out through sometimes painful experience. This is an awareness that natural resource management is a practice closely confined within a social framework. It is stewardship of natural resources *for* people and in partnership *with* people. It is also the management of people. Both the student and the practitioner sooner or later realize there is much truth in the often-quoted saying— "natural resource management is 90 percent managing the public and 10 percent managing the resource." The sooner this maxim is accepted, the sooner we can focus on the problems associated with it. The sooner we do that, the greater our chances for keeping the natural resource management professions apace with the changing times.

PUBLIC RELATIONS PROBLEMS IN NATURAL RESOURCE AGENCIES

Despite growing awareness of the human element in natural resource management, problems and failures continue to plague the technically competent resource manager. Read almost any newspaper or professional journal or listen to a gathering of managers and this contention becomes clear. Some problems simply stem from an inability to get along well with people, such as fellow workers or the visiting public; but in most cases the problems run much deeper. Today, the majority of public relations failures result not from a blatant "public be damned" attitude, but rather from the lack of ability to analyze issues, enlist citizen participation in decisions, anticipate public reactions and move skillfully with preventive measures that will eliminate or reduce conflict and ill-will.

Examples of problems are found in every discipline within the broad area of natural resource management. Many are avoidable, most could be mitigated with proper handling, and a few must admittedly be placed in the category of hopeless. Before looking at the concepts and techniques that can alleviate many of these social impediments to management, let us look at a variety of problems that are prevalent today.

In the wildlife profession, one of the frustrating issues of recent times has been the rising tide of anti-hunting sentiment. Shaw and Gilbert (1974) documented an alarming 75 percent of randomly selected college students nationwide as expressing some degree of anti-hunting or anti-hunter sentiment, with 19 percent being totally against sport hunting. Those young people are becoming today's leaders, yet few planned efforts have been mounted to counter the forces that shape such negative attitudes. Instead, we see the anti-hunting issue widening to a movement that would even prevent the sacrifice of laboratory animals for the sake of scientific research.

Some wildlife agencies are even slow in responding to increasing public interest in non-game species and the various nonconsumptive uses of wildlife. The people who photograph, paint, observe and feed wildlife around their homes need the attentions of resource managers. The support of these publics can be invaluable during these changing times, but the people in these groups are often written off as "dickey bird" watchers.

Wildlife management has a history of exemplary performance by devoted personnel. There is, however, a minority still within our ranks who, in a single act of insensitivity, may undo the entire work of an agency. An illustration may be found in the case of a law enforcement class at a major university. The students were taught the highest ideals of law enforcement and conservation work, then were given the opportunity to ride along with sheriff's deputies and conservation officers on a patrol during big game season. To the amazement of the riders, and other students who would eventually hear the tale, on two different occasions patrolling officers stopped their trucks and shot deer from the side of the road! While the circumstances did not render these acts illegal, public relations sense in these officers was completely lacking. At higher levels in recent years, we have also viewed the specter of a high department official apprehended for illegally shooting geese inside city limits, another for using state boats for private recreation, and still another apprehended for dumping trash beside a roadway. We have seen, too, the confusing effects of the U.S. Fish and Wildlife Service proposing one course of action—steel shot, for example—with state fish and game personnel publicly supporting another—lead shot in this case.

The forestry profession is rife with examples of how public relations problems can interfere with the sustained yield of timber. In the next chapter we will see that the first classic public relations failure involved a brilliant, technically competent forester who ended up causing a university to lose its entire forestry program. More recently, a poorly handled controversy over the aerial application of a 2, 4, 5-T brought this silvicultural treatment to a standstill in northern Idaho. Why? Because of a gross miscalculation of public sentiment, failure to recognize individuals and groups potentially affected by the spraying, and an unfortunate use of name-calling by a forester who told the press that most of the opposition was a "lunatic fringe."

From Maine to California, clearcutting has become to the forestry profession what doe seasons have been to wildlife management for decades. In addition, road building, off-road vehicle restrictions, "Sagebrush Rebellion" sentiment, fire management and the trend toward contracting or other involvement of the private sector in public land management are among the many problems that call for the skills and knowledge of personnel trained in public relations.

Recreation managers, with almost constant contact with the visiting public, would be expected to possess strong abilities in public relations. Many do, but who has not been ignored at one time or another by a visitor center attendant, or greeted by "Hey, can't you read?" when accidentally ignoring a sign? In recent years there has been an erosion of public confidence in land management agencies that profess multiple use but burn down historic lookout towers with little or unconvincing explanation, and fail to maintain nature trails or roadside rest areas. Then, too, it is not uncommon for tempers to flare when campgrounds are full or the lack of a permit becomes a barrier to launching a raft or taking a hike. These situations do little for the managing agency and certainly do not contribute to public understanding or the enhancement of a visitor's recreational experience.

In the burgeoning field of research, there seems to be little progress in closing the wide gap between the scientist at the leading edge of knowledge and the manager who must try to apply the researcher's findings to the solution of everyday problems. Worse yet is the gulf between researchers and the taxpayers who, in most cases, must pay the bills. This was graphically illustrated in 1978 when national television focused on complex recreation research at Montana State University. The limelight came in the form of a television exposé broadcast on the popular program *Sixty Minutes*. Biological research has at times been featured as the recipient of Senator William Proxmire's infamous "Golden Fleece" award, the senator's way of telling the public how they are being "fleeced" by wasteful government spending. Without the careful incorporation of public relations as part of every research project, this area of natural resource management is particularly vulnerable to misunderstanding by local residents, tax weary citizens, politicians, and even managers and fellow scientists.

If these cases are typical of the problem, we might next ask what are the causes? While there are no simple answers to this question, there is reason to believe that at least four factors are to blame. First, although many of the problems are not new, they have been intensified by the great awakening of public interest in natural resources. This interest reached a crescendo on Earth Day, 1970, but the effects of that intensive public and mass media scrutiny of the natural environment will be with us for a very long time. The general public found it has a voice when it comes to resource decisions. Popovich (1978), writing in the *Journal of Forestry*, warned that since the late Sixties, the public has shown remarkably little reluctance to speaking its mind on complex resource issues. Foresters, he added, have been reluctant to speak theirs. He also pointed out that foresters have not always made the effort to understand public needs, as they must if they are to convince the public of their ability to fulfill those needs. Earth Day, the National Environmental Policy Act, and similar events and eco-legislation have changed the world—for resource managers at least. An understanding of public relations—in the highest form of its evolution—is crucial to gaining or retaining any resemblance of leadership in this new era of public concern.

Perhaps the evolving nature of public relations is in itself related to a second cause of our present state of affairs. As pointed out by George Cheek, vice president for public relations at Potlatch Corporation, public relations practice has changed dramatically in recent years. While the old approach was largely oriented to image building, the new approach relates much more to issues, and depends far more on facts. This will be discussed more thoroughly in later sections, but it must be said here that many managers, agency administrators, and even some public relations practitioners still hold the erroneous view that public relations is simply the spewing out of favorable information to "the public." While this is still an important part, it is by no means the whole. In an editorial appearing in *Parks and Recreation,* Richard Trudeau (1978) of Oakland, California's East Bay Regional Park District, wrote, "No longer can we afford the luxury of having a person . . . who routinely lets the public know when our swimming pools or lakes are open, or publicizes a recreational event, or even reports what has taken place at a park commission board of supervisors' meeting. Unfortunately, what we often find is what is termed as 'flack' by newspaper editors, one whose stories are deemed 'self-serving.' What is needed . . . is the ability to be problem-solvers." Listening to the community, needling the conscience of the organization, and seeking solutions to problems is how Trudeau explains the expanded role of public relations.

The first two causes could be dealt with, were it not for a third—the neglect of public relations in the college curricula at most institutions where natural resource managers are prepared for their careers. Some schools are adding more social sciences and communication to their curricula, but these courses are rarely applied directly to the management of natural resources. An exception for many years has been Colorado State University where foresters and other majors are required to take a resource-oriented course in public relations. In 1983 the University of Idaho also made such a course required, but only for its wildlife majors. In general, reviews of catalogs for the periods 1969–71, 1978–79, and 1982–83 have shown little progress in this important area, and absolutely none at some colleges, in every region of the nation (Fazio, 1983). It appears that what little training is made available is being taken primarily by future recreation resource managers. Foresters, wildlife and fishery managers, and range managers receive little or no preparation in what is perhaps the most crucial subject they will face during their careers.

Finally, there must be the *desire* to improve public relations, and it must permeate an agency or organization from top to bottom. New employees should be hired with this quality in mind, and administrators must not lose sight of its importance. Too often the individual who does attempt a first-rate job of public relations is hampered by low budgets, lack of appreciation by supervisors, lack of training and the lack of freedom to innovate and experiment. Sometimes, too, even when highly talented and well-trained individuals are available, they are not consulted by the decision-makers until after the decisions are made. In private industry this is usually less of a problem than in government. Industry seems more acutely aware of the need to include public relations as an integral part of the total operation.

Public relations problems in the natural resource fields will not cure themselves. If ignored or underestimated, they will grow worse and undermine the best intentions and technical capabilities of the profession. If these problems are addressed with the same care and planning that are given such management challenges as the outbreak of disease, insect epidemics or fire, considerable gains could be made toward the many benefits that accrue from good public relations.

THE VALUE OF GOOD PUBLIC RELATIONS

The value of good public relations is usually not realized until it is absent. Public relations can be reflected in the morale of an organization, in the quality and quantity of goods or services produced, and by public support—or lack of it.

Good public relations may be likened to dental health. Too often we don't go to a dentist until pain makes it necessary, whereas a little care on a regular basis would usually have prevented the problem. Similarly, good public relations is not missed until needed. Sooner or later it is realized that good public relations could have prevented most of the catastrophies that have resulted from poor public relations.

Figure 1.1. Signs and other facilities often become the target of individuals who have experienced a poor relationship with a managing agency. For any management practice to succeed, public support is a necessary first step. (Courtesy of Colorado Division of Wildlife.)

Schoenfeld (1957) summed up the value of good public relations when he wrote that we must have public support, or at least sufferance, if natural resource management is to be practiced. He pointed out that a favorable climate of public opinion *must* precede management. Public support or tolerance and favorable public opinion are indeed the end products of good public relations. For private enterprise this means the privilege of doing business, the freedom to do it profitably, and the sales that make it worthwhile. For public agencies it means the ability to exercise professional judgment in the management of natural resources for commodity production and the provision of recreational opportunities.

The list of specific values resulting from good public relations is a large one. It includes being able to attract high caliber workers both in the labor force and at the management or administrative level. Within the organization, good administration is possible only through good public relations. The reward is internal harmony and lower turnover rates. Externally, an important result is legislation that allows optimal management and provides adequate budgets, personnel, and laws to do the job right. Similarly, it means good relations with governing boards and commissions so that policies are in the best long term interests of the resource and the affected publics. Importantly, good public relations can reduce prejudice, cut away ignorance or apathy, and prevent misunderstanding. It can stir the social conscience of an organization and it can offer people a way to be heard.

Today good public relations also means compromise and the avoidance of court battles that are not only costly, but erode public confidence in decision-making processes. Many in all camps are calling for an end to the escalation of resolving environmental issues in the courts. Milton Wessel, a New York attorney and author of *The Rule of Reason: A New Approach to Corporate*

Litigation (1976), makes a case for the premise that prevailing courtroom tactics are not appropriate for environmental issues. According to Wessel, deceit, procedural delays and character attacks may be "sporting" in strictly private litigations, but serve neither the public nor corporations when complex scientific issues are involved and perhaps even survival of the world as we know it. The application of modern public relations practices should be used to the degree possible to prevent or resolve issues that might otherwise lead to court action.

Finally, a value of good public relations is peace of mind or the joy of living. This seemingly simple but immeasurably important attribute is a reward to all concerned—employees at all levels, the community, and society—when the principles and practices of good public relations are incorporated into the fiber of an organization and executed with skill and consistency.

DEFINITIONS OF PUBLIC RELATIONS

One reason that public relations has not been strongly incorporated into the natural resource professions is that it is often viewed with suspicion or distrust. To many, public relations is at best synonymous with a cover-up or "white wash"—and some workers have contributed to this reputation by shady acts or outright deceit. However, such practices do not constitute public relations any more than the fabrication of survey plot data could be considered forestry or wildlife management. As will be seen in Chapter 3, the principles upon which public relations is based completely preclude dishonesty.

Definitions of public relations are as varied as the practice itself. It is a field that includes diverse ideas and involves concepts and theories as well as activities and techniques. Rules, standards and patterns are still being established, and the profession is broad, complex and not as organized as some. Under these circumstances, it is not surprising that there is such a large number of definitions. However, after careful review of this subject, we have concluded that the most concise and appropriate working definition for the natural resource professions follows closely the one given by Cutlip and Center (1978):

> *Public relations is the planned effort to influence public opinion through good character and responsible performance, based upon mutually satisfactory two-way communication.*

This definition serves as the foundation of this book. Therefore, let us look at it more closely, for each part is essential. First, it is a *"planned effort."* It is not something that happens spontaneously, or at least not if it is to be effective over the long run. Deliberate procedures must be followed, as with any aspect of management.

Ultimately, the goal of public relations is *"to influence public opinion."* There is nothing immoral about this goal and it is usually not illegal; it is an essential fact of life in both the private and public sectors. In later chapters we will see that the intended influence must be aimed not only at people outside the organization, but also at employees, bosses and others we consider part of the internal public. We will also see that this concept is compatible with the need for public involvement in resource decisions.

"Through good character and responsible performance" should be an obvious ingredient of the definition, but it is the omission of this criterion that most often leads to the misconceptions about public relations. When good character, responsible performance, or both, are missing, public relations cannot help but turn into a cover-up. Inclusion of this phrase is the keystone of our definition.

Public relations must facilitate *"two-way communication."* This may not be possible in every action taken, but it must occur at some point in working toward the goal that the action is intended to achieve. For example, two-way communication may not be possible in a persuasive pamphlet prepared for mass distribution. However, preparation of the pamphlet would be on shaky ground if two-way communication was not part of the planning process. The opportunity to communicate must also be "satisfactory" to both parties involved in any issue rather than merely being a pretense on the part of either. Many so-called public involvement schemes leave citizens with a feeling of frustration because they feel their opinions are solicited but not heard. Organizations practicing public relations will be good listeners as well as good disseminaters of information.

Two Types of Public Relations Practices

General Functions

There are two distinct ways in which public relations is practiced. The first and most common in natural resource management is the constant day-by-day contact all employees have with the public. This includes such ordinary but important occurrences as answering the telephone, greeting office visitors, driving the organization's vehicle in traffic, answering questions, and generally conducting one's self in view of others. For lack of a better term, we will identify these activities as

Figure 1.2. Any employee becomes *the* organization to someone who may have no other contact with it. The general functions of public relations are therefore as important as the organized staff function. (Courtesy of USDA Forest Service.)

general functions. To be effective, general functions should conform to the overall definition of public relations. That is, they should be conducted in at least a generally planned or certainly a conscientious manner, be based on good character and acceptable performance, attempt to include two-way communication when appropriate, and should always have as their objective the positive influencing of public opinion toward the employing organization.

The general, daily practice of public relations should include *all* employees at all times. It is easy to understand that the conservation officer, maintenance worker, receptionist, secretary or truck driver is *the* organization in the eyes of the public who may have contact only with that individual. As the contact goes, so goes the impression that an individual will have of the entire organization. One slovenly, rude, or incompetent individual can significantly affect the agency's reputation or progress toward its overall public relations goals. No employee should be exempt from the responsibilities of performing the general functions of good public relations. Subsequently, employers should be responsible for adequate training in these functions just as they undertake training in the more obvious or traditional duties of the employee. Portions of this book, coupled with individualized in-service training, should assist any employee in the improvement of the everyday business of public relations.

Staff Function

The second type of public relations practice is the *staff function.* As the term implies, this is the more structured approach to public relations and uses the services of one or more individuals who specialize in the practice. This could range from the large public relations department at Weyerhaeuser Company down to a district forester with public relations as a designated part of his several responsibilities. Within the staff function falls the job of a carefully engineered operation. Here public relations should be planned according to needs and goals of the organization. The tools available to meet these obligations should then be selected logically and used with skill. Research, time-tables, sequential steps of execution, and evaluation are all essential parts of the effective staff function.

In private enterprise, consultants or public relations firms are often used to provide at least part of the public relations staff function. There is much to be said for this approach including, as it does, more accurate perceptions or fewer prejudices by someone outside the organization. Another advantage is that the use of outside services for such things as mass mailing, opinion polling, art, or photography, can often be obtained for much less expense than would be required to develop the necessary related staff positions within the organization. In the natural resource professions this procedure is rare. When the staff function exists at all, it is most commonly a small agency staff, a single individual, or one person with many other duties. It is also often a person trained in natural resource or recreation management—not in public relations. It is primarily for this kind of individual that this book is intended.

Related Fields

Within the broad field of public relations are numerous subfields, usually of a functional nature and more commonly used in industry than in government agencies. These include *community relations, employee relations, industry relations, public affairs, information services* and others, each having its own degree of autonomy and importance depending on the size and nature of the organization. Among natural resource agencies, the following titles are being used by divisions having public relations responsibilities to one degree or another:

Information and Education	Public Affairs	Conservation Education
Office of Information	Communications	Environmental Education
Interpretive Division	Visitor Services	Naturalist Services
Public Involvement Group		Communication and Public Affairs

Unfortunately, sometimes titles are adopted wholly out of enthusiasm for change or something new rather than in an attempt to align the functions of a staff or individual with accepted definitions. Consequently, an information office is re-named public affairs; or an environmental educator is termed a community relations specialist. As long as this happens, confusion will continue to hinder a clear understanding of public relations and the utilization of its tenets. It behooves administrators to seek out the best authorities in a field before establishing job titles or re-naming organizational units. This is particularly a problem in the closely related and sometimes overlapping areas of *information and education, interpretation, conservation education, environmental education,* and *public involvement.*

In natural resource management, offices of information and education, public affairs, or similarly named units, are frequently referred to as an agency's "public relations" program. In some cases, their functions and objectives do come very close to meeting the definition of public relations practice. Usually, however, the emphasis is only on information dissemination. It is usually an effort at mass contact with general audiences, and may or may not be a conscious attempt to influence public opinion. Often there is no attempt at achieving two-way communication and, indeed, there is little need to do this if the objective is simply to announce fish or game seasons, explain where Christmas tree cutting areas are located, or to tell visitors how to obtain permits for using a wilderness area. Public relations practice goes much beyond this.

Interpretation is clearly a practice and a field of its own. Interpretation at a park or other management unit most likely will contribute to public support and a favorable public image, but that is usually a peripheral benefit, not a traditional objective. According to Freeman Tilden (1977), who was considered by many the foremost authority on this subject, *interpretation is an educational activity to reveal meanings and relationships through the use of original objects, by first hand experiences, and by illustrative media.* The emphasis is on *revelation* of larger truths underlying the obvious. The ecology of a forest or pond, for example, requires interpretation for visitors to see more than trees or a pool of murky water. Also, the primary objective is to enrich the human mind and spirit, to enhance a visitor's experience in a natural or historical setting. Many of the tools of interpretation are the same as those used in public relations, but the purposes are usually different. Some similarities and differences between interpretation and the closely related fields of conservation education and environmental education should become clear when reviewing the history of public relations in the next chapter.

Public involvement activities and agency units are also sometimes thought of as public relations efforts, but they are by no means synonymous. Most importantly, public involvement is not intended to influence public opinion—at least not in the sense of gaining support for a particular side in an issue. At its best, public involvement *shares* resource decision-making with citizens-at-large. Influencing public opinion should come *after* this step.

Public relations can be thought of as either an autonomous staff function meeting a completely separate need than the above areas of activity, or as a concept that is intimately associated with all of these. In its purest form as a staff function, public relations—like the very term—is all but absent within government agencies. The reasons for this will be explained later, but essentially they result from a combination of historical circumstances and legal constraints (especially in the federal sector). Usually the public relations function can be seen as part of other jobs under an array of titles. It is present in part in the information positions, in interpretive services and even in public involvement. In many ways it is a hidden element, as though there is something shameful about identifying it for what it is. In the process it has become an anemic function. It has not realized its potential for improving the management of natural resources.

A Further Word about Words

Two additional points need clarification. Sometimes it is said that public relations is something that is always present, and will be either good or bad. This means that for any organization a *relationship* with the public exists, and this relationship will be either a good one or a bad one. This *relationship* is one meaning of the term public relations. It is this meaning that is being used when someone says, "We should do this because it is good for public relations." This is not the same as the second meaning—public relations the *practice*. The practice is *not* automatically present, as should now be obvious from its definition.

Additional confusion arises because of the plural term, public *relations*. Even though the term is plural, it is a noun and whether used in the sense of a relationship or a practice, it is used in the singular form. Therefore, it is correct usage to say "public relations *is* important in forest management."

Lack of standardized meanings, along with sometimes shady actions passed off in the guise of public relations, have cast this subject in a somewhat bad light. This chapter has been intended to establish a foundation on which to base our exploration of public relations—and its potential—in natural resource management. The definition presented here and the principles presented in Chapter 3 are important to this goal. These form the premise on which the case can be made for including public relations as an essential component of natural resource management.

SUGGESTED REFERENCES

Effective Public Relations by Scott M. Cutlip, Allen H. Center and Glen M. Broom. 1985. Prentice-Hall, Inc., Englewood Cliffs, New Jersey.

Experts in Action: Inside Public Relations edited by Bill Cantor and Chester Burger. 1984. Longman Inc., New York.

Lesly's Public Relations Handbook edited by Philip Lesly. 1983. Prentice-Hall, Inc., Englewood, New Jersey.

2

The Historical Perspective

Vox populi, vox Dei

Public relations as a practice is a turn-of-the-century phenomenon. For those who must have a father for every movement or discipline, a journalist by the name of Ivy Lee is a likely candidate in this case. Although the term *public relations* is said to have been first used by the Association of American Railroads in 1897 (Cutlip et al., 1985), it was Ivy Lee who sparked the evolution from lop-sided press-agentry to modern public relations practice. In his *Declaration of Principles*, mailed to local newspapers in 1906, he introduced the concept of supplying accurate information "frankly and openly" on behalf of his clients in business and institutions (Hiebert, 1966). With this refreshingly different approach, Lee ushered in the contemporary era of public relations.

But the roots of several concepts and tools now used in the practice of public relations extend far back into the history of civilization. Honors for the earliest may go to the lowly trademark or logo. Trademarks were developed well before the time of Christ (Nelson, 1977), perhaps by the Phoenicians as ships carried the work of their artisans throughout the known world. The ancients recognized what some modern resource managers have yet to grasp—that it is essential to obtain widely recognized identity for your product. Babylonian kings, 3,000 years before Christ, carried this idea to the extreme. Archeologists have discovered that in some cases they had their names stenciled on every brick being prepared for new temples (Presbrey, 1929). They were taking no chances that their good deeds would go unnoticed!

Eye-catching signs and skilled barkers were also among the ancient forms of communication to attract and influence the public. Publicity agents of sorts emerged in Greece five centuries before Christ, with one Simonides being noted for selling songs of praise. The savvy Greeks, and later the Romans, also recognized the all-important concept of public opinion. *Vox populi, vox Dei*— "the voice of the people is the voice of God"—is attributed to this era.

Communication related to natural resources also has its earliest roots in the Middle East—Iraq to be precise. There, in one of the cradles of civilization, archeologists have unearthed remnants of what was an early farm bulletin that told the farmers of 1800 B. C. how to sow, harvest, and irrigate crops and how to deal with field mice (Cutlip et al., 1985).

Much later, the early kings of England had spokesmen called "keepers of the king's conscience" to facilitate communication with the people. Some early Polynesian tribes had a "talking chief" and the real monarch did not utter a word. Throughout history, publicity, advertising, public opinion and communication have played an ever-expanding role in society. Even in the Dark Ages, we find that many good knights had the equivalent of publicity agents within their entourage to spread far and wide the news of their feats!

Publicity and advertising are inseparable from the very first events in the settlement of America. Persuasive communication was necessary to find colonists for the new land, and later to sway public opinion in favor of revolt against the motherland. Thomas Paine, Patrick Henry, Samuel Adams and Benjamin Franklin were among the skilled manipulators of public thought, and every school child is aware of their tactics (the Boston Tea Party, for one) and the results.

With the industrial revolution we can view the first vestiges of public relations as a practice, but only in the sense that the practice was almost a reversed image of the definition provided in Chapter One. This period is worth mentioning, however, for it reveals how the actions of some resource managers today are as antiquated as this doleful stage of development in the Nineteenth Century.

In both industry and government, good character and responsible performance was more a matter of whim than policy. Certainly two-way communication was lacking, and other than for election purposes or sales promotions, public opinion was considered of little importance. This was the era when *press-agentry* had its finest moments in the myth factory that gave us Davy Crockett and Buffalo Bill. P. T. Barnum, still almost a household word, is perhaps the embodiment of this period. Stunts, half-truths and gaudy promotional campaigns were standard fare of the day. Disasters and decisions were treated with silence. Companies and government agencies operated largely on the philosophy that "what the people don't know won't hurt them."

The last half of the century was marked by what Cutlip et al (1985) accurately described as "the wild, frenzied, and bold development of industry, railroads, and utilities." It was a time of public rebuffs that echo to this day. These were characterized by the likes of banker George F. Baker who responded to a reporter with, "It's none of the public's business what I do;" or J. P. Morgan who said, "I owe the public nothing;" or most famous of all, William H. Vanderbilt's reply to a reporter's insistence on the public's interest in reduction of railroad scheduling— "The public be damned!" (Shadduck, 1977). When the century came to a close, illegalities, immoralities and general disregard for the public welfare were probably at their zenith in the history of our nation.

As the Twentieth Century dawned, two factors combined to hasten the development of public relations. First were the conditions described above. Next was the development of a national network of rapid communication in the form of widely circulated magazines, press services and the syndication of feature articles. The two gave rise to the era of *muckraking*.

Muckrakers were a new breed of journalist, forerunners of today's investigative reporters, and they thrived on brazen exposés. They were a key factor in the Progressive Movement and social reform, and few industries found immunity from their pens. Industry responded with defensive publicity and "whitewashing," but it was as ineffective then as such tactics are today. Not until Ivy Lee laid the foundation consisting of truth, honesty and openness did big business begin to reverse its image and effectively take the offensive in influencing public opinion.

In the years that followed the establishment of Lee's public relations agency (he did not use the term *public relations* until about 1916), notable developments marked the steady growth of the profession. President Woodrow Wilson exemplified the new public relations philosophy when he said, "Anything crooked should be out in the open. It will either straighten out or disappear." It also was Wilson who said, "We should worry about telling the people what Washington thinks, but we should worry more about telling /Washington what the people think." He employed the first presidential press secretary and started the first White House conferences to tell of his actions and decisions. These conferences have been continued by all presidents since and were the forerunners of F. D. Roosevelt's "Fireside Chats," Eisenhower's "State-Of-The-Nation" addresses, and the unrehearsed press conferences we now take for granted.

Beginning early in the Twentieth Century, people, presidents, and organizations tried to humanize themselves as well as to inform and influence. This triggered the use of large mailing lists and similar "broadside" efforts aimed at the general public. The power of organized promotion was demonstrated in George Creel's highly successful Liberty Loan drives to finance the American involvement in World War I. National promotion was equally successful in conserving food, building membership in the Red Cross, and in other ways influencing public opinion and action in support of the war effort. After the war, the techniques were applied to promotion of commercial products and in the rapidly expanding area of charitable giving.

During World War II, major advances were made in the use of propaganda. This tool for the manipulation of opinion was widely used by both sides. Indeed, psychological warfare became a most lethal weapon. "Tokyo Rose" and "Axis Sally" were known by thousands of soldiers and sailors and influenced many. The United States painted pictures in the minds of servicemen of evil, buck-toothed, sneaky, slant-eyed Orientals; or cruel, slow, stupid, ruthless Europeans. Some of these images were so firmly implanted that they still remain despite efforts to erase them. Both sides broadcast their gains widely and kept their losses quiet. The Office of War Information was created and did a spectacular job of propaganda and publicity, and the armed forces developed large information departments to promote favorable images and high morale both on the front and at home.

A part of the war effort having far-reaching effects was the development of research techniques that resulted in the sharpened ability to influence opinions and attitudes through the planned use of various communication procedures. Carl Hovland, a professor of psychology at Yale University, led the research for finding ways to more rapidly indoctrinate new soldiers and fit them with the attitudes necessary for war. Using a variety of films and presentation formats, the researchers studied their effects on carefully controlled groups of recruits. Assembling at Yale University following the war, Hovland and his colleagues continued their studies which resulted in many of the suggestions outlined in Chapter 5. Other war time advances in attitude research took place on the home front. There, group dynamics were studied to find ways of changing housewives' attitudes toward the use of liver, kidneys, brain and other organ meats to help in the vital area of food rationing and conservation.

In the years after the war, the results of this research were applied to advertising, education and any other endeavor where communication was important. In the same period, opinion polling became a highly perfected and indispensable tool of researchers, advertisers, politicians and public relations practitioners. Opinion polls and other social surveys reflected still another important development, a change in emphasis from the *broadside* approach of influencing public opinion to a more sophisticated and effective *targeted* approach. The change was similar to using a rifle instead of a shotgun, and it became essential to know as much as possible about specific groups of people who became the targets of powerfully persuasive communication. Thus, people were categorized and studied on the basis of race, religion, culture, beliefs, interests, political preferences, occupations, memberships in organizations, and anything else that could be used in tailoring a message to an intended target group.

While much of the research of this period was to perfect propaganda, or one-way communication, this was also a time when public relations practitioners learned the value of *listening* to individuals and drawing out their feelings. With the end of the war came the beginning of greater competition in business, and new techniques were developed to achieve greater internal harmony within companies. Employee attitude surveys, exit interviews, greater fringe benefits, training programs and worker-participation in management became standard procedures.

The post-war years also brought the explosive expansion of electronic media, broadening the possibilities of communication far beyond the horizons of almost anyone's imagination. Through the combination of Ivy Lee's new principles, the new tools of communication, and the sophistication of social research, the end of World War II marked the beginning of maturation for public relations practice.

A REVIEW OF RESOURCE MANAGEMENT HISTORY

Before looking at the history of public relations practice in the field of natural resource management, it may be helpful to review the evolution of resource management in America. In providing a brief overview, some roughly discernible stages become apparent, each with a social atmosphere that helped shape the development and the use of public relations.

Era of Abundance

The first period might be called the *Era of Abundance*. The wealth of resources was so great that neither the government nor most of its citizens could conceive of land use pressures that might require social action or constraint. This was a period of the rugged individualist, and a time when conquest of the wilderness was a national challenge. Vast and unmapped, the land held promise of more wood, grass, water and wildlife just over the next ridge or around the bend in the river. Through this rich natural milieu wandered the naturalist-explorers—Mark Catesby, the Bartrams, Lewis and Clark, Alexander Wilson, David Douglas and the likes. Only a few romantics voiced concern for the future. Perhaps the first was George Catlin, a widely-traveled artist who ascended the Missouri River recording the lifestyles of at least 48 tribes of American Indians. Upon his return, he suggested in 1833 a "nation's park, containing man and beast, in all the wild and freshness of their nature's beauty." Envisioned was a vast area extending across the Great Plains where the Indians and buffalo might coexist, protected by some great policy of government (Nash, 1976). Henry David Thoreau was another of the few visionaries who voiced a need for preservation of wild places, and John James Audubon believed that buffalo ought not be permitted to follow the fate of the Great Auk. Early proponents of urban parks also emerged. Immortals such as Frederick Law Olmsted helped lay the foundation of our park legacy, beginning with what is now New York's Central Park. However, except for a very few, citizens of this first era saw little need to worry about the new nation's resources.

Era of Exploitation

By the mid-1800's, a new era can be identified and appropriately labeled the *Era of Exploitation*. A wholly rural society was giving way to the growth of industrialization, and the restless sought opportunity in lands to the west. This was a period of expansion, industrialization, homesteading and destruction of vast areas of forest and great numbers of wildlife. Fire followed logging, lands were grazed or farmed then abandoned, and erosion began to reshape the landscape.

Figure 2.1. In 1864 George Perkins Marsh began warning of the dangers resulting from the destruction of watersheds. His book, *Man and Nature* drew the attention of scientists and philosophers to the problems of resource exploitation. (Courtesy of Colorado Division of Wildlife.)

Finally, alert scientists, writers and philosophers sounded the alarm and citizens and legislators began to react. One book that shook the American conscience was *Man and Nature,* in which George Marsh (1864) graphically portrayed the dangers of destroying watersheds.

Other voices led to the park movement, with Yosemite, Niagara Falls, Yellowstone and the Adirondacks being plucked from the path of exploitation. The nature study movement also was born in this period, with public school teachers like New York's Edward A. Sheldon showing the way beyond the classroom walls and into the woods and fields. The nature writings of John Burroughs began to appear, providing resource material for the schools; and magazines such as George Bird Grinnell's *Forest and Stream* rallied outdoorsmen to the cause of wildlife protection. In the legislative arena, the latter years of this period marked the beginning of stewardship for the nation's resources. One definite sign of response came in 1881 with the establishment of a one-man Division of Forestry in the Department of Agriculture for the purpose of compiling statistics and other factual information on the nation's forests.

In dividing history into periods, there is seldom a clearly defined point dividing one from the other. This is particularly true in natural resource history where the interaction of such a great number of physical and social factors gave rise to each stage of development. It can be argued that the *Era of Exploitation* extended into the Twentieth Century; in fact, depending on one's view it could be argued that in many ways it continues to this day. For our purposes here, however, we will set the close of this era in the year 1890. It was in that year that the Superintendent of the Census announced that the nation's "unsettled area has been so broken into by isolated bodies of settlement that there can hardly be said to be a frontier line" remaining. The announcement came as a distinct shock. Economically, psychologically, and politically, Americans began thinking of life in a nonexpanding land (Billington 1974). The myth of inexhaustible resources began to die.

Figure 2.2. The latter years of the Era of Exploitation marked the advent of natural resource management agencies to provide stewardship for the nation's wealth. (Photo by D. L. Gilbert. Used by permission of The Wildlife Society.)

Era of Preservation and Production

Next came the *Era of Preservation and Production* which extended from 1890 to the mid-1930's. It began with passage of the Forest Reserve Act in 1891 which provided authority to the President to set aside forested areas of the public domain. President Harrison took immediate advantage of his new power, withdrawing 15 preserves totaling over 13 million acres (Steen, 1976). These lands, held by the Department of Interior, were the start of our national forests (although called "forest reserves" at that time). In 1905, they were transferred to the Department of Agriculture where President Roosevelt had just created the U.S. Forest Service out of the old Bureau of Forestry (previous to that, the Division of Forestry). With Gifford Pinchot as its chief, the U.S. Forest Service began its long history of multiple-use management, providing "for the greatest good for the greatest number" of people. At the same time, there occurred "the great dichotomy" that remains to the present—a split between Pinchot's *conservationists* and those who saw value in the *preservation* of some areas for strictly non-commodity purposes. The preservationists followed the call of John Muir, Enos A. Mills, Stephan Mather and others who argued for parks and a distinctly different management approach than was used on the national forests. The National Park Service was the result in 1916.

Some other significant events of this period included: The Lacey Act (1900) which regulated market hunting and the import of exotic species, and prohibited the transport of illegally killed game; establishment of the Bureau of Biological Survey (1905), forerunner of the U.S. Fish and Wildlife Service; the Antiquities Act (1906) which provided for protection by executive order of areas having historical, pre-historical, scenic or scientific values; and various migratory bird treaties and acts that made possible the protection of waterfowl through what is now the national wildlife refuge system.

In the area of wildlife management, the jobs of preservation and production were done well. Restrictions became ever tighter. "Buck laws" and other males-only rules for big game species were the order of the day. Refuges became numerous. Bounty laws, artificial propagation and stocking were thought to be good management. In short, game was protected and the increase was not harvested. In addition, many abandoned farm lands and cutover forests were in early second-growth stages and afforded excellent food and cover for game such as grouse and deer. Although some species were on the decline, other wildlife populations increased beyond expectations. Budding research programs concentrated on life history studies and ways to increase populations further, in many instances already at capacity.

In forestry, purchase of eastern land for more national forests was made possible through the Weeks Act (1911), a law that clearly recognized the relationship between forests and the potential for downstream flooding and siltation. In 1924, the Clarke-McNary Act provided the means for reforestation of abandoned farm lands, creating windbreaks and generally improving the production of tree crops on private lands. This piece of landmark legislation provided the first "matching funds" approach to natural resource management. It gave the U.S. Forest Service authority to cooperate with state and local governments in a variety of expanded forestry activities. It also aided in establishing tree nurseries, providing expert advice to private citizens on reforestation, and educating the general public in matters of forest management and fire protection. At the same time, organized fire protection systems were developed by the U.S. Forest Service nationwide. On nearly every front, the principles of sustained yield forestry were replacing woodland butchery with scientific management.

In recreation, the growing number of national parks were supplemented by expansion of state park systems. It was certainly a period highlighted by both production and preservation. Production was in the form of increasing visits by recreationists, and a frantic period of facility development to provide for the visitors and their automobiles. Preservation was in the form of more land areas set aside for aesthetic reasons, *and* in the realization that some areas should have no developments whatsoever. This notion took on a lasting form when in 1918 Arthur H. Carhart, a Forest Service landscape architect, recommended that superlative wild scenery in the national forests should be managed for their value as wilderness. In 1921, Aldo Leopold gave "definite form to the issue of wilderness conservation" when he defined it and recommended its preservation in a *Journal of Forestry* article, "The Wilderness and its Place in Forest Recreational Policy."

Era of Habitat and Harvest

The early 1930's gave rise to the next discernable period, one that might be called the *Era of Habitat and Harvest*. In this period, ecological principles became more widely applied. Perhaps a beginning point was the publication of Aldo Leopold's *Game Management* in 1933, a book destined to alter the course of wildlife conservation. This was the same year Leopold was appointed professor of game management at the University of Wisconsin, one of the first such academic posts in the United States (Trefethen 1975). In the birth of wildlife management as an academic discipline, Leopold joined three "forest zoology" professors working in this area at the University of Michigan since at least 1927 (Dana, 1953). With this beginning, wildlife research and management began to concentrate on environmental manipulation based on the premise that if the life needs of a species are present (such as food, water and shelter in the required amounts), the species will exist in proportion. It followed that perpetual harvest could be provided through this kind of management. Long cherished notions, such as building up surplus populations through game preserves, began to fall and "either sex" seasons began to be promoted as a way to keep populations in balance with what the habitat could support.

Figure 2.3. During the Era of Habitat and Harvest, the "nature study movement" evolved into the more management-oriented period of "conservation education." (Courtesy of Colorado Division of Wildlife.)

Next, in 1934, the Taylor Grazing Act was passed to stop injury to public lands caused by overgrazing, and to rehabilitate these areas. Dust bowls darkened the skies in those years, carrying precious western soil as far east as Washington, D.C. A scientific crusader by the name of Dr. Hugh Bennett took advantage of this natural visual aid to persuade Congress of the need for the U.S. Soil Erosion Service, an agency which was then created in 1935 and which is now the Soil Conservation Service.

Other significant events in this period included: The Civilian Conservation Corps (1933) which replanted denuded timber land, constructed hundreds of trails, roads, fire towers and ponds; the passage of the Pittman-Robertson Act (1937) and Dingell-Johnson Act (1950) which provided federal aid to the states for research and management related to game and fish, respectively; and the creation of the Bureau of Land Management (1946) through combining the Department of Interior's General Land Office and the Grazing Service.

This era saw the old nature study movement evolve into the more management-oriented emphasis of "conservation education." Spreading out of the domain of schools and parks, it took the concepts of tree planting, erosion control and habitat improvement to scout groups, 4-H clubs, women's clubs, sporting groups and just about anyone with an interest in the outdoors. It was also the period during which multiple-use became firmly entrenched as a way of life in the U.S. Forest Service.

Harvest in this era was not restricted to consumable products. In the years following the Korean War, a recreation boom startled managers and legislators into taking a closer look at the needs and effects of the exponential increase in "nonconsumptive" users seeking intangible benefits from the nation's lands and waters. The outcome was a 27-volume report in 1962 from the Outdoor Recreation Resources Review Commission (ORRRC), a committee of prominent citizens appointed by the President. Authors of the ORRRC report cited a significant gap between the recreational needs of America and the ability to provide for them. One result was the Land and Water

Conservation Fund Act (1964) to purchase land and provide for its recreational development; another was the creation of the Bureau of Outdoor Recreation (re-named Heritage Conservation and Recreation Service in 1978) to administer the fund and promote planning for outdoor recreation. Another contribution of ORRRC was an increased awareness of potential damage to natural resources and social experiences without proper management of recreation.

The Wilderness Act was another significant piece of legislation passed in 1964, giving congressional protection to many of the last remnants of roadless areas in the United States. This act, followed by similar legislation for wild and scenic rivers in 1968, set the stage for some of the most devisive social and political decisions in the history of natural resource management.

Era of People and the Environment

On the heels of the Sixties came Earth Day, a moment in time that perhaps can be used to identify the start of a new period, the *Era of People and the Environment.* On Earth Day—April 22, 1970—an entire nation focused its attention on what was happening to its water, its land and even the very air that sustains all life. People discovered that they were inseparable from their environment. Due in no small part to the earlier publication of Rachel Carson's *Silent Spring* (1962), citizens were sensitized to things unseen—and they were worried. Insecticides, population growth, water pollution (including the ocean), and myriad other complex, highly technical issues came to the forefront of public scrutiny. An alarmed citizenry seemed to cry out— "Where are the watchdogs of society?" In many ways they felt that their government, probably controlled by big business, had let them down. It was to the Ralph Naders, Paul Erlichs and Barry Commoners that they turned their attention.

In the beginning of this era, resource managers were all but shouldered aside as citizens and legislators moved to assume the leadership in righting the direction of "Spaceship Earth." The National Environmental Policy Act (NEPA) of 1969 embodied the buildup of worry in the Sixties and the spirit of the new era—one of public awareness and insistence on having a stronger voice in decisions affecting the environment. Later acts, especially the Forest and Rangeland Renewable Resources Planning Act (1974), National Forest Management Act (1976), and the Federal Land Policy and Management Act (1976) added ever-increasing strength to public involvement in resource decisions.

This era also has given rise to *environmental education,* the third in three overlapping, developmental stages that went from nature study to conservation education to environmental education. With the new, complex issues of the Sixties came the realization that an interdisciplinary approach to problem-solving was essential. No longer could the emphasis be merely on biology. To be sure, an understanding of ecology forms the foundation of environmental education. But problem identification and the action leading to solutions of those problems requires paying attention to a wide array of social and physical considerations. Engineering, political science, chemistry, sociology, psychology and law are but a few of the disciplines that are just as important as the traditional areas of resource management or biological science. Environmental education, unlike conservation education, involves *all* citizens *and* their life styles. Furthermore, it often requires changing attitudes and behavior in an effort to bring humans into harmony with their environment.

What began as a mission believed to be necessary to save ourselves from ourselves has in recent years been tempered by economic realities and changing social values. With the Eighties has come a parsimony in government that has reduced much of the attention given to environmental matters. Voters and politicians have turned their attentions elsewhere. Environmental ed-

Figure 2.4. Environmental pollution and events of the Sixties culminated in Earth Day, 1970, and the rise of environmental education. America awoke to the fact that humans are a critical link in the ecosystem. (Photo by Rex G. Schmidt, U.S. Fish and Wildlife Service.)

ucation has even come to be viewed with suspicion or disdain in the more conservative milieu. Concerns today seem more directed at self-gain than toward public service or environmental protection. Still, perhaps spurred by the outrageous behavior of James Watt as Secretary of the Interior from 1981 to 1983, growth in environmental organizations has been unprecedented. The Era of People and the Environment continues, but only history will be able to judge if it is currently evolving into an Era of Environment Ignored, or simply adjusting like a pendulum toward some central point after going so far and so fast in one direction.

Resource management in the past two decades has become increasingly sophisticated. Computers for handling data, modeling complex situations to help with decisions, and for communication, have become more important than the Jacob's staff compass or tally sheet. Stereoscope views from the air have been supplemented with remote sensing devices in satellites that can pinpoint disease problems or aid in the planning of land use decisions. Biometrics, telemetry, wildlife behavior and nutrition, and biochemistry are bywords of today's natural resource manager. Slowly, human behavior, cultural norms, networking, and the monitoring of public opinion are also finding their way into the working vocabulary of the modern resource manager.

PUBLIC RELATIONS IN NATURAL RESOURCE MANAGEMENT

Finding the roots of public relations in natural resource management is difficult at best. As with reviewing the practice in general, this task is possible only through tracing some of the concepts and tools as they were applied—or were lacking—while resource management evolved through the centuries.

During the Era of Abundance there was little need or effort to intentionally influence public opinion toward natural resources. Communication was present, of course, almost entirely in the form of the written or spoken word. Thoreau used both, the latter being in the form of lectures he gave in Concord, Boston and other areas in New England. These were sometimes reported in local newspapers, and most ended up in his various books. But while Thoreau did indeed "speak a word for Nature" his writings were less than a smash hit of the day, and his influence on resources was more as a philosophical strand in a slowly developing land ethic than anything concrete or immediate.

The first action for park development was definitely the result of the print media. Pressure to develop Central Park in New York City began with a simple letter to the editor in 1785 complaining that the city had not a single "proper spot where numerous inhabitants (could) enjoy the benefits of exercise necessary for health and amusement" (Foss 1960). Five decades later, the physical environment in New York City had grown much worse and the social climate was right for enlisting public support for a park project. This time, writer-editor William C. Bryant took up the pen and on July 3, 1844 under the title "A New Park" started a series of editorials in the *New York Evening Post*. Landscape architect Andrew Jackson Downing supplemented the campaign, writing to a more select public in the *Horticulturist* and chastising New Yorkers for their concentration on the commercial at the expense of less tangible benefits for the citizenry. The park became a reality, and its designer-developer Frederick Law Olmsted succeeded in implementing his plan only through skillfully engaging in local politics. Personnel management was equally as important in the project, since Olmsted had a daily crew of up to 3,800 men working on the park at the height of its construction (Olmsted and Kimbal 1970)!

Art work had an early influence on resources, particularly as artists of the romantic period brought idyllic scenes of nature to the hearthsides of the home-bound. As travel systems improved after 1825, a wonderlust began to affect the American people. They wanted to see for themselves what the Eighteenth Century writers had pictured in glowing terms; and they wished to experience the surrealistic landscapes of artists like Thomas Cole and Asher Durand. A tradition began that is held dear in our culture. Summer vacation and holiday trips are now jealously viewed as a "right" and have become a significant link between people and natural resources. Such travel, for example, may be a significant reason for the interest of a Detroit auto worker in what happens to Rocky Mountain National Park.

In the Ninteenth Century, art and photography not only stimulated recreational travel, they were also used for the first time as effective tools in influencing public opinion for the cause of conservation. The classic example is found during the Era of Exploitation on the 1871 Hayden Expedition to the Yellowstone country. Artist Thomas Moran and pioneer photographer William H. Jackson were both members of that first scientific exploring party. Not only did their work dispel the last doubts about Yellowstone's wonders being fact rather than fancy, it was also used the next year by Ferdinand Hayden in winning congressional approval for our first national park. In his successful attempt to sway Congress, Hayden strategically placed the illustrations in the Capitol rotunda, adding the power of visual aids to his arguments in behalf of the proposed park.

As pointed out by Schoenfeld (1972), communication has been the handmaiden of conservation. Nothing so graphically illustrated this as George Bird Grinnell's use of his weekly magazine, *Forest and Stream,* to rally common citizens against the wasteful destruction of birdlife for women's hats. In 1886, he announced the formation of an "Audubon Society," named in honor of the husband of his boyhood mentor, Mrs. John James Audubon. Male members were required to pledge that they would refrain from "killing, wounding, or capturing any wild bird not used for food." Female applicants gave their word to eschew the use of nongame plumage for decorative purposes. The result of this early media campaign to organize citizens was that in the next three years more than 50,000 pledges were received! The magazine's small staff was so overwhelmed that they were forced to abandon the campaign, but the Audubon Society lived on (Trefethen 1975).

Other now-powerful groups were formed as the Era of Exploitation came to a close and gave way to Preservation and Production. First among these was the American Forestry Association (1875) which became a key force behind the eventual establishment of the national forest system; then the Sierra Club (1892), formed by John Muir and 26 others concerned with the depredation of Yosemite's high country. Later, other groups formed which somewhat reflected the nature of the times. For instance, as scientific forestry emerged, the Society of American Foresters was organized in 1900. As Leopold applied ecology to wildlife management, The Wildlife Society was born in 1936. Two years after the Bureau of Land Management was created, The American Society of Range Management came into existence (1948). In the wake of the recreation boom came the Association of Interpretive Naturalists (1960), the National Recreation and Parks Society (1965), and more recently, the industry-supported American Recreation Coalition.

Fernow's Oversight

Perhaps closest to the actual practice of public relations were the activities of Gifford Pinchot as he went about laying the foundation for his U.S. Forest Service. At about the same time, we had the first classic public relations *failure* in the history of resource management, and a costly one at that. For this we must credit Bernhard Eduard Fernow. Fernow was one of America's first foresters, and like many others at the turn of the century he had received his education in one of the venerable old forestry schools in Germany. In 1898 he turned over his post as chief of the Department of Agriculture's Division of Forestry to Gifford Pinchot and assumed the deanship of the first forestry college in the United States. Located at Cornell University, the New York State College of Forestry flourished and its enrollment soon exceeded even the largest forestry schools of France or Germany. Eventually funds would be sought for a new building to house the prosperous college, and all of New York would benefit from its programs of scientific forestry.

What transpired is a lesson in public relations. The details are told by Rodgers (1951), but the essence is included here because it reflects a classic error that is often repeated today by those ignorant of the past or the basic principles of public relations.

Fernow acquired for his college a 30,000 acre tract of state land in the Adirondack Mountains near Axton, New York. The tract was, in his words, "in large part isolated from tourists' resorts and tourists' travel," a factor he considered as a "point to its credit." The use of this land was to be for demonstration purposes, much like the school forests of many universities today. Fernow immediately faced a silvicultural challenge in that most of the forest was dominated by low grade hardwoods with an admixture of spruce. To the skillful German, the prescription was clear: ". . . change from the present condition . . . to spruce with an admixture of hardwoods." The goal, too, was clear: "To make the soil produce the largest amount of the most useful wood per acre . . . (for this) is the foremost aim of forestry." He did, however, recognize that the forest had intangible values as well as economical ones. He wrote that the experimental forest was not merely to be a "business forest," but that the aesthetic and "amusement phases" were to be secondary.

With this as his guiding policy, Fernow began a series of up to 30 different systems of cutting to demonstrate scientific forestry, obtain new and useful knowledge, and to achieve his objective of "reconstructing" the forest. Beginning in 1899, 15 to 30 years would be needed to complete the project and eventually it could be expected to support itself financially. Soon 1,500 acres had undergone treatment, with only 40 percent of the area needing to be planted to provide for the future spruce crop.

Then Fernow's troubles began. Despite its isolation, the demonstration forest *did* have neighbors. Among them were some of the wealthiest, most prominent citizens of the state, and they were less than pleased with noise, smoke, and fire danger brought to the woods by Cornell's expert on forestry. It did little for Fernow that the area was also a favorite hunting ground for the locals.

The result was an outcry that reached clear to the governor and found its way into newspapers of the day as articles highly critical of the management. The accusations focused primarily on Cornell's intentional "denuding" of the land. However, complaints soon spread to question the college's property rights, condemn its worker camps for violating state law against the use of oleomargarine, and even accuse it of keeping ferrets in camp, undoubtedly for the illegal purpose of hunting. The latter turned out to have stemmed from a ledger notation— "purchase of a pair of ferrets for fifty cents." Ferrets in this case were part of saddle rigging!

Cornell's president stood by his man. Following an on-site investigation by a delegation of trustees, President Schurman relayed their feelings to the governor:

> ". . . they reached the unanimous conclusion that Fernow's policy was a sound one and that, whatever might be good forest management elsewhere, in areas like those now being treated in the demonstration forest, where all the valuable softwoods had already been removed by the lumbermen, and only hardwoods, mostly rotten, remain, the wisest policy was practically to denude and then to replant, as is the practice, indeed, with more than 80 per cent of all the forests in Germany. What the critics of this policy have overlooked is that clear cutting, or what they call denudation, is only a means to an end, and that the end, which is the all-important thing, is the reproduction of wood crops. . . . It is the proud boast of Cornell University never to have failed in anything it has undertaken. It intends, too, to make this great State experiment in forestry a success. The University would not tolerate, nor could it afford to be responsible for, any other result. But it proposes to achieve this result in its own way, i.e., by securing a plan from the most eminent scientific forester in America and then adhering to it, even though ignorant critics who know nothing about forestry think that some other way should be followed (Rodgers 1951, p. 307).

When the next year's College appropriation bill reached his desk, the governor registered *his* reaction. He vetoed the bill. With a stroke of a pen, the New York State College of Forestry at Cornell University ceased to exist. Years later it was re-instituted, not at Cornell, but at Syracuse where it remains to this day. The school is now titled the College of Environmental Science and Forestry and offers not only a major forestry curriculum, but also courses in resource communication.

After reading later chapters, refer back to this case study to see what might have been done differently.

Using PR—The Pinchot and Mather Approach

The first heads of the U.S. Forest Service and National Park Service were in many ways as different as the two agencies are today. Gifford Pinchot, first chief of the U.S. Forest Service, was devoted to the principle of multiple use. While aggressively promoting the concept of productive forest management, he also aggressively opposed the creation of the National Park Service. He viewed it as being "no more needed than two tails on a cat" (Hays 1960). Instead, he believed the Forest Service could manage parks with little if any modification of their overall management strategies. Stephen Mather, on the other hand, fought tirelessly for the autonomous management of national parks, preserved and managed wholly for non-commodity uses.

Both men laid a solid foundation for their respective agencies, and both men clearly understood what Bernhard Fernow never quite grasped—public relations. From inherent ability, these two men pioneered in the use of many of the principles and tools of applied public relations. This was at the same time that Ivy Lee was establishing the principles that underlie the practice as we know it today. Both Pinchot and Mather were of wealthy families, well-schooled and familiar with the basics of business and government. Pinchot overcame childhood health problems and with dogged determination developed into a rugged individualist with high ideals and a sense of mission. Beginning in his college years at Yale University, Pinchot focused these personal characteristics toward his deepest interest—the practice of forestry. Mather began as a reporter who then achieved unparalleled success as advertising and sales-promotion manager for the Pacific Coast Borax Company. Among other things along his route to wealth, he helped create the famous trade label "20 Mule Team Borax" (Strong, 1971).

Figure 2.5. Stephen Mather (left) and Gifford Pinchot both recognized the values of gaining favorable public opinion for their opposing management philosophies. Mather, in Park Service uniform, is shown with the crown prince of Sweden; Pinchot is with President Theodore Roosevelt. (Courtesy of National Park Service and USDA Forest Service.)

FORESTERS IN PUBLIC SERVICE

Advice from Gifford Pinchot to guide the behavior of the nation's first foresters:

1. A public official is there to serve the public and not run them.
2. Public support of acts affecting public rights is absolutely required.
3. It is more trouble to consult the public than to ignore them, but that is what you are hired for.
4. Find out in advance what the public will stand for; if it is right and they won't stand for it, postpone action and educate them.
5. Use the press first, last, and all the time if you want to reach the public.
6. Get rid of the attitude of personal arrogance or pride of attainment or superior knowledge.
7. Don't try any sly or foxy politics because a forester is not a politician.
8. Learn tact simply by being absolutely honest and sincere, and by learning to recognize the point of view of the other man and meet him with arguments he will understand.
9. Don't be afraid to give credit to someone else even when it belongs to you; not to do so is the sure mark of a weak man, but to do so is the hardest lesson to learn; encourage others to do things; you may accomplish many things through others that you can't get done on your single initiative.
10. Don't be a knocker; use persuasion rather than force, when possible; plenty of knockers are to be had; your job is to promote unity.
11. Don't make enemies unnecessarily and for trivial reasons; if you are any good you will make plenty of them on matters of straight honesty and public policy and will need all the support you can get.

On becoming head of the Division of Forestry in 1898, Pinchot focused his ambitions on the transfer of the nation's forest reserves from the Department of the Interior to his own Department of Agriculture. His first action was to create internal strength. Selecting his subordinates carefully and leading his staff firmly but fairly (it all began in a two-room office with 11 employees!), he fostered an *esprit de corps* that soon became the envy of the entire federal government. He also fostered his friendship with a fellow conservationist and amateur naturalist, Theodore Roosevelt. It hurt the cause not at all when Roosevelt succeeded McKinley to the presidency in 1901, but Pinchot went far beyond his friendship with the President to win support for the Transfer Act. He triumphed, of course, in 1905. His entire campaign is a case study in the effective use of personnel management, the political process, and publicity. More than did some of his successors, he understood the need for a constant flow of publicity. Repeatedly he overcame opposition through the adroit use of personal letters, leaflets, circulars and a constant stream of news releases that resulted in an estimated 30 to 50 million newspaper copies each month carrying forestry items. He also developed an extensive mailing list to zero in on influential leaders across the country (Strong, 1971). Under the title of editor, Herbert Smith aided the chief in these pioneering efforts. Another first in a resource management agency was the employment of Enos A. Mills in 1907 as a "government lecturer on forestry" to travel about spreading the word for fire prevention.

Forest Service publicity men were given identity on May 20, 1920 with establishment of the Branch of Public Relations. Its purpose: "More careful planning of methods by which public interest may be increased in both the protection and use of the Forests. . . ." Its name was soon changed to the Division of Information and Education with Smith as its first head (Steen, 1976).

Pinchot had two prominent rivals in the preservationist camp who exploited the mass media and political system almost as well as the old master himself. Both were Pinchot's friends before the great dichotomy between preservation and utilization. One was John Muir, Sierra Club founder and a talented writer who appealed directly to the masses with eloquent statements on nature and parks. More than anyone else, he focused national attention on the need for protecting enclaves of wild beauty. His disciple, Enos Mills, spearheaded the establishment of Rocky Mountain National Park, but more importantly, laid the foundation for environmental interpretation. Mills' talks on wildlife, ranging from bluebird to bears, captivated even the President of the United States. His writings appeared in leading magazines from 1902 until his untimely death in 1922, and the 16 books authored by Mills are still treasured among the best of America's nature lore. Mills also pioneered in the area of personal presentations in the outdoors, something he termed "nature guiding." Many of the principles of modern interpretation were employed in Mills' popular walks and were clearly spelled out in his book *The Adventures of a Nature Guide* (Fazio, 1975).

Another who was skilled in the use of public relations was Stephen Mather, first director of the National Park Service. His efforts are legend and reflected his earlier career in advertising. Mather began his government career in 1915 as an assistant to Secretary of the Interior, Franklin K. Lane. His charge was to win legislation that would create an agency to manage the nation's somewhat neglected national parks. Opposition to the idea was formidable, but his success a year later can be attributed to the careful manipulation of public opinion and his creative approach to gaining legislative authorization for the new agency.

Mather's first action in Washington was a media blitz to create public awareness of national parks and promote park visitation. To help, newspaperman/magazine editor Robert Sterling Yard was hired (through a devious manipulation of funds plus some salary money from Mather's own pocket) as the publicity chief for national parks. The two men worked tirelessly promoting the parks. Mather formed an alliance with the railroads for this purpose, and among other things obtained from them financial backing for two illustrated books produced by Yard, *Glimpses of our National Parks* and *National Parks Portfolio.* The initial 275,000 copies were then sent free of charge to the most important opinion leaders in the country (Strong, 1971). The two promoters also leaned on every literary friend they could think of, resulting in a staggering 1,050 articles on parks in a two year period.

Personal diplomacy was used as never before or after. Congressmen were taken on festive outings into the parks, then entertained around the campfire with a forerunner of "living history" techniques complete with an old scout spinning Yellowstone yarns. Others were treated to sumptuous Washington dinners which included a performance by Mather's myna bird. Its tricks would conclude with an address to the assembled congressmen and cabinet officers, "What about appropriations?" Mather's showmanship also included a spontaneous pledge of $15,000 to help save the threatened redwoods—an act of generosity not lost on the wildly cheering crowd. Rich friends, including the crown prince of Sweden and John D. Rockefeller, Jr. were not overlooked, and many found themselves guests of Mather on unforgettable fly-fishing excursions (Wild, 1979). No luxury was spared on such occasions, most being financed by Mather.

This unprecedented campaign climaxed on a note befitting the dash and flare of the Mather administration. Peter Wild tells it best:

> "While the (National Park Service) bill's chief opponent, Congressman William Stafford, was flailing away on the golf links—where Mather's confederates lured him—the bill passed through the House on a drowsy Friday afternoon in August. Eager to sew up the scheme, Albright (Horace Albright, Mather's assistant) dashed over to the White House and convinced the legislative clerk to slip the bill in with others awaiting President Wilson's signature. The Park Service Act became law a few hours later (Wild 1979, p. 66).

The joyous news was then telegrammed to Mather in California where he was still entertaining the influential on behalf of his cause.

Controls and Opportunities

The free-wheeling antics of Pinchot and Mather are no longer possible in most government agencies. For one thing, few administrators have either the ability or inclination to use personal wealth to develop their agency or promote their cause. Also, our government looks askance at the expenditure of allocated funds for anything that smacks of self-promotion or aggrandizement. Pinchot's publicity campaigns attracted the wrath of some legislators who, according to Steen (1976), were perhaps "justified in slapping Pinchot down because he seemed to be using public funds to lobby." At about the same time, a congressman was "startled" to discover that the Census Bureau had what amounted to a press agent who was working under the title "expert special agent" (Cohen, 1967).

Although publicity experts had been employed by presidents as far back as Thomas Jefferson (Cutlip et al., 1985), personnel of this ilk within the federal agencies ran counter to the suspicious and parsimonious nature of early congressmen. The result was the passage of a law in 1913 which is still on the books today. It is one of two pieces of legislation that have contributed to the limited or disguised use of some techniques which could otherwise make important contributions to improved public relations practice in federal resource management agencies. The 1913 law includes the statement: "No money appropriated by any Act shall be used for the compensation of any publicity expert, unless specifically appropriated for that purpose" (5 U.S. Code 54). This has led to careful scrutiny of such appropriations. On the part of agencies, it has led to careful efforts to veil some aspects of public relations practice under the guise of information dissemination said to be solely for meeting the demands or immediate needs of publics. What often gets hidden or suppressed are attempts at image-improvement and honest methods of winning public support for management practices. Both, in the long run, would yield public benefits. Unfortunately, publicity is often thought to be nothing more than self-aggrandizement and, because most people also erroneously equate "publicity" with "public relations," the 1913 law—along with the sentiment it reflects—has led to the virtual banishment of public relations as a government title. The 1913 law has never been enforced, except by threat and innuendo (Archibald, 1967), and increasingly it is viewed as antiquated. Still, while the law endures, the work of information specialists will be a point of concern for some nervous administrators.

Suspicion and distrust have led to the severe curtailment in federal agencies of yet another activity called for in our definition of public relations practice. That is in the important process of two-way communication, hindered to a large degree by the strict controls imposed by the Office of Management and Budget (OMB) on opinion polling. This taboo received the force of law in 1942 with passage of the Federal Report Act. Today it creates a point of real irony as many laws now require "public involvement"—with the ultimate objective of understanding what people want—yet it is next to impossible to quickly or routinely sample opinion. Private organizations and industry regularly use this research method, but a federal resource manager must first clear any survey through the proper channels and receive a time-limited permit from OMB.

Another piece of federal legislation deserves mention because of its impact on the current status of public relations in many resource agencies. This is the Freedom of Information Act of 1966, a law that can have a very *positive* effect on public relations. It was designed to reverse earlier legislation under which federal agencies considered themselves free to withhold information from the public under whatever subjective standard could be articulated for the occasion (U.S. Senate, 1974). The Freedom of Information Act at long last set a standard of openness for government from which only deviations in nine well-defined areas would be allowed (for example, national defense material and personnel files). The law also gave legal foundation to the positions of public information officers (Archibald, 1967), the people who can reasonably be expected to provide public access to government on a regular basis.

Recent and Current Status

It should be clear by now why the term "public relations" is not widely used in government agencies. However, this does not negate the meritorious *concept* of public relations. Once managers and administrators both inside and outside government service understand the definition that is widely accepted in the public relations profession, most agree that the tools and the end product of public relations are badly needed for more effective management of natural resources. The fact remains, nonetheless, that to study either the history or current state of the art, it is necessary to look for titles and functions other than those actually labeled public relations. For all practical purposes, the closest relative is the field commonly referred to as either "public information" or "information and education (I & E)."

It is claimed that the first information program of a federal government agency in the United States was initiated by the Patent Office around 1830. The purpose was to inform farmers of new technology and the effort was personally paid for by Henry Ellsworth, the Patent Office Commissioner (Lesly, 1983). By 1983, the Office of Personnel Management listed 18,990 federal workers in job categories related to public relations in those agencies most responsible for natural resource management (U.S. Office of Personnel Management, 1983). A detailed breakdown of the jobs is shown in Table 2.1. "Public relations specialists", who are identified by that title in the private sector and some government agencies, number at least 90,000 (U.S. Dept. of Labor, 1984). Related occupations such as writers, editors and audio-visual specialists would expand this number many times.

Table 2.2 summarizes the relatively few studies conducted on numbers or trends of communication services within natural resource agencies. Most that have been conducted focused on state fish and wildlife departments.

Table 2.1
Numbers of Federal Employees in Positions Related to Public Relations
(U.S. Office of Personnel Management, 1983).

Job Category	Dept. of Agriculture	Dept. of Interior	TVA	All Federal Agencies
Public Affairs	412	155	102	2,667
Gen. Arts and Information	114	84	6	2,078
Exhibits Specialist	81	49	—	269
Museum Curator	—	70	—	278
Museum Specialist and Technician	—	87	—	616
Illustrating	25	61	—	1,807
Photography	75	111	70	2,545
Audio-Visual Production	21	23	—	901
Writing and Editing	134	96	3	2,037
Technical Writing and Editing	38	117	19	1,769
Visual Information	99	89	—	1,681
Editorial Assistance	85	172	—	1,341
TOTALS	1,084	1,114	200	18,990

Note: The job category "public information" is no longer recognized by the U.S. Office of Personnel Management.

In 1979 we conducted a study with Robert Mindick that for the first time attempted to distinguish between the many "conservation" agencies. For a widely-recognized guide to the major agencies, we used the National Wildlife Federation's *Conservation Directory*, supplemented by the Department of Interior's *Index of the National Park System and Affiliated Areas*. An attempt was also made to distinguish between employees engaged in various kinds of natural resource communication activities, specifically I & E, environmental education, interpretation, public relations and public involvement. Despite an attempt to define personnel engaged in these activities, it was found that confusion exists over the various roles related to each. Also, the same person frequently has a mission that fits the definition of more than one of these activities. Still, it was a necessary step toward more clearly establishing a bench mark against which change can be measured.

This study was modified slightly and repeated in 1985. The results are shown in Table 2.3. They must be viewed with all the cautions of relying on self-reported data, and it should be noted that the survey did not include the forest industries, specific state parks, or wildlife refuges. It is by no means a survey of *all* workers in the communication services. If such a survey *were* conducted, it would swell these numbers many fold, undoubtedly cheering those students who view this as the job market. Perhaps the greatest value of this survey is in comparing relative numbers in the different job categories. The emphasis is by far on providing information—not on trying to involve publics in decision-making, not on educating to transform environmental information into new attitudes and behaviors, and not on trying to favorably influence public opinion. Perhaps this is one reason why natural resource management agencies are increasingly finding themselves on the defensive and at odds with the very people they try so hard to serve and to please.

Table 2.2.
The Growth of Information and Education in State Conservation Departments[1]

Researcher	Date	Findings
Smits	1937	Information specialists and I & E departments in state conservation agencies have been in existence under various titles since the late 1920's.
Culbreath	1949	Forty-one of the 48 state conservation departments had I & E sections. Staff averaged 2 people, including the stenographer and operated with 1.6 percent of the total agency budget. The 10 largest eastern departments spent 7 percent of their budgets on I & E with 3.5 percent of their employees in this activity; 11 western departments spent 1.7 percent of their budgets and used 1.8 percent of their personnel in the same activities.
Shoman	1952	Only 14 state conservation departments had "well established" I & E programs.
Gilbert	1962	Fifty of the state conservation departments had I & E sections of some kind. The number of I & E employees ranged from a high of 36 in Michigan to 2 in four different states (average was 11) with I & E being 20 percent of the budget in Mississippi to less than 1 percent in many states (average was 5.8 percent).
Wildlife Management Institute	1968	All states except Hawaii reported having full-time staffs. Personnel ranged from 48 in New York and 42 in Texas to 1 in Ohio and Alaska. Total of 544 employees.
Wildlife Management Institute	1977	All states except Hawaii reported having full-time I & E staffs. Personnel ranged from 62 in New York, 58 in Texas and 40 in Nebraska to 1 in Ohio and Rhode Island. Total of 606 employees.
Mindick	1979	Four hundred and seven units of natural resource management agencies were surveyed, recording 2448 communication-related professionals. The majority of respondents reported college degrees in natural resource disciplines. There were indications of declining budgets. First study to attempt distinguishing between personnel in I & E, interpretation, environmental education, public relations and public involvement.

1. Conservation departments in most of these studies were primarily state fish and game departments.

Table 2.3
Natural Resource Agency Personnel (Permanents) as Reported by Type of Communication Work, 1985[1].

Agency	Units Surveyed	Percent Response	Environmental Education	Information & Education	Interpretation	Public Relations	Public Involvement	Total Employed
Army Corps of Engineers Regional Offices	11	18	0	6	0	0	0	6
Bureau of Land Management								
Washington Office	1	100	0	11	0	0	1	12
States	12	50	0	13	1	25	1	40
U.S. Fish & Wildlife Service								
Washington Office	1	100	1	1	2	1	1	6
Regions	7	71	0	14	2	4	1	21
USDA Forest Service								
Washington Office	1	100	1	11	0	0	11	23
Regional Offices	9	78	10	24	1.5	3	18	56.5
National Forests	119	83	20	116	33	41	44	254
U.S. National Park Service								
Washington Office	1	0	—	—	—	—	—	—
Regional Offices	9	67	2	4	17	4	0	27
National Parks and Monuments (Natural areas only)	110	74	20	27	263	15	9	334
Soil Conservation Service	1	0	—	—	—	—	—	—
Tennessee Valley Authority	1	100	9	13	13	2	0	37
State Fish and Game Depts.	31	88	61.5	223	3	12	4	303.5
State Conservation, Natural Resources and Lands Depts.	29	55	25	126	23	7	0	181
State Forestry Depts.	15	96	2	82	1	3	1	89
State Parks and Recreation Depts.	15	71	3	16.5	52	6	0	77.5
Canadian Forestry Agencies	8	62	2	52	0	1	1	56
Other Canadian Agencies	5	40	1	6	5	1	1	14
TOTALS	384	86	157.5	745.5	416.5	125	93	1537.5

1. From nationwide survey conducted by the senior author as a 5-year followup to Mindick's survey in 1980.

SUGGESTED REFERENCES

An American Crusade for Wildlife by James B. Trefethen. 1975. Winchester Press and the Boone and Crockett Club, New York.

Courtier to the Crowd: The Story of Ivy Lee and the Development of Public Relations by Ray Eldon Hiebert. 1966. Iowa State University Press, Ames.

Forest and Range Policy: Its Development in the United States by Samuel T. Dana and Sally K. Fairfax. 1980. McGraw-Hill Book Co., New York.

Park Naturalists and the Evolution of National Park Service Interpretation Through World War II by C. Frank Brockman 1978. Journal of Forest History, 22(1):24–43.

The Conservationists by Douglas H. Strong. 1971. Addison-Wesley Publishing Co., Menlo Park, CA.

The Forest Service by Michael Frome. 1984. Westview Press, Boulder, CO.

The U.S. Forest Service: A History by Harold K. Steen. 1977. University of Washington Press, Seattle.

3

Principles of Public Relations

Situations and even 'facts' are ever changing,
but principles can always guide the way.

For the practice of public relations to be effective, it is essential to build upon a set of principles that will serve as a useful guide under any of the wide variety of circumstances prevalent in natural resource management. Unfortunately, there are no well established, universal laws for us to draw upon as we might in ecology or the other sciences. However, we do have a definition that includes an overall goal—*the favorable influencing of public opinion.* It also includes some general ideas on how that goal may be achieved. Now it may be useful to expand on our definition, providing additional guidelines that will help clarify the concept of public relations as well as steer our efforts in the right direction under any circumstances.

In presenting the following set of seven principles, we must echo the sentiments of Freeman Tilden (1977) who claimed no finality in the six he suggested as a basis for the practice of environmental interpretation. There may be more that you would choose to list, and we recognize that some may be thought to overlap. The important thing is that they do reflect at least the minimum knowledge needed for natural resource professionals to improve their public relations skills. Some are essentially self-explanatory and need only be brought to the surface of consciousness to be helpful. Others are stated briefly, then expanded upon in following sections of the book.

PRINCIPLE 1:
EVERY ACTION MAKES AN IMPRESSION

This principle is basic to all others. Every individual or group dealing with people makes an impression on others, and the impression will be good, bad or indifferent. This impression may not be of any great significance nor may it necessarily be a lasting one. Nevertheless, each contact or deed by an individual or attributed to a group *does* influence or impress, to some degree, the person or persons contacted. Thus, everything we say or do has a bearing upon how others perceive us or our organization. Being ever conscious of this fact is important whether considering public relations as the routine, daily actions of all employees or the function assigned to specific staff members. These activities establish our relationship with others (our "public relations" used in that sense) and ultimately our image.

It is for this reason we need to be as concerned with the words and manners used in answering a telephone as we are with how we conduct a field trip or a public meeting. This is the justification for attending to such seemingly trivial details as how a driver handles the company truck in traffic or how maintenance personnel respond to visitors in a park. When training related to this principle occurs, which is all too infrequent, the basis for these skills is frequently that "you'll never know who you may be dealing with. Why, it may even be a regional officer." Although this may be true, this is only one reason for always performing at our best. In natural resources work, *service* is as much the product as any tangible commodity. Every citizen is the rightful recipient of that service and increasingly expects it as a right for which he is paying. Every action produces a judgement by citizen observers as to whether they are getting their money's worth or being treated fairly. In the aggregate, public opinion is formed.

In the private sector, the results of Principle 1 are very direct. In fact, they make the difference between profit or loss. Think of the impression a salesperson makes on you if you are undecided about an item you may purchase. This is especially important in the tourism industry where the whole idea is to sell the image of enjoyment. As an example, there is a pleasant woman who operates a small lakeside cabin resort. Potential clients are warmly greeted, but then her son takes them on a short tour. During the brief visit, he complains about how electricity rates cut into profits, what a big job it is maintaining the lawn, and the bad habits of former clients. His language is also profane. In short, it is not fun to be there, and the impression he makes drives away business.

You can think of many more examples and how you were impressed favorably or unfavorably. In meeting the public, there is no escaping this principle. Recognizing this, Principle 1 can easily be put to work in your favor.

PRINCIPLE 2:
GOOD PUBLIC RELATIONS IS A PREREQUISITE OF SUCCESS

The first principle leads naturally to the second. The image cast by an agency as a whole or any one of its employees can affect success in at least one of two ways. In Bernhard Fernow's case, he did not offend the masses. It was his ill fortune to offend the wrong individuals—a small, powerful group of them. Those people had enough power to doom his entire project and even part of the institution that sponsored it. This is not uncommon today. The realities of politics at almost any level require public relations workers to routinely use extreme care to *identify* all those with interests in a project and/or the power to influence its outcome. In the more general use of public relations, *all* employees should be trained to treat every stranger as if that person does wield such power.

The more common cause of failure is brought about through alienating large numbers of people who, in a democracy, eventually will have their say and their way. Abraham Lincoln recognized this collective power when he said, "Public sentiment is everything. With public sentiment nothing can fail; without it, nothing can succeed." In natural resource management there is a long list of good projects, management practices, or staff positions that have been scrapped or never begun because popular support was lacking. As we shall see later, this support must come from within as well as from voters, taxpayers, legislators, users or others "outside" the organization.

The notion that good public relations is a prerequisite to success can be verified by almost any experienced resource manager. All have their tales of strategies that went wrong when the human dimension was ignored. Daniel J. Decker of Cornell University even verified this concept through a research project. Leaders of a variety of organizations having an interest in deer in

Northern New York were asked to provide their opinions on the image of the Department of Environmental Conservation, the state's agency responsible for deer management. Decker found a positive and statistically significant relationship between a leader's perception of the agency and his tendency to support the agency's management efforts. On the other hand, leaders with a negative image either showed no tendency toward strong support, or were more likely to oppose management efforts (Decker, 1985).

By recognizing that success requires support, and that support comes from good public relations and a good image, the first step is taken. After that, it becomes a matter of determining the best procedures and the right tools to assure that support.

PRINCIPLE 3:
THE PUBLIC IS ACTUALLY MANY PUBLICS

One of the great basics in gaining support is to first identify the publics involved with any issue or cause. The plural word "publics" may strike the ear strangely at first, because we are so used to hearing "*the* public." But the concept is as essential as it is simple. A public can be defined as two or more people with a common interest and who may be expected to react similarly to a particular situation or issue. Consequently, when a public is identified, these people will represent a more homogenous group than the total population of which they are part. This can make communication immensely more efficient and increase the chances it will also be more effective.

Sometimes a public may contain sub-publics. For example, biologists may include range biologists, forest biologists, game biologists and fish biologists. Each of these publics can be divided further. For example, game biologists may include both big game biologists and waterfowl biologists among others.

Publics fall into one of two categories, natural or unnatural. A natural public has an inherent interest in a situation or issue. An example for a game and fish department would be a sportsmen's club. An unnatural public is one that is not normally interested but may be won over through a planned effort. An example for the same department would be a local chapter of the League of Women Voters.

An agency's natural publics can be divided into internal and external publics. An internal public is unmistakably identified with the organization family. An external public is not directly connected with the organization. All internal publics can be expected to also be natural publics.

A corollary to this principle is that for public relations to be positive and effective, it is essential to deal first with your internal publics. This and the importance of identifying publics will be included in the next chapter.

PRINCIPLE 4:
TRUTH AND HONESTY ARE ESSENTIAL

In our definition of public relations practice, a key phrase is that efforts to influence public opinion are based on *good character and responsible performance*. Truth and honesty are integral to these elements of the definition. If they are lacking, it is *not* the reputable practice of public relations. Instead it becomes a cover-up or whitewash operation; a charade at best, a fraud at worst.

No matter how powerful, how well financed or how well organized, no effort to influence public opinion can succeed on a foundation of dishonesty. Many forget, ignore, or are ignorant of this important principle, and just as many later blame fate for their misfortunes. Examples abound at all levels, but perhaps the most famous and most tragic was the fall of the Nixon presidency. Ironically, Nixon's chief spokesman, Herb Klein, understood this concept clearly. A highly respected, reputable journalist, Klein was appointed early in the president's second term of office. In one of his first public statements he told the press, "Truth will be the hallmark of the Nixon administration" (Anon 1968). Had it been, the course of history would have been different.

WHAT'S WRONG WITH A LITTLE DISHONESTY?

Nothing, according to a lot of people. In a recent survey, two out of five job applicants were admittedly "a little dishonest". What happens when dishonesty becomes the "in" thing? According to an organization called Ethics Resource Center, the possibilities range from inflation to the loss of our political freedom. Created to fight against the rising tide of dishonesty, the Ethics Resource Center can provide helpful information such as their booklet, *Common Sense and Everyday Ethics* ($1.00). Write to: ERC, 1730 Rhode Island Avenue N.W., Washington, D.C. 20036.

PRINCIPLE 5:
OFFENSE IS MORE EFFECTIVE THAN DEFENSE

The principle probably least understood by managers is that public relations can not be effective when relegated to the role of defensive action. Worse yet, many managers believe that when things go wrong the best tactic is silence. Almost invariably these attitudes lead to the worst of all possible outcomes, or at best prolong the period of public interest in the unflattering incident. Examples best illustrate this concept.

In 1978 a university television station produced an hour-long documentary called "Cedar Thief." The theme was largely a Robin Hood episode drawing heavily on local woods workers to look at the causes behind timber thefts. The down-home style interviews included a barrage of accusations against the dominant forest industry in the area. The claims focused on a variety of practices that were said to be driving "the little guy" out of honest work. During taping, industry officials were contacted to present their side of the story. Alas, they chose the all too frequent shelter of "no comment." Finally, the film went on the air and was one of the most popular local productions in the history of the television station. And salted throughout the show, usually following an emotional attack by a "little guy," the commentator made the terse statement— "industry officials refused to comment!"

Had the company participated in the film, chances are that the show would have passed with little more notice than most of the "pro and con" productions common on public television. Some who were close to the situation argue that biased editing would have negated any constructive comments anyway, but that is a risk worth taking. As it was, the newspapers had a heyday, the story made news for months, the company communication director "resigned", student and government groups borrowed the videotape for viewing, the state legislature entered the fray, and finally the company's public relations director gamely told the press that his firm "may step up its information and education efforts, hoping to present a more balanced look at industry."

Time after time, when misfortune focuses unfavorable publicity on an organization, the order goes out from top management— "Don't talk to the press," or "lay low until things cool off." With today's journalists deeply inspired by the success of Watergate reporters, such a position is like waving a red flag! The correct action is usually as simple as a Sunday School lesson—prompt, honest admission of having made a mistake, possibly adding a "sorry." Or, in the case of an accident or tragedy—prompt, honest and accurate information, including full cooperation with media representatives. Some excellent examples of the power in this approach are presented in the chapter covering the duties of emergency information officers.

To help make our point even clearer, let us look at a case study condensed from a chapter on "Converting 'Sin' into Virtue." It is from Allen H. Center's (1975) excellent book, *Public Relations Practices*. The chapter title reflects what is often an overlooked opportunity, the chance to change a defensive stance into the offensive.

In 1966, Georgia Pacific's public relations office was invaded by an outraged group of people carrying a dead bald eagle fledgling. Apparently a contract logger working for the company had felled a tree containing the eagle's nest. Technically, the action was criminal, and the angry group of citizens, including an ornithologist, knew it.

What to do? First, the PR "pro" calmed the group to gain time to do his homework as well as they had done theirs. He listened, took notes, obtained a statement from them, and promised to follow up. He also promised to reply as promptly as possible to their questions of "What are you going to do about it?"

Fortunately, the public relations man knew that top management would allow him to make good on his promises. That is essential. He was sure, because for years the company had practiced positive public relations and they were too knowledgeable to try any of the ostrich defense postures! Moving forward with the support of management, the public relations man soon ascertained that for one reason or another, a contract logger had indeed felled the eagle's nest. Then, with the skill of a true professional, he went about turning the minus into a plus for his company. He began by presenting a check for $1,000 from the Georgia-Pacific Foundation to a naturalist-photographer who worked for the Oregon Museum of Science and Industry. The grant was for eagle research, but presentation of the check was photographed (complete with a live eagle present) and was the start of a well-planned domino-effect publicity campaign that transformed the company from villian to hero.

When relying on defense as the only actions of public relations, the best one can hope for is that good fortune will smile and draw media and public attention to some other issue of more pressing importance. This is purely a gamble, and gambling is no way to run a business, nor is it the responsible behavior of a public official. Through preventative action and advance "stockpiling" or depositing goodwill with the public, the devastating effects of an adverse incident can be significantly reduced. And when it does occur, through careful analysis of the incident plus a little creativity and a knowledge of the tools of public relations, the negative incident might even be turned into a "plus."

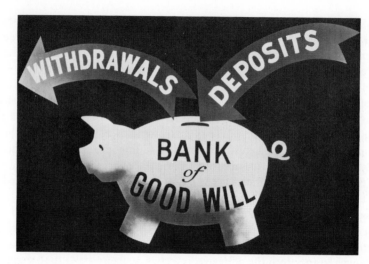

Figure 3.1. Through a planned, positive and constant effort, a public relations program is on the offensive and builds up protection against those inevitable times when things go wrong.

PRINCIPLE 6:
COMMUNICATION IS THE KEY TO GOOD PUBLIC RELATIONS

It is inconceivable that good public relations can exist or be maintained without some form of continuous communication. The more skillfully communication is used, the greater the chances that public opinion will be successfully influenced. Through this, public support—or at the very least, public tolerance—will allow management to proceed in the best interests of people and the resource. This is the ultimate objective of practicing public relations, and communication *is* the central process. For this reason, most of this book is devoted to the improved use of communication techniques.

In both professional and private life, when things go wrong the accusing finger almost invariably is pointed to "a communication gap." Poor employee performance, low morale, learning difficulties, aircraft tragedies, divorces and even wars are frequently attributable to a breakdown, lack, or poor use of communication. So central is this issue that rare indeed is the novel, comedy routine or other portrayal of the human condition that does *not* involve a plot related to confused or blocked communication. Communication is the successful transmission of messages without distortion. True communication is synonymous with *understanding*. Without this first basic step, there is little hope of influencing others or reaching agreement.

Communication is the essential ingredient for assuring public involvement in resource decisions. It is essential in building a favorable image of your company or agency. Your competent management abilities, public service and other contributions to society will mean little if people do not know about them. Communication is also essential for making your views and factual data known to legislators, board members, commissioners or others in a position to support or block your decisions, or perhaps even the very existence of your program. Notice that in the accompanying list of suggestions for how employees of agricultural experiment stations can improve their

---

**IMPROVING ACCOUNTABILITY IN STATE AGRICULTURAL EXPERIMENT
STATIONS—A HIGH RELIABILITY ON COMMUNICATION**

1. *Identify those to whom we are accountable.* Be specific. Include known characteristics of key persons.
2. *Communicate with the above people*—by the proper person with the proper information using the proper approach—to achieve, if possible, a set of expectations and anticipations on his or her part that match our proposals.
3. *Understand the expectations and anticipations* of those to whom we are accountable. Obtain a feel for the type of reporting—substance, detail and manner—that will be most meaningful and useful to them later.
4. *Manage research programs so as to accomplish predetermined objectives* in the most efficient and effective manner possible within the constraints that apply, including the expectations and anticipations of those to whom we are accountable.
5. *Report performance* accurately and effectively. Effectively means by the right person at the right time in the format and desired detail, as well as in a manner that is likely to be meaningful and convincing to each of those to whom we are accountable.
6. *Develop and actively engage in a method of communication relating to our clients, and public in general*, the total scope of State Agricultural Experiment Station activity and its impact on society and our environment. Implement processes to improve the public's image of agriculture and of the State Agricultural Experiment Stations.
7. *Develop the leadership* and obtain staff understanding and support necessary to carry out the above program.

—A statement from State Agricultural Experiment Stations, 1975.

---

research accountability, the majority of items specifically require effective communication. Finally, and perhaps above all else, communication is essential to establishing *internal* harmony, a crucial prerequisite to effective *external* public relations.

In Georgia-Pacific's eagle case, communication was used as the primary means of de-fusing an otherwise explosive situation. First the company representative *listened* carefully—an important part of communication. Then he gathered the facts, analyzed the situation and formed a plan. Next, he carefully publicized what the company was going to do. It could not bring the dead eagle back to life, but it could and *would* support research to help this species in the future. People are basically reasonable, and they could accept that action. And through aggressive publicity, including photographs and a news release of a check being presented to a respected researcher, the company made sure people knew about it. But that wasn't the end. The company then created a brochure in conjunction with the National Audubon Society entitled "Will a Bullet Kill the Last American Eagle?" That was followed by a poster designed to promote the identification and protection of eagles. The first press run of the poster was 2,500 copies. The supply was quickly depleted when a national news story made known its availability. The poster, of course, clearly included the company's identity— "Published and distributed as a public service by Georgia-Pacific/Growing Forests Forever." In addition to all that, the eagle protection story became standard fare in company speeches, magazines, films and slide shows.

Most important, internal communication was also effectively employed to make certain the external position was indeed based on a solid and truthful foundation of performance. Informational memos were sent to all public relations, timberland supervisory, and resource managerial employees throughout the company. The word was passed down to bulldozer operators, fallers, buckers, cruisers, and choker setters (Center 1975).

PRINCIPLE 7:
PLANNING IS ESSENTIAL

A public information officer (PIO) for a state park and recreation department was asked for a description of her duties. She replied, "I do everything no one else does. We work from day to day." Then she added rhetorically, "What crisis is the agency facing today?" (Baertsch, 1977). Unfortunately, this is all too common in natural resource agencies and is the embodiment of inefficiency and ineffectiveness.

Planning is a key to success in almost any endeavor, and the practice of public relations is no exception. Just as the good manager or researcher develops a detailed plan for a project in light of specific objectives, the effective public relations practitioner also plans every effort.

Planning is important in two ways. First, it keeps the organization on the offensive. Instead of the public relations function being relegated to "putting out fires," as in the case of the park and recreation PIO, long term planning can prevent many of those fires. For example, by annually analyzing public issues, as the forest industries do on a routine basis under the auspices of the American Forest Council, a plan can be developed that will allow allocation of limited finances and personnel to concentrate on priority concerns. In other words, what issues are currently on the minds of citizens and their elected leaders? Perhaps the need for new energy sources has become an issue of national concern while clearcutting has fallen to a lower priority. What, then, should your organization's position be in relation to the energy issue? How does it fit into your mission and goals? How could the issue adversely affect your mission and goals? Through careful analysis, an action plan can then be formulated to work with specific publics in a carefully scheduled and *timed* sequence and using appropriately modified techniques of communication. Planning will also include methods of evaluation so the effectiveness of the approach can be monitored and changed if necessary.

A second kind of planning is needed when an emergency occurs. The best possible efforts will not prevent an occasional "withdrawal" from the bank of goodwill. The problem might be a mass personnel layoff, the escape of a prescribed fire, or a vehicle accident. However, such incidents can be anticipated to a degree and dealt with through pre-planning. In the chapter on Emergency Information Services, we will see that public relations in a time of emergency can—and should—be pre-planned. This is no different than the pre-planning that occurs well in advance of suppression action on fires or the mobilization of personnel and equipment for rescue operations. Even when pre-planning is not possible, such as in Georgia-Pacific's eagle incident, planning should be a first step to reaction. Conscious of the basic principles of public relations, a skilled practitioner should be able to rapidly develop a series of steps that will mitigate the misfortune.

SUGGESTED REFERENCES

Experts in Action edited by Bill Cantor. 1984. Longman, Inc. New York.
Outdoor Ethics. Quarterly publication of the Izaak Walton League in cooperation with the Fred Bear Sports Club. Suite 1100, 1701 N. Fort Myer Dr., Arlington, VA 22209.
Public Relations Practices by Allen H. Center. 1975. Prentice-Hall, Inc. Englewood Cliffs, N.J.

The Tools of Public Relations

The effective practice of public relations, particularly as a staff function, requires the use of certain tools. Even if you are not part of a public relations staff, recognizing and perhaps modifying these tools can help you contribute to your organization's efforts to achieve greater understanding and support from the publics it serves.

Part II begins logically with the first step toward any successful venture—*planning*. This is followed by the tool that is necessary to facilitate planning as well as to enable us to effectively implement a public relations plan—*research*. Next is another important tool that is a prerequisite to successfully implementing public relations action—*identifying and working with publics*. Chapter 7 then introduces the tool that is at the heart of good public relations—*communication*.

4

Planning for
Good Public Relations

If you fail to plan, plan to fail.

Planning for good public relations is difficult to discuss because there is no proven right way to go about it. Each situation and each organization requires an individualized approach. The only hard, fast statement that can be made about planning is—plan we must.

In recent years there has been a definite increase in recognizing the need for better public relations. Unfortunately, what then often follows in an organization is a well-intentioned but incomplete or uncoordinated attempt to improve the situation. It is not unlike a hobbiest with a few tools, a workbench and the desire to create a piece of beautiful furniture. Despite his best intentions, without a detailed plan, a full complement of specialized tools, and the knowledge of how to use them, the finished product—if there is one—may be useful but far from perfect.

Planning is the key to success in most endeavors, and the job of promoting good public relations is no exception. Just as the good resource manager or researcher plans projects in light of specific objectives, so does the efficient public relations practitioner. The ideal is an annual plan or other long-range guide, but it is just as important to formulate a plan for each controversial issue and all short-term "crisis" situations. Planning is simply *a systematic approach to decision-making.* Whatever the method, the essential ingredient is the word *systematic*.

This chapter introduces some of the methods available to develop better public relations using a systematic approach made up of a sequence of logical steps.

THE ROLE OF PUBLIC RELATIONS IN DECISION-MAKING

Before looking at each step, it helps to take a broader view of how public relations should fit into the overall process of problem-solving. This has been put in the form of a model in figure 4.1 and makes a very important assumption. This assumption, which unfortunately is not true in many natural resource organizations today, is that the public relations person or staff is used *to counsel* decision-makers. In actual practice, the people most trained and in the best position to perform this vital function are often relegated to nothing more than public contact duties.

Here is a typical example written by an outstanding public information officer working in a national forest. This national forest, we might add, is painfully in the center of continuous land use conflicts and other controversial issues. Still, here is how this professional is utilized:

> *I write news releases; handle all public input; provide a liaison with news media personnel; maintain historical files; maintain photographic files; present speeches and slide programs; prepare brochures; provide public information advice to district personnel; and manage the Smokey Bear and Woodsy Owl programs. I am excluded from team management and other decision-making meetings.*

The information officer went on to say she believed this causes three major problems: (1) the public information function is not considered until *after* a decision, (2) despite her insights about the agency's relations with many of its publics, she has little power to influence management's decisions, and (3) she is not kept well informed. The end result contributes to poor public relations and the reason is that the person most responsible for public relations is not designated to counsel the decision-makers (management personnel).

In the more ideal situation shown in figure 4.1, public relations personnel are as important as the foresters, wildlife biologists, watershed specialists and others who provide advice on the technical aspects of a problem or controversial issue. They base this advice on appropriate research and pass it on to managers. Likewise, under the requirements of law—and common sense—the owner-publics have the right to provide input if the resources in question are managed by a government agency. While not required by law, the private sector would also be wise to consider its publics at that point in the decision process.

Managers must then assess the advice on public relations in light of other inputs and considerations. The important thing is that if this process is followed, they have the advice *before* the decision is made. They have solid information on how alternatives will affect various publics. They know what repercussions to expect, where to expect them, and perhaps how they can be dealt with. Armed with more than technical advice only on the biological or physical aspects of the problem, managers can make more intelligent, more efficient and less socially-disrupting decisions.

Once the decision is made, public relations people play another important role. This is in developing a plan that will facilitate acceptance and support for the selected course of action. Even if the plan succeeds, however, a final step is to monitor the situation lest new problems arise or public opinion sways away from being supportive. If the latter should occur then the process must begin again.

The steps for planning to achieve good public relations should begin at the pre-decision stage and continue through to the final solution. Viewed in this way, public relations can clearly be seen as an integral component of total resource management.

THE STEPS IN PUBLIC RELATIONS PLANNING

How to go about planning varies widely. Eugene Decker of Colorado State University stresses the approach that public relations planning is a component of *all* resource management planning. The two are inseparable, and the process often includes public involvement. In the private sector, *marketing strategy* sometimes is the appropriate term for what is developed in the planning stage. To sell a product or an image, the rule of thumb often used is the "Five Ms of Marketing":

1. Message-What is to be sold and said?
2. Market-To whom will we direct our message(s) and what can we find out about these people?
3. Medium-How can we best reach our market?
4. Money-How much will it cost? How much do we have to spend?
5. Measurement-What will be our definition of success?

In many government agencies, the closest thing to public relations planning is an annual work plan or program plan to provide guidance for information functions. Table 4.1 displays two actual examples.

Regardless of the approach most planning efforts involve the following four steps:

Research

Setting Goals and Objectives

Communicating

Monitoring and Evaluating

The amount of detail in each step may be elaborately developed using large staffs and taking months to complete, or they can be outlined on a sheet of paper by one or two individuals in a very short period of time. The point is that here is a structure that works. If modified to your circumstances it can go a long way toward good public relations.

Step 1: Background Research

Research in public relations takes many forms and serves several uses. Its use in planning is among the most important, and here it serves two general purposes. The first use occurs before a management decision is made. It is the challenge of detecting problems or controversial issues before they become volatile and counseling management accordingly. The second use is to help understand the publics involved and develop strategies that will build support after the management decision has been made.

Problem detection is achieved by constantly maintaining two-way communication with as many of the organization's publics as possible. It is also important that the technical staff alert the public relations people to conditions that could create problems. In short, detecting problems is a *listening* function—on-going, sensitive and crucial. It is the assessment of the social climate surrounding the problem and the reasoned anticipation of reactions to management decisions. This is no small order, but there are ways of achieving it, all involving research in one form or another.

In an example of the simplest case, analysis of a potential issue might result from a planned management action needed to safeguard a recreation resource or protect visitors from some danger. Perhaps overuse of wilderness is causing unacceptable damage to plant life, or deterioration of

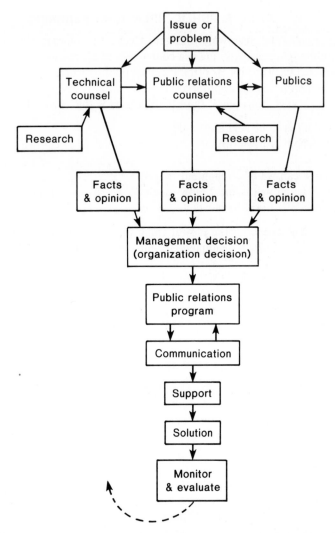

Figure 4.1. Public relations as a function in management decisions.

water quality in a popular lake. Scientists recommend to the manager that a permit system be imposed to limit use. From the public relations standpoint, analysis in this case would require listing the user groups affected, and conducting a survey to determine socio-economic characteristics, knowledge of the problem, and attitudes toward the problem and potential management strategies. If this is not possible, existing studies on these topics could be reviewed for clues. The combination of information would provide a good basis for advising managers on how a permit system would be accepted, and what kind of a public relations program would work best to head off negative reactions.

Table 4.1.
Examples of Items from Two Federal Information Program Plans.

USDA Forest Service (Regional Office)
II. *Goals, Objectives and Planned Actions*
    A. *Current Information*
        Purpose: Provide the public with current information about Forest Service Policies, programs, and activities to improve understanding and foster appropriate use.
        1. *Objectives for FY 1985*
            a. Work toward a better public understanding of National Forest management and productivity.

Additional Unit Involvement	*Planned Actions*
	(1) Evaluate the value in establishing a Regional Incident Information team and develop alternative for appropriate action (Pine, May 1985).
IS	(2) Arrange for Region 4 access to the Dialcom Computer News Service and develop a daily procedure to check into the system (Pine, Dec. 1984).
WL	(3) Implement the R-4 Wildlife Management Action Plan including:
	(a) Develop a slide-tape program (Miracle, Jan. 1985)
	(b) Develop feature for Reporter or video with RF message on commitment to wildlife values (Eldredge, May 1985).
	(c) Conduct a media tour highlighting NF habitat improvement and endangered species programs (Pine, Aug. 1985).
	(d) Develop a series of feature stories on unique or special interest projects related to habitat/T&E species programs on National Forests (Miracle, Sept. 1985)
INT	(4) Develop Educator's Field Seminar using Riparian Management theme
R-1	(Cartwright, June 1985).
	(5) Implement assigned actions resulting from the productivity task force.
	(a) Develop a slide-tape program on productivity of the National Forests (Pine, Sept. 1985).

(continued through several more action items)

Bureau of Land Management (Washington Office)
  5. *Strengthen relations with ORV industry associations.*
    Current Status: Good working relationships have developed between individuals in BLM's WO and representatives of the ORV industry. Examples of the latter include the Motorcycle Industry Council, a consulting firm called People Planners, and the Associated Blazers of California. All seem highly concerned with the need to promote principles of low impact ORV use on the public lands.
    Objectives Addressed: A, D, E
    (1) On an experimental basis, cooperate with People Planners to conduct a local or regional workshop on ORV recreation for BLM managers. Appropriate publicity directed at ORV publics should accompany the effort.
    (2) Personally visit and explain BLM's ORV management program to key officers in all Washington-based ORV industry associations. (This should be done along with personnel from the Division of Recreation). Provide copies of ORV posters, "Promise of the Land" and/or copies of other appropriate material. Explore possible cooperative efforts for FY 1983.

At the other extreme of scope, if not complexity, is the American Forest Council's (AFC) annual assessment of public relations needs on a nationwide basis. Beginning in 1976, this industrial association moved away from its more general approach to public education and began focusing on specific issues. AFC determines these issues two ways. One is through polling members of regional industrial committees, staff members, and others whose responsibilities include communicating with the industry's publics. Hundreds of people contribute their ideas which help determine priority areas of concern to be influenced through a public relations campaign. The next year, AFC's efforts focus on *those* issues. Another way AFC determines issues and analyzes public perception of them is through employing the services of professional pollsters. The results, often in the form of opinion trends on the issues, are then made available to leaders throughout the industry.

Public Acceptance Assessment

Few can afford the services of professional researchers to help detect and analyze potential public relations problems. Fortunately, there are other ways to achieve this, two of which have been designed specifically for natural resource managers. Both have the capability of analyzing issues and public response *before* managers make decisions.

One of these was described by Mater (1977) as ten steps in making a "Public Acceptance Assessment." The approach uses a series of checklists (available from Timber Press, 9999 S.W. Wilshina, Portland, OR 97225) to accomplish the following tasks.

1. *Describe the project or program.* Resources, features, planned alterations and current users of the project area are listed.
2. *Determine the impacts of the project on the public.* A checklist of whether or not project activities would have an impact on a host of activities or environmental qualities, and if so, whether the expected impact would be positive or negative. An environmental impact statement would also meet this requirement.
3. *Determine which publics care about the potential impacts.* Descriptions and estimates of how many people are in each group.
4. *Find out how the publics perceive these impacts.* The impacts from step 2 are listed, then rated as having a positive or negative effect and whether it will be "imperceptible," "moderate" or "significant." Next to each is another set of columns estimating how a specific public can be expected to perceive the same impacts. A different sheet is used for each public. Also included is how the public's perceptions were determined, i.e., letters to the editor, a survey or some other research technique.
5. *Find out why they care.* For each negative impact expected to be perceived as significant, what is involved—values, beliefs, attitudes or self-interest? Importantly, what *individuals* or groups relate to each?
6. *Evaluate how much they care.* For each public perceiving negative impacts, their 'probable action' is listed, i.e., "none," "speak at public hearing," "enter formal protest," "initiate a petition," or "institute legal action." Also listed for each is how this prediction was determined, i.e., previous actions, letters, comments, etc.

7. *Analyze whether those who care have sufficient influence to affect the outcome.* After displaying the issues, publics and key individuals who are likely to actively oppose various impacts of the proposed project, the next thing is to note which of the individuals are most influential. This is determined by identifying opinion leaders (Chapter 7) and others who have a record of past influence in the community or on similar issues.

8. *Decide what impacts you can alter.* In this step the impacts are again listed, then rated based on how readily they can be controlled. This is essentially a display of *options* that the managers face, and which, if any, will add costs to the project. Technical input is usually required here from foresters, biologists, engineers and others. Another checklist column can then be used to display what the result of a project alteration will have on public reaction.

9. *Predict the probability of public action on the project.* In this step, Mater's method sums various figures used throughout the checklists to quantify probable action, probable influence of the opposition, numbers of perceived impacts, etc. Changes in these figures can then be shown for each possible project alternative.

10. *Draw conclusions and make decisions on proceeding with the project.* This is a summary statement showing recommendations for project alterations, financial and time trade-offs, and a communication program aimed at the publics involved.

The strength of Mater's Public Acceptance Assessment is in its systematic approach to identifying and analyzing issues and publics *before* a management decision is made. In fact, sometimes it can be conducted before publics are even aware of the possible project. The system is particularly well suited to industry, but can easily be adapted to public resource management. The difference would be the requirement for more public involvement in the latter, probably at the point where alternatives are considered and selected. However, it provides any decision-maker with a much clearer picture of the public relations challenge he faces under each alternative, and some valuable data for use in planning how to overcome opposition and win support for the alternatives that are ultimately selected.

Social Impact Analysis

A similar ten step process has been developed for use by the USDA Forest Service in predicting social changes that might result from mineral, recreational or other major resource developments. The intent of the process, called Social Impact Analysis (SIA), is to help managers make better, more sensitive decisions by clarifying the social, as well as the economic, biological, and physical effects of a proposed action and its alternatives (Bryan and Hendee, 1983). It grew out of requirements imposed by the National Environmental Policy Act, specifically the need to predict social impacts when preparing Environmental Assessments (EA) or the more detailed Environmental Impact Statements (EIS). For these purposes, Social Impact Analysis is now used by most federal resource agencies.

The SIA described here was developed in 1978 by the Foundation for Urban Neighborhood Development under contract with the Forest Service's Surface Environment and Mining Program. Like Mater's procedure, this method can yield valuable information to prevent or at least keep conflict at an acceptable level. However, the public relations connotations are more veiled, sociological jargon abounds, and the emphasis is more on keeping a community stable while improving economic diversity and choice for its residents. There is also considerable focus on a socio-geographic region labeled the "Human Resource Unit (HRU)." This is an area believed to have a common physical, social and economic environment. It is used as the basis of analysis in the SIA process.

The SIA process is diagrammed in Figure 4.2. To date the recommended procedures are less concise than Mater's and depend more on narrative reporting than checklist summaries. Some brief explanations of the ten steps are provided below.

1. Seven cultural descriptions are used in providing an overall picture of the social structure within logical geographic boundaries. Included are descriptions of existing publics, settlement patterns, work routines, communication patterns, available services and recreational activities.

2. Further characterization of the area is made by compiling statistical data on how people earn their livings. Data must be collected on: population change, kinds of employment (and changes in each through the years), wage structures and the existing local labor supply.

3. In this step the many uses of forest resources by specific resident and non-resident publics are listed. Up-to-date records of current demands help immensely at this point.

4. "The resource development force" (a new mine, recreation complex, sawmill or similar development) is described by location, magnitude, timing, resource and manpower needs, technology, practices and policies of the developer, and the project's current phase of development.

5. This is the first of several predictive steps that follows description of the current situation. The purpose is to predict social impacts of proposed developments for 5, 10 and 20 year periods. Kent et al (1979) stated that each phase of a resource development activity such as mining usually goes unnoticed by resource managers until a crisis occurs. In Step 5, the phases of a development are plotted by time periods, with the specific requirements of the development described for each phase.

6. In light of the anticipated requirements in each phase of development, an estimate is made on the change that may be expected in the four economic indicators listed in Step 2.

7. Based on the above changes, the cultural descriptions in Step 1 may also be expected to change. The anticipated changes, if any, are described in this step.

8. The final three steps are designed to translate the above information into a form Forest Service management can use to determine how best to avoid disruptive consequences of the proposed developments. By identifying future demands, the manager can stay in control of, rather than be controlled by, changes resulting from resource development. He can predict future public issues by knowing in advance the resource demands the changes will bring. This allows for a public relations program that is on the *offense* rather than the more typical and disastrous reactive position. In Step 8 the changing demands for each forest resource are assessed along with likely issues and the publics they will involve.

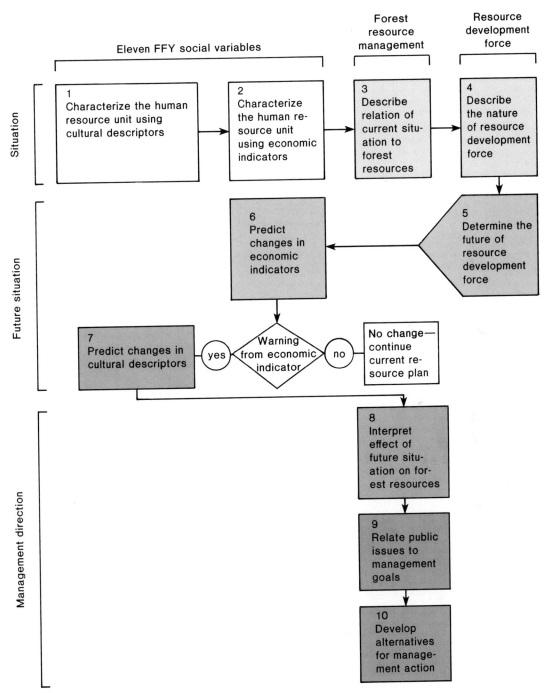

Figure 4.2. A ten-step social impact analysis process developed for the USDA Forest Service.

9. This is actually several steps that first require screening out those issues that can not legitimately be addressed by the agency, are not practical to control via agency initiatives, or are beyond addressing and resolving within given budgets. Remaining issues are compared with management goals to identify disharmony, then discussed with leaders of existing publics, and finally placed in priority for action.

10. This is another series of steps that lists alternative courses of action open to the manager, the favorable and unfavorable effects related to each, the costs, trade-offs, and individuals involved. It also requires public involvement to help select the alternatives or create new ones.

Simpler Approaches to Analysis

If the preceding methods are too complex for the situation at hand, there are other simpler methods of analysis that can be used. Remember, the whole purpose of this step is to gather enough background information on a problem or potential problem to help managers make the best decisions, or to help lay out a strategy to gain public support. In the former case, the various methods of *public involvement* may be appropriate. Another way to help with the analysis is use of the *case study* method. Both are discussed in the following chapter on research.

Sometimes all that is necessary is to draw upon personal knowledge of the case, and/or the experience of others associated with it. However, it *is* important to summarize this information on paper to share with others and to help check for erroneous data or important omissions. At the very minimum, your analysis should include:

- Brief statement of the problem and its history, and established facts.
- Publics involved and key leaders, especially opinion leaders. Who or which publics are most likely to be offended?
- Where do the publics stand on the issue (what perceptions are held), how strongly do they feel, what changes are anticipated given the management alternatives?
- Time frames and budgetary constraints.

Step 2: Setting Goals and Objectives

Once a management decision is made, the public relations function becomes one of influencing people to accept and support the decision. The same research results that were used to help make the decision can now be used to help map out an approach to successfully implement the selected alternative(s). A lot of data has been assessed to this point, but it all helps in understanding the publics that were (or might become) opposed to the manager's plans.

In developing an effective public relations program, the next step is to set goals and objectives. These are among the most important tools a person can use in just about any endeavor where achievement is important. Goals and specific objectives should be inherent in doing school work, winning a lover, winning a war, teaching, supervising, developing a career or managing a natural resource. Objectives are road maps to a goal, and without them we have no sound basis for deciding our direction, pacing our effort, knowing when to stop or judging our successes (or failures).

The terms *goal* and *objective* are often used interchangeably. However, they would be more useful if thought of as separate ideas. A goal is an end toward which effort is directed. An objective may be thought of as a mini-goal, or part of a series of efforts necessary to attain the stated *end,* or ultimate goal. An example may help make this clearer. In 1970, a large paper manufacturing firm had its collective conscience pricked by the fact that its women and minority employees were far below comparative percentages outside the company. Top management established a *goal* of meeting the company's social responsibility by having women and minorities represented at all levels, in proportions roughly equal to those in the surrounding communities.

Once the goal was established, the company quickly discovered that there were very real barriers preventing women and minorities from becoming qualified for positions in some areas of corporate activities, particularly engineering. It was obvious that to achieve the company's goal, these barriers would need to be overcome. This is where objectives came in. The barriers were listed and the ones the company felt they could remove were: (1) a deficiency in appropriate training at the high school level in mathematics and science, and (2) high college tuition costs. Objectives could then be established to overcome these problems.

Properties of an Objective

To be effective, an objective must meet the following tests:

Is it measurable?
Is it specific?
Are the expected results clearly stated?
Is the objective realistic? That is, is it challenging yet attainable?
Are time limits specified?

With these criteria in mind, it is easy to see that the paper company's attack on their affirmative action problem could be better laid out. For example, a plant manager or other appropriate executive might have specified the following objectives to help reach the company's goal:

Objective 1: By June, 1972, 95 percent of all high school students (freshmen through seniors) in Milltown will have received a color booklet on careers in paper production. The booklet will include descriptions of opportunities for women and minorities, and clearly specify the necessary college preparation.

Objective 2: Beginning September, 1972, five engineering scholarships will be awarded annually to qualified (based on high school performance) women and minorities who place highest in a company-sponsored essay contest.

Objective 3: Twelve summer internship positions will be made available in the plant's engineering division beginning in the summer of 1972. Through personal recruiting in area schools, company representatives will identify qualified women and minorities to fill at least half these positions.

In each case, the objectives provide a way of knowing if efforts were successful, and if not, by what degree they failed. They also make it easier to decide who is responsible for carrying out the necessary tasks.

Two Kinds of Objectives

The use of objectives sometimes becomes confused because there are at least two kinds. Both are necessary in public relations planning and it is important to distinguish between them so they can be expressed correctly and used effectively.

Activity Objectives   For lack of a better term, let us call the first group of objectives *activity* objectives. These are the most commonly used. They simply list the things we the public relations people, resource managers, or others in the internal public will do. These are our action items, or "do list." The Forest Service items shown in Table 4.1 are examples. Others might be:

- Reach all resident duck hunters in Minnesota.
- Place an exhibit in 75% of the county fairs in the state.
- Contact all adjoining landowners at least twice each year.
- Distribute 4,000 copies of the brochure, *Chain Saw Safety*.
- Contact all campers in grizzly bear habitat.

Activity objectives are like a shopping list. They provide a helpful way to list what needs to be done. They should also indicate who should do it and by when. In public relations work, activity objectives are usually used to help assure that we *reach the target publics*. This is a necessary step toward selecting the best media for the job and determining the budget necessary to meet a particular goal.

Behavioral Objectives   Reaching the public is only part of the job. If we stop there, we have no way of knowing if we were actually successful. It is quite easy to *contact* campers or *distribute* brochures. *Behavioral* objectives make it clear what needs to happen if we can consider our efforts truly successful. For help in this area, we can turn to educators who for years have been using *instructional* objectives.

Instructional or other behavioral objectives identify exactly what we want the *other person* to be able to *do* after we have communicated. After all Minnesota duck hunters are contacted with our message, what do we expect of them if we are to deem our efforts successful? An example might be "to have each one *be able to recall*, two months after our communication, one disadvantage of using lead shot for shooting waterfowl." An objective in grizzly country might be "to have at least one member of each party *be able to judge* whether a camping site is relatively safe from an accidental night encounter with a grizzly."

Mager (1975) warned that unless you describe what the learner will be *doing* when demonstrating that he "understands" your message, you have described very little at all. Below are listed some words to avoid because they are open to many interpretations:

to know	to enjoy
to understand	to believe
to appreciate	to grasp the significance of

In Figure 4.3 are more specific choices. Note that they reflect different levels of understanding. That is, it is one thing to have campground visitors be able *to name* poison ivy. *Identifying* it in the field reveals a higher level of understanding; and *differentiating* between it and other three-leaf plants a higher level yet. Other examples of behavioral objectives are:

-By October, to have all ORV recreationists who use the Mohave Desert be able to name BLM as the agency responsible for the area's resource management.
-After the campaign, to have 30 more landowners sign up to develop management plans.
-By the end of the course, 80 percent of the workshop participants will be able to judge which trees should be removed in an improvement cutting.

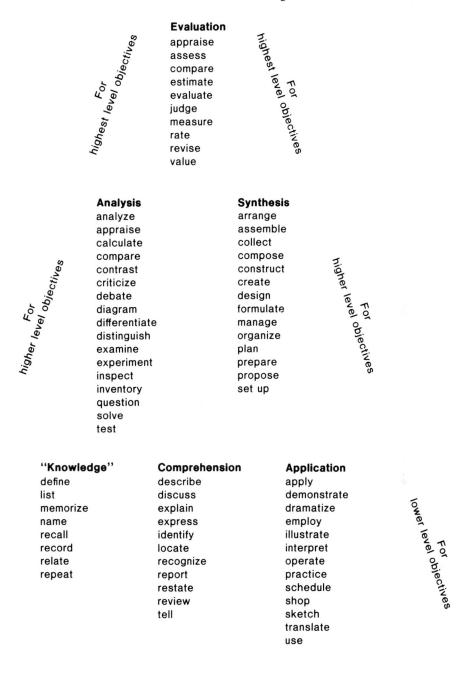

Figure 4.3. Verbs expressing levels of understanding for use in writing objectives where learning is expected.

At the beginning of any public relations project, it is important to know your overall goal(s), set activity objectives to make sure all necessary tasks are identified and will be accomplished, and list behavioral objectives so you know exactly what must be achieved as an end result to meet your goals or measure progress.

Step 3: Selecting the Communication Techniques

When analysis of an issue has been completed, management decisions have been made, and the goals and objectives for the public relations part of the project have been set, the next step is deciding how to most effectively achieve communication.

The Best Channels

Too often the media, or *channels* (see Chapter 7) that will be used to carry the organization's information are selected only on the basis of convenience. It is easy to order up a brochure or write a news release, so that becomes the standard approach. It is also one reason for so much anemic public relations in the natural resource professions.

The better approach is to be familiar with the advantages and disadvantages of each communication channel available to you. Many are described in Part III to help with this step in the planning process. Next, consider the characteristics of the key publics that were identified during issue analysis. Are the people you want to reach local, regional, or part of a national audience? Do they already know about the issue, i.e. are they *aware* of it or is this where you have to start? Or are they at the other end of the adoption sequence (Chapter 7) with their attitudes already well set in concrete? Are there other agencies involved? Should an elected official be informed?

Using a matrix such as Table 4.2, array the important characteristics of your key publics or situation down the left column. Then add x-marks based on the abilities of each medium to effectively communicate in relation to those characteristics. This is a rapid and useful way to select the best medium or—in most cases—the best combination of media to meet the needs of each public relations issue.

Many of the pertinent characteristics to consider in your matrix will be discussed in following sections. Some examples not included in Table 4.2 are knowledge levels of target publics, how different kinds of people typically obtain their information on new ideas, and whether beliefs, opinion, or values are the ultimate target of change.

The benefits of careful channel selection include: more rapid message dissemination to target publics; more effective communication since much of the "chance" element has been removed through a logical look at the options; and savings in money, time, and materials by eliminating media judged to be inefficient under the given circumstances. However, the use of several channels should always be considered as a means of assuring that the message reaches the target public. Also, when a person receives the message through more than one channel, there will often be a reinforcement effect which has been shown to be important in influencing opinion change. In some cases, a *saturation campaign* may even be in order. Like a politician's barrage at election time, this procedure uses as many channels as possible as often as possible. However, few natural resource organizations have the funds available or the need for such an extravagant spewing of information. *The better approach is targeted communication.*

Table 4.2
A Generalized Guide to the Selection of Efficient Communication Channels.

Issue-Related Considerations	Personal				Print Media					Non-Personal — Electronic Media				
	Face to Face	Field Trip	Open House	Phone	Letter	Newsletter	Brochure	Magazine	News-paper	Exhibit	Automated Sound/Slides	Television	Radio	Motion Pictures
Rapid Communication is Important	?	?	?	X	X				X			X	X	
High Level Objectives	X	X	?				X	X		?	?	?	X	X
Low Level Objectives	X	X	X	X	X	X	X	X	X	X	X	X	X	X
Point in Adoption Sequence: Awareness				?	?	X	?	X	X	X		X	X	?
Interest			?	?	X	X	X	X	X	X	X	X	X	X
Evaluation	X	X	X	X	X	X	X	?	?	?	X	?	?	?
Trial	X	X	X	X	?	?	?							
Local Problem	X	X	X	X	?	X	X		X	X	X	?	X	
Regional or National Problem					?	?		X	?			X	?	X
Potentially Offended Individual/Public	X	X	?	?	?									
Elected Official	X	X	?	X	X	?								
Internal Publics	X	X	X	X	X	X	X			X	X			
Other Agencies	X	X	X	X	X	X								

X = Usually an efficient and appropriate channel.
? = Depends largely on circumstances and how well the channel is used.

Timing Is Essential

Another important communication element to be considered in planning is *timing*. In fact, this is one of the characteristics of public relations that sets it apart from the more common information and education function. Timing is the chronological order in which different target individuals or publics receive the messages. This is a simple concept and usually easy to implement. However, it is often ignored and when it is, unnecessary problems almost invariably result.

In deciding the order in which communication should take place, the key question to ask is, "Who are the potentially offended parties in this case?" That is, who will be offended by receiving the news of a proposed management action from the "wrong" source or through an improper channel? For example, elected officials do not appreciate hearing through the mass media that a major action is being planned by some organization that will impact his constituents. This is especially true when a government agency is involved. Similarly, supervisors often resent and react negatively to a proposal or decision they are not privy to prior to its being announced to people further down the chain of command. Another common situation involves actions that affect property received from a donor. In each case, egos are at stake. When this is not recognized, public relations problems are created or made worse.

The general rule is to contact the potentially offended individuals *first,* using a channel appropriate to the situation. The safest means is through personal contact and by an individual with enough rank to be viewed with esteem by the potentially offended. In some cases a phone call or letter will suffice, in others the "wining and dining" technique may be necessary. Frequently, the potentially offended public consists of the workers right under your own roof. The importance of first gaining internal support as a foundation for wider support can not be over-emphasized. The important thing is to *plan* the order in which individuals or publics will be contacted, then coordinate this carefully with any release of information.

Publicity Planning

In addition to planning a comprehensive public relations approach to issues or specific problems, attention must also be given to on-going publicity. As will be seen in Chapter 7, one kind of planned publicity is intended to continually shed favorable light on the organization and its programs. This helps create and maintain a favorable public image, or make those all-important deposits into the Bank of Goodwill. A second kind of publicity announces and focuses attention on a specific event such as an upcoming open house, tree farm dedication or other special occasion. Either way, a concrete plan of action will assure the fullest, most effective use of communication channels to achieve the objectives of exposing large numbers of the general or specific publics to your messages.

Figure 4.4 shows some manuals that have been developed to guide publicity efforts related to natural resources. Two of them are for special events, whereas the *Tree Farm Manual* is more general. All make it as easy as possible for anyone to plan a complete and effective publicity program. Such guide books usually include factual background information on the event or program, committees needed, suggested timing, and a wide array of ideas on obtaining publicity. Also included are sample news releases (with blank spaces for "localizing" the message), proclamations for the mayor or governor to sign, exhibit and staged event suggestions, and publications, photographs, slide sets, bumper stickers, buttons and similar items available from the sponsor.

To assure on-going publicity for an organization or program, an annual plan is necessary. Different agencies have different approaches to this, but the important thing is not format but rather that a realistic plan be developed *and used*. This should include a weekly or monthly list of topics, communication channels and individual contacts, and the names of personnel responsible for each. Objectives can also be used, but these are less important in on-going publicity campaigns than in issue-oriented planning.

Below is an example of topics from a fish and game department's general publicity calendar:

Month	Topics to Stress
JULY	Fishing Report; Sportsmen of the Week; Magazine Promotion; Antelope and Bighorn Seasons (permits, etc.); Elk Permits; Conservation Courses (schools and colleges); Commission News; Grouse Season; Fur Regulations; Conventions and Personnel; Hunter Safety Report; Landowner-Fishermen Relations.
AUGUST	Fishing Report; Sportsmen of the Week; Dove Season; High Country Fishing; Hunter Safety Report; Bighorn, Antelope and Elk Drawings; Commission News; New Laws in Effect; Turkey Season.
SEPTEMBER	Fishing Report; Sportsmen of the Week; Commission News; Elk, Deer Season Preview; Migratory Bird (duck and geese) Populations; Antelope & Bighorn Review; Rabbit Season; New Hunting Access Roads; Department Activities, etc.

A similar list for specific communication channels makes planning even more helpful. For example, there can be a monthly list of topics to be included in the in-house newsletter, external magazine, regular radio or television program, exhibits and other channels regularly used by the organization. Annual personal appearances (Kiwanis Club, Career Day at the high school, Scout Camp, etc.) should also be listed to allow for the best advance planning and integration into an overall public relations effort.

Figure 4.5 illustrates one way to develop and display publicity plans for an entire year. It is a system used by Boy Scouts of America at the local level and could be used effectively on a ranger district or at a state park, fish hatchery, wildlife refuge or similar management unit. The 23″ × 30″ chart allows ample space for listing topics or objectives, who is responsible, and a few words of further explanation. This or a similar chart would go a long way toward improving on-going publicity efforts in natural resource management.

Step 4: Monitor and Evaluate

Of all the deficiencies related to practicing public relations, evaluation must rank at the top of the list. This is not unique to the natural resources field. In their excellent discussion of this topic, Cutlip and Center (1978) cited the example of millions of dollars being spent by Mobil Oil on its public relations advertising. When asked if it was paying off, a top public relations officer responded that he had no idea! In government, millions are similarly spent each year reissuing booklets and films with absolutely no checks on the effectiveness of the original efforts. So it is with nearly all efforts in natural resource public relations.

Figure 4.4. Publicity manuals can be used to assist the inexperienced in obtaining maximum publicity for programs or special events.

PUBLIC RELATIONS PLANNING CHART										Public Relations Division Boy Scouts of America
Month										
Project or Event										
Committee and Task Force Meetings										
Internal Communications Program										
External Communications Program										
News and Publicity (all media)										
Public Service Advertising										
Broadcast Programming										
Special Print Media (company, partner, ethnic, supplements)										
Exhibits and Displays										
Direct Mail										
Speakers and Films										
Recognition										

Figure 4.5. Chart used by Boy Scouts of America to plan a continuous publicity program.

Unfortunately, efforts at evaluation in public agencies are usually stymied by the official dim view of surveys. Nearly all tools of evaluation involve some procedure of systematically sampling and questioning target publics—a practice severely controlled in federal agencies by the Office of Management and Budget. However, even with this limitation there are ways to incorporate evaluation into a public relations program.

In many ways *evaluation is the common sense of learning from experience*. It provides a factual basis for corrective adjustments to guide both managers and public relations practitioners to achieve their goals. Evaluation includes constant monitoring of the entire process from analysis of the issues through to the close of a project. The process, including the public relations or publicity plan, is not inviolably set in concrete. Any part should be changed if it appears to be ineffective or producing undesirable results. Evaluation also includes a more formal look at the outcomes of a public relations effort. The key question is, *did it get results*? This can provide solid justification for dollars spent, or in the case of failures it can point to adjustments needed or ways to do a better job next time.

Pretests

Evaluating a public relations effort should begin *before* the project goes public. This simply means *pretesting* any booklets, posters, slide shows, exhibits, speeches or other means devised to influence public opinion. With written material, readability tests should be routine, including a test to see if the message is understandable (and persuasive if that is an objective). With all methods, trial runs should be made and they should not be made using your friendly office staff, but by using randomly selected members of the target public. The trial run can be equated to test-marketing a new product. Before millions are spent to market an item nationwide, a limited number are produced and put on sale in a few "typical" locations. If problems occur, money is saved and the company is spared the embarrassment of a colossal flop.

Another form of pretesting involves conducting a benchmark survey to determine awareness, knowledge and/or attitudes prior to a planned campaign. Through a similar survey during or after a public relations campaign a good measure can be taken of changes that might be attributed to the project. Telephone and mail surveys are usually used for this kind of evaluation. Analysis of unsolicited public comment prior to the project can also be valuable in assessing effects.

Documenting End Results

Once a public relations or publicity program has been implemented, it is necessary to determine at least three things: (1) Were the target publics *reached* and to what extent? (2) Was the *response* what was wanted? and (3) What is the long-range *impact* (i.e., are there lasting effects such as changed behavior or support for the agency)? By now it should be apparent that unless goals and objectives were set at the beginning of the project, there is really no way to know what to look for as end results.

The mechanics of an evaluation can take many forms. Research firms, universities and experiment stations have personnel who are best equipped to conduct or assist in these efforts, but anyone can do this to some degree.

Coverage   Coverage is the easiest result to document. It is also the least meaningful because of the old maxim that contact is not necessarily communication. Still, if the messages have not reached the target public(s), then there is no chance of communicating. Gauging coverage can begin with a checkoff of items in a plan as they are accomplished. Any plan for public relations action—whether long term publicity (Figure 4.5) or short term action at a fire or other emergency—should contain a list of individuals, publics and media to be contacted. When the contact has been made, it is noted. Simple as it is, it *is* at least a step toward evaluation. One of its benefits is that this record can quickly reveal gaps in the program's coverage.

Another common method is to monitor mass media releases that make it into newspapers, magazines, newsletters and on the air. Sometimes "clipping services" are hired to do this work. Otherwise, one or more individuals in the organization must be assigned to monitor certain publications and perhaps even selected electronic newscasts or other programs toward which communications were aimed. Combined with the audience data of those media and information of other contacts made, a rather good picture can be constructed of what messages reached how many of what kinds of people. Using expense records and a little arithmetic, it is even possible to compute costs per contact. For any particular issue, this is a form of evaluation that can be very useful for monthly or annual comparisons, or for justifying budgets and personnel.

Response   The next determination should be whether or not the messages were received as intended. That is, what was the initial response of the target publics? This is more difficult to ascertain, but without this measure how can we know if our efforts were effective? In some cases, this can be determined without survey research. For example, if a PSA offers a free booklet, a record can be kept of the number of requests. By including a code (such as Dept. A, Dept. B, etc.) in releases or ads sent to different publications and stations, it is even possible to determine which evoked the best response. In one such evaluation, a furniture company found its publicity was seven times more effective than its advertising—and that the publicity brought in 1.4 million dollars worth of inquiries (Cutlip and Center, 1978)! By taking steps to build feedback opportunities into communication, we provide the basis for evaluating response as well as providing further opportunities for communication.

Other evaluation techniques include surveys by means of interviews or questionnaires. One useful method is to determine what people have read in a publication. For example, the interviewer goes through a newspaper or magazine with a person and asks, "Did you happen to read anything on this page?" The results clearly show which messages got through and which did not. Another is to query people by phone to see if they watched or heard your program on radio or television. If they did, appropriate questions can determine if they understood the message, if it aroused their interest, changed their minds, reinforced an existing opinion, or perhaps angered or bored them. Such spot checks need not involve large numbers of people as long as they are representative of the target audience. At the very least, selected individuals can be contacted following a communication effort to determine how they respond to the message. However, because of the potential for bias and an inaccurate picture, this must be used with extreme caution.

Impact   This result is really "the bottom line." It reveals whether or not the public relations program has been successful because it measures the ultimate impact of the effort. Perhaps the effort was aimed at gaining support for the voluntary use of fire pans or portable stoves on trips down a wild river (to prevent the buildup of ashes at beach campsites). Evaluation of coverage and response would certainly be valuable in determining what communication adjustments might be needed. But, the end result is whether or not there is a reduction of ash piles on the beaches that season.

Many measures of impact can be made directly, and they *should* be made. Is litter or vandalism reduced? Do more people understand how to obtain their firewood while complying with agency rules? Have memberships increased? Have more supportive or favorable letters about some issue been received in the office? Are legislators supportive of the agency? Interviews, experiments and surveys can also be used, but the best measure of impact is to determine the actual changes in behavior that result from good public relations practice.

In every case, the measure of coverage, response and impact must be compared to the goals and objectives established at the beginning of the project.

SUGGESTED REFERENCES

An Approach to Social Resource Management by James A. Kent, Richard J. Greiwe, James E. Freeman and John J. Ryan. 1979. Foundation for Urban and Neighborhood Development, Inc. and The John Ryan Co., Denver, Colorado.

Citizens Involved: Handle With Care by Jean Mater. 1977. Timber Press, Portland, Oregon.

Effective Public Relations by Scott M. Cutlip, Allen H. Center and Glen M. Broom. 1985. Prentice-Hall, Inc., Englewood Cliffs, N.J.

Lesly's Public Relations Handbook edited by Philip Lesly. 1983. Prentice-Hall, Inc., Englewood Cliffs, N.J.

Preparing Instructional Objectives by Robert F. Mager. 1975. Fearon Publishers, Palo Alto, California.

5

Research

*Factual foundations will serve to dispel the idea
of the (public relations) practitioner as a sort of witch doctor.*
—Cutlip, Center and Broom (1985)

Research is the tool that provides answers and solid guidelines for public relations action. Some research is highly structured and technical, providing an in-depth look at national trends or social psychological relationships. Other methods, however, can be used easily and quickly by anyone with the desire to improve upon traditional guesswork as the guide to action.

In the private sector, public relations research is increasingly routine, particularly among large companies and organizations. In the government agencies, it is relatively rare. Many problems are involved with the use of this tool, but in one way or another it should be included in the planning of any public relations action.

OMB Restrictions

With the notable exception of elections and the responsibilities assigned to the Bureau of the Census, the federal government traditionally has been suspicious of attempts to gather opinions or other information from the public. In 1935 a bill was even introduced to stop such "vicious practice" by prohibiting the use of the U.S. mails for taking public opinion polls (Hawver, 1978). This attitude was reflected in the Federal Report Act of 1942 and is enforced by the President's Office of Management and Budget (OMB). In short, the 1942 law prohibits federal employees or their contractors from collecting identical information from ten or more persons outside the government without OMB's approval. This includes oral interviews, written questionnaires, telephone surveys, reports, applications, and other devices for collecting information. Standard Form 83A is available from OMB to request clearance for any proposed research of this nature, and if granted (which is usually a several month process at best), an approval number must be displayed along with its expiration date. This act does *not* apply to individuals outside the government who wish to conduct social research on federal land *if* the funding does not come from federal sources.

In recent years, various actions have weakened the Federal Report Act, but regulations at the department level and the OMB procedures still effectively screen out helter-skelter information gathering and much annoyance of forest visitors and others who would be the target of inquiries. But it also limits the federal resource manager in his ability to utilize many well tested research methods to take public pulse-readings.

Should Outside Help Be Used?

Another problem in using the tool of research is that to use it correctly, considerable expertise is often required. "Ignorance is bliss" seems to portray much of the way it is currently used. An example is the politician who conducts a poll of the constituents in his party and then proclaims the findings as the "desire of the people." In fact, they may represent only a small minority of *all* the people. Similarly, during the week when other jobs are done, a state park manager goes through the campground with his clipboard asking what the people like and dislike, and perhaps why they are there. The results of this procedure almost guarantee that such a biased response will be obtained that it really is not worth the effort to collect the data.

Excellent books are available on social research methods, a few of which are listed here as suggested references. But conducting social research and obtaining valid results is like flying an airplane—much learning must precede much practice and experience, and then to do the job right numerous factors must be considered and coordinated simultaneously. Even with that, accidents occur from carelessness or unexpected conditions. We emphasize the point because it has been our experience that managers and even biologically-oriented scientists are frequently oblivious to the special requirements and knowledge needed in social research.

Because of these difficulties, it would be misleading to present a condensed chapter on "how-to-do-research." Instead, we list some of the advantages and disadvantages of the various common approaches to research useful in public relations. From this, the practitioner can consider which may be useful and will then, hopefully, seek assistance from the outset. And assistance *is* available. In the federal agencies, the USDA Forest Service has social scientists in most of its regional experiment stations; the Corps of Engineers has a social research program at its Waterways Experiment Station in Vicksburg, Mississippi; and the National Park Service has regional chief scientists, plus several Cooperative Park Studies Units located on university campuses. State agencies have ready access to social scientists in the state colleges. In most cases, arrangements can be made to have the work done by graduate students working under the guidance of more experienced professors. This reduces costs, provides educational opportunities and usually assures the contracting agency of having the study conducted with enthusiasm and quality. Companies frequently use the services of professional research firms. These are found in the phone directories of metropolitan areas and some have been listed by Cook (1983) in *Lesly's Public Relations Handbook.* Many "consultants" are also available, ranging from college professors and Madison Avenue-type specialists to college students or individuals who perhaps have not had a single course in statistical methods. Extreme caution must be taken in using consultants, for there are no accrediting or licensing systems to assure competency.

Methods

After the above warnings we hasten to add that research should not be ignored even though it presents more problems than the other tools of public relations. Simply sitting down and reading reference materials on persuasive communications, or outlining which publics need to be considered, are forms of research. From the list of common methods below, it should be apparent that there are also other more structured approaches that in some cases can be used by anyone. Others, however, are the domain of experts. In *every* case, a clearly stated purpose of the research must precede selection of the method or the specific procedural details. Before anything else is done, be sure you can answer the questions: (1) "What is (are) the *problem(s)* we face" and (2) "What must we *know* to solve the problem?" These questions should be asked (and doing it on paper sharpens them to the point of greater usefulness) and answered as each public relations issue is faced. Importantly, no more or no less data should be collected than are needed to answer question number two.

Surveys

There are many kinds of surveys and purposes for their use. If conducted so that unbiased and adequate samples of a public are surveyed, this method is perhaps the best for gaining an understanding of the opinions, knowledge, communication habits (e.g. sources and channels used relative to a particular issue) and other pertinent characteristics of these people. Dillman's (1978) "Total Design Method" (TDM) of conducting surveys is explained in one of the suggested references and provides detailed procedures for obtaining maximum response from survey participants. Obtaining adequate returns is usually the number one challenge in using any survey method. Perhaps the greatest oversight comes from ignoring the characteristics of those who do *not* respond. This sometimes presents a serious bias because the people who refuse to respond may be quite different from those who do. This problem can (and should) be corrected by subsampling a portion of non-respondents by phoning them if it's a mail survey, or perhaps even by visiting some to conduct personal interviews.

Mail Surveys. These kinds of surveys include sending questionnaires to individuals on a mailing list, or asking that questionnaires be mailed back after they are handed to potential respondents or left on car windshields in a parking lot (enclosed in a waterproof wrapper.) For a large sample, costs per completed questionnaire can usually be kept lowest by this method, but obtaining returns is a problem. A return rate on mail questionnaires of 50 percent (after several follow-up reminders) is usually considered quite good. The TDM may be able to raise this considerably. The average response rates for 48 TDM mail surveys was 74 percent (Dillman, 1978). When highly interested publics are involved, such as wilderness users or winter recreationists, returns commonly reach 80–90 percent. Mail surveys, good and poor, have probably been the most commonly used in public relations research related to natural resource management.

Telephone Surveys. For organizations with set telephone rates, or when the entire sample is local, asking questions via telephone provides a viable alternative. Structuring the questions, however, is entirely different from designing a written questionnaire, particularly considering the necessary limitation on length and complexity. Dillman's (1978) book should be consulted before this method is attempted. Telephone surveys allow greater flexibility than mail surveys in that there is an opportunity to probe when responses are unclear, as well as to make certain that all key data are provided. They also allow more rapid collection of data, which is sometimes important in critical public relations cases.

On-Site Questionnaire Surveys. In this method, the survey participant is handed a questionnaire and is asked to complete it while the researcher waits (Figure 5.1). This has been an important method in outdoor recreation and similar research where questions must be directed to a specific public and no mailing list is available to sample from. It is a method that assures a higher return rate (commonly 90–100 percent) than by asking that the respondent return the questionnaire at a later date, and the researcher can be certain about *who* actually is answering the questions. Its limitations are usually the higher cost, weather factors, and the ethical consideration of asking a sportsman or other forest visitor to give up the half hour or so that it usually takes to complete a questionnaire.

Figure 5.1. Recreationists in the Selway-Bitterroot Wilderness Area completing questionnaires. The research benefits of a high return rate must be weighed against the intrusion on a visitor's leisure time. (Photo by J. R. Fazio.)

Personal Interviews usually take longer and are more expensive than questionnaire surveys. They also introduce the very real danger of interviewer bias, i.e., different interviewers may not record responses in the same way, or they may "color" the response according to their own feelings. They may also influence the respondent through the way they ask the question or provide clarification. *Structured interviews* are based on a set of questions which the respondent answers in his own words and which the interviewer codes into categories. *Unstructured interviews* are more free-ranging and are useful early in a study to help define the problem and decide how to design subsequent research.

Many federal resource managers believe they are circumventing OMB requirements by obtaining information through casually engaging forest visitors in conversation, then later recording what they learned. If more than nine visitors are contacted in this way, the OMB requirement definitely applies. Otherwise, it is a good technique for obtaining data from certain publics while simultaneously answering questions and visiting.

Comment Forms

Providing opportunities for voluntary comments does not obtain *average* opinion as does a survey, but it is a good way to obtain a *range* of opinions (Wagar *et al.*, 1976). For example, people who sign visitor books and add comments usually mention what strikes them as extremely good or bad about the area. This can provide valuable information to the manager, and too frequently it is completely ignored. A case in point could be found at an experimental forest in the Adirondacks. Wildlife researchers one year constructed an excellent interpretive trail for public use. The trail features included a mounted pipe to direct viewing at a distant beaver house. In time, the device loosened and pointed anywhere except at the beaver house. In addition, at least one tree with an interpretive label died. Comments about this deterioration began showing up in the registration book, but at this writing the problems have gone uncorrected. Today, the trail is still there and hundreds of people visit it annually. But the quality reflects poorly on the organization and returning visitors realize that their suggestions have been ignored.

Suggestion *boxes* may provide an even better use of this method because it then assures anonymity. These have wide application at visitor centers, campground exits, mill offices, exhibits and other places where publics of interest to the resource manager can be contacted. A related technique is to include postage-paid mail-back cards in trail guides, maps, litter bags, or other material given to visitors entering an area. However, as shown in the example above, it may be better not to invite feedback than to ignore it when it is received.

Participant-Observation

Participant-observation is a method that can help managers empathize with a particular public. It requires shedding one's true identity and actually becoming part of that public for a while. It results in allowing you to observe the agency as those people do. It is difficult to eliminate personal biases when in the role of another, and it is a time-consuming technique relative to the amount of data it normally yields. Still, it has excellent potential applications. It has been used effectively in studies of campgrounds, interpretive trails, visitor centers, exhibit halls and numerous groups. The incognito manager can observe behavior, monitor overheard comments and engage in revealing conversations that would be possible in no other way. For more information on this technique, consult Webb *et al.* (1966), *Unobtrusive Measure: Non-reactive Research in the Social Sciences.*

Locating Opinion Leaders

Rogers and Shoemaker (1971) described three ways to locate opinion leaders within a social system. All methods were found to be about equal in validity, so the method used can be the one most convenient in a given situation. *The sociometric method* consists of asking a relatively large number of people in a public or social system, "Whom did you seek (or hypothetically, "*might you seek*") for information or advice (about a given issue or item)"? Opinion leaders are those who are mentioned most frequently. *The self-designating technique* asks members of the particular public to indicate the tendency for others to regard them as influential. This is essentially a measure of an individual's perception of his opinion leadership, which to a large degree is what affects ensuing behavior. *Key informants* or judges is simply the technique of asking the opinions of those who are especially knowledgeable about the patterns of influence in a system. It must be stressed that you are asking in regards to specific issues or topics, since opinion leaders vary accordingly. Key informants will also vary depending on the circumstances. In a small, rural town, the clergy or a newspaper editor may be of help; long-time feed and equipment dealers know farmers and ranchers quite well; or it may be the barbers, bartenders, local politicians, school administrators, some combination of these, or others.

The Nominal Group Process

This method and the following Delphi technique are explained in step-by-step detail by Delbecq et al (1975). The nominal group process (NGP) involves a carefully structured group meeting which follows a prescribed sequence of problem-solving steps. It is an excellent public involvement technique for arriving at a list of priorities. An example might be to arrive at a list of preferred management priorities for a national forest. At a public meeting where the nominal group process is not used, debate on this subject could go on all night with little but frayed nerves as a result. With the nominal group process, a reasonable concensus can be reached in approximately 2–3 hours.

First the group is welcomed and the purpose of the meeting is clarified. The group is then subdivided into smaller groups of 5 to 9 people, each having a trained facilitator, news print pad, felt tip pens, and a series of simple forms or index cards for each participant. Using the above example of management priorities, the process would proceed using the following steps:

1. Group members silently and independently make a list on their worksheet of management needs as they perceive them.
2. Going around the table, each person reads one item which is then written on the newsprint pad. This round-robin continues until all items are posted. No debate is allowed, and duplicate items are not recorded twice.
3. Each item is read and briefly discussed, particularly for clarification, but comments can also be offered in agreement or opposition to the item. The facilitator makes certain all items are covered in a timely manner.
4. Each participant selects 5 to 8 (depending on length of the composite list) of the *most* important items. He writes each on an index card, then ranks the five. The ranked number is then written on each card.

The facilitator in each group collects the cards and by listing each item along with the sum of its ranked values, a final priority list has been developed. If further refinement is desired, the list can be discussed and a re-vote taken in the same way. Another extra step is to have each person rate each final priority item through such mechanisms as assigning a point score between 1 and 10 to each item, or by distributing 100 points among the items (with equal distribution disallowed).

The Delphi Technique

This method of polling opinions or judgments is somewhat similar to the nominal group process, but it is conducted through a series of mailed questionnaires. Also, it allows the researcher more control over selecting the participants. This advantage has made it a popular means of bringing together expert judgment for predicting future change and technology, setting objectives, identifying problems and solutions, and developing priorities. The technique requires considerable time (at least 45 days) and staff involvement, a high degree of participant motivation, and participant skill in written communication. Its advantages include anonymity, a means of bringing together people who are widely separated geographically, a way to prevent domination by outspoken individuals, and a means of obtaining aggregate judgments from people who are hostile toward one another.

Again, Delbecq et al (1975) or a similar reference should be consulted for procedural details. However, the series of three questionnaires can be summarized as follows:

1. An appropriate group is selected and asked to participate. Sawmill owners in the southern states might be an example. The first questionnaire will call for open-ended statements on the research topic. For example, "Please clearly list the strengths and weaknesses of extension forestry in the South."

2. Similar responses from the questionnaires are then combined. Next, a list is developed using a carefully worded statement that expresses the meaning of the items placed in each category. Continuing our example, 20 variously worded responses might have been combined under the general statement, "Not enough field foresters are available." The list is then sent out as Questionnaire 2. Participants are asked to rank the 10 most important items, and to offer comments.

3. Third, a final priority list is mailed, showing the number of votes received in Questionnaire 2. Participants are asked to again rank these in view of composite opinion and to offer comments. A variation on the third step is to ask other, related questions that might provide more useful information about the research topic. For example, "We now know that a shortage of extension foresters is a top concern of sawmill owners. Please tell us how many more are needed in your locale to provide adequate service to landowners."

Other Panels

NGP and Delphi are both methods of arriving at a consensus using a panel of sorts. In addition, panels may be used in less structured ways to poll opinions or test potential courses of action. However, extreme caution should be exercised because if used poorly this method can create a definite bias. An example might be using a group of sheep ranchers to test public opinion on coyote control. If used correctly, however, and under the proper circumstances, this can be a very useful tool. A small number of respected sheep ranchers would provide excellent insights on how most sheep ranchers would react to some proposed change in range management. Before a decision is made on a trail layout, a panel of recreationists can more easily pour over maps with the agency staff than can a large number of individuals. Wagar *et al.* (1976) found that a small panel of outsiders was a fast and effective way of evaluating an interpretive exhibit and presentation *before* time, money and effort were expended to complete the project. In this case, the panel was not made up of other interpreters who would undoubtedly think much like those working on the project. Instead, they were a variety of professional people with past experience or personal interest in interpretation. Another possible use of panels is to monitor trends. By returning to the same sample of individuals over a long period of time, it may be possible to detect attitude changes and be able to determine the reasons for these changes.

Content Analysis

This is a method to objectively determine the content of any communication. The researcher simply establishes and defines categories, then makes a count of how many sentences, paragraphs, articles or statements (in a speech) fall into each category. In recent years, this has had several applications in natural resource management. One was the analysis of public input in such controversies as the Forest Service's roadless area review and evaluations (RARE I and II). In these cases, an elaborate coding scheme was developed to classify all comments received in the tens of thousands of cards and letters. Content analysis also has been used to determine the degree of human interest in public information literature, and the kind of topics emphasized in wilderness-related literature disseminated by managing agencies (Fazio, 1979).

The American Forest Council (AFC) regularly uses this method for indirectly keeping in touch with public opinion. In one of its reports to AFC, a contracting research firm stated, "One of the key indicators of the way the public is perceiving and reacting to various issues of the day is to measure media interest in the subject" (Public Issues Research Bureau, Inc., 1976). In this case, forest-related news stories, editorials and letters to the editor in 180 newspapers across the country are categorized and ranked according to amount of coverage. By repeating this procedure at regular intervals, it is possible to determine shifts in interest. This, in turn, helps industry personnel decide on prioritizing their own public information efforts. Content analysis is a flexible tool useful for many purposes. However, it is only as good as the categories developed for classifying the articles in newspapers, parts of a speech, or numbers of specific kinds of articles or letters. Well defined categories contribute to high *reliability* (the assurance that different evaluators will place the same item in the same category). In the case of Forest Service analysis of public involvement letters, good categories and careful training has resulted in 90 percent reliability.

Secondary Analysis

Secondary analysis is an inexpensive and useful technique. It is simply reviewing other studies or existing data that may be comparable or have application in your situation. It might be the review of census data to help determine how many teenagers must be reached in a certain geographical region to provide 100 percent coverage. Another example would be if a study had been conducted elsewhere that provided information about certain adverse opinions held by high income senior citizens. If conditions are such that you believe the findings can be *generalized* to your area, you could plan a campaign to counter these attitudes. By studying census information or advertising data such as that published by *Standard Rates and Data Service,* you can determine the number of senior citizens in your area. In larger towns a mailing list might even be developed using *Polk's City Directory* to find names and addresses of retirees in the high-income neighborhoods. In the natural resource fields, a use of secondary analysis might be to examine research findings from a study conducted on visitors at a nearby park or forest. Then—with great care, because subtle differences often exist—apply the information locally to the degree possible.

For anyone who has limited abilities to conduct research in subjects related to public relations, an attempt should be made to "plug into" as many sources as possible so that useful information can be gleaned from the reports of others. Any agency office can provide the address of its research branch. The USDA Forest Service, the Sociological Studies Program of the National Park Service (Pacific Northwest Regional Office), and most natural resources colleges issue free annual listings of reports available. For the price of a stamp, interested individuals can have their names placed on the mailing lists of these organizations. Other sources of research reports include American Forest Council (1619 Massachusetts Ave., N.W., Washington, D.C. 20036) and a wide range of periodicals in the fields of journalism, public relations, interpretation, recreation management, and resource management.

The Case Study Approach

The case study is a comprehensive look backwards at a situation where public relations went wrong—or particularly well. The case study is a means of summarizing what might have been a complex series of events. It can be used as a basis for understanding the situation, communicating with others about it, and identifying what worked or where things went afoul. It chronicles the past, but it can also be used as a guide to the future.

The outline in the following insert is only one of many ways to structure a case study. In some cases, the suggested elements will not apply or can be combined or reordered; in others there will be aspects not included here. However, it has proven to be an effective guide. The items are self-explanatory and generally relate to sections of this book.

The case study is best suited for use by an uninvolved third party. It can, however, be used by those who were also participants, but an extreme effort is needed to report the facts objectively and completely. A good use of the case study is in the classroom or at in-service training sessions. By examining an actual case, the student of public relations has the opportunity to combine most of the concepts in this book and see if they apply in "the real world." We believe that each case study will turn up fresh examples of poor public relations as well as good. More importantly, the case study provides a basis to test the "why" behind each outcome. From this, the student or practitioner can move ahead toward better *planning* for good public relations.

PUBLIC INVOLVEMENT

Public involvement (or citizen involvement) is a concept and practice that has received an enormous amount of attention from natural resource managers in recent years. It is an essential ingredient of good public relations practice, and in the sense that research is a process for finding answers, public involvement is appropriately considered in this chapter. Used correctly, it is an excellent way to gather opinion and in some cases determine factual information.

The Need for Public Involvement

In some respects public involvement has been around since the advent of modern resource management. In a review of its development, Fairfax (1975) pointed out that most government agencies have always conducted business in close association with a large number of private groups and individuals. However, discontent and disenchantment with resource management (and government in general) during the 1960's gave rise to new demands that a wider spectrum of citizens be given access to the decision-making process. This was reflected in no uncertain terms in legislation of the period, especially the National Environmental Policy Act of 1969 (NEPA), the Forest and Rangeland Renewable Resources Planning Act of 1974 (RPA), the National Forest Management Act of 1976, the Federal Land Policy and Management Act of 1976 (FLPMA), and other laws at the federal, state and local levels.

Despite the fact that most agencies have long involved private citizens—primarily through advisory committees and informal contacts—a lack of trust developed. People felt insulted that clearcuts marred the view from their picture windows in Montana's Bitterroot Valley. They felt

CASE STUDY OUTLINE

1. Introduction
   A. Geographical setting and time period
   B. Principal organization(s) involved
   C. Brief synopsis of the issue or problem
2. History
   A. Detailed background information on events and conditions leading to the problem or surfacing of the issue
3. Situational Details (These may be combined in above if their explanation in chronological order helps clarify the case)
   A. Legislation and policies
   B. Budgets
   C. Statements
   D. Results of relevant surveys or other research
   E. Public involvement
   F. Politics
   G. Equipment, procedures or other technical aspects relevant to the case
   H. The basis for arguments (pro and con)
4. Publics Involved and Their Characteristics
   A. Proponents
      1. Internal publics—(and subpublics)
      2. External publics—(and subpublics)
   B. Opponents
      1. Internal publics—(and subpublics)
      2. External publics—(and subpublics)
   C. Opinion leaders and other key individuals
   D. Relevant sociological factors
5. The Campaign and Communication
   A. Plans and strategies
   B. Persuasive message content
   C. Media used and how (publicity, advertising, regular programs, etc.)
   D. Other techniques
      (1) Research
      (2) Propaganda
      (3) Emotion
      (4) Personal contacts and presentations
      (5) Meetings
   E. Timing
6. Analysis of Results
   A. Successes and failures
   B. Were goals and objectives met?
   C. Effectiveness of media, techniques and timing
   D. Other reasons for successes and failures
7. Alternate Solutions
   A. Management alternatives
   B. How public relations could have been handled differently
8. Summary and Prediction for Future
9. References
   A. Literature cited and personal communications
   B. Bibliography

ignored when little attention was given to song birds and other nongame wildlife. They felt betrayed that their watchdog government allowed the air and water to be fouled to the point of near disaster. In short, the true involvement of citizens in decisions related to their environment was felt by many to fall far short of what was desired.

Perhaps at this point it would be well to review our definition of public relations in Chapter 1 and the essential principles in Chapter 3. It should be clear that the modern practice of public relations *without* public involvement is inconceivable. Certainly the primary intent of public relations is to influence opinion and develop a climate of understanding. However, this requires successful *two*-way communication. It also requires honesty and responsible performance, which in turn implies that management of public resources will reflect the will of their owners—the people. Even in private enterprise, performance must reflect the will of the people if it is to be allowed by our democratic society to continue. Public involvement can go a long way toward contributing to good public relations.

The need for public involvement and its relationship to public relations are well illustrated in both "public acceptance assessment" and the "social impact analysis" described earlier. In public acceptance assessment, publics are "listened to" carefully, and where possible, management adjustments are recommended to accommodate expressed concerns. In social impact analysis, steps nine and ten specifically require involvement of publics in identifying appropriate issues to address and the selection of the best alternatives. The roles of both public involvement and public relations are also shown in Figure 4.1. Notice in the model that input from various publics is sought *before* the management decision. Also, the double arrow between "public relations counsel" and "publics" indicates that publics must not only be heard, but must be informed of technical data, and other background fundamentals of any issue. This part of the public relations function should help lead to more informed opinion. The USDA Forest Service appropriately labels this dual organizational function *Inform and Involve*. After the management decision, the public relations job continues to use two-way communication, but now it becomes more a matter of gaining acceptance for the selected management alternative.

The Nature of Public Involvement

In the late sixties when interest in public involvement was skyrocketing, Sherry Arnstein (1969) developed a model to show that there are many degrees to which publics can be "involved." In fact, she pointed out that sometimes public involvement is nothing more than a play on words. Her concept was put in the form of a hierarchy, or ladder, that depicts the possible levels of participation (Figure 5.2). From the categories in Arnstein's ladder it is clear that only in some cases do citizens really have an opportunity to influence management decisions. In the worst cases, they are essentially being fooled into believing they are participating, whereas in reality they are being manipulated into accepting the preconceived ideas of powerholders.

Public involvement that is conducted as a ritual without intention of giving some degree of power to the participants is a sure route to poor public relations. Disappointment, frustration and anger are the inevitable results. Since this has been known to occur in natural resource management (as well as in public housing projects, schools, senior citizen homes and other diverse settings), it needs to be emphasized that public involvement—like the practice of public relations—must be based on truth and honesty. As the saying goes, "Don't ask for advice unless you are ready to heed it."

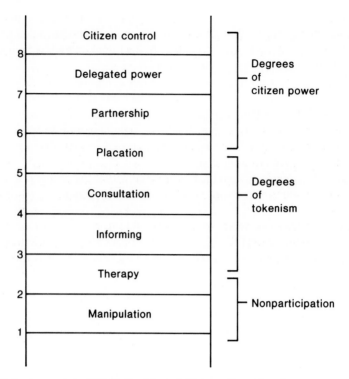

Figure 5.2. Arnstein's (1969) Ladder of Citizen Participation. (Reprinted by permission of the *Journal of the American Planning Association*, Volume 35, No. 4 (1969).)

Other problems with the way public involvement has been structured include the massive volumes of information citizens are expected to digest, and the bewildering jargon in which it is often presented. Reflecting the feelings of many citizens who would like to have a voice in national forest planning, an editorial in the March 19, 1984 issue of *High Country News* stated:

> Although editorial writers are supposed to be omnipotent, we have no clear idea of what to do. We understand the Forest Service's game: the agency requires that we become experts in the economics of forestry, in the life cycle of aspens, in the real estate laws which govern land swaps, in the jargon in which they write their reports, before we can even begin to talk about forest management.

Zeller (1984), writing in *Audubon Actions,* complained:

> Only 90 days were allowed for review of (a) three-volume, 600-page document, which had taken the Forest Service staff years to prepare, and which (contained) pages of barely decipherable phrases, conflicting terminology, and incomprehensible charts. . . .

In all documents and presentations on the input side of "inform and involve," agency personnel must find ways to condense factual information, present it clearly and concisely, and do all in their power to help citizens understand the basics needed for helping with the decisions at hand. Anything less will not only negate the research results possible through citizen participation, it will also lead to mistrust, lack of support, and poor public relations.

Techniques of Public Involvement

There are many ways to implement public involvement, some of which use the research tools previously discussed. No two situations will necessarily require the same procedures. Therefore, the progressive resource manager or public relations person will consider the many ways to obtain as much public involvement as possible and select the approach most suited to *why* public involvement is needed and *what* is desired from it. Heberlein (1976) stressed these as two prerequisites to any public involvement effort. A number of the possible methods for achieving public involvement are presented in Table 5.1 along with a relative rating of how effective each is in serving various purposes. The table is adapted from one presented by Heberlein (1976) and uses the following definitions of the four functions of public involvement:

Informational—Disseminating information to and obtaining it from publics.

Interactive—Joint work between agency and publics on an issue or problem with information rapidly going back and forth.

Assurance—The goal of the agency is to make sure that a group knows that its views have been heard and that it has not been ignored in the planning process.

Legalistic—An attempt to involve the public to satisfy legal requirements or social norms only and to allow input from any sources which may have been inadvertently overlooked. The goal is to convince others (besides the affected public) that there have been open mechanisms for public involvement. The publics' involvement must be "traceable," or verifiable.

Figure 5.3. A citizen takes advantage of an opportunity to provide input prior to a management decision. Good public relations can result only if the agency is sincere in listening and sharing its decision-making power with its publics. (Courtesy of USDA Forest Service.)

Table 5.1
Forms and Functions of Public Involvement (Adapted from Heberlein, 1976).

Form of Public Involvement	Function of Public Involvement					
	Informational		Interactive	Assurance	Legalistic	Representativeness
	To Give	To Get				
Open Public Meetings	Good	Poor	Poor	Fair	Yes	Poor
Workshops (small)	Excellent	Excellent	Excellent	Excellent	Yes	Potentially good
Presentations to Groups	Good	Fair	Fair	Fair	Yes	No clear assurance
Ad Hoc Committees	Good	Good	Excellent	Excellent	Yes	Potentially good
Advisory Groups	Good	Good	Excellent	Excellent	Yes	Potentially good
Key Contacts	Excellent	Excellent	Excellent	Excellent	No	No clear assurance
Analysis of Incoming Mail	Poor	Good	Poor	Poor	Yes	Poor
Direct Mail From Agency to Public	Excellent	Poor	Fair	Good	No	Potentially good
Questionnaires and Surveys	Poor	Excellent	Poor	Fair	Yes	Potentially excellent
Behavioral Observation	Poor	Excellent	Poor	Poor	No	Potentially Excellent
Reports From Key Staff	Poor	Good	Poor	Poor	No	No clear assurance
News Releases and Mass Media	Good	Poor	Poor	Poor	Yes	Potentially fair to good
Analysis of Mass Media	Poor	Fair	Poor	Poor	Yes	Potentially fair to good
Day-to-day Public Contacts	Good	Good	Excellent	Fair	No	Poor
Nominal Group Process	Poor	Excellent	Poor	Excellent	Yes	Potentially good
Delphi Technique	Fair	Excellent	Fair	Excellent	Yes	Potentially excellent

Benefits of Public Involvement

True involvement of publics in the decision-making process is intended to lead to *better* decisions and to decisions that allow wise management to proceed efficiently. Specifically, involving your publics early in the process of any major management action can yield the following benefits.

1. New factual data may be brought to light about the resources involved.
2. Preferences, conflicts and unknown social complexities will be made known.
3. People will accord greater respect and confidence to an agency that openly invites their participation in management.
4. The likelihood is reduced that management decisions will be reversed in court, by new legislation, or by superiors.

The public relations person can help make this happen, and can help make it a *quality* experience for both sides. In addition to the immediate benefits to management, the process can yield valuable insights for later public relations programs designed to "close ranks" and gain the support necessary to proceed. When these benefits are more widely recognized, fewer resource managers will see this part of their job as merely a bothersome requirement. As this occurs, and better ways are sought to involve a broad spectrum of publics on a continuing basis, and as citizens' ideas and concerns are taken more seriously—a more harmonious relationship will result. A sincere, planned effort at public involvement is essential to good public relations.

SUGGESTED REFERENCES

Citizen Participation: Practice in Search of a Theory by Norman Wengert. 1976. *Natural Resources Journal* 16(1):23–40.

Foundations of Behavioral Research by Fred N. Kerlinger. 1973. Holt, Rinehart and Winston, Inc., New York.

Group Techniques for Program Planning: A Guide to Nominal Group and Delphi Processes by Andre L. Delbecq, Andrew H. Van de Ven and David H. Gustafson. Scott, Foresman and Co., Glenview, Ill.

Lesly's Public Relations Handbook edited by Philip Lesly. 1983. Prentice-Hall, Inc., Englewood Cliffs, N.J.

Mail and Telephone Surveys by Don A. Dillman. 1978. John Wiley and Sons, New York.

Methods of Social Research by Kenneth D. Bailey. 1978. The Free Press, New York.

Public Participation Handbook. 1980. USDA Forest Service, Washington, D.C.

6

Identifying and
Working with Publics

There is no such thing as the public.

Trying to practice public relations without first identifying specific publics is like shooting at a blank piece of cardboard, then drawing target rings around the hole. All too often, public relations efforts that might otherwise be highly effective are dissipated into worthlessness by not zeroing in on specific groups of individuals and the characteristics they possess. That is the unfortunate result when a well-meaning resource manager directs his efforts at that amorphous mass we hear called "*the* public."

The third principle of public relations defines a public as *two or more people with a common interest and who may be expected to react similarly to a particular situation or issue*. By breaking down the hopelessly infinite characteristics of the general public into smaller, more homogenous groups, the chances of influencing the opinions and behavior of those people increase tremendously. By identifying publics, it becomes easier to:

- understand the people who are affected by some issue and know where they stand on it.
- reach these people through communication, including informal networking.
- tailor message content for effectiveness in meeting specified objectives.
- evaluate effectiveness of public relations efforts.

Recognition of specific publics is simply a matter of targeting, and it is essential if good public relations is to be achieved. Unfortunately, in natural resources management, the identification of publics is usually not understood or its value is highly underestimated.

Before making a list of publics, four things should be kept in mind. One is that a public is identified relative to *your* position in the analysis of a situation. If you are a district forest ranger, your staff can be considered an internal public. To the logging company down the road, *your* staff is an *external* public.

Second, the identification of publics can be used to greatest advantage when identified in relation to a specific issue. Therefore, it is necessary to re-classify individuals each time you face an issue and wish to plan your approach. For example, in trying to implement a new management program to resolve conflicts on a network of winter recreation trails, it would be important to identify as many snowmobilers and cross-country skiers as possible (and/or their leaders) and to consider these people as belonging to two separate publics. This procedure would be far more effective than simply addressing "recreationists" or "winter users." In a different issue—for example, opening an area to mining—it might be appropriate to lump all recreationists into a single category. The point is that publics must be considered in light of each issue.

It should also be pointed out that people need not be included in every issue. Taking the example of the winter trail conflict further, it can be seen that members of a garden club or a cattlemen's association, probably would not need to be considered publics. This would avoid wasted time and expense, and it would prevent bothering disinterested citizens (unnatural publics, in this example) with information not relevant to their needs or interests. In recent years, as government agencies have attempted to meet legislative requirements for public involvement in decision-making, some citizens have been inundated with a flood of information and requests to provide "input." Untargeted information may sometimes do more harm than good, particularly when an expressed interest in one issue brings the citizen an endless flow of requests and information in areas of no interest.

Third, it should be remembered that any public, like all of humanity, is part of a continuous parade through time. Therefore, as new issues emerge, it is necessary to update lists of who constitutes a particular public. The individuals and leaders interested in the quality of cross-country skiing today are not the same as those who will be interested if an issue re-emerges five years from now. Importantly, attitudes, knowledge and other characteristics may also be quite different.

A fourth important factor is that publics must be categorized in a way that will help meet your objectives. Everyone can be labeled as belonging to a public that is internal or external, natural or unnatural. This, of course, is helpful in determining how they should be approached and in what order. Beyond that, categories can be created to serve the needs of the situation. This may require no more than a separation into traditional user groups associated with the resource, or it may be helpful to identify target publics by cultural differences, religion, family conditions, political affiliation, financial status or some other socio-economic characteristic. In some cases it may be helpful to know the beliefs, values, knowledge levels or other intricate characteristics of the people with whom you are dealing. The following are a few of the many useful ways "the public" can be grouped in order to facilitate better public relations.

INTERNAL PUBLICS

It would be hypocritical at best, and foolish at worst, to attempt to seek the goodwill of external publics while ignoring those who are the very lifeblood of an organization. For the most part, internal publics *are* the organization. For this reason, it is essential that any idea or planned action must receive internal acceptance before the external operation can succeed. Strife or dissension within an organization or the professions it represents, easily can be detected by those on the outside, particularly representatives of the mass media. When discord is present, the question is then asked by outsiders, "How can this idea be good if they cannot agree on it themselves?" Hence the idea is often rejected by external publics whose concurrence and support are necessary.

Internal publics are not limited to employees of an organization. As shown in Table 6.1, the list may include others who work symbiotically with the agency or organization. There are any number of ways to define specific internal publics and again this should be done based on the issue or need.

Table 6.1.
Some Internal Publics of Three Natural Resource Agencies

State Game and Fish Department	U.S. Forest Service	National Park Service
Administrators (Director, Chiefs and Staff Assistants)	Administrators (Regional Forester, Forest Supervisors and Staff Assistants)	Administrators (Regional Directors, Park Superintendents, Division Chiefs and Staff Assistants)
Wildlife Conservation Officers	Rangers and Assistants	Rangers and Naturalists
Researchers under Pittman-Robertson and Dingell-Johnson Funding	Forest and Range Experiment Station Scientists	Park Researchers and Biologists, and Cooperative Park Studies Unit Personnel
Labor/Construction Crews	Labor/Construction Crews	Maintenance Division Personnel
Office Staff	Office Staff	Office Staff
Retired Employees	Forest Service Alumni Association	Retired Employees
Seasonal Staff	Seasonal Staff	Seasonal Staff
License Agents	Dude Ranchers and Fire Wardens	Concessionaires
Game and Fish Commission	Forest Service Advisory Boards	Park Service Advisory Boards
State Legislators	Federal Legislators	Federal Legislators

Other Land—Use Agencies

Publics lying somewhere between being internal and external are those in land agencies that might be termed "sister agencies." These are colleagues in the same profession, doing similar work, but for a different agency or organization. This could include wildlife biologists working for game departments in other states, or it could describe the relationship of the U.S. Forest Service with the National Park Service or Bureau of Land Management. In the private sector, forest industries are acutely aware of this natural bond and frequently use it to great advantage. Similarly, groups like Sierra Club and The Wilderness Society recognize the advantages of dealing with each other as internal publics much of the time. Common examples of the image presented when these kinds of internal publics are *not* in harmony are presented in Figure 6.1.

Land-use agencies involved in natural resource management must give each other cooperation and respect. Each should have a voice in management practices that affect other land-use agencies. For example, all should be allowed input when hunting seasons are set for lands under their management. In Colorado, for example, personnel from the U.S. Forest Service, National Park Service, Soil Conservation Service, and Bureau of Land Management are present when Game, Fish, and Parks Division officials make the initial season recommendations. Supervisory personnel of these organizations also are present at the final meeting before the seasons are firmly set by the Commission.

Figure 6.1. When internal publics disagree, it is difficult to gain the understanding and support of external publics. For the purposes of public relations planning, it is wise to consider sister agencies as internal publics.

In the same accord, any changes in forest or range management planned by one agency should be known and approved by all agencies that may be affected directly or indirectly by the operation. In some states, however, situations still exist where cooperation does not occur. Programs of browse spraying by one land-use agency may directly oppose the policies of another. Vast quantities of deer food are destroyed to provide more grass. Other examples include organizational disagreements which have resulted from water impoundment projects; clearcuts that have destroyed the visual quality at camping areas; and the allocation of wilderness.

Between sister agencies, communication often lags and causes many conflicts. Other land-use agencies should be kept informed of happenings of interest and be encouraged to do likewise. Newsletters and magazines should be exchanged regularly. A "natural resources club" of all land management agencies in a community has served the purposes of contact and idea exchange in some areas. Also, a chance to help one agency should never be turned down by another agency. For example, in many states, U.S. Forest Service personnel and game and fish department employees cooperate in solving mutual problems. They work together in analyzing big game-range plots instead of arguing about range conditions and doing nothing to reach a mutual agreement. To gain the respect of external publics, it is essential that resource managers keep their own house in order. With so much at stake, and so much of common interest, this should not be difficult to accomplish.

Employees

For want of a nail a shoe was lost; for want of the shoe a horse was lost; for want of the horse the battle was lost. This old adage has an important parallel in working toward internal public relations. When considering employees, no detail is too small if it has bearing on the support of objectives, job satisfaction, and the general relationship among co-workers. Like the lost horse-shoe, ignoring public relations with the employee public can lead to disasterous consequences. Practicing good public relations can lead to a harmonious operation which will be reflected not only in morale and support of objectives, but also in the quantity and quality of production or services rendered.

It is also necessary to consider *all* employees in a well planned public relations program. An instance is known where the custodian of a Forest Service building also was the commander of the local Veterans of Foreign Wars chapter. A secretary may be the leader of a parent-teacher association, or a seasonal laborer may be a teacher during the school year. *Every* employee is influential in some way, and every employee needs to be part of the public relations effort.

Supervision is a critical factor in employee relations. Frequently, this important responsibility is delegated without proper training. The topic is beyond the scope of this book, but excellent references are available at most libraries. There are however, some general concepts in supervision and personal management that are presented below to help in working with employee publics. Perhaps the most fundamental concept is to recognize that employees have needs and wants that they expect to have fulfilled on the job. Hofstede (1972) showed that these needs can be ranked, but that the ranking varies drastically between kinds of workers. For example, self-actualization and esteem needs such as challenge, training and autonomy were ranked highly by professionals and managers, but meant little to clerical workers and unskilled plant workers. Social needs (co-operation, good manager, friendly workers and efficiency) ranked highest with the clerks, whereas security and physiological needs (physical setting, security, earnings and benefits) were most important to unskilled workers. Understanding these needs is a first step toward good internal public relations.

Employee needs also vary considerably between individuals within any worker group. Whenever possible, a supervisor should try to determine on an individual basis what is most important to a worker. This requires a conscientious attempt at two-way communication—not guessing—

Table 6.2.
Employee and Employer Ratings of Nine Employee Needs[1]

Needs	Employee Rating	Employer Rating
Recognition and Appreciation	1	8
Status and Participation	2	6
Help on Personal Problems	3	9
Working Conditions	4	4
Wages and Fringe Benefits	5	1
Interesting Work	6	5
Advancement Possibilities	7	3
Loyalty of the Organization	8	7
Stability or Security	9	2

1. Used by permission of The Wildlife Society.

√ TEN QUALITIES OF A GOOD SUPERVISOR

_____ Provide clear direction.
  a. Establish clear goals and standards.
  b. Communicate group goals, not just individual goals.
  c. Involve people in setting goals.
  d. Be clear and thorough in delegating responsibility.

_____ Encourage open, two-way communication.
  a. Be open and candid. "Level" with people.
  b. Be honest and to the point.
  c. Establish a climate of openness and trust.

_____ Be willing to coach and support people.
  a. Try to be helpful in dealing with people.
  b. Work constructively to correct performance problems.
  c. "Go to bat" for subordinates with "higher ups."

_____ Provide recognition, objectively.
  a. Recognize good performance more often than criticizing poor performance.
  b. Relate rewards to performance, not by seniority or personal relationships.

_____ Establish ongoing controls.
  a. Follow up on important issues and actions.
  b. Provide feedback to subordinates on how they are doing.

_____ Select the right people for your staff.

_____ Understand the financial implications of decisions.

_____ Encourage innovation and new ideas.

_____ When the time comes, be decisive; give subordinates clear-cut decisions.

_____ Earn respect by consistently demonstrating a high level of integrity.

—By Robert A. Stringer
Harbridge House, Inc.

Used with permission of
Skies West Publishing Company

---

for often an employer's initial perceptions are quite different from what employees consider to be important. In a lecture at the University of Michigan, Wooding illustrated this point by listing the discrepencies shown in Table 6.2.

Herzberg (1976) provided an interesting and helpful perspective on working with and motivating employees. He stated that true job *satisfaction* comes from a different set of conditions than those that merely prevent *dis*satisfaction. Based on studies of 1,685 employees in a variety of fields and at several levels within their organization, the conditions presented in Table 6.3 were identified and should be considered as ways to move employees higher on the scale of job satisfaction. Items in both columns are important, but those in Column A serve only the function of *preventing* dissatisfaction. If those conditions are not met, internal problems undoubtedly will result. If they are handled reasonably well, employees will be near the central part of the scale—a rather neutral position where individuals are less than highly motivated or "self-actualized."

When the conditions in Column B are met, employees have the opportunity to become all of which they are capable, a state of self-actualization enjoyed by probably less than 15 percent of us. This is total job satisfaction, one of the ultimate goals of good public relations with employees.

In the practice of public relations, employee needs are recognized and planned efforts are made to help meet these needs. For example, merit awards for outstanding service or for years of performance are ways to recognize achievement. When possible, this should include public recognition in the news media and internal publications. How the employee perceives the importance of his job is often determined by the factors of status and participation. Perhaps more today than ever before, employees want to participate in management decisions. The wise manager will view this as an opportunity rather than a nuisance. There is no better way to obtain internal accord than to make people feel that an idea was theirs, or that they were included in the planning of an action *before* it was implemented. Participation may even mean nothing more than calling in supervisors to give them a piece of information before it is given to their workers or the news media. This is especially important if the information is bad news, such as an impending layoff. Careful selection of *who* relays information prevents threats to status and provides for a sense of participation.

Another way to instill a sense of participation and to simultaneously make each employee a good public relations representative is by making it clear how his or her job fits into the total operation. An outstanding example of this approach can be viewed in the film *My Job* which was produced by Hugh Crandall for the National Park Service. Crandall used the example of three stone cutters and how they perceived their jobs while helping to construct a cathedral. When asked what they were doing, one stated he was cutting stones; another said he was building a cathedral; but the third said he was glorifying God. Foresters, maintenance people, typists and all other employees at *every* level need an understanding of their organization's structure, mission, current projects, and guiding philosophies. This should be a standard part of an orientation process for new personnel, as well as an annual update or review. The latter might include a woods tour for the office staff, or a meeting with top management for the field crew.

The public relations practitioner will be alert to ways for improving all the inherent qualities of an employee's working situation. It is assuring the loyalty of the organization when things go amiss in the employee's personal life; it is seeking fair wages, fringe benefits, and prompt travel reimbursements; it is providing opportunities for satisfying social experiences for families; it is establishing grievance committees and credit unions; and it is assuring that promotions are based on merit, not politics, and that job security is there for all who deserve it. The public relations person should even be concerned with optimum work loads because overloads cause anxiety, family troubles, resentment and eventually, "burn out." Too little work can be as harmful as too much, as it leads to boredom and is the breeding grounds for rumors, loss of pride and similar troubles. Finally, an important consideration is to assure opportunities to improve and to qualify for advancement. This is possible through scholarships, educational leave, travel, apprenticeships and in-service training schools. The accompanying checklist provides suggestions for applying a variety of public relations techniques to help motivate employees through meeting their needs that lead to job satisfaction.

✓ EMPLOYEE RELATIONS CHECKLIST

Selected Public Relations Techniques	Primary Contributions to Job Satisfaction											
	—Prevent Dissatisfaction—							—Satisfy / Motivate—				
	Policies	Supervision	Interpersonal Relations	Money	Job Security	Work Conditions	Status/ Participation	Achievement	Recognition/ Appreciation	Advancement Opportunities	Inherent Job Qualities	Learning/Growth
___ In-house Publication—(Newsletter, magazine; family-oriented)			●				●		●			
___ Employee Manual—(Policies relating to personal benefits such as sick leave, insurance, social opportunities, etc.)	●	●	●									
___ Policy Manual—(Clear explanation of policies)	●	●										
___ Orientation Program—(For all new employees at all levels)	●	●	●									
___ Bulletin Boards/Exhibits—(Current, interesting, well organized)	●	●	●			●	●		●			
___ Physical Surroundings—(Pleasant, clean, safe)			●			●						
___ Meetings—(Well organized, enjoyable when possible, appropriate top managers present)	●		●			●	●		●			●
___ Open House—(For relatives, external public)			●				●					
___ Tours—(For employees, to unfamiliar part of operations)			●				●					●
___ Other Organized Activities—(Socials, sports, etc.)			●			●						
___ Continuing Education—(Training sessions, study leaves, sabbaticals)			●	●	●	●	●	●		●	●	●
___ Awards—(Merit, longevity, etc.)			●	●	●		●	●	●			
___ Publicity/Advertising—(Establish good image in media, announce awards, etc.)			●			●	●	●	●			
___ Grievance Committee—(Mgt. and employee representation)		●	●		●	●	●					
___ Suggestion Box—(Anonymity guaranteed)						●	●					

Table 6.3.
Factors Contributing to Job Satisfaction

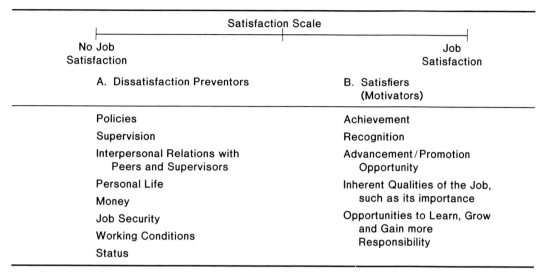

Satisfaction Scale

No Job
Satisfaction

Job
Satisfaction

A. Dissatisfaction Preventors	B. Satisfiers (Motivators)
Policies	Achievement
Supervision	Recognition
Interpersonal Relations with Peers and Supervisors	Advancement / Promotion Opportunity
Personal Life	Inherent Qualities of the Job, such as its importance
Money	
Job Security	Opportunities to Learn, Grow and Gain more Responsibility
Working Conditions	
Status	

Retirees

Retired employees or alumni groups should not be ignored as an internal public. Such a group can have a great deal of influence, good or bad, on current employees and on a wide range of external publics. Their knowledge and experience can be extremely valuable. In some cases, continued service as a consultant or volunteer can not only aid the organization, but contribute to the health and continual growth of the individual. Retiree clubs also help maintain the linkages that have been part of the employee's life for so long. At the very minimum, retirees should be kept informed and in turn can help the organization keep abreast of current employee attitudes.

The National Park Service achieves this through devoting space in *Courier,* the agency's employee magazine, to the activities and opinions of its retirees. Reunions, trips and other services also are offered to make its retired employees feel that they are still a valued part of the organization.

Researchers

The researcher in a natural resource agency or company may present a special headache to the organization. He is a specialist trained to do a highly specialized job. Although there has been considerable improvement in recent years, it can still be said that the researcher often lacks conception of the importance of other happenings and positions. Many lack patience when their findings are not immediately implemented as management practice. This internal public often does not realize that research results, like any other action, must be accepted by other departments within the agency, and by outside publics. Before that is done, the findings must be weighed to determine how they will affect the enterprise as a whole. For example, from the public relations standpoint, it may be completely foolish to poison the fish in a lake (at a certain time) to remove undesirable species. Research may prove this feasible, but public pressure may be so strong at the time that it would be unwise to carry out the operation. Or, perhaps a dense stand of sagebrush is to be chained to open it up and allow grass to grow. This, according to research findings, is the most effective way to increase cattle production. On the other hand, if this stand is converted to grass, it may destroy a popular sage grouse strutting area. Again, it would require careful consideration of the public relations effects before putting the research results into practice. The researcher public needs to be made aware of the social implications from what are frequently biological findings.

Another challenge in working with the researcher public is to encourage the dissemination of results to the people "paying the bills." Researchers are often more interested in giving talks or distributing publications to their peers than to legislators, media personnel or other lay groups. Broader communication would help convert research into information that could be put to use. It would help close the technology transfer gap that usually sees implementation lagging well behind the leading edge of knowledge. The job of translating the research results from technical jargon to plain, useable information is often where the public relations person can help most.

Certainly research is important. Research in the natural resource professions has provided the modern techniques, ideas and principles being used today. There always will be need for research and researchers to provide additional knowledge plus new and better ways of getting the management job accomplished. But all the investigations and researchers in the world will not advance management one bit beyond our effectiveness in communicating the results and considering them in light of good public relations.

Governing and Advisory Bodies

Somewhere in the structure of most natural resource organizations is a governing or advisory body. Their powers range widely. In some companies, the board of directors may make major decisions on a regular basis. In a conservation association, the board may do little more than meet annually and embellish the masthead of the group's magazine with a list of prominent citizens. In federal organizations, advisory groups are common and they serve primarily as sounding boards for managers' ideas or as one avenue of more formalized input for public opinion. In state organizations, commissions or governing boards usually have major roles in setting policy. This is true in most state fish and game departments as well as in park and recreation departments. These will be discussed here because they provide an example of how policy-makers and administrators must define and respect each other's roles if good working relationships are to be maintained.

In state agencies, a typical governing board consists of 4 to 10 people from various parts of the state and who have avocational interests in natural resources or outdoor recreation. Theoretically the body is non-political and usually includes the governor or other top official as an administrator or ex-officio member.

The primary duty of these boards is to establish policies. A policy can be defined as *a guide to conduct* or *a pathway to action within the broader charges of law which established the particular agency*. It also can be shelter to hide behind in case of trouble such as undue pressure from special interest groups, or criticism of procedures from a legislator or the mass media. Policies should be based on the best available information and advice from both internal and external publics. The importance of two-way communication is obvious. If information to aid in policy formation does not come from the publics to be served, how can these policies be established to serve the best interests of all? Good public relations starts with good policies.

Current public thinking, alternative courses of action, possible impacts and public reaction should be a part of policy planning. Therefore, it is advisable to have someone from within the agency present who has public relations responsibilities. This person can then hear first hand the opinions of board members, and can also provide counsel by predicting the results of decisions in social terms. This is rarely the case, however. It is also a good idea to be aware of the policies of other agencies before making changes or additions. This prevents conflict of interests among sister agencies and in the long run, improves the quality of resource management. When the need arises, representatives of other agencies should be invited to attend commission or board meetings.

Once policy is established, it is important to make it known to all employees in a clear, simple, concisely written manual. A policy manual should not be clogged with legalese, but rather should include only essential information, and in an easily understood format.

Administrators and all supervisory personnel are responsible for carrying out the policies established by the commission or governing body. Internal strife results when agency personnel and the policy makers try to do each other's jobs. Too many commissions and boards interfere with administration, management activities and personnel matters. Commission and board members should realize that their job is an avocation and not a vocation. Therefore, they should leave the action program to professionals in the field. The authority of the agency head to handle personnel and operations must be recognized, respected and maintained by commission and board members. Conversely, after a policy has been established, it should be followed and not openly questioned by the agency head, supervisors or other employees. Once the policy is firm, it is necessary to close ranks and manage within the new guidelines. The alternative for dissidents is to find employment in another agency with ideas more compatible with their own. However, most dissent can be avoided if members of an organization are informed of the *reasons* behind the policies. This should be done quickly and simply so there is no doubt why a policy was established. Communication channels for informing personnel should be determined at the time a policy is made. Unless this is done, the policy process is not complete and poor internal relations are likely to result.

Legislators

Legislators, either at state or national levels, should be considered an internal public by employees of government agencies. These elected officials usually control the budget, create licenses, establish laws and fees, and approve land exchanges.

The legislator public should be kept informed constantly, whether in or out of session. Newsletters and other published materials should be sent to them. Personal contact of legislators at critical times and on critical issues should be made only by high ranking, respected administrators who are confident and capable.

Officials of the natural resource organization should be aware of the legislators' attitudes and actions. This is absolutely necessary so that the techniques of influence and of changing opinions can be used to facilitate desired action at the proper time. The reason behind desired legislation, if explained properly and at the right time, will do much to obtain the desired results. Similarly, it is often necessary to influence legislators when detrimental laws are proposed. Good natural resource management can be good politics because so many people are interested and legislators constantly think in terms of vote counts. Therefore, good management should easily be sold to a capable politician. Many satisfied people mean many votes at election time.

The influential position held by legislators must be recognized by anyone with an interest in public relations. This is so important that Chapter 12 has been devoted to understanding the political process so it can be used to advantage.

Catalyst Publics

Catalyst publics are those who act in behalf of the natural resource organization, but are not actually part of it. These groups constitute potentially important allies or enemies of any natural resource organization, but are frequently neglected as a communication link with recreationists or other user publics. The catalyst publics often have great influence on the ultimate users of the resource, and this influence should be used to advantage. In Table 5.1, the examples given for a "catalyst public" are license agents, dude ranchers and concessionaires. Others could be added to this list, such as guides and outfitters, consulting foresters, ski slope operators and a variety of special use permitees who sell services or goods to recreationists or others who utilize natural resources.

Catalyst publics need to be made to believe they are part of a team, and an appreciated member. Periodic banquets, meetings or conferences to inform them of happenings would contribute to winning their confidence. The reasons behind actions and regulations should be explained clearly and simply so that correct information can be passed on to license buyers or visitors. Explanations of happenings and regulations should be made through frequent and regular contact. In the case of concessionaires, agency personnel should offer to make a presentation each year at orientation sessions for seasonal employees.

License agents, and to some extent concessionaires, guides, outfitters, dude ranchers, and consulting foresters, should be included automatically on selected, internal mailing lists and should receive newsletters. More and better aids (posters, displays, and literature) should be given to these people to assist them in selling the organization and its values.

Catalyst publics can also provide excellent feedback information. From their contact with customers, the opinions, beliefs and attitudes of catalyst publics will often reflect those of private land owners, sportsmen and various other recreationists. Therefore, the opinions of these groups should be listened to in establishing policies or planning public relations programs.

Cooperative Extension Service

The Cooperative Extension Service is a public that lies in the grey area between being internal (as a sister organization) or external. It is included here because of the unique opportunities it presents to natural resource managers. In some states, full advantage is taken of this network of professional educators that includes branch offices in every county. In other areas, there is little working relationship between natural resource managers and Extension, the latter focusing only on farm crop agriculture and home economics.

The Cooperative Extension Service came into being in 1914 with passage of the Smith-Lever Act. This act provided federal funds to be allocated on a state matching basis to land grant institutions. The act was to be administered by the U.S. Department of Agriculture and stated that money was to be used to conduct research and to disseminate results and information. It was to "extend" the university to people throughout the state.

Professions originally incorporated under the Smith-Lever Act were agriculturally and home economically oriented. This has played an important part in the success of modern agriculture. County agents are an accepted part of most rural communities. Since its inception, the act has been broadened to include other professions such as horticulture, agronomy and some areas in the broad field of conservation or natural resource management.

The structure of Cooperative Extension includes a staff of experts in Washington, D.C. and others located at each state land grant institution. Nearly every state includes forestry and wildlife specialists, and some also have fisheries, range, recreation and forest product specialists. At the county level, often located in the county government office complex, are county agents. These people may specialize in agriculture, home economics or youth services (4-H), or they may have a combination of functions. The state and county personnel are all members of the university faculty, a factor that provides a degree of freedom from political pressures. Funding and policy guidance is shared by the county, state and federal governments—thus the term *Cooperative.*

To the alert natural resource manager in any organization, extension personnel represent a highly organized and usually effective force of communicators. To win the respect and cooperation of these individuals in working toward common goals is to gain a powerful ally. Both state-level specialists and county agents usually have detailed mailing lists, regular publications, and well established contacts with agriculturists, business interests, community leaders, recreation groups and many others. In addition, extension professionals often have prestige that is associated with faculty status at the state's major university.

At times the information specialists in natural resource organizations view Cooperative Extension as competitors. This is unfortunate, since there are plenty of challenges to go around and many angles from which to approach problems of common interest. Even more unfortunate are those states that are so dominated by agri-business interests that there is little emphasis given to forests, wildlife or recreation. By recognizing this important public, learning about its structure and functions, and becoming acquainted with its personnel, natural resource management agencies have an opportunity to extend their influences and efficiently reach many more publics.

EXTERNAL PUBLICS—TRADITIONAL IDENTITIES

External publics are neither part of the organization, nor are they closely related as are legislators, license agents or Cooperative Extension personnel. Traditionally, resource managers place external publics into rather broad categories. These frequently will suffice for planning an effective public relations program and they are more easily identified than the more detailed breakdowns discussed later. In determining a public, the main thing is that it should be useful to *your* needs in improving public relations. Following are some of the more traditional publics associated with public relations efforts in the natural resource fields.

Communities

A community actually is an aggregation of many publics living in close association. It is a social group of any size whose members reside in a specific locality. A community's members usually have a comparable culture and a common government. Our nation is composed of communities, and state and national opinions originate in communities. Public relations with a community, sometimes referred to as *community relations,* can be considered quite simply as neighborliness.

The trend of big business, large organizations and some natural resource agencies has been to decentralize authority and to attempt to become a part of a community. In addition to increasing operating efficiency, decentralization reduces the air of supremacy and bureaucracy which accompanies large organizations. Being within the community also increases the opportunity to serve the needs of citizens at *their* convenience. This is the reason that many Forest Service ranger stations have been moved from their previously isolated locations on national forests to more accessible accommodations in towns adjacent to the forest lands.

An organization of any kind has an *image* in the community. An image in the public relations sense is the way people perceive something, be it a product (the image of Wheaties is that of producing champion athletes), a person (John Wayne was the macho male and super patriot), or an organization (the Red Cross is equated with the saving of lives). An image may be accurate or inaccurate—it is solely how the people think it is or how they *perceive*. Natural resource organizations are subject to the phenomenon of images. Thus, an agency or company may be viewed by its neighbors as friendly or aloof, clean or dirty, a prestigious place to work or employment of last resort, a boost to the community or a detriment. Image in the community can have a profound effect on the ease of daily operations, the quality of job applicants and the quality of goods or services produced. And image is to a very large degree dependent on the practice of public relations.

Both the community and the organization can expect fulfillment of certain conditions. Any organization wants good employees to hire, fair treatment, adequate transportation and housing, police protection, good schools and churches, hospitals, friends, and a way to satisfy cultural and social needs. The community, in turn, expects jobs for residents, adequate wages, taxes, patronage of local businesses, contributions to community causes, leadership and participation in civic efforts. In short, they want a good neighbor.

Specific ways in which any natural resource organization might participate in community affairs include free use of equipment such as airplanes and snowmobiles when needed for emergencies; formation of a rescue team; employees speaking to school groups and others on request or helping and joining service clubs such as Lions, Rotary and P.T.A.; and personnel becoming part of community affairs, such as becoming scout leaders or counselors.

Companies often have a committee or even a paid staff specialist to handle public relations at the community level. Industry spends millions of dollars a year to finance education, sponsor conferences, build facilities, bring cultural events to the community, promote safety and offer career guidance in schools. Personnel of the businesses act as chairmen of drives and campaigns for community betterment and are encouraged to hold public office. They operate speakers bureaus and finance educational motion pictures, radio shows and television shows. Community effort awards are donated by businesses and chambers of commerce. Contests for community causes are funded and promoted. They sponsor floats in parades and displays at community gatherings, and they spend many dollars on beautification, playgrounds, parks and pollution control.

Brion (1967) gave an example of a business, in this instance a construction company, which used an ingenious idea and a little extra work to turn around an unfavorable situation and promote good public relations at the community level. A landmark building had to be torn down and the company was under severe criticism for this and for creating an unsightly area. A fence barrier was constructed for safety while the new construction was proceeding. And then the offensive effort! This was that holes were cut in the barrier fence for people to use in observing the construction in progress. In addition, segments of the fence were portioned out to community clubs,

Figure 6.2. Company or agency equipment can sometimes be used to assist with search, rescue or similar missions, thus fostering good public relations in the community. (Courtesy of USDA Forest Service.)

service groups and schools for use in a company-sponsored art contest. The whole idea was publicized in newspapers and goodwill was won instead of lost. The company's image in the community was enhanced.

Efforts used in community relations work by industry are not always applicable to governmental natural resource agencies. Nevertheless, most agencies could do much more to further the cause of good public relations at the community level. The truth in this was underscored by proponents of the so-called Sagebrush Rebellion who attempted to wrest control of western lands away from federal land managers. A major part of the problem, according to James Watt as he accepted the post of Secretary of the Interior, was "arrogant" land managers who failed in conducting their business as "good neighbors."

Not only is a good neighbor policy essential, it is equally as important to constantly publicize the organization's good works and the value of its presence in the community. From children to the city council or county commissioners, no sub-public should be missed in these efforts. In working with the community public, deposits should be made in the "Bank of Goodwill" as often and in as many ways as possible so they can be drawn upon in those inevitable times of need.

Consumptive Users—The Harvesters

Every man, woman and child is a consumptive user of natural resources—a fact often forgotten by those who would relegate resource management to a second rate occupation! Of these millions, however, the publics with which managers most frequently interact are the harvesters. These are the publics who come on-site to take possession of the natural wealth which belongs to all citizens, and which is the "bottom line" of why we are natural resource managers in the first place. They are among our most important publics, and can also be the most difficult with which to work. To ignore them in planning public relations is pure foolishness, for they can be our greatest allies or they can do the most damage either as opponents, or out of ignorance if they fail to understand resource management and the role of the agency. The harvester public includes loggers, miners, sheep and cattle grazers, irrigation interests, hunters, fishermen, Christmas tree cutters, berry pickers, and similar commercial or recreational primary consumers.

Commercial harvesters are the easiest to identify because in most cases they must contact the resource manager for a permit or contract. Frequently, this public includes the same individuals over a long period of time. With them, the techniques of personal contact can be used to highest advantage. They are also business people, and as such, most will accept rationally presented information, especially when it is put in terms of economic opportunities or limitations. The economic reasons or implications behind an agency action, or planned action, can become an important factor in influencing the opinions of this important public.

Commercial harvesters usually have strong influences within the political structures at all levels. There are at least two reasons for this. One is that our system of government is based on the principle of free enterprise. Resource managers, particularly younger ones, often forget this because their education has largley prepared them for service-oriented careers, and usually in government agencies. The other reason for political influence is simply—money. Within the framework of "disclosure laws", it is quite acceptable for businesses—either individually or collectively through their associations—to donate money toward a politician's election campaign. Human nature and politics being what they are, this means that the contributor will be listened to very carefully at some later date.

Commercial harvesters have a powerful domino effect on other publics. Not only do they have a strong influence on their own employee public, they also are important to other business interests in the community. Some, like the wood cutter who sells firewood in a park campground, or an outfitter who supplies guides for sportsmen, are looked at by their customers as possessing considerable authority. What they say is gospel to many forest visitors. This is why earlier it was suggested that if these harvesters operate as concessionaires or special use permitees, they should be treated as an *internal* public.

Recreational harvesters provide a greater challenge in making contacts and planning the best approach to achieve communication and influence. Also, their interest in the resource is not an economic one, so managers must find other points of focus to gain the attention and understanding of these people. Perhaps most difficult to overcome is the fact that with this public, a manager is often dealing with a person using leisure time—a highly cherished and personal thing that the individual associates with free choice and pleasant experiences. Any interference requires a carefully planned approach, and it is here where interpretation (sometimes referred to as "attractive communication") can play such an important role for managers. Readers who are unfamiliar with the concept and special approaches of environmental interpretation should consult as a starting point, *Interpreting our Heritage* (Tilden, 1977) and *Interpreting the Environment* (Sharpe, 1982).

Recreational harvesters can be powerful allies. For one thing, the individuals in this public span the spectrum of our citizenry. The bearded, blueberry picker on an Adirondack mountainside could be a newspaper editor from New York City; the hunter in Texas may be a prominent heart surgeon; the angler on a Georgia river could be . . . . Not only is this public made up of people from all walks of life, they are people who may have an emotional involvement with the resource that supercedes even economic dependency. To favorably influence this public is to gain active support for your programs.

A special problem with recreational harvesters involves the promotion of landowner—sportsmen relations, a major challenge in the wildlife management profession. The problem of keeping private land open to hunting and fishing, and getting sportsmen to respect the rights and property of landowners is at the roots of a perennial conflict that directly influences the conservation department in many ways. The conservation agency acts as the "middle man" in attempting to settle these differences.

Many attempts at facilitating good landowner-sportsmen relations have been described. Titus *et al* (1939) described the Williamston plan started in Michigan in 1929. This appears to be the first attempt at such organized cooperation. Leopold *et al* (1939) advocated a test which must be passed before a hunting license could be purchased. Wagar (1958) suggested that a firearms safety examination should be included. Shick (no date) suggested that rewards offered by sportsmen for apprehension of violators is an effective technique. Bromley (1945) explained a working approach to the landowner-hunter problem in New York. The plan, entitled "The Fish and Wildlife Management Act," was simple, easy to manage, financially sound, protected the landowner and provided remuneration. Land areas were leased from private landowners for long periods and small sums were paid by the state conservation department for the leases. These areas were posted by department personnel to mark boundaries. This method, still in operation today, also allowed the lands to be used for research and demonstration.

Other attempts to build better relationships have included sportsmen-landowner-manager councils, bumper stickers, hunter safety workshops and various programs to post safety zone signs around houses and barns. Some programs have elicited cooperation through promissory notes given by sportsmen to the landowner. For example, the Colorado Wildlife Federation issued a "Sportsmen's Guarantee" against doing damage. For years, each member of the federation carried a wallet card he would show to the landowner. It promised that if the holder was allowed to hunt or fish, he would do no damage to property or livestock. If damage did occur, the federation would pay the landowner $100. To our knowledge, the federation was never asked to pay one claim. Another technique is shown in Figure 6.3. Here, the sportsman leaves his signed pledge with the landowner, complete with vehicle and other data. In turn, the landowner signs a permission card that grants access to the sportsman.

Recreational harvesters, like their commercial counterparts, often take a proprietary interest in a resource. Rather than viewing this as a kind of intrusion, managers should use this interest to build better relations. One important way is through seeking input on seasons, zones, special hunts or fishing methods (flies-only streams, for example), and similar policy and regulation matters. The request for involvement should be sincere, not cosmetic. Good ideas or grounds for compromise often result from the collective thinking of many people, particularly from those who are as familiar with field conditions as most active recreationists.

The leaders, formal or informal, of the harvester publics should be known, contacted, and sold on ideas or issues of importance to the manager. These leaders, be they bankers or janitors, cattlemen or beet-growers, must be the avenue used to reach their respective groups. They must be kept informed. If an agency or company works through the leaders of a public, the leaders will be more likely to favor the ideas being proposed. A majority of the harvester public simply does not care one way or the other about most issues. The agency, or opposition, whichever makes the first and proper contact with a public's leaders, has the greatest chance to succeed.

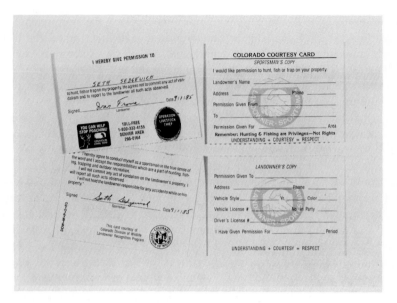

Figure 6.3. "Colorado Courtesy Card," provided by the state's Division of Wildlife, is an attempt to promote better sportsman-landowner relations and keep private land open for recreation.

Harvesters, including hunters and fishermen, as with most publics, need help to realize their potential. The power they can exert, if organized, is tremendous. In most areas, however, they are not organized. Rod and gun clubs seem to limp along, doing nothing unless someone comes to their aid, or acts as a catalyst for action. That someone can be from the natural resource agency or company and he can sell his organization's principles and practices and outline specific ways a club can help. The resource manager should consider it a professional responsibility to keep conservation-oriented clubs from becoming involved in selfish projects or those which flout good resource management principles. Some examples are promotion of bounties, introduction of unsuited exotics, most artificial feeding, and prizes for the largest kill or catch. In many instances the so-called "kids' fish-ponds" projects, which are so popular, do more harm than good. The crowded conditions and prizes offered for the first, largest, or most, really do not further the cause of wise management and good sportsmanship. Too often those of the younger generation aren't interested in learning how to fish, where to fish, the sport involved, or courtesy for their fellow anglers. They want fish, prizes and recognition. The sight of children scooping trout out of gutters with their hands certainly does not promote the ideals of good natural resource management. Sadly, in this case, the gutters were filled with water and the project promoted by the local rod and gun club. Similarly, adult fishing contests are sometimes sponsored which jam a lake or stream with beer-guzzling anglers more interested in a raucous good time than in the responsible use of a valuable resource. While such activities are often viewed with approval by chamber of commerces, they do little to promote good sportsmanship, environmental understanding or relations with the growing numbers of nonconsumptive wildlife users.

Instead of the above, projects can be designed to help both the club and the agency. A few examples are the promotion of ethics, safety programs, stream cleanup and development and sportsmen-landowner cooperation ventures. One such venture included the placing of signs along property boundaries before hunting season. The unique signs were color-coded to go with the following wording:

STOP—No Hunting (Red)

GO AHEAD, BUT ACT LIKE A GENTLEMAN (Green)

CAUTION—ASK PERMISSION BEFORE ENTERING (Yellow)

For aesthetic reasons, the project could include removal of the signs when the season is over.

Other worthwhile projects include liability insurance for landowners, insurance for landowners which covers wildlife damage, wildlife education scholarship funds, conservation education workshop sponsorships for teachers, junior conservation club sponsorships, and various action projects to improve or create habitat. Recreational harvester organizations can aid in fish stocking, habitat improvement, clean-up campaigns, rifle range development and conservation parades and displays. Many bulletins and articles are available that list excellent projects and make suggestions for club success.

When important local harvester publics have been identified, meetings of that public should be attended by one or two (not an army) of organization officials. Too many resource people at a meeting may be counterproductive. Similarly, while it is a good idea to join in cases where there is open membership, it is best that the resource manager abstains from holding office.

Nonconsumptive Recreationists

Until recently it could be said that this public was of relatively little importance except perhaps to the National Park Service. Today, it is an increasingly vocal and crucial public which may eventually shape the future of resource management everywhere. Nonconsumptive users include photographers, painters and bird watchers, plus a variety of more active recreationists ranging from hikers and backpackers to canoeists, snowmobilers and off-road vehicle enthusiasts.

These are the people who use the outdoors and natural resources without physically harvesting anything. In Idaho, for example, it was found that 9.2% of a statewide random sample of residents used the state's wildlife resource solely for nonconsumptive purposes (Fazio and Belli, 1977). Nationwide, nearly 55% of all Americans 16 years of age or older engage in nonconsumptive wildlife activities at least part of the year (Shaw and Mangun, 1984). In addition, what documentation is needed for the massive growth in numbers of recreationists who take to the outdoors on wheels, skis or just about anything else that rolls, glides, floats or flies? Can this public be ignored? Incredibly, many tradition-bound resource managers do just that. Some forestry schools, in fact, do not require a single course in wildland recreation management, a course that could provide valuable information on understanding recreationists and working with them successfully and to the advantage of all.

Many sub-publics exist among the nonconsumptive recreationists, and many of those are in conflict with each other. As with other publics, categorization must depend on the uses and public relations needs of a given area or situation. It will also take a special effort to ferret out formal organizations of some groups (hang gliders, for example) to take advantage of communication

Figure 6.4. Non-consumptive recreationists are an increasing and influential public that can no longer be ignored. (Photo by Bruce Andersen.)

opportunities using their publications and meetings. Others, like artists, photographers, and cross-country skiers, may tend not to be "joiners." These, and large numbers of *any* public will need to be reached through other ways. Suggestions are included in following chapters.

When organizations among nonconsumptive user groups do exist, they usually are highly receptive to the attention of resource managers. All too often they are given the impression that fish and game departments are for hunters and fishermen only, or the Forest Service is for loggers and car campers only. In some states, "trail councils" have been developed to provide an alliance of all recreation interests related to trails. They include representatives of all user types on the governing board and as members, and also provide for equal participation by representatives of the land management agencies in the state. Newsletters, symposia and other meetings of these and similar recreationist coalitions provide excellent opportunities for managers to learn about the users and to communicate with them.

In recent years, the proliferation of organizations and corresponding special interest media has kept pace with the rise in numbers of nonconsumptive resource users. *Mother Earth News, Country Journal,* and similar publications reach thousands of young people who, in many cases, may harbor unrealistic ideas about natural resources. Resource managers have not begun to understand or work with these people, just as in many cases they ignore local Sierra Club chapters and make disparaging remarks about the "dickey bird watchers" of the Audubon Society. Four hundred thousand men and women, many of them extremely influential, count themselves among the dickey birders—a public no manager can afford to slight.

Landowners

Like the commercial harvesters, the landowner public fills an important niche in our economic system. These are the taxpayers of highest magnitude, and they are usually the most stable, well established individuals in any community. Private land in the United States annually provides more than half the game shot by hunters, while 60% of the nation's commercial timberland is controlled by private interests with the majority of the acreage in the hands of small, non-industrial owners. The landowner public is easily contacted—the county tax books providing a ready mailing list to anyone who wants it. Like others, landowners belong to many publics simultaneously, but their interests in local government, living quality and economic prosperity of the community form an important bond that can be used by the resource manager. Most are also interested in information that will help them meet their own personal objectives for use of the land.

Traditionally, the landowner public has been thought of as the ranchers, farmers and large timber producers. In addition to direct contact, the best means of reaching these people have proven to be meetings of the Grange, cattlemen and wool-grower associations, and landowner cooperatives. Cooperative Extension works largely with this public, and a technique found useful is to hold a meeting at one of the local ranches or farms and, of course, during the season of least agricultural activity. A series of small meetings with several neighbors may be better attended and more effective than trying to get all the landowners to attend one large meeting in the county building. Wherever the meeting or whatever the occasion, it is essential that the resource manager working with this public speak the rancher's or farmer's language. To gain the respect and trust of these individuals, it is important to have a working knowledge of equipment terminology and crop management, and to be familiar with the many problems that face these producers of food and fibre. One way to do this is to regularly read publications such as *Farm Journal, American Agriculturalist* or the stockmens'/farmers' tabloids that are published most places for statewide distribution (*Michigan Farmer,* for example).

The problems of this public frequently interface with those of the resource manager. One is damage to private property by game animals, a particularly knotty problem that must be handled with tact—especially when trying to determine which claims are just and which are falsified. Sportsmen access and conduct is a major problem discussed earlier. Who can blame the landowner for posting his property when cattle are turned loose by a gate left open, when holes are shot in equipment or buildings, or when litter is left behind? For that matter, what right does a person have to even walk on private land without first asking the owner's permission? These are the kinds of messages that must be put across to outdoor recreationists of all kinds to prevent the closing of private land, and landowners should be made aware of your agency's efforts in their behalf.

In some cases, a resource manager may be able to encourage sportsmen clubs, snowmobile groups or other outdoor recreation organizations to sponsor projects to alleviate this problem. Annual sportsmen-landowner banquets, furnished by the sportsmen, have been successful in some areas in breaking down barriers and keeping private land open to responsible recreationists.

Today, an increasingly important landowner is the urban escapist. These consist of several subpublics that are quite different from each other. One is the absentee, or second home owner. In New York and New England, for example, vast areas of abandoned farm land of marginal agricultural quality have been purchased by city dwellers. From Buffalo to New Haven, these people leave their apartments or city lots on weekends and during vacations to spend time on their 40, 80, 160 acres or more in the country. Most of this land supports potential forest crops, wildlife and even fishery resources.

In a study of absentee landowners from Buffalo and Rochester, New York, Dickson (1970) found that many of these people have the desire to manage their land to yield resource crops. For example, he found that 35 percent of his respondents were involved in Christmas tree production or the sale of wood products. Over half of the owners stated an intention to initiate or continue

Figure 6.5. Littering and other poor conduct of campers, hunters or other users on private land cause landowners to close their land to all recreationists. This adds more pressure on public lands and should be of concern to every resource manager. (Courtesy of Colorado Division of Wildlife.)

thinning and pruning trees, managing fish habitat or providing food and cover for wildlife. Dickson also found that certain characteristics separated those individuals who were more likely than others to voluntarily seek help from resource professionals. These characteristics included: ownership of more than 30 acres, or as low as 5–20 acres if plantations were present; having a dwelling on the property; spending more than 10 winter days and 100 days annually at the property; and having professional-type careers. It was found, however, that even those who wanted help had some difficulties obtaining it. Some of the reasons for this were agency office hours that did not coincide with times absentee owners were usually in the area; "anti-absentee" tendencies on the part of local agency advisory committees; inadequate numbers of foresters available; and a lack of field personnel adequately educated to establish rapport with the more highly educated segment of this public.

Cabin owners without manageable land comprise another group to be recognized. Although they may own but a few acres or even a 50 × 100-foot lot, this public can have a tremendous impact on local resources, particularly water quality. In many areas, these people sorely lack understanding of ecology or resource management, yet by virtue of their affluence they can have considerable influence on the outcome of resource-related issues.

Similarly, but often at the other end of the economic scale, there are the young, back-to-the-land enthusiasts. Armed with *The Foxfire Book, Mother Earth News, Organic Gardening* and similar "how-to" publications, these free-spirited individuals buy a few acres in their search for an alternative to lifestyles left behind in the city. As the USDA Forest Service found out in north Idaho when it wanted to reduce brush competition on its land using a herbicide, this new public can be vocal, highly savvy in swaying public opinion, and in the aggregate can consist of far greater numbers than may be realized. This public's rather purist approach to environmental manipulation creates a barrier between the "back-to-the-landers" and many resource managers. However, in most cases there is common ground that can act as a beginning point for dialogue and good relations. This may be wood as an energy source, soil stabilization, wildlife protection or similar topics. It behooves managers to include this group in their public relations planning.

Business Community

This public actually includes many landowners, commercial harvesters, dude ranchers and concessionaires, but it also includes the grocery store operator in a small town, the service station owner, motel manager and others who may feel quite divorced from natural resources. As with all commercial interests, these people need to be constantly reminded how important natural resource management is to the businesses in the vicinity. Many economic studies have been conducted and all point out that natural resources in the community area mean much to the prosperous condition of that community.

To use an extreme example, what are the natural resources of Yellowstone National Park worth to the businessmen of West Yellowstone or Gardiner, Montana? What is the deer season worth to the residents of northern Michigan? Dollars and cents figures may not be easily available, but many of these business people go south to rest for the winter after the short tourist or hunting season is over. If you have tried to get service in a restaurant during the rush hours of the opening day of deer season, there would be no doubt regarding the importance of sportsmen to the business. Nor is it necessarily as sporadic as the fall seasons. Many states have year-round fishing seasons. Hiking, backpacking, bird watching, skiing and other resource-dependent recreational activities make contributions to the business community far greater than realized by many. There is a major challenge in convincing the business community to be sensitive to the environmental conditions sought by these recreationists, otherwise, in a desire to expand and develop, the very attractions become destroyed by those dependent on them for a livelihood.

In addition to the use of mass media with messages tailored to business interests, resource managers can associate with the business community through organizations that are usually found in even the smallest towns. These include Junior and Senior Chamber of Commerce groups, service clubs such as Lions, Rotary and Kiwanis, and fraternal organizations such as Elks, Moose, Masons and others. Membership and attendance are an investment in understanding people, and understanding is a first vital step toward influencing.

Natural resource agency personnel should also try to patronize local business operations whenever possible. This not only promotes goodwill, but also gives an opportunity to exchange ideas and information.

Youth and Their Leaders

A cynical wildlife biologist once said, "Work with the kids and hope you outlive the rest of 'em." For certain, the youth public is the hope for environmental quality of the future. From the public relations standpoint, they not only are the opinion leaders of tomorrow, they can significantly influence the opinions and behavior of their parents today. They are also enthusiastic and open to working with anyone from a resource agency not lacking in energy and vitality. But while moxie is a quality necessary for anyone who is to work with this public, it in itself is not enough. As Freeman Tilden (1977) pointed out, presentations to children will fail if they are merely dilutions of presentations to adults. A special approach is required and we will address some considerations.

First, however, we need to consider the terminology quagmire that has been present since the advent of environmental education around 1970. Some teachers and other youth leaders understand the difference between conservation education and environmental education (Chapter 2). The resource manager who promises the latter and delivers the former, or who still views everything as conservation education, will lose credibility for himself and his agency. On the other hand, many teachers are not yet aware of this important conceptual difference. In these cases, the resource specialist can do a service by clarifying the two. We also need to be honest about the difference. For example, if a state game and fish department has as its objective "public understanding of harvestable game management"—and nothing more—then it is best to label it conservation education and do the best possible job of meeting *that* objective. Do not call it environmental education, because it does *not* involve a solution-oriented approach to discovering and alleviating (through interdisciplinary approaches and behavior changes) far-reaching environmental problems. For the most part, resource agencies and associated industries have done an outstanding job in the field of conservation education. As society's needs broaden to all aspects of environmental protection (air, water, and nuclear contamination, for example), we have much to learn, and we must recognize what we can contribute and what we can not.

Whatever the purpose, working with youth begins with working with their leaders. Be certain there is a clear understanding about what you are to do and to accomplish, when, where and with what assistance. Visit the leader at his convenience and plan out all details, in advance, recording them so a copy of a plan or outline can be made for both parties. Suggest that pre-work be done to prepare the youngsters for any field work, and have ideas ready for post-trip work to make the experience more meaningful. Also insist that one or more of the regular leaders assist with the project, or at the very least be responsible for handling discipline. In the case of field trips, have an alternate plan ready in case of inclement weather. This may be a rain date or an alternate indoor activity or tour.

Teacher education should also be given serious consideration in lieu of working directly with children. By providing leadership, materials and perhaps facilities or an outdoor setting, many of the public relations benefits can be obtained while efficiency is improved through the "multiplier effect". A group of teachers, properly trained, can work with many more children than the resource manager can ever hope to reach while meeting his other obligations. Teacher workshops are well established in some areas of the country, but completely lacking in others. To be successful, not only is an interesting and exciting program needed, it also must be at a time convenient for the already time-scarce teacher. The ideal (and most difficult) is to arrange with administrators for release time so teachers can attend during the work week. Early summer is probably the second best alternative. Weekends will discourage all but the most highly motivated. It also helps if sponsorships can be arranged to defray costs. Sportsmen's groups and companies have been very generous in this regard. Another incentive is college credit. Many school districts require teachers to obtain a certain number of credits on a continuing education basis, and the teachers often look for non-traditional courses that will be enjoyable as well as educational. It will be necessary to cooperate with a local accredited university or college to make this possible.

Working effectively with young people is not automatic nor is it based on some instinctive quality that grows out of being a parent. The job should be entrusted only to those having enough interest to plan, read, experiment and modify in order to improve their style and abilities. A good starting point is two publications written for interpreters but applicable to anyone working with children. One is a Forest Service booklet, *Educational Principles and Techniques for Interpreters;* the other is from the National Park Service, *Children's Interpretation: A Discovery Book for Interpreters.* References for both follow this chapter.

Besides enthusiasm for both the task and the subject, the two keys to working with children are *organization* and *involvement.* Detailed organization is essential even in a so-called unstructured exercise, like a walk in a bog. The area should be walked and studied in advance of taking the group. Objectives should be thought out, as well as the means for meeting those objectives. What about transportation to the site, lunches, nets, traps, hand lenses, first aid equipment and toilet procedures? How will you close the session? Rather than drifting back to the buses, a meaningful wrap-up should signal the end and make certain the objectives were met. Every detail must be planned in advance.

Involvement means just that. Every session should involve the children—and as many of their senses as possible. An *interesting* film produced for the age level with which you are working or a short set of *good* slides would be the minimum for this principle. Better yet are small teams exploring for creatures, soil layers, leaf types and similar physical features; or allowing the children to handle a snake, measure a tree or feel the talons of a mounted hawk. In addition to *instruction* (the film or slides) and *action* (exploring and handling), Machlis and McDonough (1978) suggested using *fantasy* as a powerful tool to achieve understanding. Storytelling, reading an historical diary, role playing and puppetry are all ways of triggering a child's fantasy to help with the task of communicating.

Finally, the cognitive or mental development of this public must be carefully considered both in planning and conducting any efforts. A common error is to speak "over the heads" of young people, or ask them to do reasoning for which they are not ready. Table 6.4 may be of some help in matching content to age level. It is also important, at all levels, to stress *usefulness*—not a very difficult task in the field of natural resource management.

A common encounter with youth and their leaders is when a resource manager is approached for ideas on projects. Many books and pamphlets are now available and should be collected as references. "Project Learning Tree" is a set of particularly useful materials developed by the American Forest Council (1619 Massachusetts Ave., Washington, D.C. 20036). More recently, this has been supplemented with "Project Wild" which is available through most state fish and wildlife departments. The National Audubon Society, Soil Conservation Service, U.S. Fish and Wildlife Service, Forest Service, and many others also have material available.

For those working regularly with young people, it would be wise to subscribe to *Ranger Rick's Nature Magazine,* (National Wildlife Federation, 1412 16th St. N.W., Washington, D.C. 20036), and to publications for teachers such as *Science and Children,* (National Science Teachers Association, 1742 Connecticut Ave. N.W., Washington, D.C. 20009). A list of local projects which could utilize volunteer labor might also be kept on file. For any project, learning and/or public relations objectives should be listed and met. Even with trail maintenance, litter clean-up, or tree planting, efforts should be made to show a tie-in with broader concepts of environmental management.

The potential for public relations endeavors with young people and their leaders is unlimited. Working with this public is a worthwhile investment of time and should be considered an important function of any agency or company involved with the mangement of natural resources.

Table 6.4.
Stages of Cognitive Development in Children (Adapted from Machlis and McDonough, 1978)

Stage	Age	Key Concepts
Early Childhood	0-2	Exploration of Immediate Surroundings Learning is Active Sensing, Not Thinking
Pre-School	2-7	Likenesses and Differences Some Classifications Cannot Reverse or Conjecture Senses are Important Intuitive Thought Begins
Elementary School	7-11	Classification Ordering Conservation (of qualities through changes in shape or position) Reversibility Internal Manipulations with Concrete Data Inductive Thinking Increasing Interest Span
Junior/Senior High School	12-18	Abstract Thought Processes Concern for Reasons and Proof Deductive Thinking

Media Representatives

To many natural resource managers, one of their most frustrating relationships is with the representatives of the mass media, especially reporters. "I didn't say that!" or, "She quoted me wrong!" are common statements. Others watch in vain for news releases that never appear after being sent to the local paper, or wonder why the television station doesn't provide coverage of their activities. Resource agencies need publicity, accurate news coverage, and a healthy relationship with media representatives. Actually, the agencies are important to the media as well, for there are interesting and exciting stories in the routine business of resource management, and stories are the raw material of the media. The opportunity exists for a mutually beneficial relationship.

The important subject of working with the mass media is covered in detail in Part III. The main tenets, however, can be summarized as: (1) Before news breaks out, make yourself acquainted with the *appropriate* individuals at radio, T.V., newspaper and wire service offices, as well as with local free lancers and "stringers" working for periodicals or distant media; (2) Know and adhere to the needs of the media, including deadlines, style, preferred formats, and the kind of story or slant each usually uses; (3) Be truthful and helpful always, and treat competing media equitably.

The General Public

To make a point, it is sometimes said in public relations work there is no such thing as "*the* public". Whenever possible, *specific* publics should be identified and worked with on the basis of their special characteristics. Sometimes, however, people can be placed in no single category, or an idea is applicable to *all* external publics. Only in these cases is the term *general public* an accurate one. Understanding or communicating with such a broad spectrum of human beings is extremely difficult, so the temptation to lump publics into this category should be avoided whenever possible.

IDENTIFYING PUBLICS—A DIFFERENT APPROACH

Throughout this chapter we have stressed the importance of categorizing people into publics in any way that aids the public relations effort. Publics are *dynamic,* with individuals being part of many publics at once, and being shifted from one to another depending on the issue at hand. An employee by day may be a youth leader by night and most likely is also a landowner and/or member of the community, to mention a few. What the public relations practitioner is really interested in is identifying as many people as possible who may be affected essentially the same way by a particular act or policy of the organization, *and* who are likely to react or otherwise affect the organization similarly (through opinion or action). Again we stress that grouping individuals in such a way makes the job of understanding and influencing enormously easier. Still, it is a step in the public relations process often shortcut by natural resource organizations, especially in the public sector.

Usually the traditional, easily observed characteristics will suffice. As an example, consider the case of a decision to reestablish the Oregon Trail for recreational enjoyment. In this hypothetical situation, assume that public involvement has taken place in the decision-making process and that the decision has been made to go ahead with the idea. The public involvement stage revealed very divided opinions on the proposal; certainly there was no consensus among the people living or working along the route of this historic trail. In planning a public relations campaign to implement the project, it may suffice to recognize that a "landowner public" will need to be dealt with. If a breakdown of publics were used at all, that would be the traditional approach. But perhaps a more helpful way to prepare for working with this public would be to further classify the landowners. Some useful groupings might include: those with the trail route crossing their land and those living nearby; those who work their land and those with recreational holdings; or those having *values* strongly oriented toward "patriotism," and those oriented toward the "need for social recognition," or "wisdom." Or, it might be helpful to know where the individuals in this public stand in their *attitudes* toward the trail or different features of the proposal. It is quite likely not all the landowners will be alike in any of these characteristics. When the differences are known, appropriately different approaches can be taken to win their support of the trail idea and its successful operation.

In the following pages, a few of the many possible approaches to delineating useful characteristics are outlined. Others, ranging from simple two-category divisions to complex social-psychological analysis can be created and used depending on the scope, nature and importance of the issue or project, and the manpower, expertise and money available to conduct the necessary research.

Intellectuals—The Thought Leaders

In a publication titled *The Engines of Public Opinion,* John E. Benneth (1967) suggested that there is a group of people who "roll the intellectual rocks that initiate landslides of mass public opinion. . . ." These thought leaders, he pointed out, are the nation's intellectuals, men and women who are interested in and critically evaluate the broad spectrum of issues, morals and values in society. They are the workers of mind, not hand, and they find vitality in ideas. Usually, but to an increasingly lesser degree, they are also in positions free of the responsibility for administering society's public and private business. Benneth listed three sub-publics among the intelligentsia. These are summarized in Table 6.5.

It was the intellectual public to whom Germany's Volkswagon Company directed its efforts in the early 1950's when it made its entry into the U.S. market. The results, of course, revolutionized automobile sales and manufacturing in this country. The Sierra Club, masters at influencing public opinion, also use this approach. Benneth listed the following publications as carefully selected intelligentsia contact points used by the Sierra Club in its campaign to stop the construction of a dam in Grand Canyon: *New York Times, Scientific American, Harper's, Ramparts, National Review* and *Saturday Review.*

The point of Benneth's article was that most of the thought leaders are divorced from the realities of resource management; they are preoccupied with the aesthetic and are blind to production needs and methods. His suggestion was that the resource management professions need to recognize these "trigger points" of opinion and work more directly with them.

Innovators or Laggards?

On a more formalized basis there are various theories of how ideas diffuse through society. One of these is the *adoption-diffusion process* as described by Rogers and Shoemaker (1971). This theory attempts to explain how a new idea, or an "innovation" such as a mandatory, back-country permit system, or a new hybrid that produces pulpwood quicker, flows through a social system. Within this social system, people may be classified based upon a time sequence in which they usually accept new ideas or practices. Knowledge of this theory may in some cases provide a practical way of defining publics to help speed the acceptance of a new idea.

Table 6.5.
Characteristics of Sub-publics among the Intelligentsia (Adapted from Benneth, 1967).

Group	Relative Size	Occupation	Characteristics
I	Smallest	Various	Giant thinkers / Often original Articulate / Influential Speak to small groups of other intellectuals through elitist publications
II	Larger	Leading Editors, Broadcasters, Playwrights, Novelists, Artists, Scholars, Clergy, Some Business Leaders	Thinking heavily influenced by Group I Disseminators of new concepts and styles
III	Largest, Hundreds of Thousands	Academic and Professional (Physicists, Economists, Lawyers, Doctors, Engineers, Educators, Clergy, Etc.)	Avidly consume products of Group I & II Wield influence over millions

Rogers and Shoemaker explained that adopter distributions follow a bell-shaped curve over time with the continuum of adoption divided into five categories. These categories, along with a summary of characteristics determined largely from agricultural studies, are shown in Table 6.6.

The *Innovators* are the first to try and the first to accept an idea, and are known as the "experimenters" or "people always trying out new things." These are the information seekers. They usually have money, prestige and already have "arrived." The innovators usually are influential in an area larger than a community. Their activities, interests, contacts, and positions may extend to the county or state level. Their main sources of information are the agencies, departments or scientific organizations where the idea originated, or they may originate the idea themselves. The innovators are few in number and are willing to take risks. However, they are rarely the persons that most people go to for advice.

The *Early Adopters* often include community leaders among their ranks. They may be elected officials of a formal group or leaders of an informal group; they have wide social contacts and belong to formal organizations. They usually are relatively young, well educated and well informed. They read more bulletins, magazines and newspapers than the others. Both innovators and early adopters prefer factual and "why" information as opposed to the "how" and "what" answers sought by the later adopters.

The *Early Majority* includes many informal leaders who operate not on an elected basis, but rather within cliques or other small social groups. They may not even be recognized as being leaders by others. They usually are older than the early adopters, cannot afford financial setbacks, and in their personal and social characteristics are very similar to the majority. They are looked to however, as having good judgement, and are slower to adopt than the innovators or early adopters. Their main sources of communication are the media, neighbors and friends.

The *Late Majority* are the "followers." They have a "wait and see" attitude that makes them highly dependent on their peers in the early majority. They often are less well established in the community, have less education and are older. They have few social aspirations and participate less in public or community affairs. Change for them is difficult and a large degree of communication is through neighbors and friends.

Laggards are so tradition-bound that change is very difficult to accept. They adopt only with greatest reluctance. They are often older people with the least education, lowest incomes and lowest social status. They cannot afford risks. Neighbors and friends of like status and values are their primary means of communication. In a given social system (loggers, for example) laggards tend to drop out, particularly if they refuse to adopt at all.

The rate of adoption and the acceptance or rejection of an idea by individuals are dependent on many factors. The adoption sequence is discussed further in the next chapter, but for more details on many variables not included here, consult *Communication of Innovations* by Everett M. Rogers and F. Floyd Shoemaker.

Socioeconomic Characteristics

Social and economic characteristics provide another way that the broad population may be broken into useable categories. For any geographic region, Bureau of the Census publications can be consulted for that kind of information. Newspapers, television stations and radio stations also usually have statistics of many kinds for their areas of coverage. They use this information in trying to show prospective advertisers the numbers of people they can reach having any given

Table 6.6.
Summary of Adopter Characteristics[1]

Adopter Category	Salient Characteristics	Personal Characteristics	Communications Behavior	Social Relationships
Innovators (First 2.5% to try out idea)	"Venturesome"; willing to accept risks	Youngest age; highest social status; largest and most specialized operations; wealthy	Closest contact with scientific information sources; interaction with other innovators; relatively greatest use of impersonal sources	Some opinion leadership; very cosmopolite
Early adopters (Next 13.5%)	"Respectable"; regarded by many others in the social system as a role-model	High social status; large and specialized operations	Greatest contact with local change agents	Greatest opinion leadership of any category in most social systems; very localite
Early majority (Next 34%)	"Deliberate"; willing to consider innovations only after peers have adopted	Above average social status; average-sized operation	Considerable contact with change agents and early adopters	Some opinion leadership
Late majority (Next 34%)	"Skeptical"; overwhelming pressure from peers needed before adoption occurs	Below average social status; small operation; little specialization; small income	Secure ideas from peers who are mainly late majority or early majority; less use of mass media	Little opinion leadership
Laggards (Last 16%)	"Traditional"; oriented to the past	Little specialization; lowest social status; smallest operation; lowest income; oldest	Neighbors, friends, and relatives with similar values are main information source	Very little opinion leadership; semi-isolates

1. Adapted with permission of The Free Press, a division of Macmillan, Inc. from *Communication of Innovations: A Cross-Cultural Approach,* 2nd Edition, by Everett M. Rogers and F. Floyd Shoemaker. Copyright © 1971 by The Free Press.

characteristic (age, sex, income and education to name a few). Advertising agencies also carefully maintain this kind of information in their files. In most social research, including studies of resource users, socioeconomic data are routinely gathered and correlated to such variables as preferences, opinions, activities, knowledge levels, experience levels or whatever else serves as the focus of the study. Natural resource specialists could use the insights provided by these user profiles to help tailor communication to specific publics.

Cognitive Styles and Complexity

The concepts of cognitive styles and cognitive complexity provide valuable insights on matching certain communication techniques to individuals who will respond best to the given techniques. Most of the research with these concepts has been conducted with youngsters in teacher-learner situations. However, the ideas are probably just as applicable to adults. In either case they can be of value to natural resource specialists who often find themselves in the role of teacher, a highly appropriate role in the context of public relations as used in this book. The description and tables that follow are adapted from a paper by Norris, Heikkinen and Armstrong, 1975.

Cognitive style is a person's preferred way of interpreting, organizing, transforming, and reporting information. "Reflectivity" and "impulsivity" are two of the styles reported by educational researchers. The reflective student, as the term implies, tends to give careful, well thought-out answers. Learners in this category are likely to consider several sources of information, and to weigh the relevance and importance of various bits of discrepant input. Impulsive individuals tend to make decisions based upon whatever occurs to them first. Subsequent discrepant information is usually rejected without consideration. The same teaching approach used with both types of learners will *not* be equally successful. Research indicates that students who are impulsive tend to learn better in a structured atmosphere, while reflectives thrive in the unstructured setting (Walters and Seiben, 1974).

Cognitive style is associated with *cognitive complexity,* which may be thought of as referring to any of four stages of moral and cognitive awareness evident in humans of adolescent years and beyond. These stages, or levels of cognitive complexity, are summarized in Table 6.7.

Students having an impulsive cognitive style show many of the characteristics of levels one and two; reflectives tend to resemble levels three and four. The usefulness of recognizing these differences when working with young people (or adults) is that it allows selection of an approach that will have the greatest chance of being successful. Without having knowledge of cognitive complexity and the cognitive styles of your group, effectiveness will be greatly reduced. For example, you may be quite proud of yourself for developing an ingenious simulation game to make youngsters aware of the problems of land use planning. For the reflective types, and especially the few at complexity level four (only 10 to 15% of all adults are said to achieve this level), you will probably be highly successful. Unfortunately, you will probably be creating in the rest of the group an inpenetrable indifference! Conversely, a technique such as lecturing or showing a film may work well with the majority, because most youngsters in our society—particularly in rural and more conservative regions—are likely to be functioning at complexity levels one and two. Those at level three will not hear you; those at level four will *possibly* be interested. To remove the guesswork or to provide a variety of approaches that will interest students along the entire spectrum of cognitive complexity, consult Table 6.8 for a guide to instructional methods. To determine your own biases for or against specific instructional styles, a self-administered test (Canfield Instructional Styles Inventory) is available from Humanics Media, Liberty Drawer 7970, Ann Arbor, MI 48107.

As with any categorization, care must be taken to not oversimplify. Many individuals exhibit characteristics of more than one level of cognitive complexity, and people move from one to another. Complex personality factors, as well as cultural and environmental influences frequently create exceptions in the most careful schemes to classify human beings. Still, the recognition of differences, and the skill to be able to group people accordingly, is one of the most helpful foundations for the practice of good public relations.

Table 6.7.
Summary of Characteristics of Youngsters in Different Levels of Cognitive Complexity

Level	Characteristics
One: Stereotypes	1. Respond to the adult world's promotion of role expectations that fall neatly into specific stereotyped occupations. 2. Lack the basis for forming individualized opinions regarding career choices. 3. Do best in course work that relates to real world jobs, skills, or careers. 4. Like learning activities such as programmed materials, workbooks, worksheets, text related readings, structured or teacher directed laboratory assignments. 5. Short attention span. 6. Generally inattentive. 7. Less self control. 8. Confused easily. 9. Not too interested in school.
Two: Opinionates	1. Strong concern for cultural conformity. 2. Most enjoy low-level memory or factual information. 3. Often competitive. 4. Right-wrong, black-white specifics are most appreciated. 5. Like to impress the teacher with questions. 6. Most comfortable with clear explanations of what to do, and how to proceed; grade anxious. 7. Prefer learning from lectures, handouts, teacher directed discussions, workbooks, structured labs, reports, films, Learning Activity Packages. 8. Future or past oriented—finds living for the moment difficult.
Three: Existential	1. Now oriented. 2. Rejects most information which alludes to historical positions or ideas. 3. May be expressing themselves with alternative dress, religious expression, and questions about what is worth studying. 4. Prefer learning that which is now-oriented and that which allows for freedom and flexibility. 5. Prefer contracts, open-end problems, experimentation.
Four: Autonomous (Also called creative or self-actualized)	1. Interact largely with selves. 2. Interested in information. 3. Accept the idea that all behavior represents the possibility of choice and of exposing one's self to change. 4. There is an accepting that one is responsible for determining one's own destiny. 5. Require verification of ideas with data. 6. Self-directing with little need for adult acclaim or reinforcement. 7. Can accommodate input from multiple sources. 8. Can construct new ideas to assimilate new information, and reorganize the entire framework according to changing circumstances. 9. Students at this level can successfully utilize any degree of structure, from the most highly structured to entirely unstructured, depending upon inclination of the student.

Table 6.8.
Instructional Methods Appropriate for Different Cognitive Styles and Levels of Cognitive Complexity.

Cognitive Style	Level of Cognitive Complexity	Appropriate Instructional Methods
Impulsive	One (Stereotypes) and Two (Opinionates)	Demonstrations Workbooks Films/Filmstrips Programmed Learning Lectures Structured Laboratories Directed Discussions Single Texts Learning Activity Packages Directed Projects Notebooks
Reflective	Three (Existential) and Four (Autonomous)	Problem Formulation Open-ended Problems Discrepant Events Games Simulations Unstructured Laboratories Student-led Discussions Student Oriented Projects Multiple Text Reading Assignments

Values

Milton Rokeach of Washington State University has done considerable work with values and attitudes, and their relationships to beliefs and reality. Of the myriad theories and models of human behavior within social systems, Rokeach's ideas seem to have particular merit and are included in this text as one way to conceptualize the basis for public opinion and action, and how it might be altered. Understanding *values* can help and is one more tool in dividing the general public into more specific publics, with known characteristics. In this case, there is even an easily-administered testing instrument available to allow people to rank order their values. It is shown in Figure 6.6 and is available for purchase.

Rokeach (1968) defined a value as an enduring belief that a particular mode of conduct (*instrumental* values) or that a particular end-state of existence (*terminal* values) is personally and socially preferable to alternative modes of conduct or end-states of existence. This differs importantly from an *attitude,* a term more frequently and often loosely used in natural resource management. An attitude is also based on enduring beliefs, but focuses on a specific object or situation, predisposing one to respond in some preferential manner.

Again from Rokeach's (1968) explanation, a value is a standard that tells us how to act, what to want, and even what attitudes we should hold. A value is a standard we employ to justify behavior, to morally judge, to compare ourselves with others, and to decide on what we need to influence others (so they will share our values). To stress the difference between attitudes and values: a value transcends specific objects and situations, while an attitude focuses directly on

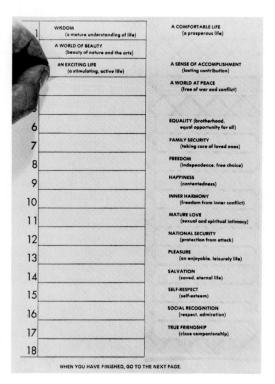

Figure 6.6. Value survey forms consist of two pages of gummed labels representing "modes of conduct" and the "end states of existence" (shown here). When respondents rank order the values, those having similar rankings may be considered a public for certain approaches to public relations. (©Milton Rokeach, 1967. Reproduced by permission of Halgren Tests, NW 1145 Clifford St., Pullman, WA 99163.)

specific objects and situations; and unlike an attitude, a value is a standard, or yardstick, guiding not only attitudes, but also *actions,* comparisons, evaluations, and justifications of self and others. Also unlike an attitude, it is a distinct preference for a specified mode of behavior or end-state of existence.

A value *system,* according to Rokeach, represents a learned organization of rules for making choices and resolving conflicts. Similarities of culture, social system, sex, occupation, education and religion are a few of the variables that are likely to shape in similar ways the value-attitude *systems* of large numbers of people. Importantly, any change in any part of the value-attitude system will affect other parts; also, any change in the value-attitude system should lead to behavioral change. Now, consider his contention that an adult possesses many thousands of attitudes—as many attitudes as he or she has had encounters with specific objects and specific situations—but far fewer *instrumental values* (perhaps 60–72) such as ambition, broad-mindedness, and courage which in turn are in the service of and related to 18 basic *terminal values* (See Figure 6.6 for examples).

This may be an important key to influencing others. Here is how it would work. Humans have an inherent need not only for physiological consistency (body temperature, for example), but for mental consistency as well. When we encounter a discrepancy in our cognitive system, a tension is established, known as *cognitive dissonance.* The normal reaction is to try to resolve this conflict (Festinger, 1957). This resolution of the conflict can take place in many ways, including a *change* in our value-attitude system. For example, a particular terminal value may be brought into a dissonant relation with another terminal value, or with an instrumental value, or with an attitude. Such experienced dissonant relations should give rise to motivational forces leading an individual to change his values and attitudes in such a way that they would become more psychologically consistent with one another (Rokeach, 1968).

Further elaboration on Rokeach's theory is presented in *The Nature of Human Values,* including specific examples of induced changes in values, attitudes and behavior. One of these examples was an experiment conducted by Hollen (1972) who demonstrated the ability to bring about a significant increase in the terminal value "a world of beauty." The research group was college students and the test for the change was conducted a month after the experimental treatment. Hollen succeeded in altering this value merely by pointing out to the students that "young people and better educated people tend to rank 'a world of beauty' higher than the general public ranks it." Moreover, increase in this value was accompanied by positive changes in attitude toward various ecological issues such as highway beautification programs, the banning of non-returnable bottles, and the banning of automobiles from cities (Rokeach, 1973).

In natural resource work, value surveys have been used in at least two cases. The first was in 1974 at the start of a public controversy over placement of Idaho's Priest River in the National Wild and Scenic River System. According to James VanLeuven, University of Idaho researchers were able to predict with at least partial success what stands potential leaders in the controversy would take on the various alternatives proposed by the resource managers. The prediction was based on the consistency between the respondent's high-ranked values and the values served by each of the managers' alternatives.

Value surveys were again used in 1977, but this time as social indicators to show the extent to which different publics were satisfied with the management of the Clearwater River, one of the nation's first wild and scenic rivers. In this case, Rokeach's value inventory was administered to 280 selected representatives of the nine interest groups involved in the river management program. The inventories were then combined into a composite as well as tallied separately for each of the publics. The results are shown in Table 6.9.

Some interesting asides from the results of VanLeuven's study were: the longer a Forest Service employee lived in the area, the greater were the chances he would mirror the values of landowners; elected officials, although in a strongly Democratic area, came very close to reflecting the value rankings of business leaders (who tend to be Republican); and the two publics who differed the most from the overall rankings were environmental club members and outdoor club members.

Table 6.9.
Rankings of Terminal Values by Selected Interest Groups in a Study of Satisfaction with Management along the Clearwater River, Idaho (VanLeuven, 1980).

Terminal Values (Alphabetical Order)	Composite Ranking	U.S. Forest Service Personnel	Other Agency Personnel	Landowners along the river	Loggers	Outdoor club members	Environmental club members	Elected Officials	Businesspeople	Other Individuals
A Comfortable Life	14	14	14	13	8	13	17	8	12	12
An Exciting Life	15	13	12	17	15	18	5	16	14	7
A Sense of Accomplishment	4	2	3	6	7	5	2	4	3	6
A World of Beauty	12	12	11	14	13	6	1	14	13	10
A World of Peace	5	6	10	3	12	10	7	3	6	4
Equality	11	8	13	10	14	9	14	9	15	7
Family Security	1	1	1	2	2	4	8	1	1	1
Freedom	2	4	2	1	1	7	3	2	2	2
Happiness	6	11	5	5	4	8	11	6	5	8
Inner Harmony	8	7	7	8	6	11	9	12	10	14
Mature Love	13	9	9	12	11	16	10	15	16	11
National Security	10	15	15	7	5	1	16	10	9	3
Pleasure	16	16	17	15	17	17	15	17	18	16
Salvation	18	18	18	16	16	15	18	11	8	18
Self Respect	3	3	4	4	3	3	6	5	4	5
Social Recognition	17	17	16	18	18	14	13	18	17	17
True Friendship	9	16	8	9	10	12	12	13	7	13
Wisdom	7	5	6	11	9	2	4	7	11	15

A Concluding Thought

Research in values, attitudes, cognitive styles and similar social and psychological phenomena is relatively new. Its incorporation into public relations practice is even newer. There is much to be learned, and only a few approaches to categorizing publics have been included here. However, anyone with a sincere interest in improving public relations will not only be acutely aware of the need to define and work separately with different publics, but will also be ever alert to more effective ways of doing this.

SUGGESTED REFERENCES

Action Strategies for Managerial Achievement by Dalton E. McFarland. 1977. American Management Associations, New York.

Children's Interpretation: A Discovery Book for Interpreters by Gary Machlis and Maureen McDonough, 1978. U.S. Gov't. Printing Office, Washington, D.C.

Communication of Innovations by Everett M. Rogers and F. Floyd Shoemaker, 1971. The Free Press, New York.

Educational Principles and Techniques for Interpreters by David F. Boulanger and John P. Smith, 1973. USDA Forest Service Gen. Tech. Report PNW–9, Pacific Northwest Forest and Range Experiment Station, Portland, OR.

Managing People at Work by O. Jeff Harris, Jr., 1976. John Wiley & Sons, Inc., New York.

Teaching for Survival by Mark Terry, 1971. Ballentine Books, Inc., New York.

The Nature of Human Values by Milton Rokeach, 1973. The Free Press, New York.

SUGGESTED REFERENCES

7

Communication

Resource management agencies will be better off when they realize that contact is not communication.
—Douglas L. Gilbert

When planning, research and identification of publics are completed, the task turns to reaching and communicating with people. Communication is the very heart of public relations. In fact, it is often equated with public relations, but by now you know that it is only one of the several tools used in the practice. Nonetheless, it is such a large part of public relations that most of this book is devoted to understanding and using this tool more effectively.

THE NATURE OF COMMUNICATION

Communication may be defined as the successful transmission of thoughts or ideas, without significant distortion, so that understanding is achieved. This is so simple, yet so terribly complex. It is a phenomenon taken for granted like the air we breathe, yet it is usually at the root of our problems in every avenue of life.

A key element of the above definition is *understanding*. Communication has taken place only if a thought is reconstructed in the mind of person B (the *receiver*) very much the same as it occurred in the mind of the *sender,* person A. In most public relations work, the process must go a step further. Not only must the thought or idea be transmitted clearly and with minimum distortion, it must help in the task of influencing public opinion, so in most cases it will need to convince or persuade. This special branch of study and use is known as *persuasive communication.*

One more point of semantics. The above *process* of thought transmission is the singular, communica*tion.* The plural, communication*s*, refers to more than one act or instance of transmitting, or to a system (like a telephone network) established for the purpose of communicating. Therefore, correct usage would be: "Effective communication with employees should be a goal of managers" and "In the past, communications placed on the bulletin board have not been successful."

Perhaps the best way to understand what takes place, or does *not* take place, during an attempt to communicate is to view a graphic model of the process. Dozens of models have been developed for this purpose, but we have selected one of the more simplified versions for illustration in Figure 7.1. It contains all the essential elements of the process and assumes the case of an agency representative communicating with a recreationist.

Most models of the communication process contain, in one form or another, the following elements: (1) a sender, sometimes referred to as the information source, who (2) encodes (3) a message that is sent through (4) some channel and then (5) is decoded by (6) a receiver. If understanding is to be achieved, there should also be opportunity for the process to be reversed, a feature referred to as *feedback*. Also, for the model to be complete, an array of physical (sex, age, etc.), psychological (attitudes, motivations, etc.), and social (culture, residency, etc.) factors must surround both sender and receiver.

The Sender—Credible Source of Information?

This book is written from the perspective of potential senders, i.e., natural resource managers who seek to practice good public relations. Importantly, characteristics of the sender can either expedite or inhibit persuasive communication. One of the most important of these characteristics is *credibility*. If the sender of a message is believed by a receiver of the message to be a credible source of information, the chances of effectively influencing the receiver are greatly improved. The keys to credibility are many and depend a lot on the nature of the target audience, that is— the eye of the beholder. Status, race, religion and many other factors all play a role in the receivers' perceptions. However, *trustworthiness* and *authoritativeness* are the key characteristics people are looking for and will tend to define based on their own particular circumstances (Hovland et al., 1953).

To judge a source as trustworthy, the receiver must believe that the communicator is telling the truth and usually that he has his (the receiver's) best interests at heart. In natural resource management, examples abound of communication failing because of low source credibility based on lack of trustworthiness. Following former President Carter's announcement of his first national energy plan (which he labeled the "moral equivalent of war"), the Department of Energy failed in its attempt to persuade Americans of the impending crisis. One investigation concluded: "There is no real education program under way to help the American people understand the energy

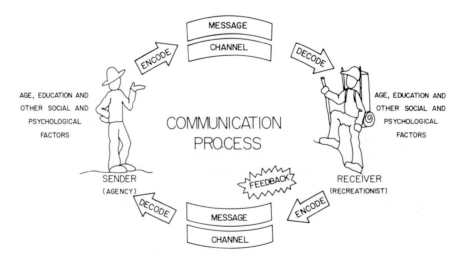

Figure 7.1. A simplified model of the communication process.

problem." Press releases, pamphlets and fact sheets were regarded by the general public as "propaganda." It was also found that the department's "statements and statistics" were "regarded by literate people as serving the narrower interests of the agency or the Administration" (Anderson, 1978a).

Source credibility is linked very closely to Public Relations Principle 4: Truth and honesty are essential. This is prerequisite. Also, this basis for credibility must be consistent, and it must be made apparent to our publics. Jay Gruenfeld, a forest product marketing consultant, expressed this well in his address at the 1978 national meeting of the Society of American Foresters. He said:

> To develop credibility the other party must understand what you are conveying and hear it in a credible context. Professionals have a special responsibility to be wise enough to be credible. The world is full of statements that are truthful but not believed.
>
> Credible communications will help the professional forester reduce the public distrust of the forest land managers. Specifically there is a distrust of the ability to manage for commodity values while protecting non-commodity values. Managing for timber and wildlife or timber and scenery are examples. To overcome this distrust and to achieve our other professional goals, we must *act* as though we believe that communication is important. We must communicate factually, analytically, credibly, often, and effectively. But first we must perform effectively on the ground.

Authoritativeness, the second key to credibility, is simply whether or not the sender is believed to know what he is talking about. Is the person competent, intelligent and well trained? This should be an easy criterion for most natural resource managers to meet when dealing with topics in their field. However, it also points to the need for breadth of knowledge in today's complex world. It may also serve as a warning to organizations that are turning more and more to professional communicators who have no background in natural resource management. This consideration of credibility should be important in selecting public speakers, exhibit attendants, media liaison persons and especially in hiring public relations or information specialists.

There is also some evidence that attractiveness of the sender may be an important factor in influencing others (Schneider, 1976). Neatness, personal cleanliness, and attire or personal styles matching those of the target audience are some of the factors that can be of influence in oral communication. It is possible that the quality of printed material may also follow this principle of attractiveness and appropriateness for the occasion.

Encoding and Decoding

When the sender *encodes* a message, he or she selects a series of visual or audio symbols we think of as printed or spoken language. Other forms of encoding are through imagery, such as pictures without words, and personal expressions. A frown, a kiss, or nervous avoidance of eye contact can often communicate messages very accurately.

Naturally, the encoding must be done in a way that allows *decoding* by the intended receiver. Winking at a blind person has no chance of succeeding as communication, nor does speaking French to someone who knows only English, or distributing printed material to illiterates.

The Message

The *message* is the content part of the process, i.e., *what* is being communicated and how it is put together. Dick *et al.,* (1974) summarized and referenced many of the principles that can affect the persuasive power of a message. Although these principles are not universally accepted or applicable, the summary is presented here in the form of a check-list to help guide the improvement of message content. For more details, the original source and suggested references should be consulted.

The Channel—Conveying the Message Effectively

Any message must be transmitted through some medium, or *channel.* Channels may be the spoken word, such as speeches, campfire programs, meetings, rumors, press conferences, training sessions, radio broadcasts, or discussions with friends and relatives. Written or printed channels include newspapers, books, magazines, pamphlets, in-house publications, newsletters, bumper stickers, posters, bulletin boards, direct mail literature, and similar material. Visual channels include television, slide shows, motion pictures, exhibits, models, drawings and viewing personal expressions such as the wink. Tactile channels might be a firm handshake, pat on the back, a kiss, or a slap on the face! Frequently, combinations of channels are utilized for maximum efficiency.

Selection of the most effective channel is essential if communication is to succeed. The most important factor, within the constraints of available budget, is that the channel must be one that will both reach (*contact*) individuals in the target public *and* facilitate understanding. If an objective was to reach a large number of housewives, radio and television in mid-afternoon would be a better choice of channel than the same media at 5:30 p.m. or a publicity article in a farm journal. To reach young people, a youth-oriented radio station after about 3:30 p.m. would be worth a try, whereas the same message in an agency brochure distributed in the ranger station would be likely to miss most of this public.

It should be stressed that *contact does not mean communication,* and *communication does not necessarily mean success in persuasion.* Mass media messages may reach many people, but often few are motivated enough to even think about the message to the degree necessary for understanding to occur, let alone to act, or to change their behavior. The effectiveness of a message should be measured in results or impact, not by the size of the audience or the time involved in the effort. One thousand more brochures distributed this year than last year is *not* a good measure of success or effectiveness in communication.

In an experiment we conducted to determine the best channel to use in communicating with backcountry recreationists in Rocky Mountain National Park, the same messages on low impact camping were disseminated using several different channels. We know from available statistical data that by using the mass media channels of television and newspapers, a minimum of 68,000 viewers and 251,829 readers in Colorado were reached with the test messages. But in this case, only seven of 665 backcountry users (the *target* public) could recall seeing or hearing the test messages. Clearly, these were not the correct channels for reaching that particular public, at least on a "one-shot" basis. Brochures also were tested, since these are often viewed by managers as the panacea for all problems requiring public communication. When some of the park visitors obtained their backcountry use permits, they were handed a brochure containing the test messages and were asked to read it. Contact using this channel was made with 132 of the recreationists. This was by far the *easiest* channel to use, but pre- and post-testing revealed that knowledge and

---

√ **CHECKLIST FOR STRENGTHENING MESSAGE STRUCTURE**

_____ Design your message to get attention immediately, then hold attention. Contrasts, potential rewards and threats can help, but these must be at optimal levels. Too much of anything can be bad.

_____ Use words, symbols, analogies, situations and stereotypes that can be understood by your target audience.

_____ Relate your message to known interests of the target audience.

_____ Incorporate facts and evidence into your own wording and in a smooth, coherent way. Remember, a good speech is as necessary as concrete data.

_____ If you seek to change opinion, first make statements that you know your audience will agree with. Begin where the audience is and attempt to reshape slightly, thus making many subtle changes over time. Moderate difference in opinion has the best chance of resulting in a shift in the direction desired by the presentor.

_____ Arouse needs in the receiver and outline specific routes of action to satisfy those needs. Otherwise, appeals for action tend to be ignored. For example, persuasion regarding the need for chain saw safety is more effective if accompanied by procedures to attain it.

_____ For any strong fears you arouse in the audience, provide ways for relieving those fears. Otherwise, the audience will tend to ignore or minimize the importance of the threat that aroused the fear. Talking about the effects of acid rain will be most effective if you tell people what they can do about it.

_____ State your conclusions explicitly if addressing lay audiences. When dealing with complicated issues or topics unfamiliar to the audience, this is usually more effective than relying upon the audience to draw its own conclusions. In the case of highly informed or highly intelligent audiences, however, let _them_ arrive at the conclusions.

_____ If your audience will be exposed to counter arguments, or if you know they will initially disagree with your position, include both sides of the argument. This "inoculation" technique is believed to be important in sustaining long-term attitude change.

_____ It is a good idea _not_ to forewarn your audience of the manipulative intent of your presentation. That will only increase resistance to it.

_____ Include visual illustrations whenever possible.

—Adapted primarily from Dick et al. (1974)

---

acceptance of the low impact camping messages was no higher than in a control group that took the pre- and post-visit tests but were exposed to none of the experimental channels. Ninety-eight other recreationists watched a short automated sound-slide show when they received their use permits. In this case, testing showed that their knowledge and acceptance of low impact camping did improve significantly (Fazio, 1979). In this study, the sound-slide show was the only effective channel for persuasively communicating with the backcountry users. However, no testing was conducted to determine if _behavioral_ changes followed acceptance of the new information. That would have been the ultimate test, for it has been found that on many occasions knowledge or attitudes may be changed but behavior is not. That is, people _say_ one thing but do another.

In addition to matching the appropriate channel with the target public, an input-output ratio must always be considered. Input is the effort (in time and cost) needed for preparation of the messages for their presentation through a particular channel. Output consists of two parts. One is the _number_ of people contacted; the other is the potential _impact_. To illustrate, writing a newspaper article requires less input than preparing a motion picture film. However, if the film is suitable for television or will be widely distributed and available for many years, it will reach more

Table 7.1.
Communication Methods Ranked by 269 I & E Executives in Natural Resource Agencies
According to Their Importance in Achieving Agency Goals.

Importance Ranking	Medium or Method
1	Newspaper articles
2	Publications (brochures, etc.)
3	Informal, unscheduled field contacts
4	Slide talks
5	Show-me trips
6	Lectures or talks
7	Exhibits/Displays
8	Radio broadcasts
9	Television broadcasts
10	Slide tape programs
11	Film showings
12	Magazines (externally produced)
13	Magazines (internally produced)
14	Miscellaneous others

people in the long run. In addition, a film may have greater appeal, retention value, and persuasive power than a newspaper. If the goal of the communication is to change attitudes on an important topic over a long period, the film would probably be the best choice if the money and necessary expertise were available. If the goal were merely to make people in a community *aware* of something, the newspaper article with its lower input costs would be the best choice.

Many more variables than those mentioned above must be considered in channel selection. This is one reason why the more important channels are discussed in greater detail in following chapters. For now it may be interesting to note how natural resource management agencies perceive the importance of different communication channels. The data shown in Table 7.1 are from a nationwide survey conducted in 1985 by the senior author. High level personnel in the information offices of state and federal natural resource management agencies were asked for their opinion on the importance of each of the media or techniques in achieving their agency's I & E or public relations purposes. Each of these methods are discussed later as we suggest ways to improve the use of communication to achieve better public relations.

The Feedback Loop

As may be seen in Figure 7.1, *feedback* is simply a reversal of the sender-message-receiver process with the message going from the former receiver to the original sender. Feedback provides the receiver with the opportunity to ask questions, to seek clarification, to contribute ideas, or to reveal points of disagreement. It is essential to achieving understanding, and it is the element that makes communication a *two-way* process.

Providing publics with the opportunity for feedback is possible (and important) in newspaper articles, television, exhibits, nature trail booklets or just about any other channel. However, in interpersonal communication the opportunity is clear and immediate. Moreover, it allows instant modifications of the messages. This is *flexibility* and this is what makes interpersonal communication the most powerful of all our communication options. It means that when people ask questions or respond with blank stares to a comment on the dichotomous branching of mule deer antlers, you can back up, drop the jargon and try again with an illustration of the Y-shaped pattern. Feedback and flexibility also allow the sender to field counterarguments or to quickly follow up to reinforce points of newly achieved agreement. These qualities underscore the need for interpersonal communication when lay individuals or small groups must be won.

The Receiver—A Need for Empathy

In viewing the model of communication, it can be seen that this leaves only the *receiver*. The receiver is an individual, and one who is often a member of a target public. Like the sender, the receiver is shrouded in experiences and other physical, social and psychological characteristics that affect his beliefs, attitudes, and behavior. The more a sender knows about these characteristics, the more skillfully he can fashion the informational or persuasive messages. It is no accident when a presidential candidate pulls into Spineyridge, U.S.A. and opens his speech by congratulating the town on its Hedgehogs winning the state softball championship! He and his staff have done their homework. Few things are more flattering or warm up an audience faster than revealing an understanding of their successes or their problems. The key word is *empathy,* for to influence is to first put yourself in the position of the other person. By viewing the situation through the eyes of your target public, you will discover areas of agreement from which to begin, you will know how much of a change in attitude or behavior is needed, and you will gain valuable clues on how best to facilitate the change. If careful identification of target publics comes first, and attempts at understanding them follow, there is a much firmer basis for planning effective communication than would otherwise be possible.

Barriers to Communication

It should be obvious by now that at every step in the process of communication *barriers* can intrude to prevent successful achievement of mutual understanding or desired changes in the receiver. Generally, if a communicator is aware of this potential problem, it can be prevented or eliminated.

A barrier is anything that distorts the message, prevents understanding from being achieved, or in the case of persuasive communication, prevents the desired change from resulting. Sometimes barriers are physical; sometimes they are mental. Talking too rapidly, or boring an audience by talking too slowly, can prevent understanding. So can a letter with typographical errors, static in a public address system, or using words in an article that only an English professor could love. And, of course, persuasive power is lost by ignoring the many principles determined through research that were discussed earlier.

Of the almost endless array of potential barriers, some of the most common that plague communication in natural resource management result simply from poor word usage. Those might be termed *semantic barriers*. If the subject matter is not clear and if points are not understood, failure will result. Words used by the sender may be too technical to be understood by the receiver.

The dialect spoken may not be familiar. The vernacular in an area and the educational level of the audience or readership should always be determined well in advance of a speaking engagement or writing assignment.

Clarity of meaning is necessary to avoid barriers in understanding. Many words mean different things to different people. To illustrate, the word "cat" can mean a tractor, a lion, a domestic pet, a "hep" person, a malicious woman, a prostitute or a bobcat. To use an example from natural resource management, an area is known where sage grouse commonly are called "sage chickens" by the local people. To use any other term in promoting a hunting season for sage grouse would immediately brand the individual as an outsider and a barrier would be raised.

There are times when another word or a new word must be used to increase clarity. One such word used to replace palatability (a word with many meanings) is "eatability." It is not in the dictionary, but no one should confuse the meaning. "Popullution" came into use around the first Earth Day as a way to indicate the pollution effects of population. "No nukes" would have meant nothing a few years ago. Now it is a catch phrase that expresses the sentiments of people opposed to nuclear energy sources, or it can be used to label that group.

Another language barrier occurs when we fail to use words that match the level of understanding of our audience. Evidence will be provided in the chapter on written communication, but the problem exists in oral presentations as well. Flexibility and adjustment to the specific audience is a key to success.

Another common group of barriers to communication are those that are *physical*. These include noise, poor visibility, discomfort, and distracting odors (bad or good!). They also include more subtle barriers such as using a channel that is not available to the target public, typographical errors in a news story, scheduling meetings at times that conflict with other obligations, or the incorrect speed in making an oral presentation.

Social barriers include the aura of biases, apathy, values, status and similar characteristics that surround us all. Examples include race, sex, wealth, religion, appearance and others. All are grounded in a learned system of interconnecting beliefs and attitudes. Being aware of these through identifying publics, empathizing to the degree possible, and understanding the principles of persuasive communication, can go far in overcoming the problems.

Feedback barriers also are important and often quite subtle. These arise from not providing the opportunity for receivers to respond in some way to the sender. It may be ending a campfire program in a park without asking for questions from the audience, or placing an exhibit in the county fair with no identification of your organization, or publishing an article urging action or change, but not providing readers with a way of obtaining more information. By not carefully providing for feedback, a sender often suffers from an *illusion of communication*. This simply means thinking that the message has been at least understood, and at most effective in its purpose, when in actuality it has *not* been. This can result from no feedback, or inaccurately perceiving what feedback you do receive. A common example is the speaker who believes he did a fine job because two or three well-meaning people congratulated him after the presentation. Meanwhile, 40 more honest people left without saying anything.

Communication is highly complex. Any dissection of its parts runs the risk of diminishing the fact that all parts of the process are interrelated. It is comparable to the study of ecology. Still, both its parts and the whole warrant careful study as a foundation for using communication to develop good public relations.

Figure 7.2. Visitors at a historic site in Great Britain carry headsets that plug into "listening posts" throughout the area. Such devices could be used to communicate messages in different languages, or to different age levels, or even to visitors with different interests such as those of hunters and non-hunters at a wildlife refuge. (Courtesy of British Information Service.)

COMMUNICATION RESEARCH—SEEKING A FOUNDATION FOR ACTION

Research in the field of communication and attitude change has been considerable, but is still at the stage of inventing the proper thermometer. The task calls for measuring the human mind, and no challenge to science is more complex. Results to date have been both inconclusive and inconsistent. Frequently there is not even agreement on such basic terms as *opinion* or *attitude,* and certainly there is little agreement on the relationship between attitudes and behavior. Some social scientists have made sweeping generalizations from their data only to be shown later they were not even measuring what they had intended. Others have concluded that it is impossible to change attitudes through use of the mass media (a charge not in agreement with those who spend millions of dollars each year on advertising!). Books that summarize much of the research in this important area are listed at the end of this chapter. In the pages that follow, we have attempted to provide a brief overview of a few influential schools of thought on communication that may prove helpful in the practice of public relations.

The Adoption Sequence

Recall that in Chapter 6 we presented the *adoption-diffusion process* that explained how new ideas (or practices) may flow through a social system. A small segment of the social system, the *innovators,* accepts or rejects the idea more quickly than the *early adopters,* and so forth down to the final few who may never even give the innovation a try. Another enduring part of that theory is that individuals in all categories of the adoption-diffusion process go through a definite sequence of events in arriving at their own conclusions on whether to accept or reject the new idea. Moreover, different channels of communication are used more than others at each step in the sequence. The five steps, listed below, are easy to conceptualize if you think back to some new product you recently purchased or decided against purchasing.

1. **Awareness** This is when the individual first learns of the idea, product or practice. From the public relations standpoint, this result is the quickest and easiest to attain. Mass media can be effectively used to bring a public to the awareness stage in an issue.

2. **Interest** We are aware of thousands of ideas in which we have no further interest. The mental process simply ends there. However, if our curiosity is aroused and more information is desired, we have entered the interest stage. To bring people into this stage, mass media can again be used effectively. It is more difficult to get people interested, and it requires creative thinking to provide some vital link between an idea and the newly aware person. In other words, it is necessary to show *why* a person should be interested.

3. **Evaluation** In this stage, a person consciously weighs the pros and cons. In the classic diffusion studies, mass media became relatively unimportant at this stage, whereas friends and neighbors became the most used source of information. Significantly, at this point, the appropriate agency may be looked to for advice or information, as they were in agricultural studies reported by Lionberger (1960).

4. **Trial** At this stage, if we are dealing with a product or practice, the individual sees enough merit in it to give it a try. In the farming studies, this meant trying a new practice (growing hybrid corn) on a small scale. Friends and neighbors and the appropriate agency have been shown to be the most important information sources at this stage.

5. **Adoption or Rejection** If the idea or practice passes the personal tests of preceding stages, a favorable attitude has developed and the individual adopts the innovation (a behavior change). If it does not pass the tests, the idea is rejected.

Solo and Rogers (1972) regarded these stages as functions of: *knowledge* (1 and 2), *persuasion* (3), and *decision* (4 and 5). They also suggested a function that follows adoption or rejection. This is *confirmation,* and we all recognize it as an attempt at self-assurance that we "did the right thing." Conceivably, this provides the persuasive communicator with continuing hope that through a change in tactics or the situation of the receiver, a rejected idea may yet be adopted. Conversely, *discontinuance* is a decision to cease use of an innovation after previously adopting it (Rogers and Shoemaker, 1971). This points to the need for public relations practitioners to continually reinforce the opinions of those who have accepted a new idea or practice favorable to the organization's position. Mass media has been shown to be particularly effective for this purpose (Klapper, 1960).

The relative use of channels by individuals in different stages of the adoption sequence is shown in Table 7.2. As with any research, care must be taken in generalizing results to situations not actually tested. However, by 1971, 18 out of 20 studies conducted supported the conclusion that mass media channels are relatively more important during the knowledge function and interpersonal channels are relatively more important during the persuasion function. It should be noted, however, that in cases where the new practice or idea is perceived to be very complex the

Table 7.2.
Stages and Relative Importance of Communication Channels in the Adoption Sequence
in Agricultural Studies. (Adapted from Lionberger, 1960)

Ranked Importance	Stage of Adoption				
	Awareness	Interest	Evaluation	Trial	Adoption
1	Mass Media	Mass Media	Friends and Neighbors	Friends and Neighbors	Personal Experience
2	Friends and Neighbors	Friends and Neighbors	Agricultural Agencies	Agricultural Agencies	Friends and Neighbors
3	Agricultural Agencies[1]	Agricultural Agencies	Dealers and Salesmen	Dealers and Salesmen	Agricultural Agencies
4	Dealers and Salesmen	Dealers and Salesmen	Mass Media	Mass Media	Mass Media
					Dealers and Salesmen

1. Cooperative Extension, vocational-agriculture, etc.

relative advantage of mass media is decreased. In those cases, interpersonal "change agents" such as extension personnel or farm foresters may be necessary to even achieve awareness and interest. It has also been found in 8 out of 10 studies that mass media channels are relatively more important than interpersonal channels for earlier adopters than for later adopters (Rogers and Shoemaker, 1971).

The *rate* of adoption depends on many complex factors. Rate is usually a measure of a specified number (percentage) of receivers who adopt a new idea in a specified time period. Some hypothetical examples of how the factors of complexity and cost may affect the rate of adoption of an innovation among natural resource-related publics is shown in Table 7.3. Other important factors that affect the rate of adoption are: relative advantage, compatibility, trialability and observability. These phenomena are explained more fully by Rogers and Shoemaker (1971) who also made the following conclusions:

1. At the knowledge stage, the innovation's complexity and compatibility should be most important.
2. At the persuasion stage, the innovation's relative advantage and observability should be most important.
3. At the decision stage, the innovation's trialability should be most important.

Flow Theories and Opinion Leaders

Many theories have been developed in an attempt to explain how information is disseminated through a social system. Some of these are summarized below from Rogers and Shoemaker (1971).

First came the "hypodermic needle model" of the 1930's and 1940's which ascribed great powers of influence to the mass media. According to this outmoded notion, to influence public opinion, you merely need to reach as many people as you can and these passive masses will conform. This idea began its decline in 1940 when studies of voters found that people changed their opinions very little because of mass media, but were instead influenced by interpersonal sources.

Table 7.3.
Hypothetical Examples of Rates of Adoption Dependent on Complexity and Cost Factors.

Relative Rate (1 = Fast, 4 = Slow)	Proposed Change Ranked by Increased Complexity and Cost	Examples by Public			
		Ranchers	Sawmill Operators	Campground Operators	Game Department
1	Material/Equipment	Cattle Food Supplement	Automatic Stacker	Bicycles For Patrolling	Safety Color Requirement
2	Improved Practice	Hereford to Black Angus	Scaling by Weight	Carryout Garbage Policy	Statewide Tagging Regulation
3	Improved Practice, More Extensive Change	Rest-Rotation Grazing	Different Sawmill Set-up	Tenter/Rec. Vehicle Sections	Seasons/ Limits on Zoned Basis
4	Enterprise	Cattle Ranch to Dude Ranch	Sawlog to Pulp Operation	Convert to Living History Farm	Closed Season or New Either-Sex Season

Such sources have come to be labeled *opinion leaders*. This discovery gave rise to the popular *two-step flow model* to explain the process. It is a helpful but oversimplified concept that depicts opinion leaders obtaining an idea from the mass media, then by virtue of their status among peers, passing it along to the 3, 4 or more individuals with whom they hold influence.

A *multi-step flow model,* as reflected in the adoption sequence and innovation-diffusion research, portrays communication flow as a sequential relaying of information, but allows for a variable number of relays. Depending on the individual, he may accept the information directly from the source or a mass media channel (one step), or he may receive the information two or more times removed from the original source.

In both the two-step and multi-step models, the role of opinion leaders is clear. In the transmission of information, these individuals will have an important effect on how the message will ultimately be viewed by large numbers of people. Is steel shot instead of lead shot a good idea for hunting waterfowl? A wildlife agency may say it is essential to prevent bird losses from lead poisoning. But as the information diffuses through the hunter public, it will largely be the opinion leaders who gain or lose support for the proposal. In one study, Arndt (1968) found that people receiving favorable word-of-mouth communications from opinion leaders were three times as likely to buy a particular new product as were those receiving unfavorable comments.

So who is an opinion leader? This is a difficult question to answer, although some suggestions for locating these people in a given social structure are offered in the following section on research. All the characteristics of opinion leaders are not agreed upon by researchers, but one thing is certain. There are *not* two classes of people—the leaders and the led. Instead, in modern specialized societies, there are individuals who are sought by a circle of friends or acquaintances for their opinions *depending on the topic*. This tendency for an individual to act as an opinion leader for only one topic has been termed *monomorphism*. It is the opposite of *polymorphism,* wherein a guru-like individual is sought for opinions on *all* matters.

Opinion leaders then, should be sought out on every issue and within every social system of concern to the public relations person. Since they are not necessarily elected officials or otherwise plainly visible, this is no easy task. In fact, it is so formidable that Lesly (1983) suggested concentrating instead on "the mass media from which the opinion leaders tend to derive the fuel for the development of the opinions they pass on to others." He goes on to suggest not using mass media in general, but those selected for their ability to reach potential leaders on the issue of concern. It all goes back to the idea of identifying publics, and carefully matching channels with target receivers.

Difficult as the task may be, there are occasions when it is possible to identify individual opinion leaders. This is particularly true in small towns and rural communities, within organizations such as sportsmen's clubs, office staffs, classrooms and other settings where the people are known over a long period of time. Based on considerable research, Rogers and Shoemaker (1971) offer the following generalizations about opinion leaders that may be helpful in separating their characteristics from those of their followers:

1. They attend more to mass media.
2. They are more cosmopolitan.
3. They have greater contact with change agents (extension personnel, educators, professionals).
4. They participate socially; they are accessible to the people who look toward them as opinion leaders.
5. They usually occupy a higher social status.
6. They are generally more innovative, but may or may not be in the innovator category described in Chapter 6.
7. When a social system's norms favor change, opinion leaders are more innovative; but when the norms are traditional (as in primitive cultures or more conservative regions), opinion leaders are not especially innovative.

The Yale Approach

World War II was the stimulus for much of the research in what is now considered persuasive communication. At the end of the war, researcher Carl Hovland and many of his compatriots continued their work at Yale University. This body of work is often referred to as the Yale attitude change studies, and they were characterized by an approach still widely used in communication research. Using highly controlled situations, research subjects were asked their opinions about some selected topic. They were then exposed to a message or messages presented different ways (the independent variables), then re-tested for comprehension or retention of the messages, and any change in attitude. The resulting attitude change was then attributed to the independent variable in the study.

Most of the ideas presented earlier about source credibility and structuring messages resulted from the Yale studies. The studies also concluded that there are four processes determining the extent to which a person will be persuaded by a communication. These are: *Attention* (the sex, humor or startling events used by advertisers to attract your attention); *Comprehension* (making the message understandable to the target public); *Acceptance* (the results sought from the persuasive nature of the communication, e.g., the opinion influence sought in public relations); and *Retention* (the preceding do little good if your messages or their effects are not remembered very long).

Below are some additional findings of the Yale studies that may be helpful in resource public relations work. They are presented here with the usual caution that they are not consistently true, and that Hovland *et al* (1953) should be consulted for more complete explanations.

1. People tend to selectively seek and expose themselves to information consistent with their position, but they do not necessarily selectively avoid information dissonant to their position.
2. Some people are generally more persuadable than others; low self-esteem being a particularly notable characteristic of these individuals. Easily influenced people are likely to be equally influenceable when faced with counterarguments.
3. The effects of a persuasive communication tend to wear off in time—thus the need to continually repeat or otherwise reinforce.
4. Either complex or subtle messages produce slower decay of attitude change.
5. Attitude change is more persistent over time if the receiver actively participates in, rather than passively receives, the communication.
6. Repetition tends to prolong the influence of a message.

Group Dynamics

Another area of communication that grew out of the war effort and is pertinent to natural resource public relations is the *group dynamics* approach. Zimbardo *et al* (1977) summarized this school of thought and with their permission we paraphrase below to provide the useful essentials.[1] Serious public relations practitioners would do well to review group dynamics in more detail, for it represents a powerful force that can work against you, or be put to work for you.

In contrast to the research methodology of the Yale tradition, the group dynamics approach assumes that the individual is more than an isolated, passive processor of information who derives his final attitude from logical combinations of well-presented arguments. Led by Kurt Lewin of the University of Michigan, group dynamics views the individual as a social being, intimately dependent on others for knowledge. Importantly, according to this approach, a major factor that causes people to change their perceptions, beliefs and attitudes of the world around them is the *discrepancy* that exists between an individual's attitude or behavior and the *group* norm.

Experiments, as well as real life situations we are all familiar with, make clear our reluctance to be rejected or disliked because we are different. So we try to conform to group norms if the particular group is of importance to us. Specifically, other people do not even have to persuade you by argument; they need merely hold a position different from yours. If you are aware of that discrepancy, and need their acceptance, approval and recognition, it is very likely you will change your attitude. Can you imagine a cattleman wearing tie-on shoes and a three piece suit to a stockmen's association meeting, or an Audubon member proposing 2–4–5T treatment of the local marsh?

Unlike the learning view held in the Yale tradition, in the group dynamics approach change is said to occur because it is motivated by various socially based *needs*—the need to compare oneself to peers, to evaluate one's own abilities and attitudes, and to reduce discrepancies between

1. Zimbardo/Ebbesen/Maslach, Influencing Attitudes and Changing Behavior, 2/E, © 1977, Random House, Inc., New York, pp. 62, 103–105. Used with permission.

Figure 7.3. Up at dawn, executives jog while attending a company seminar at Walker's Cay in the Bahamas. Research findings in group dynamics help explain how individuals are persuaded to think and behave like others. (Courtesy of Precision Valve Corp.)

one's own position and group norms. Faced with a discrepancy in attitude, an individual seems to have three choices: (1) change in direction of the group norm, (2) try to influence the group norm, or (3) reject the group as irrelevant. The second choice places the group member in jeopardy of being rejected, and if the group is important to him, the third choice will be ruled out.

To the public relations worker, the potential relationship between persuasive communication, opinion leaders, and group dynamics should begin to underscore the importance of a carefully planned and timed "rifle approach" to trying to influence public opinion. The shotgun-type spewing of information to "the public" can succeed only by pure accident; whereas more effective influence can be brought to bear through an understanding of how individuals can be persuaded, how change flows through a social system, and how unseen pressures tend to make people conform to groups that are personally important.

From Zimbardo *et al* (1977) and Kiesler and Kiesler (1969), the following summary has been prepared to share a few of the useful findings from various studies on the effects of groups on attitude and behavior changes:

1. People's opinions and attitudes are strongly influenced by the norms and goals of groups to which they belong and want to belong.
2. People are rewarded for conforming to the standards of the group and punished for deviating from them.

3. Members of groups have more influence power over each other when they are part of groups that are high rather than low in cohesiveness.

4. The sheer frequency of communication by the group's members is a major determinant of interpersonal influence. People who talk most and say positive things are most likely to emerge as influence leaders.

5. The influence of neighbors increases with their proximity.

6. Groups may facilitate the release of normally inhibited behaviors in members by diffusion of responsibility, imitation, anonymity, and behavioral contagion.

7. The structure of communication networks within a group affects the way in which information is processed (filtered through a central position or shared by all in decentralized networks).

8. People who are most attached to the group are probably least influenced by communications that conflict with group norms.

9. Opinions that people make known to others are harder to change than opinions that people hold privately.

10. Audience participation (group discussion and decision making) helps to overcome resistance to persuasion.

11. The support of even one other person weakens the powerful effect of a majority opinion on an individual.

12. The need to maintain group consensus can lead to "group think" in which individual critical evaluation is suppressed and personal opinions are disregarded.

SOME FUNDAMENTAL DEFINITIONS

Belief—A state of mind . . . in which trust or confidence is placed in some person or thing. (Webster's New Collegiate Dictionary).

—Any simple proposition, conscious or unconscious, inferred from what a person says or does, capable of being preceded by the phrase "I believe that . . ." (Rokeach, 1968a, p. 113).

Attitude—An enduring organization of several beliefs focused on a specific object or situation, predisposing one to respond in some preferential manner. (Rokeach, 1968a; p. 550).

Value—An enduring belief that a specific mode of conduct or end-state of existence is personally or socially preferable to an opposite or converse mode of conduct or end-state of existence. (Rokeach, 1973; p. 5).

Opinion—A verbal expression of some belief, attitude or value. (Rokeach, 1968a; p. 125).

Value System—An enduring organization of beliefs concerning preferable modes of conduct or end-states of existence along a continuum of relative importance. (Rokeach, 1973; p. 5).

Rokeach's Belief System

The possibility of changing attitudes through creating discrepancies within an individual's value-attitude system was described in Chapter 6. Milton Rokeach (1968, 1971 and 1973) demonstrated that intentional manipulation of a person's values can be a powerful modifier of attitudes and behavior. According to Rokeach, there is a very limited number of values which are directly connected to a much larger number of attitudes. By making a desired change in one value, presumably all attitudes related to that value will be changed.

Going the other way, it is proposed that a very extensive system of beliefs form the foundation for a person's whole interconnected network of attitudes and values. Also, beliefs may be conceptually arranged in such a way as to provide insights on what may be happening under certain conditions of persuasive communication. What Rokeach (1968a) termed the "central-peripheral dimension" of such an arrangement is illustrated in Figure 7.4.

According to Rokeach and most other social psychologists, not all beliefs are equally important to an individual. The more central a belief, the more difficult it is to change. Then, due to the connectedness of the system, the more central the belief changed, the more widespread the repercussions in the rest of the belief system and, consequently, in any attitudes based on those beliefs. Presumably this follows through to the behavior that might be predicted from the attitude.

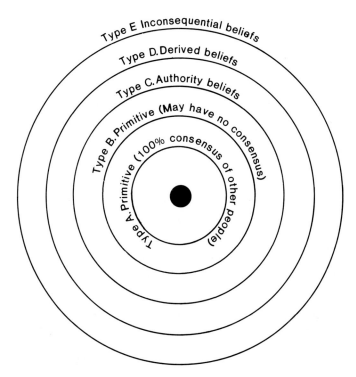

Figure 7.4. Conceptualization of beliefs arranged to show that some are more central and strongly held than others. In persuasive communication, an attempt may be made to change one kind of belief by linking it to another.

Rokeach's (1968a) belief system, fully described in his earlier work, *Beliefs, Attitudes and Values,* consists of five classes of beliefs. The most central, type A, are those learned by direct encounter and reinforced by the unanimous consensus of others. Under normal circumstances, these kinds of beliefs are beyond questioning. Examples are that you believe your name is . . . , or that your parents are. . . . To disturb these important functions of trust would be to disturb our self-identity, our self-consistency—our very mental balance.

Type B beliefs are also very central and learned from direct encounter, but are not dependent on the consensus of others. Basically, they are impervious to persuasion, even though they may not be true. Examples include phobias, delusions, hallucinations and various ego-enhancing and ego-deflating beliefs arising from some experience. Self images such as "I am a reasonably intelligent person" or beliefs like "I believe my son is honest" are illustrative.

Type C beliefs bring us closer to the relevance of this model for improving public relations in natural resource management. These are the *authority beliefs,* i.e., beliefs about the reference persons or groups who we decide *could* or *should* know about something. These are the authorities we decide can be trusted as our world expands beyond our parents. They are the ones we will look to as we go about our daily lives seeking information about the world. Can you now see more relevance in working with children?

Type D, quite logically, are the *derived beliefs* that emanate from people or other sources we decide are authorities in some sphere of life. Thus we believe a history book even though we did not experience the Civil War. A Catholic believes what the Pope says; a respected teacher will be believed by his students; and opinion leaders or hero-figures will be believed by their followers. This is the basis for the tremendous success of testimonial advertising. If an authority figure appears on television and attests to the virtues of a product you believe he should know about, the chances are good that you will adopt a derived belief about that product.

Finally, on the periphery of a person's belief system lie the *inconsequential beliefs*. They are said to originate through direct experience with the object of belief and they may be held very strongly. The reason type E beliefs are called "inconsequential" is because few, if any, other beliefs will change if these change. They are a person's tastes or preferences, such as buying a Winchester rifle instead of a Remington, believing trout fishing is a better sport than bass fishing, or that a vacation should be spent at a wilderness lake instead of a comparable non-wilderness lake.

Frequently, advertisers will use self-images strongly held as type B beliefs to alter product preferences which are in the realm of type E. Rokeach (1968a) suggested that actually there are two kinds of type B beliefs—those reflecting positive self-images, or the things of which we are capable of (B+), and those of a more negative nature such as things we fear (B−). People with many self-doubts or low self-esteem may be particularly vulnerable to appeals directed at B− beliefs. Examples abound among the soap and deodorant commercials on television, such as one that brings all sorts of social condemnation on the person who has a dirty shirt collar. The happy, zestful "Pepsi Generation" and "Things Go Better With Coke" commercials appeal to B+ beliefs that usually guide our aspirations to become better, more well rounded individuals and more open to fun-filled experiences.

In summary, any given attitude may be considered a "package" of interconnected beliefs. To influence opinion, which is the verbalizing of an attitude, it is necessary to consider what *beliefs* and *values* affect the attitude and determine how these might be altered to bring about the desired attitude change (or reinforcement).

Other Research

It is not possible to include here all the research and theories that have a bearing on communication as a tool of public relations. For additional useful information the public relations practitioner would do well to explore the marketing, sociological and psychological literature. Especially important may be the research of Fishbein and Ajzen (1975) in which they have attempted to account for certain variables, and their interactions, not included in the traditional studies of persuasive communication. Among other things, this research considers initial discrepancies about specific elements of the message (*belief statements*) that exist between source and receiver before the message is transmitted. Based on measures of the initial discrepancies, probability curves have even been determined to help predict how readily the receiver might accept what is being said or written by the sender. Fishbein and Ajzen also take on the problems of the many influences that intervene when we try to communicate. These include source credibility, receiver characteristics, and such message factors as order of presentation, emotion vs. logic, and the countless others.

New ideas are constantly being generated in the social sciences, but rarely do they filter into the natural resource fields. More frequently, promising theories or concepts are seized upon by advertising and sales organizations. Some find their way into education and recreation management. Unfortunately, most are highly complex, difficult to understand by people not schooled in social science, and the results are scattered through the literature of many disciplines. Nevertheless, from the mass of research may come one small fact or a broad, revealing theory that can aid in developing better public relations. As advertisers are acutely aware, it may pay high dividends to invest the necessary time and effort to stay in touch with research in the area of persuasive communication.

PROPAGANDA

It is stretching the term communication to include a discussion of propaganda under its heading. However, propaganda can be considered a form of communication even though some kinds exclude the *two*-way nature of true communication. Also, despite some ethical questions about the use of propaganda, some *is* used in the practice of public relations.

When you think of "propaganda," do you envision Hanoi Hanna, Axis Sally, or Nazi leaflets warning about poisonous Kreuzotter snakes that crawl under blankets and sleeping bags at night? Propaganda is a word loaded with evil connotations. Surprisingly, it is a word originated by the Catholic Church in 1622 to describe the missionary work of "propagating" the faith (Cutlip et al., 1985).

Some believe that *all* public relations work is propaganda. Others believe that education, too, is propaganda. We believe there is a difference between education and propaganda, and that not even all persuasive communication is propaganda. We also agree with Harlow (1957) who wrote that the public relations person uses *all* these things; he informs, represents, educates, interprets, *and* tries to persuade people.

Education, in the finest sense, provides learners with the tools and information for making sound judgments. Samuel Johnson said the supreme end of education is expert discernment in all things. Zimbardo *et al* (1977) wrote that ideally educators teach students not *what* to think, but only *how* to think. Unrealistic as that may sound, especially to students, the fact is that it is poor education that does not present both sides of any issue.

If propaganda and education are not the same, the key difference is that propaganda is a conscious and deliberate effort to manipulate others through persuasion and an appeal to emotions. The connotation that must be quickly added is that this deliberately persuasive effort employs techniques that do *not* provide the target person or public with all the information needed to make a fair judgment. Education provides information, evidence, facts and the ability to reason logically. Propaganda usually provides partial information, one-sided evidence, only some facts, and the attempt is to make only one side of an issue seem logical. This is certainly how it is used in psychological warfare. Propaganda can be—and frequently is—used in public relations work. However, not *all* public relations efforts, or even all attempts at persuasive communication, can be called propaganda. Recall, for example, that one technique of persuasive communication *is* to provide both sides of an argument ("inoculation" against counterarguments). We would also argue that assuring accurate, truthful messages disseminated by credible sources cannot be considered propaganda.

Types of Propaganda

There are many different techniques of propaganda recognized in the literature on this subject. Whether to use these techniques, or *any* persuasive technique, requires an ethical judgment as well as a technical one. One thing is certain, however. The techniques of propaganda will be used against you, just as they are commonly used against resource management everywhere. Especially for that reason, below are some propaganda techniques that should be of interest to professionals in natural resource management:

The Band Wagon Approach. This is the suggestion that *everyone* is doing it, or at least all of some particular, desirable group. Group dynamics are at work here, for people do not want to be different. Many commercials use this technique: "More people use brand X, take pill Y or drive car Z." Therefore, it *must* be the best product to use. Or how many times have you heard, "Come on. We are *all* going down for a beer after work." People like to be part of bandwagons, they don't want to feel left out even if they are not particularly enthused with the ideas or activities of others on the bandwagon. In natural resources, this type of propaganda is frequently used in messages designed to get children to work on litter clean-up, or by reminding them that "Smokey's friends don't play with matches." Sometimes this technique is used in trying to sell game seasons: "They have either-sex deer seasons all over the West and in many states in the East, so why not here, too?" This technique is also used against resource managers when such statements are made as "All those forestry-types will be taking a 'no wilderness' stand. Join other conservationists as we mount a campaign to balance the opposition." For or against, the bandwagon approach is an effective tool under the right circumstances.

Card Stacking is the technique of telling half-truths. In this willfully deceptive approach, information that could be counterproductive to the persuasive cause is carefully censored. This is commonly employed every day in communication ranging from conversation with friends to advertising used cars or promoting the image of a political candidate. Like most other techniques of propaganda, card stacking is sometimes used *by,* as well as against, natural resource interests. To illustrate, a field trip might be taken to the worst area of range where the most deer have starved. Or a concerted effort may be made to show only the data for the year with the worst deer starvation losses. Mention might not be made of the years when starvation did not occur. The other side of the story is not told or is curtailed greatly. In another example, the reproduction of 64 percent of

Figure 7.5. A mock certificate used to raise funds and rally opposition to herbicide spraying. It resulted from an incident of name-calling that backfired.

the deer may have been adversely affected, but only two percent died and this was not mentioned. A sign of a truly educated person is when he routinely and critically examines every communication for the information *not* given!

Name calling is a technique designed to "label" or categorize opponents so others will identify them with something undesirable. This is commonly used in political campaigns. Candidate A speaking in a conservative farming region may call Candidate B a "free-spending liberal." Meanwhile, Candidate B is addressing a university group and calls Candidate A an "unrealistic obstructionist." This is a dangerous and questionable approach, and it is not a practice becoming professional resource managers. It can backfire quite easily and end up being used in the media or by the opposition to permanently brand *you* as belonging to one category or another. It can also easily lead to insult that will be used by the offended party or parties to arouse even more intense opposition than existed previously. Figure 7.5 is used to illustrate an example. In what may have been a slip of the tongue rather than intentional name-calling, a Forest Service employee told a newspaper reporter that "much of the opposition to spraying (herbicides) is coming from a 'lunatic fringe' within the public" (Johnson, 1978). The comment incensed those students, doctors, recreationists, housewives, professors and just about anyone else who did not favor the spraying. The active anti-spray public picked up on the remark and made mock certificates which they then sold to raise funds to intensify their campaign against the herbicide project.

Loaded Words are closely related to name-calling. This is a technique used in an attempt to add a subtle connotation that the sender knows will be applied because he knows how the receiver will perceive the particular word. To illustrate, "frugal" and "stingy" may mean essentially the same thing, but the former is usually flattering whereas the latter is not. Similar pairs include: elected official-politician; scent-stink, or stink-stench; trees-timber; predators-killers; doe-mother deer; visitor-tourist. Used with care and skill, loaded words can help in persuasive communication. They may be particularly effective when used with publics who tend to agree with your position. Receivers who tend to disagree, however, may notice the loaded words and recognize them for the propaganda they are.

The Red Herring technique is to lead a public down a side track, to divert its attention to favorable conditions or information and away from an unfavorable situation. The manipulator attempts to make the public forget a bad situation (smoke from slash-burning after a clearcut) in the light of a new idea favorable to the cause (the regeneration of the forest and money coming into the community from lumber production).

The Testimonial was mentioned previously as an example of how persuasive attempts can take advantage of authority beliefs to alter derived beliefs. When someone who you perceive *should* know something about skis (a former Olympic champion, for example) recommends brand X because they are faster or safer, it is likely you will look favorably on purchasing a pair of brand X skis. In a logging magazine, regional ads often feature a logger from that same region standing next to his rubber-tired skidder giving testimonial to its hauling capacity, good traction under local conditions, and its low amount of downtime. This testimonial will mean much to other loggers considering the purchase of a new skidder. The testimonial method has several variations. It may use the recognized authority (the Olympic champion), a peer (a known local logger), or an endorsing organization such as a state parks and recreation department endorsing a snowmobile event. There is considerable potential for this technique in developing more effective public relations in natural resource management.

Emotional Appeal can be a strong tool if not over-used, if not used with the wrong public, and if not used at the wrong time. Those are a lot of *ifs*. Too much emotion, such as presenting too great a fear-appeal, will probably be "tuned out" by your audience. Some publics, such as a scientific group, usually will react negatively to an emotional rather than a logical appeal based on factual information. However, used in moderation and along *with* supportive evidence, emotion can probably work just as well *for* natural resource management as it often is used against it. Emotions of hunters can be aroused at the prospects of deer starving to death instead of being harvested for sport and meat if an either-sex season is not established. On the same issue, non-hunter emotions could be aroused if the inhumane aspects of starvation were pointed out and illustrated. The issue of wilderness preservation has brought out considerable emotion on both sides. The skillful use of emotional appeals entails understanding publics and many of the principles of persuasive communication.

Money has universal appeal. As a propaganda technique it can be used alone or in combination with card-stacking, testimonials, or emotion. It is simply pointing out the economic effects of an issue. Examples are common. "Locking up more of the Adirondacks in 'forever wild' status will mean the loss of jobs. Mills will shut down. Everyone will suffer so a few environmentalists can backpack!" Several types of propaganda techniques are evident here, but the overriding one is economic. Similarly: "City folks are discovering the restorative powers of wild waters and woods.

The 'forever wild' Adirondacks offer such a place. Where freedom and beauty beckon, there will be healthy communities where outside dollars in large quantities will buy goods and services on a year round basis."

Especially when communicating with commercial publics and tax-weary landowners, focusing on money can be a very helpful tool for nearly any cause. The real strength, however, lies in backing up one's contention with examples or projections based on hard economic data. Counterarguments will then be more difficult than if generalities are used as was done in the Adirondack examples.

In recent years money has found a new way to talk. This is in the form of *political action committees* (PACs). Business, labor, and other special interest groups—and politicians themselves—have found this to be an effective way around post-Watergate campaign laws. Groups of citizens with a common cause are allowed by law to form PACs and solicit funds for the purpose of electing or defeating political candidates pertinent to a particular cause. A PAC can be formed by a small group of sawmill workers who oppose wilderness, or by thousands of environmentalists fighting air and water pollution. Millions of dollars are raised each year by these proliferating "committees," and grateful elected officials are increasingly sensitive to what these organized groups of donors have to say.

Repetition has been used as a propaganda technique in recent wars. "Brain washing" methods employ repetition. Something repeatedly heard or seen makes an impression on the mind. Advertised items, slogans, billboard posters, radio or television announcements or articles in the newspapers will eventually penetrate the life sphere or inner consciousness of a public. It is also an important way of overcoming noise and other barriers that may be present. Repetition, however, can be overdone. The public may get sick and tired of seeing or hearing too much about something. What has been accomplished can be erased, and more, if such an operation is not stopped in time.

Is Propaganda An Ethical Tool?

In summary, there are differences between propaganda and education, and both have a place in public relations practice. Also, while all propaganda is persuasive in intent, not all persuasive communication is propaganda.

Is propaganda dishonest or bad? This is something only the individual manager or public relations practitioner can answer. In our opinion, there are times when it is a legitimate and useful tool. For example, after a management decision has been made with due public involvement, the practice should be promoted so it will be accepted by all. If a testimonial is in order, or an emotional appeal, or an appeal to the pocketbook—so be it. This does not mean every type of propaganda technique will be appropriate and certainly any that is unethical in a particular circumstance should not even be considered. But it does mean that propaganda cannot be ruled out as a public relations tool. Certainly the opposition, and there is always some, will not hesitate to use persuasive techniques, including propaganda. Many good, sound, natural resource proposals and practices have been rejected by publics who were propagandized by groups or individuals with a strong desire to prevent the idea from working. A knowledge of propaganda techniques can help detect when it is being used against you. This alone can be an important means of planning a more effective approach to influencing others.

PLANNED PUBLICITY

Like propaganda, *publicity* does not fit neatly under the heading of communication. It is usually a one-way dissemination of information and can be thought of as a spotlight that focuses public attention on an individual, organization or an object such as a product. Unfortunately, there are two kinds of publicity. One is uncontrolled, the other is controlled, or *planned*. Uncontrolled publicity can by coincidence be favorable to the organization, but generally it is not. Usually, uncontrolled publicity places the organization in a bad light and on the defensive, whereas planned publicity can be highly effective in taking the offensive approach to good public relations.

Being featured in Jack Anderson's syndicated exposé column, "Washington Merry-Go-Round," is nearly always a guarantee of unfavorable publicity—and on a national scale. Consider his column of August 21, 1978, giving the Corps of Engineers some unwanted publicity for their visitor centers. In the lead paragraph: " . . . the eager beaver Engineers have dipped into the federal pork barrel for about $10 million to promote themselves." He went on to explain in his razor-sharp style that the money for this "grandiose propaganda scheme" was slyly set aside for the construction of 11 visitor centers throughout the country "so that the Corps could butter up the taxpaying public" (Anderson, 1978b). No organization wants that kind of publicity! But where public relations is not routinely and actively practiced, uncontrolled publicity usually is the only kind that is ever received.

Planned, or controlled, publicity is quite a different matter. This tool of public relations is a mass *contact* technique used by the practitioner primarily to create awareness or interest. There may or may not be provision for feedback—but usually the overall objective requires only that public attention be favorably focused on the organization or one of its particular functions. In many ways it is what every elected official knows must be done— "keep your name before the public at all times," and in a positive way.

The methods of accomplishing planned publicity are as limitless as the imagination, but some common ones include posters, bookmarks, open houses, ceremonies, tours, and above all others—making news happen. Lesly (1983) suggested 42 different ways to create news, many of which are as applicable to government agencies as to private enterprise. In the publicity sense, the sponsor *plans* an event he believes to have news value, then must try to convince the news media that it is indeed "news." To illustrate, the Forest Service may want to publicize the fact that much of the agency's time and funds go to *planting* trees, not just harvesting them. A publicity event might be to have the forest supervisor plant the first tree at a spring planting camp. Using that unique angle—complete with photos—the rest of the story can be told of men, women, money, mice and the thousands of nursery-raised seedlings that go into the annual drama of this sustained yield management program. The Corps of Engineers could put their visitor centers in the news each year using visitor statistics, special guided walks, invited guests such as local politicians, announcements of new displays or slide shows and what went into their production, routine event scheduling, *ad infinitum*. A good example of creative publicity was when personnel at the Forest Service Cape Perpetua Visitor Center created news for their visitor program by feting the millionth person to enter the building.

One of the easiest and most common methods of publicity is to give an award and then publicize the occasion through appropriate media. In the case of awards to personnel (length of service, outstanding performance, suggestions, etc.), the publicity not only focuses favorable attention on the organization, it helps meet the job satisfaction needs discussed previously under

Figure 7.6. Awards not only provide incentives and build morale, they also create excellent opportunities for publicity in the mass media. Here, an outstanding senior receives a plaque from a college administrator at an annual banquet. (Photo by George Savage.)

employee publics. Many awards are conjured up by parent organizations or associations for its member units. These often foster a competitive spirit or motivation for higher performance, but they also provide a recurring opportunity for publicity. State and regional newspaper associations annually give awards in numerous categories ranging from best proofreading to outstanding photography, reporting, advertising layout, and just about every function of newspaper work. In addition, there are sometimes different classes depending on circulation size of the newspaper or whether it is a weekly or daily. It seems that about every paper goes home from the annual meeting with at least one award, and the ensuing local publicity helps sell more advertising space and subscriptions. In another example, the Western Wood Products Association takes advantage of award publicity at its annual meeting, including the presentation of an attractive plaque for "Plant Appearance." A media release is issued along with a photo of the recipient, using the winning of the award for its "news" value. However, sandwiched in with the news are many lines of copy about the mill's contribution to local employment, the economy, and the company's sensitivity to the visual environment.

The value of most awards, in addition to the incentives and need satisfaction they provide through recognition, is *not* in the certificate, plaque or check itself, but in the potential for publicity. Anyone who conducts a ceremony or sends a check and does nothing else is guilty of public relations neglect.

Trademarks, Emblems, Logos and Slogans

The power of symbols has been recognized since humans began to communicate. In a moment's glance, a visual symbol transmits meaning and serves the function of reminder. The crucifix, star of David, Red Cross, and the American flag are examples of visual symbols. *Trademarks* are symbols that designate the origin or ownership of merchandise or services for sale. Under the Trade-Mark Act of 1946, these symbols can be "registered" with the U.S. Patent Office and protected against encroachment. The tiny letter R next to the symbol designates this legal protection.

Commercial interests recognize the value of symbols to stimulate instantaneous recall and identity. It is for this reason that firms have been known to pay nearly $1 million for the development and testing of a trademark. The stylized N of NBC television is said to have cost the network $750,000 when they decided to replace their old peacock symbol (Keerdoja, 1977). Needless to say, with investments on that scale, trifling with a trademark is not taken lightly. Moreover, once developed, no opportunity is passed over in placing the symbol in public view.

Insignia or *emblem* is more correct than the term trademark when describing the visual symbols of nonprofit organizations and government agencies. These correspond to trademarks in purpose and appear not only on literature and signs, but also on badges, shoulder patches, hard hats, vehicles, and other equipment. Publics come to rely on the familiar emblem and the accompanying color scheme. They expect cleanliness and quality when they see a campground sign with a Forest Service emblem, and the agency should make every effort to provide a set standard of quality anywhere the emblem appears. Conversely, it is a questionable practice to develop separate emblems for different visitor centers or other units of an agency. Clever and distinctive as some may be, identity value for the parent agency is lost or reduced. In Figure 7.7 a case in point is illustrated. The Lavalands Visitor Center near Bend, Oregon, uses a distinctive symbol on its literature, entrance sign, and throughout the area. Many visitors will not clearly or instantly associate this $750,000 center with the good works of the agency making it available.

Publics *do* take emblems seriously. When the Department of Interior attempted to modernize its famous buffalo-and-sun design in 1968, such a protest was raised that the effort was abandoned (Figure 7.7). The bison lives on, and emotions run high to preserve this fitting symbol.

In a case of lost opportunity, a roadside sign is recalled that was placed—we think—by the Bureau of Land Management on a heavily traveled Utah highway. The pullout where it was located was a welcome rest spot, and it adjoined a wide expanse of grazing land. The sign, with the heading "YOUR PUBLIC LANDS," did a nice job of explaining the many benefits of multiple-use land management. Unfortunately, nowhere on the sign was an emblem or any other piece of identification that would indicate the name of the agency providing all those fine benefits and good management!

A *logo* (short for logotype) is a rendering in type or handlettering of the name of a sponsor (Nelson, 1977). The name, or term, may or may not accompany a trademark or emblem. Sometimes it is called a *signature*, and essentially it is just that. In no unmistakable way, the logo states that the message in this literature, or this sign, poster, film or slide set, is presented by. . . . As with trademarks and emblems, it is important that design and lettering, as well as the quality the logo represents, are carefully standardized. Figure 7.8 illustrates the emblems and logos of several organizations. In most cases institution policy prohibits variation from these formats except in size.

Figure 7.7. Top row: Emblems used at Lavalands Visitor Center, one of the most elaborate centers operated by the USDA Forest Service. At right, the traditional Forest Service emblem. Separate symbols may prevent identity values from being attributed to the parent organization.
Bottom row: Sentiment toward the traditional Department of Interior emblem (left) was so strong that an attempt in 1968 to modernize it had to be aborted.

Slogans are a type of symbol that can continually help to publicize an organization or its cause. The "Black Power" slogan gave rise to a whole generation of powers: Flower Power, Children Power, Peddle Power and others. To promote tourism there are myriads of catchy one-liners like "Virginia is for Lovers," "Colorful Colorado," and "I Love New York." When Idaho's Department of Commerce and Development added this slogan to its advertising literature, it brought in a record number of inquiries from potential vacationers: "Idaho is What the Rest of the World

Figure 7.8. Emblems and logos (the names or "signatures") of three organizations. Standardization of type style and positioning helps provide identity for the organization.

Would Like to Be." In natural resource management, there have been many slogans used through the years. "Hunt Like a Gentleman" is a slightly sexist one that needs updating; "Don't Be a Litterbug" has been successfully catchy; and "Wood Is Wonderful" was an effective contribution to the forest products industry from Corley Manufacturing Company, a maker of timber processing equipment. But of all the emblems and slogans in recent times, both inside and outside the natural resource professions, none has had the tremendous success enjoyed by Smokey Bear and his "Remember—Only *you* can PREVENT FOREST FIRES."

The Smokey Bear Campaign

Smokey Bear has become part of our heritage in natural resource management. He also exemplifies how symbolism in a publicity program can effectively focus attention on something—in this case, forest fire prevention. Many of the early events in this long-lasting campaign were recorded by Mal Hardy, retired from the USDA Forest Service, and Ray L. Bell, former New Mexico state forester. Much of the following came from presentations by these men at the First National Smokey Bear Workshop which was held in Atlantic City, New Jersey, in January, 1970.

It all began with World War II and the realization that fires in the forest would divert valuable human and material resources from the war effort. Many firefighters had been enlisted, bulldozers, and other equipment were under priority freezes, and the Japanese added to the concern by hitting the coast with a few shells near Santa Barbara, California. In the spring of 1942, the threat of a bad fire season with enormous losses was very real.

The U.S. Forest Service responded to the threat by giving a trial effort to a fire prevention campaign directed at the four national forests in southern California. Arnold Larson, an ex-newspaperman working for the Angeles National Forest, came up with the idea of asking advertising agencies to see if their clients would contribute posters and/or incorporate fire prevention messages in their ads. At about the same time a War Advertising Council (now the Advertising Council) had been established to contribute the talents of private advertising specialists to the war effort. Its Los Angeles branch took on the fire prevention campaign. In that first year, $43,000 of government money and at least an equal amount of donated time from the advertising industry went into the 1942 campaign materials: 10 million envelope stuffers; 5 million air raid warden leaflets; 2 million bookmarks; 1 million "fag bags" (red denim containers for cigarette packs with warning messages attached); 20,000 car cards (for use in trolley cars and buses); 10,000 posters for display at service stations; 5,000 billboard posters; a series of radio spots and short programs; and a motion picture trailer. The theme of the campaign was war and the message grim— "Careless Matches Aid the Axis."

A particularly significant event that first year was that Perry Merrill of Vermont and Joe Kaylor of Maryland came forward and volunteered the members of their State Forestry Association to coordinate the "Wartime Forest Fire Prevention" program in their respective states. This was the beginning of the three-way cooperation that today is the foundation of the nation's fire prevention program—the Advertising Council, USDA Forest Service, and National Association of State Foresters.

The wartime theme continued in 1943, and Walt Disney temporarily loaned "Bambi" for posters in 1944. There were too many complications with continuing the use of Bambi, but the animal theme was here to stay. For the 1945 program, squirrels were suggested by some, but others argued for an animal that could stand upright to demonstrate good practices. According to Hardy (1970), Dick Hammatt, Cooperative Forest Fire Prevention program director for the U.S. Forest Service, spelled out what was wanted. In a memorandum dated August 9, 1944, he wrote that a bear was to be the characterization. He stated it should have a short nose (panda style), brown or black fur, with an appealing expression, a knowledgeable but quizzical look, "perhaps wearing a campaign hat that typifies the outdoors and the woods." Prospective artists were warned to avoid simulating "bears drawn by Cliff Berryman of the Washington Star (Teddy Bears); used in Boy Scout publications; used by Piper Cub airplanes; the bear that symbolizes Russia; or the bears on a Forest Service bookmark then in use."

Figure 7.9. Smokey Bear, one of the most famous symbols in history, as he appeared on the first poster in 1945 (left) and in the 1985 campaign.

Albert Staehle, a New York free lance artist, was selected to do the rendition. Somehow the name Smokey was given to the creation. Some believe that Smoky Joe Martin, a retired New York City assistant fire chief, was inspiration for the name, but this is not certain. Bill Bergoffen, former audio-visual chief for the Forest Service, is credited for "putting the pants on Smokey."

The first Smokey Bear poster appeared in the 1945 campaign (Figure 7.9). In 1947, the advertising firm of Foote, Cone and Belding added the lasting slogan, "Remember, only *you* can PREVENT FOREST FIRES." During that same year, Jackson Weaver, a Washington, D.C. radio personality, put his head in a barrel and created the well known voice characterization for radio and motion picture. Smokey matured in 1948 when new artwork transformed the awkward, clumsy, almost comical Staehle bear into the present face that appears everywhere inspiring trust and affection.

Enter the live Smokey Bear. By 1950 some who were associated with the fire prevention program had expressed the desire for a real bear to supplement existing publicity techniques. Others had misgivings. Live bears die—then what? It became a mute point thanks to events on a windy New Mexico mountainside May 9, 1950. It was on that day that Ray L. Bell, who was then chief of law enforcement for the New Mexico Department of Game and Fish, became step-father to a frightened, badly burned bear cub found clinging to a snag in the 17,000-acre Capitan Gap Fire. He named it after the bear in the posters, and thought it "might have a good future with a name of Smokey and the experience it had had in the fire" (Bell, 1970). His plans almost went awry when a local newspaper did a story on the fire and the orphaned bear cub, and called him "Hot Foot Teddy!"

Bell promoted the name Smokey, however, and called in a photographer to take pictures of the fire. The story became nationwide news. The state of California even telegrammed stating they would like to have the cub as a living symbol of their flag. But Clint Davis, the Forest Service's chief of the Smokey Bear Campaign, wrote, too, asking that the cub be placed in the National Zoo in Washington, D.C., as a living symbol of the fire prevention poster.

This added a new dimension to an already phenomenal publicity campaign. Amid great fanfare, the recuperated bear cub was feted at a party in Santa Fe attended by agency and advertising officials, Girl Scouts and Boy Scouts, and a representative of the Piper Aircraft Corporation. The next day, Smokey was flown off to Washington in a Piper Pacer, the picture of a bear with its arm in a sling painted on the fuselage. The rest is statistical. For example, he became one of the most popular exhibits in the National Zoo with nearly 5 million visitors a year to his cage. The campaign added an animated television series, is featured annually before 100 million people in Rose Bowl parades, receives over 3,000 letters a week (so much mail that Smokey was given his own ZIP code—20252), and has brought in more than $2 million to the Forest Service in carefully guarded license agreements to use his image with commercial products (Anon., 1976). Moreover, millions of children through the years have signed Smokey Bear pledge cards to help prevent forest fires. By 1968, a survey indicated that nine out of ten people in the United States knew who Smokey Bear was (Anon., 1977), a statistic any politician would view with great envy.

In terms of the ultimate objective of all this publicity, the program can be called nothing short of a complete success. Smokey is credited with reducing man-caused fires to about one-fourth their 1942 level, saving unknown numbers of human lives, wildlife, and more than $21 billion for the taxpayers (Cockrell, 1985). Sadly, however, by 1985 the Forest Service watched human-caused fires—particularly in the south—again increase to such alarming numbers that the decision was made to supplement Smokey Bear publicity with new "get tough" messages. As a tribute to the popularity of Smokey, when the new campaign using a law enforcement theme was released, there was reaction ranging from an editorial in the *Los Angeles Times* to remarks on the *Johnny Carson Show*—most concerned that Smokey Bear was being set aside. The Forest Service, however, views the new emphasis as "helping Smokey," not replacing this super-successful campaign.

Old Smokey, the original living symbol of forest fire prevention, died in his sleep at his retirement home in the National Zoo November 9, 1976 at the age of 26-going-on-80. The touchy public relations problem of using a mortal symbol had been partially solved on May 2, 1975 by having a frisky 6-year-old Young Smokey take over the official cage when the old bear developed arthritis. A media campaign announced Smokey senior's retirement and plans were for him to be quietly moved back to New Mexico for his inevitable demise. His death came before Congress got around to allocating funds for his new grotto, but in a tribute befitting one of the nation's most popular animal symbols, he now rests in the Smokey Bear Historical State Park in Capitan, New Mexico.

The PSA

Considerable potential for publicity revolves around what is variously termed "public service advertising," or the "public service announcement." Either way, the concept is widely recognized by its initials, PSA.

Usually the PSA is a short announcement of 10, 20, 30 or 60 seconds on radio or television, or advertisement-like placements of various sizes in a newspaper or magazine. Unlike advertising, however, the time or space is not paid for by the sponsor, but rather is donated by the medium[2] in which it appears.

The Federal Communications Commission (FCC) defines a PSA as: " . . . any announcement for which no charge is made and which promotes programs, activities, or services of federal, state or local governments (e.g. recruiting, sale of bonds, etc.) or the programs, activities or services of non-profit organizations (e.g. United Fund, Red Cross blood donations, etc.), and other announcements regarded as serving community interests, excluding time signals, routine weather announcements and (station) promotional announcements" (FCC, 1974, p. 8).

Use of PSA's by broadcast media is closely related to the concept that airwaves are public property. Because of the public property concept, a government regulatory agency, the FCC, currently has the authority to license individuals and corporations to operate on a frequency in a given location. With this as a powerful lever, the FCC grants (and renews) licenses only on the condition that broadcasters operate a radio or television station in *the public interest*. The FCC has further defined this public interest obligation as the "affirmative responsibility on the part of broadcast licensees to provide a reasonable amount of time for the presentation over their facilities of programs devoted to the discussion and consideration of public issues. "One of the ways a station can meet this obligation is to give "free time" to nonprofit organizations, and using an organization's PSA is one way to do it. (Other ways include public affairs programs, news, instructional programs, and religious programs.)

Each day a small flood of PSA's is received at a station from organizations around the country. Station personnel have the right to select which they will use (except in the case of network PSA's, which are transmitted along with nationally broadcast programs). The selection process is made

---

2. Medium is the singular form of media. Television is *a medium* and one of several of the mass *media*.

on the basis of technical quality, and in the case of local selections, on the relevance of the PSA to that particular community. In all, this adds up to an important opportunity for natural resources personnel.

First of all, many station managers report a dearth of material that is clearly oriented toward the local audience they serve. Of course, a PSA with the theme "Fight Cancer with a Check-Up and a Check" is universally applicable. But a PSA on the safe application of agricultural chemicals is going to more clearly serve the public interest mission of a small town station in Iowa. For that same reason, a station in Hamilton, Montana, will look favorably on a PSA promoting hunter-landowner cooperation or safe driving on logging roads. One Forest Service ranger found the radio station in his town so eager to have *local* material that station professionals helped the ranger's staff produce an excellent series of PSA's on low impact wilderness use.

Another way the natural resources PSA can successfully meet the competition is to have a nationally produced tape, film, or script delivered to the local station by a local person. For example, the Society of American Foresters (SAF) may produce a radio tape on multiple-use. Rather than mailing them to stations all over the country, if they are mailed to local SAF chapters for personal delivery, there is a higher chance they will be used. Any agency with regional and local offices also can take good advantage of this delivery method.

About 40 percent of all PSA's originate with the masters of PSA creation—the Advertising Council. Each year the Ad Council selects about 25 campaigns that it feels are of national interest and importance, and which will not offend the regular advertisers who use the agencies that make up the council. Once selected, the campaign is turned over to a member firm who charges only production costs. Then, with the Ad Council's respected logo clearly imprinted on the material, it is distributed to media personnel who may then print or air the PSA as a public service. Each year millions of dollars worth of donated space and time complete the efforts of the Advertising Council in behalf of the "public interest."

Most of the 60 percent of all PSA's that are not produced by the Ad Council are done under contract to advertising firms, or produced inhouse by agency specialists. Some, like the radio tapes about wilderness ethics, are done by individuals at the local level, and sometimes with production assistance from a local station or university. Like PSA's produced for the Smokey Bear campaign, most attempt to quickly gain attention, provide awareness or a reminder, and motivate the listener or viewer to some kind of action. With the public interest requirements that must be met by radio and television stations, and with approximately 1 of every 43 minutes of air time contributed to some nonprofit message (Paletz *et al.,* 1977), this is a tool that should be considered by all natural resource organizations seeking publicity for their cause.

A Coordinated Approach

Publicity provides one of the most interesting and creative challenges in public relations work. It is also an endless task. Not a month should pass without the implementation of planned publicity, with each effort designed to meet certain objectives. In the national fire prevention campaign, meetings are held regularly to assess progress and problems and to plan the next moves. This is essential to any effective program, and Figure 4.5 in the chapter on public relations planning provides an easily adapted example used by the Boy Scouts of America for generating publicity on an annual basis. For specific events, a complete set of suggested activities and guidelines will help assure that no opportunity for publicity is lost.

Some publicity methods, of course, are part of the daily routine of doing business. Emblems, stationery and postage meter marks are examples of these standard procedures. But even these need periodic consideration and coordination with a well-balanced, *total* campaign designed to continually shed favorable light on your organization and its projects.

ADVERTISING

Advertising is paid publicity. To use this tool of public relations, the practitioner simply *purchases* the use of some communication channel. Usually the purchase is space in a newspaper or magazine, or air time on radio or television.

Advertising has many advantages. One of the most important is that it allows the user to reach *any* target public at any time. If top business leaders nationwide must be reached, space in *Business Week* or *The Wall Street Journal* can be acquired on very short notice. Snowmobile dealers will read ads in *Snow Goer* and similar trade journals; the elite among amateur naturalists will see a message in the pages of *Smithsonian, Audubon* or *National Wildlife;* and small woodland owners can be contacted through *American Forests.* Similarly, messages can be transmitted on radio and television on stations and at times that are perfectly matched to the specific audience you want to reach. Actually, channel selection is no different than it is for the use of publicity or news dissemination, but with advertising the element of chance is removed. Within limits, an editor or station manager cannot decide against using the material. Space or time has been paid for, and with few exceptions the submitted material *will* be used. Therefore, channels can be selected and used with fine-tuned accuracy.

Similarly, material submitted will be used the *way* it is submitted. It will not be edited or otherwise altered. Persuasive techniques will be transmitted exactly as planned. If photographs or film footage is submitted, the advertiser can be sure it will appear.

In short, advertising can do anything that can be done with publicity, but with much greater certainty that it will reach the target public and in an unaltered form. This, however, also creates some *dis*advantages. For example, much greater care must be exercised since the natural screening process will not be there. Poor grammar, low quality photography, and inaccuracies may appear for the world to see and with no one but the advertiser to be blamed. A case is known where a forest industry placed an ad showing the crystal clear water of a well known river. The message was that effluent from the pulp mill was sufficiently clear to allow such unblemished beauty as was shown. Unfortunately for the sponsoring company, a reader recognized the scene as part of the river mentioned, but a stretch of it far above the mill and under wild and scenic classification! In this case, an error had been made and it caused embarrassment and some loss of credibility. Legal requirements for "truth in advertising" also come into play when advertising is used, making it particularly crucial that nothing is put forth that cannot be proven as factual.

The greatest disadvantage of advertising is cost. Usually, cost is proportionate to the number (and kind) of people an advertiser can reach in a single effort. Therefore, a national magazine such as *Newsweek* with a paid circulation of 3 million readers charges approximately $30,000 for a full page black and white ad placed only once. The rate jumps to $46,000 for full color and is higher yet for a preferred location in the magazine such as the inside of a cover. For regional editions of *Newsweek,* lower rates are available. Similarly, a more limited-interest national magazine such as *American Forests* (1984 circulation 55,000) charges approximately $600 for a one run, full page black and white ad, or $814 for color. A small town daily newspaper may cost an advertiser from $250–$800 for a full page ad with no color.

Prices for the use of broadcast media also vary by listener or viewer numbers, as well as by the time of day. Radio is the least expensive, with 60 seconds of time on a national network costing under $2,000. A local radio commercial in a small town may be around $6.00 per minute if used 50 times in a week. It is slightly higher for less frequent use. Television costs are rather astonishing. One minute for a commercial on national, prime time television (8:00 P.M.–11:00 P.M.) will cost at least $60,000. Double that amount during events such as the Rose Bowl game! Daytime television costs are much less, and on a small city station this could be as low as $50–$100 per minute.

Who's who in the woods.

We'd like you to meet four of the best tree people in Arkansas.

In or out of the forest.

Larry Mallette knows every inch of the 150,000 acres in his area and what's going on in each one. When to harvest and replant. How to guard against erosion. And the best time to fertilize and thin each stand.

Dr. Roy Hedden's specialty is finding ways to keep the Southern Pine beetle, and other nasty little critters, from destroying our trees.

Dora Harden works in our regeneration center, keeping track of over 35 million seedlings by age, specie, origin, and planting cycle. So when it's time for Larry to replant, Dora's the one who fills his order.

And Bob Barrett's job is to see that every log coming into the mill is used to its best potential. So that all the work that Larry, Roy and Dora have done isn't wasted.

Now we all know who gets the credit for actually growing trees.

But Mother Nature doesn't really care about society's demand for more and more wood products.

So, we give her all the help we can.

Weyerhaeuser

The Tree Growing Company

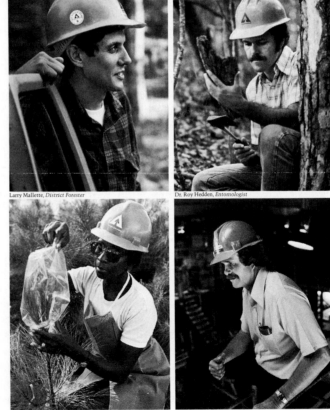

Larry Mallette, *District Forester*

Dr. Roy Hedden, *Entomologist*

Dora Harden, *Nursery Crewman*

Bob Barrett, *Mill Superintendent*

Figure 7.10. An example of corporate image advertising.

With costs such as these, advertising is out of the reach of most resource management agencies. In many cases, the expenditure of public funds for this purpose is also prohibited by law. Advertising is almost always the province of private enterprise where the expense for a minute of time or page of space can at least be equalled by the additional profit it brings. In the natural resource fields, such use has generally been limited to the forest and tourism industries.

Corporate Image Advertising

As a public relations tool, the forest industries have gone beyond buying space to sell lumber or paper products. They have, in fact, been among the national leaders in *corporate image advertising.* Figure 7.10 is an example of the kind of advertising intended to promote the image of a company in the broadest sense. It can probably be assumed that such ads also have a positive carry-over effect on public perception of the entire industry. For example, in 1964 St. Regis Paper Company launched a corporate advertising campaign under the theme "The Tree and the Forest" (Figure 7.11). In the first two years of the campaign, St. Regis received requests for nearly 150,000 reprints of their colorful, educational ads—despite the fact they had never mentioned the availability of reprints or even the company address.

Figure 7.11. One of a series of advertisements in a corporate image advertising campaign that was highly popular among magazine readers.

So encouraged by the magnitude of public approval and response, St. Regis personnel than produced 37,500 sets of posters and sent them to high school and college science departments all over the United States. In addition, 12 of the ads were reproduced in booklet form and were distributed by the thousands (Fazio, 1967). Such advertising campaigns possibly have more positive effect on the public image of industrial forestry than any other tool of public relations.

Advertorials

A so-called *advertorial* is space or time that is purchased to present some point of view, usually in an attempt to stir action related to social or political issues. Essentially it is unveiled advocacy, and undoubtedly the most direct attempt at influencing public opinion via the mass media. Resource managers may sometimes find themselves the object of such advertising, or in some rare instances may be able to use it.

One example of an advertorial was a one and one third page newspaper spread purchased by a woman who planned to open a "School of Country Living" near a small, conservative community. To counter rumors and adverse public opinion, she purchased space and printed a 4,000 word rebuttal to 30 topics such as "Carla smoked pot last summer," "There will be sewage running into the river," and "The forest will be set on fire."

Advertorials are somewhat common in the print media, but with the exception of political campaigns, to date they have been almost nonexistent in the electronic media. One reason for this is that some broadcasters argue that by accepting such ads they would be required to air opposing views under regulations of the Federal Communications Commission. Companies that have had their time purchases refused complain it is a violation of their rights of free speech. But Gene Mater, vice president of CBS, has responded that the public interest is best served when views on issues are presented in a journalistic format rather than through advertising. He also stated, "We don't want to throw the public forum open only to the person with the biggest purse" (Carter *et al.,* 1979).

Mater is probably guilty of an overstatement, because when controversial issues are presented, there *are* ways to counter opinions expressed on the air. Stations are not required to air controversial issues (nor are they required to accept all advertising), but if they *do* present one side of an issue, the "Fairness Doctrine" requires that they provide time for the opposing view.[3] This doctrine is actually a law, a 1959 amendment to Section 315 of the Communications Act of 1934. The law states that broadcast stations must operate not only in the public interest, but must also "afford reasonable opportunity for the discussion of conflicting views on issues of public importance" (Commun. Act Amend., 1960). The Fairness Doctrine can provide an important access route to the electronic media to counter advertorials. Countering views in the less regulated print media are pretty much limited to either buying space or writing a "letter to the editor." Both can be rejected at the discretion of the editor, and the latter can be reduced in length or otherwise modified. However, most reputable newspapers and magazines welcome opposing viewpoints and will publish them if they are signed and well written.

---

3. The Fairness Doctrine should not be confused with the FCC's "equal time" provision. This provision applies to political candidates and requires broadcasters to afford equal opportunity to all rival candidates if they provide it to any.

SUGGESTED REFERENCES

A Guide to Effective Interpretation—What the Forest Service Can Learn from Marketing Research by Murial E. More. 1983. USDA Forest Service, Washington, D.C.

Advertising—Its Role in Modern Marketing by S. Watson Dunn and Arnold M. Barban. 1978. The Dryden Press, Hinsdale, Illinois.

Advertising Media Planning by Jack Z. Sissors and E. Reynold Petray. 1976. Crain Books, Chicago.

Advertising Strategy in Tourism and Recreation by Michael J. Etzel and C. R. Michael Parent. 1977. Tourism and Recreation Review 6(3). Utah State University, Logan.

Beliefs, Attitudes and Values by Milton Rokeach. 1968. Jossey-Bass, Inc., San Francisco.

Communication in Organizations by Everett M. Rogers and Rekha Agarwala-Rogers. 1976. The Free Press, New York.

Communication of Innovations by Everett M. Rogers and F. Floyd Shoemaker. 1971. The Free Press, New York.

Influencing Attitudes and Changing Behavior by Philip G. Zimbardo, Ebbe B. Ebbesen and Christina Maslach. 1977. Addison-Wesley Publishing Co., Reading, Mass.

Putting Knowledge to Use by Edward M. Glaser, Harold H. Abelson and Kathalee N. Garrison. 1983. Jossey-Bass Publishers, San Francisco.

Social Psychology by David Schneider. 1976. Addison-Wesley Publishing Co., Reading, Mass.

The Design of Advertising by Roy Paul Nelson. 1985. Wm. C. Brown Company Publishers, Dubuque, Iowa.

PART III

Media and Techniques for Better Communication

To achieve good public relations through effective communication, it is necessary to first select the best techniques. This is not unlike an artist selecting colors from a palette. Next, the task becomes one of applying the techniques with skill and patience to achieve the desired effect. To do the job right, the necessary skills are acquired through both study and practice.

In the chapters that follow, the major communication media and methods are discussed. This is an opportunity to be introduced to the strengths and weaknesses of each, and the basic "how-to" aspects of communication. These chapters are also intended as reference sources for professional resource managers who find themselves faced with the actual challenge of public communication.

8

Communication Techniques—
Interpersonal

Speak clearly if you speak at all;
Carve every word before you let it fall.
—D. W. Holmes

Interpersonal communication can be considered synonymous with face-to-face communication. Primarily because of its air of intimacy and flexibility, this form of communication has more potential for contributing to good public relations than any other method. It is also one of the methods most commonly used by both managers and public information specialists in the natural resource professions.

FACE-TO-FACE WITH VISITORS

Some interpersonal communication is the one-to-one contact at the information desk, in the field, or across a desk in the office. Each requires unflagging diplomacy, a large measure of empathy, and constant realization that every contact, every action and every word contribute to the public relations effort. It requires a special effort to remain cheerful, interested and helpful at the information desk. In addition to frequent breaks and rotations of duty, it helps to remember that each question represents a *new* experience for the visitor. It may be the one hundredth time you have heard the question "Where can I camp?", but it is the *first* time for the other person. Respond accordingly, just the way you want someone to help you when you are in a strange place for the first time.

Law enforcement also presents a particularly difficult challenge in public relations. Here again, even in the face of tension or verbal abuse, it is the sign of a professional when he remains calm, polite, and as considerate as the circumstances allow. The outcomes of many law enforcement actions depend to a great extent on how the initial contact is made. For example, an inquiry of "May I see your license?" is better than "Do you have a license?" The first approach implies trust rather than doubt.

It is possible to make either a good friend or a vicious enemy for the parent organization, depending on how borderline cases are handled. For example, unknowing violators of big game tagging regulations can be hauled into court and fined. The department probably will have made

Figure 8.1. Whenever possible, warnings should be issued instead of citations for marginal offenses. By trying to win friends and explaining *why* laws exist, the result can be good public relations as well as future compliance. (Photo by J. R. Fazio.)

a few dollars, some enemies, and certainly no friends. Or the violators can have the regulation explained to them in a courteous manner. They can be told why the law exists. Then they can be made to tag their animal in the correct way. Thus, friends are made for the department.

It should be the objective of *every* employee to convert every visitor into a friend and supporter. This is the underlying philosophy of the USDA Forest Service's "Good Host" program which was developed in recent years to assist visitors in enjoying the national forests. To help Forest Service employees become more sensitive to their roles as the "host," an excellent booklet using a modernistic and humorous approach was written by Nord C. Whited and may be obtained from the California Region of the Forest Service (630 Sansome St., San Francisco, Calif. 94111).

Often interpersonal communication can be enhanced by initiating conversation in a friendly but meaningful way. That is, when approaching a visitor, instead of talking about the weather for openers, try touching on something personally important to the visitor. Perhaps a bumper sticker reads: "Join the Marines." You might ask if he was a member, where he served, etc. Visitors welcome comments on their recreational equipment, and by making a knowledgeable comment about the type of tent, gun, or other item it is possible to gain their respect as well as their attention. Motorized recreationists are sometimes even paranoid about their equipment, believing that resource managers are categorically opposed to it. *Knowledgeable,* friendly remarks about four-wheeling, or a dirt bike, can completely surprise and mentally disarm an otherwise defensive individual. Similarly, conversations with horse users (or any other recreationist) go better after the visitor can say, "Hey, this guy's all right. He *knows* horses." It should be part of every professional's responsibilities to get to *know* the publics with which he will be working. Participant-observation research is an excellent way to achieve this.

An instance is known where a man and woman entered a manager's office to discuss something of importance. The manager sat down and leaned back, put his feet on his desk toward them and lit up a cigar! Undoubtedly he thought he was being informal, which many people equate with cordiality. Instead, he was erecting immediate barriers to communication. Office manners, like contacts in the field, are essential to good public relations. They include making guests feel welcome and comfortable, and removing piles of books or other psychological barriers in the line between conversation participants. When possible it is good practice to sit *with* the visitors instead of being separated from them by a desk, counter, or other authority symbol. Privacy and quiet also aid dialogue, and attentive *listening* is essential.

Whether in the field or in the office, the success of good interpersonal communication depends largely on courtesy, sensitivity to the other person's needs, and a bit of common sense. Resource managers should consider this standard procedure in their approach to improved public relations, and they should insist on similar performance from *all* employees under their supervision.

PUBLIC SPEAKING

Every professional in a natural resource organization is called upon at some time to disseminate information to a public through personal appearance. Responsibilities as a speaker will continue to increase with responsibilities in the profession. Many courses are offered in public speaking and most progressive resource curricula have one within their requirements. Therefore, only those points will be presented here which have been found to be especially important and helpful.

Zelko (1970) listed the steps in giving a speech as planning, organizing, developing, practicing and presenting. Perhaps purpose should be added as a first step. Definite objectives should be decided upon *before* the other steps can follow. Also, two additional steps at the end are needed— evaluation of the presentation, and filing of notes, handouts, visual aids and ideas for future efforts.

Getting Organized

No two people prepare their presentations the same way, and the important thing is to do it the way that is most effective for you. If you have not yet developed a style to your own satisfaction, you may want to consider the following procedure used by Sam H. Ham, instructor of interpretive methods at the University of Idaho:

1. *Narrow down your topic.* It is rare when a request specifies exactly what is wanted. The common error is to approach a topic too broadly. Such a presentation is frustrating to prepare, and frequently turns out to be boring or less than useful. For example, if a request is for "a talk on birds," perhaps you could suggest narrowing it to "local nocturnal birds."

2. *Develop a title.* Unless the sponsor already has one selected, suggest a specific title for your talk. This will help attract an audience, and it will prevent the embarrassment of ending up with a title being publicized that does not communicate what the talk is actually about. The *title* certainly needs to be more appealing than the *topic,* "local nocturnal birds"! How about: "Wings of the Night"?

3. *Express your objectives and a short theme.* Write these out, as they will serve as your guides, or the "sideboards" for the whole talk. The theme can also be used in promotional publicity. Some examples:

(Objectives) To have the audience. . . .

   a. become aware of local nocturnal birds.
   b. appreciate basic adaptations for nocturnal living.
   c. know about the interesting aspects of an owl's life history.
   d. be able to discount falsehoods and superstitions about owls and nighthawks.
   e. support efforts for protecting local nocturnal birds.

(Theme)

   One of the more interesting groups of birds are those which become active during the twilight hours. Many of them, like the owls and nighthawks, have unusual adaptations for this kind of life. Nocturnal birds are seldom seen because of their secretive habits and period of activity. This lack of familiarity has fostered many superstitions and legends about them, often to their detriment. Birds of the twilight are an interesting, beneficial and important part of the natural community and they deserve our protection.

4. *Prepare an outline.* The three parts of any presentation are: (1) the introduction, (2) the body, and (3) the conclusion. Ham's procedure is what he terms the 2, 3, 1 method, working on the parts of the speech in that order. He finds that it allows him to more efficiently develop a stronger introduction, and one that ties more closely into both the body and the conclusion. When finished, the outline assures that there is cohesion throughout the presentation. The details and visual aids can then be developed for what has a very good chance of being a high quality presentation. For the objectives and theme used above, a completed outline might appear as follows:

(*Introduction*—Sets the mood, establishes an air of friendliness. Gains the attention of the audience and focuses it on the topic. The introduction should include a "grabber" and may include jolting statements, a brief, interesting or humorous story, or perhaps a rhetorical question.)

   1. *Opening remarks, including "grabber"*
   2. *The variety and kinds of birds that become active during twilight*
       a. *Where they stay during the day.*
       b. *Many replace diurnal birds which fulfill similar functions.*

(*Body*—The main points, concepts and examples needed to meet your objectives. Incorporate supporting statistics, analogues, anecdotes, testimony, humor and logic.)

   3. *Adaptations for nocturnal living.*
       a. *Eyes and eye shine.*
       b. *Wings of owls.*
       c. *Rudimentary feet of nighthawks.*
       d. *Development of song instead of bright plumage.*

4. *Life histories of selected species common to this area.*
   a. *Habitat and places where they can be observed.*
   b. *Care and feeding of their young.*
   c. *Mating and vocalization of owls.*
   d. *Food and food habits.*
5. *Legends and superstitions.*
   a. *Reason for these.*
   b. *Owls and pellets (their use).*
   c. *Nighthawks and witchcraft.*

(*Conclusion*—A brief, smooth summation of the main points and concepts established in the body. It should tie the presentation together and make certain that all objectives have been met. It also provides a lasting impression of you and your organization, so it deserves very careful attention. In addition to a summation, an effective conclusion may include an inspirational message, another short humorous story that fits into your objectives well, or a question such as "Where do we go from here?" In all cases, the conclusion should answer the question, "So what?")

6. *The role of nocturnal birds in a natural community.*
7. *Problems and solutions.*
   a. *Bounties and other control attempts.*
   b. *Persecution.*
   c. *Protective measures by agency.*
   d. *How citizens can help.*
8. *Summation and closing statement.*

Practicing and Presenting

Not even a veteran speaker should make a presentation without practicing. In fact, most accomplished speakers rehearse at least once or twice before a presentation, and the inexperienced should plan on more. When practicing, speak out loud, use a room as nearly like the actual one as possible, record yourself and listen to it. But *don't* let it become a "canned" program that sounds memorized. Be sincere, and let the desire to do a good job be your motivation.

Casualness and calmness are important attributes of a speaker. A helpful method used by some to retain confidence is to remind yourself that you probably know more about the subject than the audience or you would be listening rather than talking. A good solution for the individual desiring more confidence and speaking ability is to give presentations at every opportunity. One way that can be done is to join a Toastmaster's Club. Toastmaster clubs center their public speaking training around dinners and other enjoyable activities. They are found within most communities or personnel in an agency or company may form their own. In these clubs, constructive criticism is offered by friends for each speech given. The quickest way to become proficient at speaking is to do it often and to try constantly for improvement.

No matter how much some people try, pre-speech nervousness never goes away. There is nothing wrong with this. In fact, it is quite normal and if the nervous energy is harnessed, it can actually be an asset. It will help encourage practicing, and it can provide the alertness needed to do the job with enthusiasm and energy. When a person is not nervous to some extent before a speech, he should probably not be giving it.

Cockiness and overconfidence lead to disaster. A cocky approach creates a barrier in the minds of the audience and they look, and hope, for the show-off to fail. An overconfident person is also courting trouble because he tends toward less preparation.

To use notes, nothing at all, or a whole prepared speech—that is a question of endless debate. Again, each person must develop his own style. Memorization by itself should be ruled out, as memories often fail under stress. Memorization that does not sound like such is sometimes used effectively if done in conjunction with notes or a script. The best approach, however, is to use notes that simply jog your memory and get you started on each consecutive point.

Speeches can be read completely from a script on very formal occasions, or if it is someone else's speech being delivered, or if it is too complicated or crucial to be delivered any other way. Also, some people prefer to have the entire typewritten speech in front of them because it gives them a feeling of security. It is there if they need it, but the accomplished presenter will use it the same as notes rather than reading it word for word. A written copy of any oral presentation should be triple spaced. This allows for notes and additions to be made and makes the copy easier to follow at a glance. Segment or topic headings should be used freely, and highlighting in yellow or red can be used to designate the more important points. Pauses also can be shown on the manuscript.

Reiteration of important points is essential. A good speaker tells something, explains what he said, then summarizes what he talked about. Reiteration especially is needed for figures and statistics. These, however, should be kept at a minimum.

Gestures, expressions and emphasis are important, but they can be overdone. Keep them to about the same level you would use in talking with a good friend. A jittery, running delivery can be as bad as a stoic, deadpan lecture. The audience will concentrate on the characteristics or actions of the speaker and not on what is being said. Relief devices, such as looking up for eye contact, pausing for effect, walking out from behind the podium, or asking a question, break monotony and aid the speaker in retaining the interest of the audience.

Timing is another of the many qualities that comes with practice. A good rule of thumb is to "send them away wanting more, not less." One of the worst sins of a speaker is to drag on too long. Thirty to 40 minutes is about as long as most public presentations should last, and approximately 175 words per minute is a rate that is not too fast, yet is not so slow that attention wanders or the audience dozes off. Another cardinal rule is to end the presentation on time, even if you were forced to begin late. This is only fair to the audience and to any other speakers who may follow.

Promote Thyself

Few would argue that if done well, public speaking engagements offer an excellent opportunity to communicate with various publics, and to develop understanding and goodwill for the conservation organization. In general, they can do much to foster good public relations. Why, then, sit back and wait to be asked? Why not make this part of an overall public relations offensive? Resource management organizations always have topics of interest to many diverse publics, but frequently the organized groups in those publics are not aware of the possibilities of obtaining speakers.

TEACHING/RESEARCH/SERVICE
Wildland Recreation Management
(208) 885-7911

University of Idaho
College of Forestry,
   Wildlife and Range Sciences
Moscow, Idaho 83843

February 1979

RESOURCEPOOL

It is time once again to announce topics available during the spring semester through "Resourcepool." As you probably know, Resourcepool is a service to Moscow teachers and youth leaders to provide volunteers for conservation and environmental education programs. Our purpose is twofold: (1) To provide a public service by making available competent student volunteers to assist with programs related to their fields of academic training, and (2) to provide our students with practical experience in the important areas of public communication and environmental interpretation.

Access to our pool of volunteers is through Sam H. Ham or James R. Fazio, program coordinators. To arrange for a student volunteer, simply phone 885-7911 or circle the topic(s) of interest listed below and return this form. The selected student will then contact you to plan for the session. Please note that our semester ends May 11 and no requests can be filled between then and next fall.

If you have questions or suggestions, please contact us.

1. Edible Plants
   (Jr. or Sr. High School)

2. Pollination
   (Jr. or Sr. High School)

3. Bird Study
   (Grades 5 or 6)

4. Tree Identification/Botany/Wildflowers
   (All levels)

5. Camping/Survival Skills
   (All levels)

6. Low Impact Camping
   (All levels)

7. Earth Sciences/Geology
   (All levels)

8. Bats (All levels)

9. Ecological Principles/Plant
   Succession (Grades 4-12)

10. Endangered Plants in Idaho
    (Grades 6-12)

11. Outdoor Safety/Hypothermia Etc.
    (Grades 6-9)

Date(s) and time(s) preferred: _____

Your name: _____

School _____ Grade(s)_____ No. of Students____

Your phone number _____ Best time(s) to call_____

Figure 8.2. Sample of a mail-back publicity letter used to promote speakers on natural resource topics. Any agency could develop similar publicity rather than taking a passive position toward public speaking.

This problem of "low identity" is easily solved. We suggest that resource organizations do what the American Medical Association, EXXON and other professional and commercial organizations have done for years—publicize the availability of speakers. After consulting with those who will be involved, a list of topics can be printed and mailed to local schools, civic groups, churches, youth leaders, recreationist clubs, volunteer coordinating groups and others. Figure 8.2 illustrates a publicity list used to make teachers and youth group leaders aware of natural resource students who volunteer each semester to give presentations. In this case, the student can indicate with what grade level he prefers to meet. The students' names are omitted so that a central control point is established to serve as a "clearinghouse" for requests, and to monitor quality and the number of contacts made each year.

Introductions

One author, while working for the Colorado Game and Fish Department and about to present a slide show, was once introduced as, "Some guy from the Forest Service here to show us a film about something." In retrospect, he was sure the resulting program suffered, perhaps not on purpose, but because his heart wasn't in the presentation!

There are only two cases when an audience should be subjected to a speaker "who needs no introduction." One is when it can be said, "Ladies and gentlemen, The President of the United States." The other is when the speaker is one of a daily working group, such as the foreman, fellow worker, or a student in a class. Even in the latter case, there are times when an introduction is in order.

All introductions should be short (no more than three minutes long) and carefully planned out *before* the date of the presentation. A standard form can be sent to the speaker in advance, or a letter requesting a resumé.

The introduction serves the two-fold purpose of preparing the audience and making the speaker feel good about being there. Specifically it should include:

1. the speaker's *name*—pronounced correctly!
2. the speaker's organization, title and/or other background data that provide a *sense of place,* i.e. where he is from.
3. the *topic* or title of the presentation.
4. *why* the speaker is qualified to present the topic. This may include some information on educational background or other "pedigree" details, but these should be selected for *their relevance* to the topic and/or the specific audience.

It requires an extra degree of sensitivity when introducing a substitute speaker. Rather than emphasizing the would-be speaker or the details of why a switch was necessary, simply mention gratitude for speaker X being willing to stand in on short notice for speaker Y, and proceed to introduce speaker X following the guidelines suggested above.

√ **CHECKLIST OF TEN DON'TS TO IMPROVE INTRODUCTIONS**

DON'T. .

1. . . . take chances on accuracy. Double check pronunciations, titles, and his or her organization name with the speaker.
2. . . . look at the speaker while making the introduction. Address the audience, then wait at the podium until the speaker arrives there.
3. . . . use trite or over-used expressions.
4. . . . apologize to the speaker for low attendance.
5. . . . overbuild the speaker. This may make him or her nervous, or set the audience up for a let-down.
6. . . . embarrass the speaker with inappropriate tales or demeaning jokes.
7. . . . stress his or her oratory skills. This will draw attention away from the message.
8. . . . try to be a star. It's the speaker's show.
9. . . . steal the speaker's thunder. Let the speaker cover *all* topic material.
10. . . . take up the speaker's time with a lengthy introduction or announcement.

USING VISUAL AIDS

Researchers agree that learning and understanding are increased in proportion to the number of senses employed in the communication effort. The process of learning, as determined by psychologists, generally is about 83 percent dependent upon sight, 11 percent on sound, 3 percent on smell, 2 percent on touch and 1 percent on taste. It seems logical, therefore, to use as much sight as possible in trying to influence public opinion.

A visual aid is an object used by a speaker to incorporate the sense of sight and perhaps movement in the communication process. Thus, the clarity of the presentation should be enhanced. A visual aid is just what the name implies, an "aid." It is not a panacea, but if used correctly it will increase understanding.

Visual aids can accomplish several things for a speaker. First, they create and retain audience interest. Second, they increase clarity. Third, they heighten retention because more than one sense is used. Fourth, there is greater chance for motivation and action by an audience that clearly understands the subject. Fifth, the use of visual aids, if publicized, may increase attendance. And sixth, and perhaps as important as any reason, visual aids can be a great help to the speaker. They can take the place of notes as a reminder of what should be said next.

Too many visual aids can complicate and confuse rather than clarify, and may be worse than none at all. Only those which truly illustrate what is being said will help the presentation; others may detract.

In preparing to use visual aids, an outline of the talk should be constructed to determine the major points to be stressed. Visual aids then should be developed or acquired to stress those points. If a choice is possible, the visual aid that has movement and will employ the greatest number of the senses should be used. To illustrate, an "active" graphic, one that is built up or torn down as the talk progresses, usually is better than a "static" graphic if quality is comparable. A real object that employs the sense of touch may be better yet.

A visual aid should have appeal as well as being technically correct. Cartoons and carica-tures can add humor and increase interest. Bright colors and a brief message in simple words make understanding easier. One style of letters should be used for one effort, and a simple, bold style is suggested.

All parts and letters should be of relative size and large enough for the audience to see them easily. If the visual aid cannot be seen, it should not be used. Too often the first comment con-cerning a photograph, chart, or slide used in a lecture is, "You can't see this, but. . . ." Why show it if it can't be seen?

As a guide to letter size for individuals with normal vision:

¼ inch is visible for about   7 feet
½ inch is visible for about   15 feet
1 inch is visible for about   30–35 feet
3 inches is visible for about 90–110 feet

Line spacing should be about 1½ times letter size. Letters should be from ¼ to ⅐ wide as high, depending upon the boldness desired.

It generally is best to have materials too large than too small. Before the talk, the speaker should go as far back as the farthest seat and see how the visual aid appears from that distance.

Color in Visual Aids

Colors have powerful psychological influences. For example, it has been experimentally found that a box or other weighty object painted red is believed to be heavier than the same thing painted green. Similarly, people in a red room overestimate time; those in a green room tend to under-estimate. In natural resources work, the two most important attributes of color are aiding *identity* and providing *meaning*. Color helps provide identity the same way that consistent design does in emblems and logos. Consistent color schemes should be used in signs, vehicles and structures to help publics associate these with the providing organization.

Color can help lend meaning to an object, design or the wording in a visual aid. Thus, it can help speed and focus the communication process. In our culture, some useful meanings often as-sociated with colors are:

Red—Heat, the extremes of passion (love or hate), danger.
Yellow—Caution, warmth, bright and cheerful, sunny, importance (as letters or symbols highlighted in yellow).
Orange—Festive or silly, Halloween, fall (leaves and hunting).
Violet—Royal, stately, pompous.
Blue—Coolness or cold (icy), relaxed or passive, distant.
Green—The forestry color! Freshness, growth, coolness, life.
White—Purity, truth, clarity, snowy.
Black—Depression, gloom, death, heaviness or formality.

In selecting a color scheme to use with visual aids, first consider colors on the basis of their meanings and relationships to the theme of the message. Then consider how the possible combi-nations harmonize and contribute to legibility. The most legible combinations are black on yellow (thus, their use in highway signs). How others compare to each other is shown in Table 8.1. Often,

Table 8.1.
Color Combinations Ranked by Legibility

1. Black on yellow	7. Yellow on black
2. Green on white	8. White on red
3. Red on white	9. White on green
4. Blue on white	10. White on black
5. White on blue	11. Red on yellow
6. Black on white	12. Green on red

the best background color is something "neutral" like gray. Letters, or small objects, tend to stand out or "advance" toward the audience if rendered in warm colors on a neutral, cool background. In fact, a good rule of thumb is, the smaller the object or graphic, the brighter it should be made to appear. Another good rule is to limit your use of different colors to two or three with one being dominant to present the message. Color should not be the attraction in itself, but rather should be used to subtly influence effective transmission of the message.

In using visual aids, it is important that the audience does not see or examine the materials before the time of their use in the presentation. For example, if a handout is to be used, passing it out at the beginning of the presentation will cause a severe distraction. People will read the handout rather than listen to the speaker. Have it ready and hand it out after the presentation or only when ready to go over it with the group. Similarly, other kinds of visual aids should be kept out of sight until you are ready to use them. When that time does come, it is important to stand out of the line of vision between the aid and the audience, and to keep it present only as long as it is relevant or useful to the discussion. In the case of graphs or tables, the speaker should read or interpret it and simultaneously point to the applicable parts.

Selection of which visual aid to use depends on many factors. First, what is the nature of the presentation and the theme to be developed? What talent is available for developing the visual aid and using it? What supplementary equipment is necessary to use a particular aid, or is there money available for its acquisition? Are good visual aids of one kind or another already available? What is the size of the audience and the room where the presentation is to be given? Most important of all is the question, which visual aid will do the best job of illustrating the points in the presentation?

The Different Kinds of Visual Aids

Visual aids can be divided into five categories (Figure 8.3). All have their particular advantages and disadvantages, and each must be used with forethought and skill if the presentation is to be effective and reflect favorably on the organization.

Actual objects. Nothing can substitute for the real thing. When its use is feasible, an actual object can be one of the most effective visual aids. However, it must be large enough for all to see or abundant enough for each person to have one. For example, if a forester is explaining the difference between the acorns of red oak and white oak, one pair would be an inadequate visual aid. However, having a supply so that each person could have his own would be an effective aid to the discussion. If the actual object is too large, too small, too scarce or otherwise not suitable, then there are many other options open to the speaker who wants to improve his presentation.

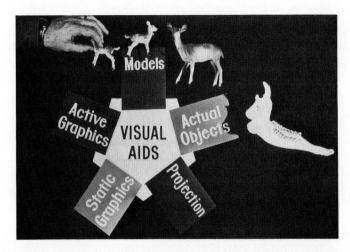

Figure 8.3. An active graphic (hook and loop board) used to illustrate the five kinds of visual aids. (Used by permission of The Wildlife Society.)

Static graphics are flat pieces that do not move or require active manipulation by the speaker. Essentially, they are just put in place and sit there while the speaker refers to them. Examples are still photographs, charts, graphs, maps and posters. They are often already available and inexpensive (a map, for instance), easy to transport and store, and no additional equipment is necessary for their use. Color and size considerations are important, of course, and simplicity is a must.

Graphs are probably the most abused static graphic because the rule of simplicity is ignored. All parts must be visible and understandable, and no more than three comparisons should be attempted in one graph. No graph should be simply lifted from a scientific report and used with a non-scientist public. As shown in Figure 8.4, interest should be added through the use of illustrations and design that would be as inappropriate in a scientific report as a graph from the report would be as a visual aid at most public presentations.

Maps are also frequently abused. The area under discussion should be outlined ahead of time in a highly visible color. If more than one area, the colors should clearly contrast with each other and the background. Mounting the map on cardboard also makes it more visible and less awkward than trying to hold one that has been newly unfolded, or trying to tape it to a wall or chalkboard.

In most cases, the use of static graphics should be limited to small audiences. Of course, any static graphic can be photographed and projected for use with a larger group.

Models are three dimensional representations of an object, usually constructed to scale. They allow control of size if an object, either too large or too small for actual use, is duplicated in facsimile and used in the talk. Models can be made so they can be dismantled. They also offer possibilities for internal illustration if constructed so parts can be removed to show the inside (as with the human heart). Another possibility is animation to show working or component parts, such as the inside of an internal combustion engine. An elk trap is too large and bulky for the classroom

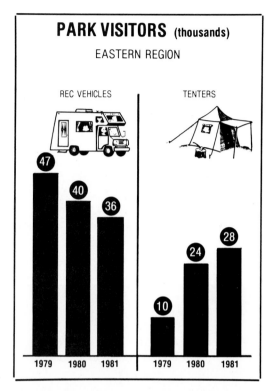

Figure 8.4. A graph on poster board with no movable parts is a static graphic. Graphs should be simple, clear and visually interesting.

or studio, but a model will show the trap almost as well as the actual trap (Figure 8.5). Excellent plastic models of some biological objects, ranging from atoms and cells to bumble bees and the human body, are available commercially.

Active graphics are visual aids that can be put together or taken apart, step by step, as the talk progresses. The key is movement and building up to the climax or completed illustration. Examples are use of chalkboards on which objects are drawn as the talk progresses, magnet boards, flannel boards, charts or graphs with movable parts, and hook and loop boards.

Flannel boards and the more useful hook and loop boards (Velcro being a well-known brand name) work on a friction principle. In the case of hook and loop boards (Figures 8.3 and 8.6), tape with thousands of tiny hooks is glued to the back of a visual aid. When placed against a board covered with loop material (thousands of tiny loops), three dimensional objects adhere as easily as flat graphics such as signs or words. These aids are not only useful and easily portable, they are also so seldom used that they have considerable audience appeal simply from the standpoint of novelty.

Like any visual aid, there is the smooth, professional way to use a hook and loop board, and there is a sloppy, distracting way to use the tool. The box insert warns of the seven common errors to avoid in its use.

Figure 8.5. Comparison of an actual elk trap and a model of the same device. Models can simplify explanation and are useful when the actual object is too large or too small for use with an audience. (Courtesy of Colorado Division of Wildlife (above) and Colorado State University.)

Figure 8.6. A hook and loop board can be used to display both flat and three dimensional objects. Its use should be smoothly coordinated with the presentation. (Photo by J. R. Fazio.)

BEWARE THE SEVEN SINS OF HOOK AND LOOP BOARD USE

Digging	Not having graphics or objects laid out in order of intended use. Very un-professional!
Waving	Using a graphic as a pointer or waving it about while gesturing.
Exposure	Waving leads to exposing the back side of the graphic. This should be avoided at all times, as the hook tape and non-illustrative portions of a visual aid are its private parts!
Petting	This is the excessive smoothing of the graphic once it has been placed on the board. It is unnecessary and it causes blocking.
Blocking	Blocking is a common sin in the use of many kinds of visual aids. It means that the speaker stands in front of what is intended for the audience to see.
Speeding	Placing graphics or objects on the board before the time comes to talk about them. They then become the focus of attention before there is anything for them to reinforce.
Creeping	The opposite of speeding. The graphic or object is placed on the board after the discussion it was intended to illustrate or reinforce.

A ferriergraph or "strip-tease" is the opposite of the "slap" boards where objects are stuck on as the talk progresses. In this case, material is *uncovered* as the presentation continues. For example, five reasons for raising user fees may already be on a chalkboard, flannel board, or other backing. Each point is covered with blank paper taped or clipped lightly over it until the speaker is ready for its unveiling. Cloth draped over parts of a large model or real object would work on the same principles of focusing attention on one part at a time and holding attention through the use of suspense.

The chalk board is an active graphic that is used widely, sometimes well, sometimes poorly. Neatness, letter size and writing speed are important in obtaining effectiveness. Colored chalk and art ability also help. For example, colors might be used to illustrate rock layers and uplifts in a talk on geology, then by erasing, the effects of erosion or a road cut can be shown.

Projected visual aids are by far the most used of any kind. They are versatile, easy to use, easy to store, and relatively inexpensive and long-lasting. Moreover, they allow contact with larger audiences than any of the other visual aids. These are the familiar opaque and overhead projections, motion pictures and transparent slides.

With an *opaque projector,* the projected material does not need to be transparent. For example, pages from a book can be projected on a screen. This is accomplished with a series of mirrors and requires a completely darkened room. If the room is not dark, the quality of the image will be inferior. An added person is needed to operate the projector if the speaker wants to face the audience and talk from in front of the room. An opaque projector is usually large, heavy and clumsy, but does project an exact duplicate of material that otherwise would need to be processed in preparation for projecting.

An *overhead projector* allows the operator to draw with a wax pencil or felt tip pen or to lay transparent materials on a glass area for projection onto a screen. With this type of projection, the speaker faces the audience, maintaining eye contact and the freedom to use gestures or facial expressions. Also, the room need not be darkened. The projector is placed close to the front of the room and is operated by the speaker without the necessity of turning out the room lights completely (thus allowing note-taking or reference to other materials). Image clarity and adequate size usually are no problem, but strongly upward angles will cause "keystoning" of the projected image unless the screen is tilted outward at the top to compensate for the projector angle. That is, if any screen is vertical and a projector is tilted upward, an image which should be rectangular will be wider at the top than at the bottom. To prevent this distortion, it is necessary to keep the line of projected light perpendicular to the screen.

For use with the overhead, lettering or drawings are done on transparent acetate sheets of approximately 8½ × 10½ inch dimension, or on a continuous sheet of acetate that runs between rollers on both sides of the projector. Cardboard frames are available for single sheets and provide a place for penciled notes as well as serving to stabilize each transparency. Colored acetate sheets and tapes are also available, as are colored wax pencils and inks for drawing on clear sheets. Several overlays, superimposed, can give the projected images the advantage of added colors and of active graphics in that the visual aid is added to as the talk progresses. A piece of paper over part of the overlay sheet to be projected can be moved to uncover each point, segment or step. Thus, the ferriergraph is duplicated and can be highly effective for certain presentations.

Line drawings and pages from books can quickly and easily be converted to overhead visuals. The usual procedure is to duplicate the page, perhaps using a Xerox machine, then run it through a dry copier such as Thermofax along with an acetate sheet manufactured for that purpose. The image is then transferred to the acetate and is ready to project. Several other kinds of office copiers may also be used for this process.

Because the use of slides and motion pictures is so universally popular, separate sections will be devoted to the improved use of these projected visual aids.

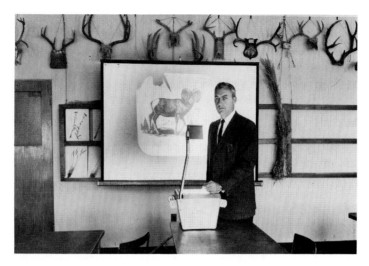

Figure 8.7. An advantage of the overhead projector is that it allows the speaker to face the audience in a room that is not darkened. (Courtesy of Colorado State University.)

THE SLIDE TALK

For natural resource professionals, slides (color transparencies) probably represent the greatest of all technological contributions in the area of public communication. When compared with other visual aids on the basis of potential impact and depiction of reality, slides must be ranked as the easiest of all to create, store, transport and use. They are also very inexpensive, can be shown to audiences numbering in the hundreds or even thousands, and can be quickly sorted and modified to match the presentation to different publics. Today there are many speakers who use slides with a high degree of skill and impact. This, coupled with the prominence of television and its excellent visual quality, have made the expectations of audiences quite sophisticated. A poorly done slide talk will be noticed by almost any public and it will reflect poorly on the speaker and his organization. With a little care in preparation and presentation of slide talks, resource professionals can take full advantage of the wealth of visual topics available to help them promote better public relations.

The Script Comes First

A top quality slide show rarely results from simply throwing together a set of slides that are conveniently lying around the office. Instead, like anything else in public relations work, quality comes with careful planning. In the case of slide talks, a script is the first step. After that, slides are selected to illustrate the words.

The format of a script is not too important if being done only as a guide for one's self. Often, however, the script also will be used by others who will help compile or shoot the necessary slides to accompany the narrative. One technique is to use the "storyboard." Cards (4 × 6 inch index cards work well for this) are used for segments of the script and to depict the slide that will best illustrate each script segment. These cards can be changed and moved about to add a new subject or to experiment with a different order in the presentation. The result is a logical script from which the photographer will know what pictures are wanted. A variation to this approach is the use of storyboard sheets. These have a column of rectangular frames down the left side of a standard 8½ × 11 inch page. The needed slides are sketched there and the narrative portions are written to the right of each frame. This method lacks flexibility, but the sheets are easier to handle and can be duplicated for team members to use in the production of major slide shows. Samples of both methods are illustrated in Figure 8.8.

A third technique that combines the best of both methods is to type the script using a computer word processing program. By using a half-page format, the plain side can be used for sketching the slide. With some computers, even the visual part can be done electronically and parts of the script can be shifted around almost as easily as sorting index cards.

Each slide talk should be developed with one central theme or objective in mind, using the principles of public speaking discussed earlier. It is better to tell one story completely than to tell several half-way. As difficult as it may be to do, the proposed number of slides to be included usually should be reduced. This is because an impression of hurriedness in a talk distracts greatly. A few good slides are better than many mediocre ones. *Poor* ones should be purged!

Many people want a rule of thumb to follow in deciding exactly how many slides should be presented in a given time period (*rate of presentation*). An average of 30 seconds per slide is sometimes suggested, but there is really no single answer to the question. The *rate* should reflect the tempo of the presentation, and it should vary during any showing. For example, if the presentation is on the environmental impacts of the Winter Olympics site in Lake Placid, the talk

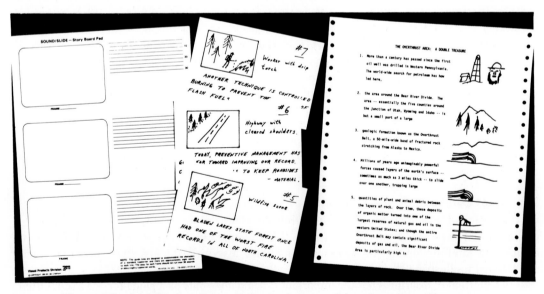

Figure 8.8. An effective slide talk begins by organizing thoughts and developing a script. The three methods shown here are (from left) story board sheets, index cards, and computerized word processing.

might open by establishing the location of Lake Placid. A rather rapid succession of slides could go from a New York state map to an Adirondack map, then perhaps to some highway scenes of a few seconds duration showing the Northway Interstate Highway, a secondary highway sign, then a Lake Placid sign. Then the tempo would change and perhaps two or three minutes would be spent discussing the impossing ski jump looming on the skyline. A varied rate can add meaning, impact and audience interest. Planning the rate should be part of the storyboarding process.

The sequence should be edited and arranged with care. Some truly excellent pictures at the start act as "attention grabbers" and are extremely important to catch and hold interest at the beginning of the presentation. Anecdotes, poems, quotations or a challenging statement also create attention and interest. Lighter commentary and pictures interspersed occasionally will help the speaker to attain and retain attention and interest. But, the "fun stuff" shouldn't be overdone. It is possible to detract too much from the main message of the talk. The old gimmicks of nationality jokes, nude scenes, or anything close to a sexist remark should not even be considered—regardless of the public being addressed.

Titles and Slide Graphics

A touch of professionalism can be added with a title slide, illustrative graphs, wording that reinforces main points, and a credit slide at or near the end to guarantee maximum exposure for your organization. Slide graphics can be done many ways. The easiest is to simply have the art work and lettering done in proportion to the size of a slide frame and photograph it on a copy stand or by holding a camera by hand in sunlight. The viewing area of most 35 mm slides is $1\frac{3}{8}$ inches wide by $\frac{7}{8}$ inches high. This rectangular proportion can be easily maintained for producing artwork of any size, or for checking magazine pictures or other existing art for useable proportions. This is done by drawing a diagonal line across a slide frame as illustrated in Figure 8.9. The proportion is the same whenever projected side lines intersect the projected diagonal.

Figure 8.10 shows a copy stand being used to photograph what will become a title slide. In this case, the background was cut out of a magazine and raised letters were arranged over it. Lettering for this purpose might also be done in free hand, with a Leroy lettering set, or with transfer letters ("rub-ons") available at most stationery or art supply stores. Real objects such as sea shells, leaves, bullets, diameter tape or anything else appropriate to the title can be added to provide dimension and stimulate interest.

Slides having white letters on blue or other brightly colored backgrounds are usually produced by a special darkroom process. Similarly, specialists can produce excellent titles through the use of slide duplicators and a double exposure process. Also, graphic shops have various ways of backlighting and photographing lettering on semi-transparent papers or acetate.

Computers now offer a wide range of possibilities for slide graphics. Figure 8.11 shows one of the least expensive options—Kodak's Instagraphic CRT slide imager. The imager, on a cone-like system that fits over common-size computer screens (9-, 12-, 13- and 19-inch diagonals), uses an electronic shutter and special lens that partially corrects for screen curvature. The device snaps a color picture of whatever is on the screen and self-develops the picture which is ready for projection in a matter of minutes.

More expensive units, sometimes called video image recorders, are available that tap directly into the computer's electronic system, thereby yielding sharper pictures. This is done on either conventional 35mm films, or through the use of modified equipment that houses the Kodak Instagraphic and its "instant" film.

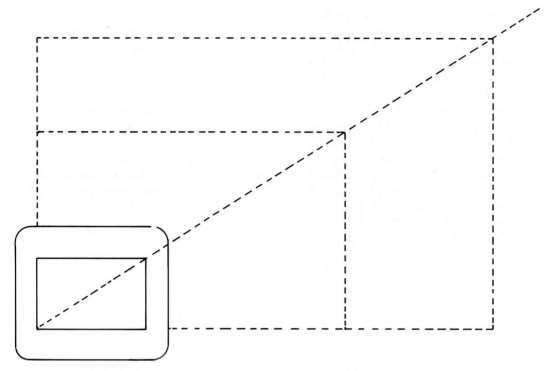

Figure 8.9. A method for diagramatically projecting format proportions to be used in preparation of artwork for title slides or other slide graphics.

Specialized, highly flexible, and very expensive systems are also available specifically for the production of computer generated graphics. These units can be purchased or leased, or a terminal can be acquired and used with a modum to take advantage of someone else's film recorder or large computer. Details, including a list of companies that manufacture computerized slide equipment, are available in Audiovisual Notes from Kodak (1982).

Still another option for high quality graphics is to have them produced by one of the commercial concerns specializing in this. Xerox's Reproduction Centers and General Electric's Genigraphics offer such services, with branch offices in many larger cities.

Most natural resource managers would do well to sketch what is needed, then seek assistance from a graphic specialist or employ a commercial service. However, the copy stand process can be used by anyone with a camera and some creative imagination. Additionally there are four "quickie" methods to producing slide graphics that might be considered:

Natural Scenes. Excellent slides to accompany the introduction of a slide talk can include entrance signs, interpretive signs, or similar identifying scenes. Shields and emblems make good credit slides to close with. When in a hurry, the use of Kodak's Ektachrome film will allow 24 hour service at most film processors.

Figure 8.10. A raised-letter title slide being photographed on a copy stand. With care, the slide could also be made outdoors with a hand-held camera. (Photo by Bruce Andersen.)

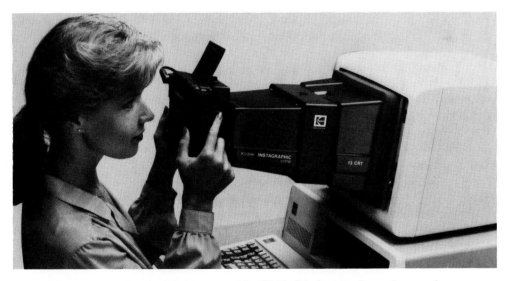

Figure 8.11. The Kodak Instagraphic CRT slide imager is used to produce color slides of computer graphics in a matter of minutes. (Courtesy of Eastman Kodak Company.)

Write-on Slides. These are commercially available in many colors. The material accepts pencil, ink, felt-tip pen and typewritten words. These are fast and easy, and suitable for adding important figures or key words to reinforce points. Their use should generally be limited to emergencies.

Stencils. Like write-on slides, these are usually acceptable only in a "squeeze." Simply type a title, statistics or wording within a clear 1⅜ inch × ⅞ inch area of green or blue mimeograph stencil. Cut out a slightly larger area and enclose in a plastic or paper slide mount.

Acetate Transfer. Various office copiers can transfer black and white letters or sketches to clear or colored sheets of acetate. Overheads can be made this way, or if the black and white original is made small enough to fit within a slide frame, the acetate reproduction can simply be cut out, mounted and projected.

Lettering by any method should be large enough to be read easily *on the slide* with the naked eye. Color selections and the rules of simplicity apply as much to slide graphics as they do to any other visual aid.

The Physical Arrangements

When the script is finished and the slides have been shot or compiled, the first steps are complete. Preparation continues with *practice,* and it continues by making sure that no detail has been overlooked to insure a flawless performance. Whenever possible, slides ready for the actual presentation should be kept in the same trays they were in during practice. This assures they will be in the right order. Rushing to fill a tray at the site of the presentation is an invitation to disaster.

There is no excuse for slides being out of order, upside down or backwards. During practice, be certain the slides are in the tray with the emulsion side (tiny bumps or a dullness can be seen when examining the slide) toward the screen.[1] When all are in order, number them in the upper right corner so they can be reloaded later if tray switching is necessary or if they are accidentally spilled. It is also a good idea to label all slides, including the date, and names of photographer and owner. A blank (opaque) slide should start and end every set so that the eyes of the audience are never assaulted with the blinding flash of a pure white screen. Blanks can be cut from cardboard having the thickness of other slides.

Two or more personal rules that should be held inviolate are: (1) *always* set up and check out equipment at least 30 minutes before starting time (sooner if more than one projector is used), and (2) *always* be as self-sufficient as transportation to the site allows. Both rules counter the inevitability of things going wrong. By setting up equipment early, a malfunction can be found in time for replacement and everything can be ready when the audience begins to arrive. It also prevents the audience from previewing as you align and focus slides. Previewing reduces the element of anticipation. Moreover, instead of fussing nervously with equipment as the starting time arrives and people interrupt, advance set-up allows a brief period to relax and exchange pleasantries with the hosts or audience.

Self-sufficiency means having all your own equipment, including projectors, trays, extension cords, spare bulbs, a three-prong to two-prong adapter plug, and in some cases, even a portable screen. When it comes to equipment, do not rely on others!

---

1. This is for front projection or rear screen projection using one mirror. If rear screen projection is used and no mirrors are included, the emulsion side is toward the projector lamp.

Room arrangements are an important consideration to facilitate smooth delivery and to prevent communication barriers. The room should be visited in advance of the presentation date, if at all possible. Adequate darkening facilities should be checked as well as seating capacity, external noise sources, ventilation, and acoustics (including the public address system if one will be used). Stand in the spot where the presentation will be made. Get a feel for the place. Find and check the electric outlets and light switches.

Screens

The screen can be the weakest link in the chain of a good presentation. Old, discolored, creased, or dirty screens assure that a slide presentation will be less than ideal. The alert speaker will avoid using such screens. Even more so, knowing the qualities of three or four basic kinds of screens will help match the right one to any occasion.

Beaded screens are widely used and are adequate for small groups and for long rooms that have a narrow viewing cone. With a beaded screen the ideal viewing angle is no greater than 30 degrees from a line mentally drawn from the center of the screen and at right angles to it. Viewers should sit in this 60-degree viewing cone (two 30-degree angles, one on either side on the imaginery line) but should sit no closer than two times the width of the screen. The most distant viewer should be no farther back than six times the width of the screen (Figure 8.12).

Silver lenticular screens get their name from their ability to capture and redirect light that is normally reflected to the sides, ceiling and floor. The image they reflect is of comparable brightness to that rendered by a beaded screen and lenticular screens have the added advantage of a wider optimal viewing cone—90 degrees, or 45 degrees on either side of the midpoint. Although this type of screen surface allows a brighter image in partially lit rooms, it has the disadvantage of distorting color balance in the projected image.

Matte screens are ideal multipurpose screens. They diffuse light evenly over a much wider area than either beaded or lenticular screens and have a smooth surface which can be vigorously cleaned. Matte screens do not render as bright an image as the other two types but in an ampitheater or when a room can be completely darkened this is a negligible factor. Furthermore, matte screens are invariably the least expensive of the three types.

Daylight, or *high gain screens* are a relatively new innovation that allows projection in extraordinarily bright conditions. "Ektalite" screen is an example. This special aluminum screen surface will reflect an acceptable image even in full room light. It is clearly a special purpose screen and possesses several disadvantages: (1) it is expensive, (2) it comes in only small sizes, (3) it has an extremely narrow viewing cone (about 40 degrees); (4) it is easily damaged, even by fingerprints; and (5) it is fixed to a rigid frame, limiting mobility.

Rear projection screens use a special translucent material allowing the projector to be placed *behind* the screen. Plain shower curtains have sometimes been used as a cheap—but inferior—substitute. Rear projection screens are useful in visitor centers or other display spaces, conference rooms where projector noise or physical presence of equipment is disturbing, or in cases when it is necessary to project in lighted rooms. Since there is usually limited space behind the screen, wide angle rear projection lenses are needed.

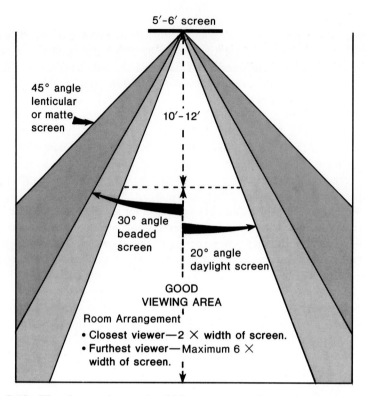

Figure 8.12. The closest viewer should be no nearer than twice the image width. The maximum for the farthest viewer is six times the image width. The ideal viewing cone varies with screen type.

The Projector

The projector should be far enough back so the picture almost fills the screen with no overlap on the sides. A square screen is advantageous because both horizontal and vertical slides can be shown from the same distance without having part of the picture miss the screen. Both vertical and horizontal slides should be checked during set-up.

The focal length of the projector lens dictates the extremes of distance that can be tolerated with a certain size of screen and a corresponding size of image. This is illustrated in Table 8.2 which is useful for selecting the correct projector and lense for circumstances ranging from projection in an automated exhibit to a large auditorium. *Zoom lenses* allow modification of the focal length (and image size) within a certain range and without moving the projector.

In addition to the type of screen, brightness depends upon other factors such as wattage of bulb, projector design, cleanliness of optics and nature or denseness of the material to be shown. Very seldom is a projected image too bright. However, it can be too light or "washed out" due to the slide being overexposed.

Projectors require specific size (wattage) bulbs. A projector with a 500-watt bulb is adequate for short distances and correspondingly small groups (Table 8.2). A 750– or 1000–watt lamp and projector are suggested for long projection distances and large audiences. For extra dark, dense

Table 8.2.
Suggested Blub Wattage, Approximate Projection Distance, and Image Width Based upon Focal Length of Lens, 35mm. Projectors (Used by permission of the Wildlife Society).

Projector Distance in Feet	Focal Length of Lens							Suggested Minimum Bulb Wattage
	9.0 (mm.) 3.5 (in.)	100 4.0	120 4.75	150 6.0	175 7.0	200 8.0	250 10.0	
	Image Width in Feet							
5	1.75							
10	3.75	3.50						
13	5.00	4.50	3.75					500
16	6.25	5.50	4.50	3.75				Watt
18	7.00	6.00	5.25	4.25	3.25			(To 25
20	7.75	7.00	5.75	4.50	3.75	3.50		feet)
23	8.75	8.00	6.50	5.25	4.25	4.00	3.25	
26	10.00	9.00	7.50	6.00	5.00	4.50	3.50	
30	11.75	10.25	8.75	7.00	5.75	5.25	4.50	750
33	12.75	11.50	9.50	7.50	6.00	5.75	4.75	Watt
36		12.50	10.25	8.25	6.75	6.50	5.25	(To 50
40		14.00	11.50	9.25	7.50	7.00	5.75	feet)
43			12.50	10.00	8.50	7.50	6.00	
46			13.00	10.75	9.00	8.25	6.50	
49				11.25	9.50	9.00	7.00	
52				12.00	10.25	9.50	7.50	
56					11.00	10.00	8.00	
59						10.75	8.25	1000
62						11.25	9.00	Watt
65						11.50	9.50	(Over
69						12.50	10.00	50
72						12.75	10.25	feet)
75						13.50	10.75	
85							12.25	
95							13.50	
110							15.00	
150							20.00	

Distances from projector to screen also can be computed with the following equations (Eastman Kodak Co., 1967). All estimates or measurements must be in inches or the results will be confusing.

1. $\dfrac{\text{Desired Projection Distance}}{\text{Image Width}} = \text{Factor}$

2. $(\text{Factor x Image Width}) + \text{Lens Focal Length} = \text{Projection Distance}$

3. $\dfrac{(\text{Projection Distance} - \text{Lens Focal Length})}{\text{Factor}} = \text{Image Width}$

and underexposed slides, the projector can be moved closer to the screen, but this results in a smaller image. A projector moved to one-half the original distance will project an image four times the original brightness.

The Presentation—A Time To Excel

Slides should not be a crutch for the ill-prepared speaker. They should supplement a presentation made following all the guidelines of a good speech, including introductory comments made while the lights are still on. Pre-arrangements should be made for someone other than the speaker to turn on the projector and turn off the lights when the time comes for slides to supplement the presentation. As in any presentation, the speaker should *stand* (not sit) in the *front*.

Slide changes should be controlled *by the speaker* with a remote changer (remote control). Few things are as disrupting as an ill-prepared speaker who must click a clicker, stomp his foot or say "next slide please" everytime a new slide is needed! Most remote changers have extension cords that can reach the length of any auditorium, but some are now battery operated and transmit a signal without the need for cords. Some even have "off-on" switches that allow complete control of the projector from a distance. All better remote control units allow focusing, but if this is not available and the projector does not have automatic focus, a *pre*-arrangement should be made with someone to sit next to the projector to handle this function.

A smooth commentary is essential to a good slide presentation. Triteness and redundancy must be avoided. Common errors include many "uhs," "this is a slide of," "as you can see here," "this is a view of," or "look closely and you will see." The audience can see what the slide depicts and what is on the screen.

Ideally, one should be so familiar with the slide sequence that the scene coming next is always known and the projected slide will be slightly behind the speaker's words. But memories fail, and the second best method to insure smooth commentary is to let the talk *slightly* follow the change of slides. In this way, one can be saying the last words about the preceding picture when the next one is flashed on the screen. The speaker will be sure what slide is next, and the flow of words will be smooth, flowing along without a break in the commentary.

Pointing to details in a scene should be done with a yardstick or a telescoping pointer that can be purchased commercially. A flashlight pointer is even better and can be part of the equipment carried by the self-sufficient presenter. By no means should the speaker walk into the scene pointing with a hand or pencil. It is detracting to the audience and indicates a lack of preparedness.

When using slides, there is rarely a need for a script to be read. Under normal circumstances, the slides should serve as the speaker's notes, triggering what is to be said next in the pre-planned sequence. Note cards and scripts cause lighting problems and are unnecessary if the presentation has been well planned and practiced.

Ending the slide set calls for special attention. "The end" is less than subtle, and like the sunset scene is probably much overworn. With some thought, substitutions for those old themes can be found which tie into the topic, or variations can be tried ("The End" written in beach sand; a bird or ranger silhouette, perhaps reflected in water; or some suitable sequence of several slides without commentary). The credit slide can then be put on the screen, or it in itself can serve as the ending slide. Room lights should be turned on by someone assigned this task ahead of time while the final slide is still on the screen, or as the blank slide darkens the screen. At that point,

√ SPEAKER EVALUATION
(The Slide Talk)

	Very Strong Point	Strong Point	O.K.	Weak Point	Very Weak Point
1. Facilities/Equipment Controllable by Speaker					
a. Proper visual aids for size of room/group	5	4	3	2	1
b. Equipment ready when audience arrived	5	4	3	2	1
c. No loose cords for people to trip over	5	4	3	2	1
d. Podium or speaker positioned well	5	4	3	2	1
e. Distractions minimized	5	4	3	2	1
f. At end, had projector (fan) turned off immediately	5	4	3	2	1
2. Introduction					
a. Established theme of presentation	5	4	3	2	1
b. Aroused interest, gained audience attention	5	4	3	2	1
c. In retrospect, tied into conclusion	5	4	3	2	1
3. Body					
a. Continuity through unifying theme	5	4	3	2	1
b. Well organized	5	4	3	2	1
c. Spoke to level and interests of audience	5	4	3	2	1
4. Conclusion					
a. "Brought message home" to a neat ending	5	4	3	2	1
b. Persuasion/other objectives met	5	4	3	2	1
c. A definite ending recognized by audience	5	4	3	2	1
d. Allowed time/handled discussion well	5	4	3	2	1
e. Closed on time	5	4	3	2	1
5. Delivery					
a. Volume adequate/speed varied and comfortable	5	4	3	2	1
b. Good eye contact/confident	5	4	3	2	1
c. Free of "uhs" and other distractive mannerisms	5	4	3	2	1
d. Enthusiastic and friendly	5	4	3	2	1
e. Spoke to audience, not the screen	5	4	3	2	1
f. Slide viewing time appropriate	5	4	3	2	1
g. Used pointer/did not block screen	5	4	3	2	1
h. Remote control handled by speaker	5	4	3	2	1
6. Slides					
a. In focus and filled screen; no slop over	5	4	3	2	1
b. Good quality slides only/all right-side up etc.	5	4	3	2	1
c. Title slide, other graphics simple, clear, attractive	5	4	3	2	1
d. Blank slides used to prevent lighted screen at start/finish	5	4	3	2	1

Total Scores: 145-130, Excellent Presentation; 129-101, Good; 100-60, Needs Improvement; 59 or less, Terrible!

an assigned person should also turn off the projector. With today's equipment it is *not* necessary to let the fan cool down the bulb. Even if it were, a shorter-lived bulb is less expensive than a speaker's time and the wasted communication effort caused by a noise barrier.

Follow-up in the form of final remarks or a question and answer period is much better than simply ending the show abruptly. Questions should be answered concisely so that there is time for as many as possible. However, when the alloted time is over, it is the speaker's responsibility to politely call for one last question, then bring the session to a close.

Slide Care and Storage

To protect particularly valuable or frequently-used slides, they should be mounted in glass. This is usually too expensive for use with all slides, but it is the best way to protect the surface from dirt, scratches and fingerprints. If a tray contains slides that are all glass mounted, the need for frequent focusing is also eliminated. Refocusing is usually necessary because of (1) different thicknesses of slide mounts, (2) heating which causes the film to warp slightly, or (3) a slide in backwards.

When glass mounts are not feasible, it is sometimes suggested that only duplicates be shown so the original slides are preserved. The problem with this is that frequently duplicates do not possess the color quality of originals. Another alternative might be to make certain that everyone with access to a slide collection first receives a briefing on how to *handle* slides (e.g., by the edges only). Pressurized air cans or soft hair brushes with an air tube can be used to remove dust particles, and special cleaning fluids may be purchased in photo stores.

Three of the most popular storage methods are shown in Figure 8.13. Slide file cabinets allow the review of about 130 slides simultaneously, but the cost is high and storage capacity usually ranges from 4,000 to 6,900 slides. Loose leaf notebooks have the same advantage and disadvantages on a smaller scale. Each plastic page holds 20 slides, with a capacity of approximately 25 pages, or about 500 slides in a 2-inch notebook. Also, some plastic pages have been known to discolor slides, so it is important to obtain established brand names from reputable dealers rather than to try to save a few cents. Also, a strong plastic odor is a clue that unstable chemicals may be present to cause troubles. Pages with slots that open to the side are easier to use in notebooks than those opening at the top. Some people file these pages in regular file drawers rather than storing them in notebooks. Either way is better than stacking notebooks because the latter method adds unnecessary pressure on the slides. A third method of storage is the metal tray where slides are held compactly on end. Viewing at a glance is not possible, but the trays are inexpensive, dust resistent, easily stored and each holds up to 900 slides.

In any system, especially with metal trays, it is essential that a good cataloging scheme be developed. Unfortunately, none has been uniformly accepted, and each organization has its own system or systems. Whatever is developed should be simple and each slide must be coded appropriately. This allows the speaker to make a list of the slides used in a presentation. The list can then be filed with the presentation notes as a start on a similar program next time. If slides are coded and systemized, it also allows a busy professional to turn them over to a secretary, aide or student assistant for filing after the presentation. Balsley and Moore (1980) offered some excellent tips about systems used by professionals.

Figure 8.13. Three popular methods of slide storage. (Photo by J. R. Fazio.)

Single Projector or Dissolve Slide Show?

Dissolve slide shows are becoming increasingly common. Dan White (1979) surveyed eight equipment depositories in the USDA Forest Service, National Park Service and Bureau of Land Management and found that seven of them had dissolve equipment (sometimes called phasers or lapse dissolve). This equipment allows one slide to phase into the next without a momentarily blank screen. As the advance button is pushed, a rheostat system dims the light of one projector while brightening a second one that has the next slide ready. The first projector then cycles to the next slide and the process is reversed when the advance button is again pushed by the speaker. In some models, the speaker can control the *rate of dissolve* from instantaneous (under 1 second) to slow (8 seconds) or even slower.

Dissolve adds new life to the old slide show. It allows a smoother transition from slide to slide and, if a sequence of photos is taken and mounted with dissolve in mind, they can be shown with an illusion of movement. But sophistication does not come without cost. Two projectors are needed instead of one, plus a dissolver. It takes more time to set it all up, and exact superimposition of the two projected images adds even more time to the process (zoom lenses become particularly helpful when dissolve is used). Although dissolve equipment is becoming more reliable, compact and easy to use, there is still considerable opportunity for error, particularly in trying to keep the two trays sequenced correctly. In a way, the chance for problems is doubled.

Why, then, should dissolve projection be considered? This is a question each organization must face, especially in light of tight budgets. For one thing, if done flawlessly, it gives the speaker an air of professionalism. Also, the dissolving of scenes is standard fare on the home T.V. set, and people today are rather sophisticated viewers. It also allows contrasts to be shown with impact (a beautiful, clear pond dissolved into an ugly, open sewer) and can provide the illusion of movement without the expense of motion picture production. Finally, Miles (1979) found that in an experimental situation people who watched an automated slide show in dissolve had significantly higher recall of information immediately after the presentation than when seeing the same subject matter through single projection.

POOR PERSON'S DISSOLVE UNIT

To obtain an effect similar to the electronic dissolve:

1. Cut a piece of cardboard to these dimensions

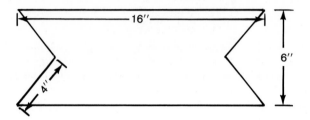

2. Align two side-by-side projectors, with slides alternating in the trays.

3. Project slides 1 and 2, but begin by covering projector B.

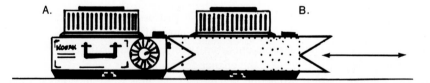

4. When you are ready for slide 2, slowly move the cardboard to cover projector A and reveal projector B. Advance projector A to slide 3, and continuously repeat the process. This method works best with the help of an assistant.

Slide Show or Motion Picture?

To use slides or a motion picture—this is another question that must be answered each time a request for a public appearance is received. Frequently the motion picture is selected simply because less work is involved. If improving public relations is an objective, what is *easiest* is the worst possible criterion to use in the decision.

The motion picture is the best choice only when it lends itself perfectly to the requested topic and to meeting public relations objectives. The slide show is a more personal medium and will usually stimulate more discussion (feedback). When done well, a personal presentation with slides will help give credibility to the speaker and his organization. It is also flexible and can be modified to include local scenes or other slides that help pinpoint the message and match it to the specific public. When speaker ability is a problem, as claimed by many resource agencies, then training should be undertaken to correct the deficiency.

Motion pictures have some definite advantages, too. One is the connotation of entertainment and almost guaranteed quality. These features often serve as an attraction to people who might not take a chance on spending an evening with what could be a boring speaker. A film also can be used to ease the pressure when personnel are over-extended or have conflicting engagements that prevent a personal appearance. Finally, the film has the inherent qualities of life, realism, drama and impact that are rarely as possible with slide shows. Testimonials from authority figures can come to life on the screen, and where the careful sequence of message presentation is critical, the film has no rival.

SHOWING MOTION PICTURES

The invited speaker who merely shows up, turns on the switch of a movie projector or taped sound/slide program, then goes home, does a great disservice to the audience, the host, and the public relations effort of his organization. When the motion picture is selected for presentation, it should be considered a visual *aid*. Its use requires careful planning and conscientious showmanship.

Showing a film begins with *a preview* before taking it before an audience. This should be done every time the film is shown so that the speaker is certain it is not scratched, broken or otherwise defective. The preview is also the time to become thoroughly familiar with the projector. Most projectors are relatively simple to operate—*after* the first time. A person should be sure that spare parts, including bulbs and fuses, always are available. He should know what might go wrong and how the fault can be remedied. A list of common problems (see box insert) can be taped inside the lid for use if needed. Lenses and tracks can be cleaned in this preview operation, and it is the time to take notes so that a meaningful introduction to the film can be made.

In the introduction the speaker has the opportunity to tailor commentary to the specific public, thereby bridging a gap between the audience and the content of the film. Comments on the main message of the film, or "what to watch for," help make the entire effort more productive.

Actually showing the film requires some forethought, too, and the room considerations described for slide talks are equally applicable with film presentations. The speaker should arrive early, bringing all his own equipment when possible, including a sufficiently large take-up reel. By the time the audience arrives, the projector should be set up, checked thoroughly by advancing

Figure 8.14. Film previewing, familiarity with the equipment and setting up before the audience arrives can prevent scenes like this. A poorly presented film can destroy credibility and contribute to poor public relations. (Used by permission of The Wildlife Society.)

and reversing a few feet of film, and advanced to the first frames of title or scenes to be shown. The *volume* also should be checked and left turned on at the desired level so that when the *lamp* and *forward* switches are turned on, sound will begin at the same time.

When a separate speaker is part of the projector equipment, sound will be best synchronized and most audible to the entire audience if the speaker is placed near the screen and is high enough to be seen by all (ear level). A low-positioned speaker causes loss of quality and is difficult to hear in the back of the room without people in the front row being blasted out of their seats. If the acoustics of the room leave much to be desired, a corner or part way back location for the speaker may improve the sound. Poor acoustics also can be improved by having the sound tone set at maximum treble. However, the sacrifice for crisp speech will be the loss of fidelity in music.

During the showing, sit near the projector so that trouble can be detected and corrected quickly. The sound level should also be monitored so that it is just loud enough for the most distant person in the audience to hear comfortably. If the film should break, advance the broken film around the take-up reel and proceed with the showing. A note in the film can or box should alert maintenance personnel to splice the break before the next presentation. It should never be spliced with anything except splicing tape.

As the film ends, slowly reduce the volume while "The End" or the final credit line is still on the screen, then switch off the equipment completely. Do not rewind the film until the entire program has ended, and check the instructions first since some loaners prefer to rewind the film after its return. This is the way they can most efficiently check for damage and clean the film.

When the film ends, the presenter should return to the front, continue his commentary and reinforce the main points of the film. A question period should follow, handled with care the same as with slide talks. Finally, the film should be promptly returned so the next person will have it on time.

√ **TROUBLE SHOOTING CHART**
(Motion Picture Projector)

1. Projector won't run.	1. Check power supply, fuses in building, circuit and projector fuse.
2. Automatic threader won't operate	2. Check that automatic threading lever is in correct position. Clip off end of film so it is square. Thread manually.
3. Projector runs but bulb won't light	3. Replace bulb.
4. Projector runs but no sound.	4. Make sure separate sound switch is turned on.
5. Loud speaker hums but there is no sound.	5. Check for loose speaker connections. Check if the exciter lamp is burning. If not, replace.
6. Exciter lamp burning, loud speaker humming but no sound.	6. Possibly photo-electric cell inoperative. In most instances turn over to repairman. Check that film is tight on sound wheel.
7. Picture flickering.	7. Press reset lever or button or rethread; film probably not engaging properly. Reform loops behind lens.
8. Sound garbled.	8. Film not tight or poorly aligned around sound-head.
9. Lip movement and sound not synchronized.	9. Projector improperly threaded, too long or too short length of film between aperture and sound-head. Check size of lower loop.
10. If the film breaks.	10. Do not pin, tape or in any other way join the film together. Run off about two feet of the film and overlap the film on the take-up reel so that the friction between the two pieces of film will hold it together. Continue the show after this has been done. Indicate breakage when returning film.

When you show a motion picture without "incidents", without lost time or obvious fussing with the equipment, you gain the confidence of your audience. A poor show lowers your professional stature. You may not be a professional projectionist but you can offset that by careful attention to the points covered in this chapter.

PUBLIC FIELD TRIPS

Public field trips are especially applicable to natural resource management use. This method of direct contact affords the opportunity to take the leaders of various publics and others who are interested into the field and show them why such a particular practice or facility is necessary. "Show me" trips are effective with teacher groups, adult clubs, youth groups, and many other publics. Through this interpersonal approach, it is possible to clarify many points and to promote many good conservation and management principles while in the field. Examples can be made vivid and pointed. All senses, including sight, sound, touch, taste and even smell, can be used. People are interested and are more easily influenced when reasons are explained and shown to them right in the field.

For example, "show me" trips can be used to explain deer seasons to employee publics, legislators, sportsmen's clubs and other influential persons in the community. By taking them to overused deer range, pointing out browse lines where food is gone as high as deer can reach, explaining how overuse affects soil erosion, and perhaps even showing carcasses of starved animals, it is possible to explain why a liberal, either-sex season is needed. An added inducement to agreement is to perform a necropsy on an animal, pointing out parasites and signs of disease or malnutrition.

Forestry field trips are also powerful persuaders. For example, an Oregon chapter of SAF took members of a school principals' association into the field to see a typical high lead logging operation. Old growth stands were visited so deterioration could be illustrated, and managed areas such as reforested clearcuts pointedly showed the basis for professional forestry. Elsewhere, effective trips have shown thinned plots, genetic improvement projects, nurseries, techniques of harvesting, slash disposal, erosion control, Christmas tree production, and just about everything else that needs to be understood by lay publics.

Public field trips must be adequately and carefully planned. They should click like clockwork. They can be just as effective in creating *dis*favor for the organization or proposal if something goes awry. Arrangements should be made for enough transportation, for rest stops, for lunch, for hot drinks on cold days and cold drinks on hot days. People should be briefed before the trip starts. Written notes and an itinerary help in presenting background information and keeping the discussions focused where desired. Every stop must be coordinated with distances timed in advance and roads checked for passability. Enough time should be allotted to do the job, but events must not be allowed to drag. Minor things, such as rough roads, or too much dust, can put accent on the hardship rather than on the ideas being presented.

Figure 8.15. Whether for children or adults, careful planning of every detail is the key to success. (Photo by David E. Goeke, U.S. Fish and Wildlife Service.)

One common problem with field trips is that people often cannot see what is going on or hear what is being said. Small groups and a battery-operated loudspeaker will help to alleviate these obstacles. Portable loudspeakers, however, can create more problems than they solve unless checked out in advance and used properly. These and other common problems to avoid are effectively illustrated in an animated film, *Conducted Tours,* available from the National Park Service.

Many of the problems encountered with public field trips could be prevented by following a few simple guidelines:

1. Through letters or other publicity, be sure that you explain exactly when and where to meet; clothing, equipment, food to bring; any rules, such as no children under a certain age; and when it will end.
2. Orient guests to the trip with a brief discussion of the purpose and plans. Set the stage, take care of introductions, be friendly and professional.
3. When arriving at points of interest, wait until everyone is there before starting to speak. Be sure everyone can hear and see. Stand on a rock or stump if necessary.
4. Lead the group by staying in front. A colleague or appointed member of the group should bring up the rear and keep the group moving.
5. Be sure the audience is not looking into the sun. Keep stops brief, interesting and comfortable.
6. Be safety conscious, know first aid and have a medical emergency plan in mind. It is always good to have a two-way radio along.
7. Repeat questions so the entire group can hear. If you don't know the answer, say so.
8. Have fewer stops during the latter part of the trip.
9. Remain flexible and take advantage of spontaneity. If the purpose of the field trip is to view bark beetle damage and a porcupine is encountered, forget bark beetles for a while and discuss porky. That's where the audience's attention will be anyway.
10. *Involve* the group, don't just lecture.
11. Make the last stop a conclusive ending. As with any public presentation, bring all the parts together, briefly summarize the points necessary to help meet the objectives of the trip, and attempt to reach common agreement or understanding.

HOSTING A PUBLIC MEETING OR CONFERENCE

The natural resource professions are rife with meetings and conferences. Sooner or later, you will find yourself in charge of one. The results can enhance or diminish your personal reputation, and they will certainly reflect on the sponsoring organization one way or the other.

Each meeting or conference should have definite, clear objectives for a specific audience. Decisions as to potential audience size and who will want to attend must be made before speakers and facilities are arranged. If these objectives and decisions are not clear or cannot be made, the meeting probably should not be held. Many people could become heroes by standing up at the critical moment in the planning stage and saying, "This meeting is not necessary", or "This conference is a bad idea!"

When the need or advantage is determined, setting of a date, times, location, and speakers becomes critical to the success or failure of the effort. Time conflicts should be avoided by checking that no other events are planned elsewhere that would compete for the attention of the target public. Times should be convenient to that public. For example, evening meetings that begin at seven o'clock often are too early for people who work until five o'clock. The location, too, should be convenient to the target public, *not* the host. County courthouses and other locations of authority may actually deter attendance at public meetings. To attract community attendance, the local Moose Club or Legion Hall may be a better selection. For scattered professional people, facilities with easy access by air become important.

The person responsible for the meeting or conference also has the responsibility of making sure the facilities are clean and neat with comfortable chairs, good ventilation, adequate lighting, good acoustics, and ample room. Even between sessions, ashtrays should be emptied, coffee cups should be picked up and the meeting room generally made neat and comfortable. An uncomfortable person will not be able to concentrate on what is being said and anything that detracts from presentations will detract from the overall effectiveness of the meeting or conference.

Above all, speakers should be selected with care. Speaking ability and knowledge of the subject should carry more weight than a title. Speakers of unknown ability are a risk, and those who hesitate when contacted or seem disinterested should be quickly dropped from consideration. Specifics on what is to be covered, how expenses will be handled, and the amount of payment or honorarium, if any, should be made very clear with the first contact. Once agreement has been reached, every courtesy must be extended to the speaker, including assistance in making lodging reservations, local transportation, and other details as requested. And, of course, a resumé should be secured in advance so an appropriate introduction can be prepared and delivered.

Publicity in every form is necessary to assure good attendance. Releases to most magazines should be made at least six months prior to the event. It will often take two to three months to appear, then there must be time for interested persons to inquire, obtain travel funds and register. Additional publicity can be released at two to three week intervals for newspapers and the electronic media, if these channels can effectively reach the target publics. Posters and brochures should also be used and must be taken to the printer months in advance. Direct mail regularly proves to be the best publicity channel for many meetings and conferences. Maps, lodging information and a detailed agenda or program should be made available either in publicity packets or when people inquire. By requiring advance registration, an idea of attendance will be obtained, but for most public meetings this will not work and it may even discourage attendance.

A word about *proceedings*. The advantage of this form of published record is that it greatly extends the benefits of the presentations. Those who can not attend can read about what took place. Others can use them as reference and can concentrate on the speaker instead of taking notes. For the sponsor, proceedings can provide excellent publicity and prolonged credit for a job well done. But proceedings are expensive! Typing, printing and mailing costs must be anticipated and included in registration fees. Depending on sales alone is to invite financial disaster. To reduce the mammoth task of recording and transcribing the sessions, speakers should be required to provide copies of their presentations. Getting busy people to do this is a major task in itself, and then it opens the door to having speakers read their presentations word by word to the audience. These factors must be weighed carefully before a decision is made, and it *must* be one of the first decisions made.

Before the event begins, everything should be checked so that equipment, including projectors, extension cords, screens, lecterns and other materials needed by the speakers are available. This equipment should be in good working order with spare parts, such as projector bulbs, immediately available. Most speakers will not arrive as well prepared as those who follow the sug-

√ **CHECKLIST FOR A SUCCESSFUL PUBLIC MEETING OR CONFERENCE**

Before the Event

_____ Firm up entire program well in advance; a year if possible.

_____ Be certain speakers know their topic and time requirements.

_____ Outline program contents for publicity channels, including places and dates. Allow several months for magazine insertions.

_____ Complete planning for all physical facilities:
a. Meeting and banquet rooms, and break arrangements.
b. Hospitality and press rooms, and adequate exhibit space.
c. Registration supplies and personnel.
d. Audio-visual equipment and assistants.
e. Signs and bulletin boards for guidance and directory purposes.

_____ Arrange for and invite displays and exhibits.

_____ Line up local city support and participation—use your convention bureau or Chamber of Commerce.

_____ Provide for dues collection and an employment contact desk or bulletin board in lobby or registration area.

_____ Line up staff of hosts and hostesses, transportation facilities to and from stations and airports and local points of interest.

_____ Printing of brochures, programs, tickets.

_____ Facilities for handling money at registration and ticket sales periods.

_____ Arrange for photography, both formal and informal shots.

During the Event

_____ Start sessions promptly; announce at the beginning that this will be standard procedure!

_____ Keep sessions and speakers on schedule.

_____ Public address, recording and audio-visual equipment:
a. Have it ready and warmed up beforehand.
b. Have qualified operators available.
c. Assign persons to turn lights off and on.

_____ Provide hallway display panel announcing current session inside meeting room.

_____ Keep program on schedule (beginning to get the idea?)

_____ Make a good photographic record of each feature of the program.

_____ Keep the program on schedule (got it?)

_____ Make adequate recording of important parts of program *if* a future use has been determined for them.

_____ Staff hospitality and press rooms and transportation desk.

_____ Arrange for press, radio, and T.V. coverage of meeting, interviews with outstanding personalities in attendance, and take advantage of other promotional opportunities.

_____ See that sponsoring officials are given due introduction and credit.

After the Event

_____ Personalized thank you letters to speakers and assistants.

_____ If proceedings are to be published, do it promptly.

_____ Publicize important statements and actions, as well as the next meeting or conference.

_____ Return all borrowed equipment.

_____ Compile budget summary and evaluations for future use.

gestions made earlier in this chapter. Accidents relative to equipment should also be anticipated and planned for by having extras of everything in nearby storage. Water should be easily available to the speaker because a dry throat or cough will detract from a talk.

The person responsible for a meeting or acting as program chairperson must be sure the time schedule is adhered to. Speakers should know how long they have and should not be allowed to exceed that time limit. One speaker going over his allotted time will cause others to start late, and the entire conference or meeting will be out of phase. Someone will be cut short at the end, and goodwill is not the result. One approach to keeping speakers on schedule is to used a belled timer or alarm clock. This is effective, but is not too delicate. With some speakers, it may be too much regimentation. Some may become confused and perhaps insulted, so this method of control should be used with care. A slip of paper given to the speaker five minutes before his time is up may be quite unobtrusive but can also be effective. Another technique is to have a closed circuit with a blinker light at the podium. The chairperson flashes the light when time is up. No one sees the signal but the speaker.

From the standpoint of many in the audience, break time is as important as the program. This may seem strange, but it is during the breaks that business contacts are made, friendships renewed, and discussion occurs. Adequate time and space for these must be allowed. Refreshments help, too, with beverages other than coffee being available for non-coffee drinkers. Placement of the refreshments should be streamlined for efficient self-service. No detail (sugar, stirring spoons, trash recepticals, etc.) can be overlooked.

Follow-up publicity during and after the meeting is almost as important as advance publicity. Photographs of speakers add human interest. Results and highlights of presentations are publicized for those who could not attend. This late publicity also sets the stage for the next effort at another time. Finally, no meeting or conference is complete until *individualized* thank you letters are sent to all speakers and others who assisted.

For large efforts, it is necessary to assign committee members to be responsible for different aspects of the effort (publicity, facilities, equipment, speakers, etc.). The ultimate responsibility, however, rests with the person in charge. Staging a well conducted meeting or conference is an exhausting chore, but it also can be highly rewarding and provide for the effective use of interpersonal communication.

COMMITTEES

Committee meeting! The very phrase makes some people blanch. For many, the word committee is analogous with diluted authority, a waste of large portions of the working day, less than rewarding evening responsibilities, and other negative feelings. Unfortunately, there is often good reason for this. The cause is that too many committees function in a slow, cumbersome manner that rarely results in either efficient production or goodwill. It need not be that way.

Usually there are two kinds of committees. The *standing committee* is normally appointed for one year to handle recurring matters. Bylaws or policy statements usually designate the name and purpose of the committee and how members are to be selected. A *special committee* or *ad hoc* committee is appointed by someone with authority, usually only when a one-time need arises. Any committee must have an achievable purpose or it should not exist.

SHOULD A COMMITTEE BE USED?

Yes, To . . .

1. Gather information and facts from various sources.
2. Disseminate information rapidly and simultaneously to many varied receiver groups, and be able to clarify questions.
3. Increase creativity, participation, involvement.
4. Test ideas and get reactions to plans and programs.
5. Train, teach, get acquainted.
6. Keep track of progress toward goals and prevent duplication of effort.
7. Gain cooperation of several groups.
8. Legitimize a decision.
9. Satisfy the ego of participants of groups they represent.
10. Provide opportunity for constructive criticism and resentment to be aired.

No, To . . .

1. Make a final decision between alternatives.
2. Serve as supervision of an individual.
3. Most situations where time is of the essence.
4. Make routine decisions covered by policy.
5. Dilute accountability.
6. Work out details implementing a plan or program.
7. Serve unplanned and non-specific purposes.
8. Situations where individual creativity and motivation will be replaced.
9. Situations requiring disclosures of personal information, or where violent clashes might be expected.
10. Involve those not concerned or affected.

Besides an enthusiastic and dynamic chairperson, nothing can contribute to efficient committee functioning like an *agenda* for each meeting. An agenda provides direction, a record for measuring progress, and it prevents the random introduction of items not germane to the committee's purpose or immediate objectives. The chairperson should solicit agenda items from all members (and perhaps outsiders) by setting a date by which they must be received (by mail). Ideally, those who submit items should also be asked how much time they feel should be allotted to it. If more items are suggested than there is time to cover, they should be prioritized. A typed copy then is passed out at the beginning of the meeting and members should have the opportunity to decide if the priority should be changed or if late items should be added. Once set, the agenda should be followed and time allocations should be adhered to if these are included. Even if they are not, the chairperson should keep track of time and prevent one or a few items from monopolizing a meeting. The meeting should be kept moving. Agenda items not reached when the *pre-established* ending time arrives become candidates for the next meeting.

The satisfactory functioning of a committee depends on a conscientious chairperson and competent, responsible members. If these elements are present, the chairperson can organize the work, assign parts so that the load will be equally shared, and set deadlines. Instead of trying to do everything himself, the chairperson should spend his effort stimulating and assisting the members so the tasks are completed, and *on time*. The chairperson is not the "boss", but rather a catalyst, making sure that everyone is part of a team effort. Convenient meeting places and times, as well as the agenda, should be arranged by the chairperson. Also, regular summations of meeting discussions/actions and reports of progress toward pre-established objectives are his responsibility.

To accomplish all this, committee members must do their share. If they are not willing, they should remove themselves or be replaced. Most committee failures occur because of weak links in the chain of cooperation. The member's responsibilities include faithful attendance at all meetings, completing tasks on time, and entering discussions but without dominating them or introducing irrelevant matters. It is also important, and a sign of maturity, that the committee member not get angry when the group makes a decision contrary to his desires.

Time is a person's most valuable possession. Wasting it serving on ineffective or unnecessary committees is a guarantee of poor public relations, internal or external. Both chairpersons and committee members must strive to streamline operations and work together for genuine accomplishment.

TELEPHONE MANNERS

Technically the use of the telephone is not "face-to-face" communication, but it is similar enough to have it placed in a chapter on interpersonal techniques. It is also a very *important* form of communicating. The person answering the telephone is a representative of the organization more times each day than most public information or public relations professionals. How this person handles the job should be an object of training and constant concern to any supervisor or administrator.

A case is recalled where a 10:00 a.m. call was made to a local natural resource agency office. After asking for a specific individual, the caller received the reply, "He ain't showed yet." The secretary should not tell the world that Mr. Doe was late to work! Her grammar was atrocious and a nasal twang didn't add much to the conversation. Needless to say, impressions of the organization, Mr. Doe, and the secretary all dropped considerably.

But perhaps this was not the fault of the secretary. Why not have a secretarial applicant talk over the telephone before hiring occurs? A pleasant voice can set the stage for an enjoyable and beneficial conversation. The administrator also was lax in that he apparently had not instructed the secretary in how the telephone should be answered.

It is suggested the caller be told the name of the organization or the department, immediately. A good format for answering is, "Good morning, California State Parks. May I help you?" If the location is a private office, the person's name should be given if the call first went through a central operator. If not, both the organization and the person's name should be part of the greeting. Thus: "Good morning, International Paper, Mrs. Smith's office."

Sometimes phones can be answered in a distinctive way that helps put across a message or contributes to projecting an image of the organization. Some examples:

"Good morning. Syracuse University beat the Mountaineers!"

"Good morning. U-Haul. We can help you."

"Good morning. Please be careful with fire. Can I help you?"

There is not full agreement on this point, but it seems rather impertinent for a secretary to ask "Who is calling, please?" or "May I say who is calling?" The temptation is to reply, "No!" Why should it matter? What does the caller think if the person is then found to be out of the office? This common practice serves very little purpose and the potential for public relations damage overrides the slight benefit of alerting the recipient to who is on the other end of the line.

The secretary or switchboard operator should know at all times who is in or out of the office. If it is a small office, standard procedure during business hours should be for the secretary to know when a person leaves, where he is going, and the expected time of return. This aids communication considerably. Some offices use a "location board" with each person's name in a column down the left side. To the right, their location is noted by a system of cards, tags or chalk. At a glance, the secretary or anyone else knows exactly where the others are.

When the phone answerer does not know, tact should be used. Even if it is 10:00 a.m. and the person has not yet arrived, the reply should be, "Mr. Doe is not in the office right now. May I take a message or would you like him to return your call?"

A call-back message should be placed on the employee's desk, door or other location where it will be noticed immediately upon his return. It is then important that the call be returned promptly. Much goodwill is lost by not returning calls, or by giving the caller an impression of being low priority by taking a long time to phone back.

When an employee has a visitor in the office, it is unfair to interrupt with a phone call. A secretary would not escort a second visitor in while another is talking business, so why should a caller be given that privilege? "I'm sorry, Mrs. Smith is in conference (or has someone in her office right now)" should solve this problem and a message can be taken.

Telephone protocol should be established for the benefit of all concerned. Once decided upon, it should be followed as policy. The main two points, however, are to be courteous and helpful at all times. Other helpful ideas suggested by General Telephone Company are:

1. *Answer during all business hours.* The phone should never be left unattended or un-plugged.
2. *Answer promptly*—on the first ring, if possible. Display alertness and efficiency.
3. *Be prepared.* Keep a notepad and pencil by the phone and take accurate and complete messages.
4. *Transfer properly.* If you must transfer, do so properly and make sure the caller understands he is being transferred, knows why, and knows the number to phone if accidentally cut off.
5. *Place your own calls*—this personal touch saves time and creates goodwill.
6. *Explain delays.* Ask the caller if he wishes to wait while you obtain the information or whether he would prefer to have you call back.
7. *Don't abandon your caller* who has been placed on hold. Make periodic reports on the progress at least every 30 seconds.
8. *Terminate calls pleasantly.* "Good-bye" is still the best term to use. Allow the caller to hang up *first,* then place the receiver down gently.

LISTENING

One of the most important yet neglected parts of interpersonal communication is *listening.* When others do not listen, it affects our effectiveness in trying to impart messages and influence opinion. When we fail to listen, or to listen well, it is often the cause of misunderstandings between resource management organizations and the public that should be served. Images, business, friendships and wars have been lost because someone *heard* sounds but did not truly *listen* to the message. Improved listening will pay high dividends toward improved public relations.

It is strange that not more emphasis is placed on the skill of listening. A classic study on listening behavior was conducted by Rankin (1929) and clearly indicated its importance. For example, listening was found to be the most frequent communication activity engaged in by the subjects in his study. He arrived at this by using adults in a variety of occupations and asking them to keep a log of their verbal communication activities at 15-minute intervals throughout the waking part of their days. Here are the results:

Communication Activity	Percentage
Listening	42
Talking	32
Reading	15
Writing	11

In a variety of situations, many other studies confirmed the rather startling amounts of time spent listening, among them Wilt, 1949; Bird, 1953 and 1954; and Breiter, 1957.

Formally defined, listening is the selective process of attending to, hearing, understanding, and remembering aural symbols (Barker, 1971). Certainly it is a skill, and certainly it demands active participation to do it well. The first step toward improvement and toward understanding when and why people are not listening to you is to understand some common listening faults. These are summarized below and are adapted from Nichols and Stevens (1957) and Barker (1971):

Uninteresting Subject. This problem usually arises from preconceptions. Through biased assumptions we create a block to listening because we "know" whatever is said is going to be uninteresting. The speaker may overcome this by using a visual aid or some approach that stimulates our interest in spite of ourselves. If not, we can rid ourselves of disinterest through recognizing it as a problem, then *right at the beginning* of the speech or conversation, forcing ourselves to listen and "get into" what is being said.

Faking Attention. Through politeness we often subject a speaker to a mask of attentiveness. Professors know the feeling well and students have often experienced it when seeking help from advisors! It is often an effective method of hiding the fact that something else is on our mind. Unfortunately, it is habit-forming and becomes a regular barrier to communication. View it as bad manners and treat it like any other bad habit.

Hop and Skip Listening. There are many reasons for this, but it is an ineffective means of listening. It frequently is used when the subject matter is difficult to understand. We tend to "tune out" whatever increases the demands on our mental energies and listen only to the easy parts. This must be overcome through the same perseverance as in dealing with an uninteresting subject. It may also help to jot down questions to seek clarification of the parts you don't understand. From the speaker's side, "reading the audience" can reveal when this barrier crops up. Clarification before moving on can then help to retain the group's attention.

Jumping Ahead. This is much like the above except for the opposite reason. Instead of inconsistent attention due to the message's difficulty, we think we already know what the speaker is going to say. Thus, instead of listening we start formulating questions, objections or clever comments. An embarrassing result often is the classic "dumb question" that was already answered by the speaker. As will be discussed later, the reason for this listening laxity is due to the difference between speaking and thinking speeds.

Listening for Facts. This bad habit comes from the multiple choice testing mentality of many professors. We begin to form our listening patterns so we hear everything in terms of items that are likely to make good exam questions. This is counterproductive to critical thinking in which statements, concepts and lines of thinking should be analyzed. If the situation is such that facts only are important, then of course listen for these. Otherwise, it is important to listen *evaluatively* so as not to miss concepts, symbolic meanings, the chance for multiple interpretations that can cause problems, and other subtleties that can affect successful communication.

Critiquing the Speaker. Hopefully the public relations person will strive to be a good speaker through being sensitive to all the points of appearance and delivery that have been shown to be effective. However, we must not spend our listening time looking for these qualities, or lack of them, in others. If we do, there is a good chance we will miss the message. Instead, try to accept the person and listen for what is said, not how it is said.

Distractions include noise, odors, discomfort and other physical factors that are common barriers to communication. The simple solution is to alter the environment or conditions to remove the distraction. If this is not possible, then a conscious, extra-effort to completely concentrate on the speaker is necessary. With practice, "tune-out" exercises can develop remarkable powers of concentration on one sound source to the exclusion of all else.

Emotional Deafness is a difficult problem to control. When a preservationist hears someone speak about "locking up" wilderness, or a forester hears a speaker suggest we need to "save our trees," much of what follows may not be heard, or not heard accurately. The more ego-involved the listener, the more likely this is to happen. Certain words, phrases or value statements can strike the emotion gong in the calmest of people. This must be dealt with and controlled to be an effective listener. One way is what some stress psychologists call "anticipatory coping." Simply by anticipating what the speaker might say that will anger you, it is possible to dissipate the emotion that might otherwise take over. Other methods include efforts to empathize with the speaker, and to defer judgement until you have heard everything the speaker has to say. Of course, yet another way to cope with emotional deafness that can go a long way in public relations work is to stay flexible, realizing that the other party may have a good point.

In addition to the above techniques, Barker (1971) and others have suggested the following ways to overcome listening problems:

1. Watch your physical condition. Fatigue reduces the ability to listen.
2. Be prepared. Research shows that if you read material in advance, think about it, and are generally familiar with the topic, learning becomes more efficient and lasting.
3. Use your listening time wisely. Most speakers talk at a rate of about 150–200 words per minute. We can think at a rate of over 400 words a minute. This is perhaps the root of most listening faults. Instead, the rate difference should be used to advantage. This can be done by mentally reviewing points made by the speaker, anticipating *then comparing* what the speaker actually says, searching for subtle or hidden meanings, and trying to identify the developmental techniques being used by the speaker.
4. Be polite. Give the speaker your full, courteous attention, and ask questions when clarification is necessary.
5. But be selfish! Think of how the information might be personally useful.
6. Listen for the *main* points a speaker is trying to present, rather than attempt to memorize all the sub-points or examples.

7. Concentrate. Keep your mind on the speaker and the topic. Item 3 above should help.
8. Practice and improve. As with any other skill, improvement comes through actual practice. Ways that might help include making a check list using suggestions in this chapter, and listening to difficult expository material. The latter may be a presentation by a scientist or by someone speaking on a complex topic in which you have no natural interest. Improvement in listening also comes through continually building a better vocabulary. In addition, for several minutes each day, try focusing on a single sound source to the exclusion of all else.

WHEN THINGS GO WRONG

Despite the great potential of interpersonal communication for efficiency, impact and the achievement of understanding, any resource manager will attest that problems often arise. In the practice of public relations, such problems are anticipated to the extent possible and preventative measures are taken. When prevention does not work, other actions are required that will mitigate the problem or keep it from becoming worse. A few common problems involving interpersonal relations and communication are discussed in this section.

Rumors and Their Control

Rumors are complex forms of informal communication. Some messages transmitted as rumors have absolutely no grounding in truth, others are distortions of truth, and in rare occasions rumors are accurate. Schneider (1976) pointed out that rumors have three characteristics: (1) they are a social and collective process; (2) they arise in ambiguous situations; and (3) the rumor is an attempt to find meaning or define a reality, and results from the use of whatever rational processes are available. Let us look at this more closely. An ambiguity can be viewed as something that is unclear. Perhaps three men are laid off at the local sawmill. If other workers do not know why this happened, they try to find meaning for the action. Usually, they turn to others in trying to resolve the mystery. Then, for a variety of reasons, someone may suggest the mill is going to close down. Another, who harbors negative attitudes toward preservationists, may add that "those environmentalists caused it". The rumor picks up pieces of information, and before long the three lay offs grow to 6, 12, 20 or more.

In time of emergency, the opportunity for ambiguities to arise is increased and rumors spread at an accelerated rate. At fire camps, rumors always seem to crop up about the size and seriousness of the fire, accidents that have happened, and how long it will be until the crews can go home.

Rumors are powerful means of message transmission and they frequently lead to unfortunate attitude formation and even actions. Perhaps the men at the mill start looking for other employment, or production drops and home life suffers as morale goes down. In truth, the three men who were fired may have been repeatedly caught drinking while on duty. In emergency situations, including fires, problems are abundant enough without rumors. These usually lead only to low morale, panic or disappointment.

What is known about rumors suggests that the best control is the dissemination of accurate information and the provision of open channels for feedback. Essentially, it is the practice of much that is suggested throughout this book. In the mill example, foremen should have been called in for an accurate explanation of the action before or when it took place. They, in turn, could have communicated the information to their workers. The dismissals could have been used to focus attention on the policies that were violated and the corrective actions that had been tried but were ignored by the three. Newsletters are especially good at preventing or correcting rumors among internal publics. It would seem inappropriate to publicize the firings, but perhaps interest in the incident could have been channeled into an article on alcoholism and available help. In fire camps, successful methods of rumor control include camp newspapers, bulletin boards, and frequent briefings. In addition, if an employee knows he has access to authorities, if good rapport and an environment of openness exist at all times, then the person can turn to a reliable source when the need exists to clarify an ambiguity.

Rumors among external publics are more difficult to control, but many of the same principles are true. In the mill town, regular publicity on the economic health of the mill and the forest industry could have had a dampening effect on the closure rumor. A quick, candid and *truthful* announcement from a *credible* person in top management can also convert a rapidly growing rumor back into factual information. Delaying tactics, false denials about unflattering incidents, or a reputation for previous lies or inaccuracies only add fuel to rumors. In short, the consistent practice of public relations is probably the best weapon in rumor prevention and control.

Complaints

Resource management is largely the business of dealing with people, and especially the providing of goods and services to people. Anyone in such a position is exposed to complaints. They are inevitable despite the best efforts to prevent them through quality performance, and they come from individuals in both internal and external publics. Complaints can lead to public relations disasters, or they can be parlayed into goodwill. The attitude you take and the procedure you follow will make the difference.

First of all, every complaint should be viewed as an opportunity and a challenge. A voiced (or written) complaint, well-handled, will prevent a build-up of dangerous resentment. It also will stifle the "ripple effect" (see box insert). Turning a disgruntled person into a satisfied friend of the organization is a most rewarding experience. Complaints also can reveal where genuine problems exist and need correcting, or how service can be improved.

HELP STAMP OUT. . . .

The Ripple Effect—This is the result of one disgruntled person sharing bad feelings with another who passes them along to yet another. The similar spread resulting from positive feelings never seems to travel as far.

The Ping Pong Phenomenon—This occurs when a visitor or person with a problem is bounced from one office to another. Participants in this process may or may not have good intentions, but the phenomenon results because no one bothers to determine for certain where the hapless victim can find the needed assistance.

Buck Passing—Similar to the above except that the participant simply does not want to take responsibility for a decision or solution.

The Policy Mask—Policies are necessary, but not when they are the only thing preventing an otherwise logical solution to a problem. "We can't help you because our policy is . . ." reveals the mask is being put in place to save someone the trouble of trying to find out what *can* be done.

The two prerequisites for successfully handling a complaint are: (1) stay calm, and (2) listen. Most complainers are emotionally charged at the moment of contact, and it is difficult not to become equally affected. Law enforcement officers constantly face this challenge of remaining polite and calm under a barrage of verbal abuse. But the incident will pass, the individual will calm down and perhaps even be embarrassed later about his irrational behavior. The professional who can "ride out" this storm preserves his dignity and through exercise of self-control is rewarded later by a satisfying feeling of accomplishment. In short, don't take it personally! But *do* listen, and make it clear that you are taking the complaint seriously, even if it is something you consider trivial or unjustified. It helps to get out paper and pen and take notes. Get the facts down, and read back your account of what you believe the person has said. Ask the individual to help you get an accurate record of the problem.

The National Park Service and some other agencies have special complaint forms that are completed by the complainer. It is questionable whether, from a public relations standpoint, they are as effective as a concerned employee listening and writing down what is bothering the other person. Either way, the next step is to determine what remedy will satisfy the person.

At this point, it may be necessary to check the facts, obtain "the other side of the story", or determine if the conditions of a possible solution are possible. If time is needed for this, it is essential to explain to the complainer that you intend to investigate the matter and give it your full attention. Assure the person you will get back in touch later. Then *do* it, and promptly. Filing a form away for some year-end statistical count is not enough.

If the complainer's demands are unreasonable, suggest some alternatives that are possible. An incident is known where a camper returned to his reserved (and paid for) campsite only to find another party fully occupying the site. Someone in the reservation office had double booked the site. All other sites were full and the first camper had carefully selected it early because of its privacy. With blood in his eye and voice at a high pitch, he demanded that the other party (who had also paid) be thrown out. A calm and skillful reservations clerk got the facts, determined an error had been made, apologized for the error and came up with an alternative to dislodging the second party. A group camp nearby was not in use that week. It was separate from the main campground and was usually off limits to individual parties. Under the circumstances, it was offered to the camper and he ended up with an ideal spot to camp and a favorable impression of the agency. He is still talking about it today!

If compromises or solutions are offered begrudgingly, they may as well not even be offered at all. Capitalize on solving a problem by doing it willingly and cheerfully. Sometimes, as in the case of Georgia-Pacific's eagle problem described in Chapter 3, follow-up publicity may even be possible to gain further public relations benefits from the incident.

It would be naive to think that all complaints can be converted to goodwill. Some people defy rational solution of their problems, and others may even fabricate a problem or be chronic complainers. In cases like this, you can only do your best, then take solace in the knowledge that others usually recognize these people and soon learn to discount their stories. In the majority of cases, however, problems *can* be solved and complaints *can* be converted to goodwill. Like other aspects of public relations, it rarely will result by accident. Training for employees at all levels is needed to make them aware of the procedures suggested above. Many films are available for this purpose, largely in the commercial sector, including the excellent series *Winning With Customers*.

This is available from the Bureau of National Affairs, 9401 Decoverly Hall Rd., Rockville, MD 20850. Although oriented to private enterprise, the principles in these films are equally applicable to government service.

The Bad Apple

The bad apple is a common problem that involves tact and determination. In short, this is the internal situation involving an employee who will not conform to established policy, does not cooperate in the team effort, defies authority, is unproductive or unconcerned about quality, or generally causes a disruption within the organization. An even more delicate problem is the person who continually "bad mouths" the organization.

State and federal civil service systems, as well as labor unions, have made this a much more difficult problem than it once was. However, even in a small commercial enterprise where a "firing" is still relatively easy, from a public relations standpoint the dismissal of an employee is the action of last resort. Regardless how unconforming, disruptive, or bizarre a person's behavior may be on the job, he is respected in some circles or publics, and goodwill will usually not result from the firing. Still, in fairness to other employees and the welfare of the organization, the bad apple can*not* be tolerated.

Corrective measures are the best approach. Try to unobtrusively determine *why* the person behaves the way he does. Often this is all that is necessary and the situation can be corrected. Sometimes the reasons may not be apparent and it is necessary to discuss it with the individual. If this is the case, it is important to project concern, not threat, and a willingness to help correct the situation. It may be a temporary problem, like the throes of divorce, and a little patience and understanding will help as time brings a return to normalcy. If unobtrusive investigation or friendly discussion does not work, stronger measures are necessary.

Involve the employee in discussions of the problem. Be sure it is clear to him that the behavior *is* a problem, *why* it is, and what is expected of him. However, be sure to always provide a "face-saving way out." That is, rather than confronting him with conclusions or the damning facts of a matter, at least first provide a chance for explanation, even if it is not the first such discussion. Ask for his suggestion of what to do about the problem, and try to reach a mutual agreement about corrective steps to be taken. In some cases, it may be best to have a written record of the "agreement" with copies for both parties. On a more routine basis, this is essentially the nature of an annual performance record as used by most state and federal resource agencies. In disciplinary cases, additional documentation may be helpful.

In all cases, a detailed record must be kept of times and dates of all incidents and corrective actions. This will be essential if the situation continues to deteriorate and dismissal becomes inevitable. Early in the situation, consider the alternatives. Is it possible to change the person's duties? Would different hours, more or less responsibility, more or less assistance, or other changes be possible? Would a leave of absence help? One company we know of provided a six week leave of absence with pay to send a valued employee to an alcoholism treatment center. He has been completely cured and is still with the firm today. Sometimes a transfer out of an area is a solution, but if this tactic simply passes the problem on to another part of the organization it should not be considered. If nothing works, the next to last solution is to suggest resignation. This is a common means of getting rid of the person without the stigma of being fired appearing on his record (although some job applications do ask about "forced resignations"). The last resort, then, is dismissal after a final review with the person of the reasons and the documentation of those reasons.

If a forced separation involves only one person and the person is not a key official, no external public relations effort is necessary. It is a case of just hoping that people will be understanding of the situation and that enough previous deposits have been made into the bank of goodwill. For multiple firings or the dismissal of key individuals, a public relations plan is essential. By taking the offensive, informing key persons such as a union official, being candid with the news media, and doing it in a carefully timed sequence, the incident will probably pass quickly and with little attention.

The Hostile Audience

No resource manager gets very far into his career without facing a hostile audience or some hostile individuals in the audience. Perhaps no aspect of public relations is more difficult to handle, and there is only limited guidance that can be provided. A wildlife biologist in Pennsylvania had his own solution which, like most others, was unique to the time and circumstances. He had presented an evening program on the local deer population when one member of the audience repeatedly attacked his knowledge of the topic. The loud, angry individual put forth his own views, laying claim to many years as a hunter to back up his contentions. The audience wavered between the two points of view. Finally, the biologist asked, "Sir, what do you do for a living?" "I'm a plumber," came the response. To that the biologist replied, "Well, I've been flushing toilets for 26 years and I wouldn't think of trying to tell you about *your* business!" This brought down the house in laughter and the story goes that it also quieted the hunter. We do not suggest the use of sarcasm, but sometimes humor can relieve an otherwise tense situation.

What *can* a speaker do who finds himself standing before an openly hostile audience? Books on public speaking are full of summaries of the tested principles of persuasive communication discussed earlier. These, of course, need to be applied whenever it is expected that the audience will be hostile to the message. Monroe and Ehninger (1974) went further and recommended ten other ways to set the stage for changed attitudes *and* better personal rapport:

1. Show a genuine friendliness, liking, and concern for your listeners.
2. Maintain an attitude of fairness, flexibility, modesty, and good nature.
3. Refer to experiences which you hold in common with them.
4. Point out your honest agreement with some of their cherished hopes, beliefs, attitudes, or values.
5. Be honest and straightforward.
6. Demonstrate that you have genuine expertise and experience concerning the subject you are talking about.
7. Quote or indicate your association with persons known to be respected by the group.
8. Avoid behaving in a conceited or antagonistic manner.
9. Use humor that is pertinent and in good taste, especially if it can be employed at your own expense.
10. Try to make sure that the nonverbal elements (gestures, facial expressions, etc.) of your presentation reinforce rather than contradict or negate your verbal meaning.

In exceptional situations, the best strategy may be to decline an invitation to speak. When severe hostility erupts during a presentation, it is best to remain poised, perhaps stopping and staring at the worst hecklers. Group pressure or the host will usually take care of the offenders when it reaches that point. Another tactic is to ask a persistent arguer to see you after the presentation to continue the discussion.

There are no easy solutions to facing the hostile audience, but like handling the irate complainer, the key seems to be remaining calm and establishing common ground. Fortunately, hostile audiences are rare, and rude ones even more so.

SUGGESTED REFERENCES

Audiences, Messages and Speakers by John L. Vohs and G. P. Mohrmann. 1975. Harcourt Brace Jovanovich, Inc., New York.

Interpretative Skills for Environmental Communicators by John W. Hanna. 1975. Texas A&M University, College Station.

Interpreting the Environment edited by Grant W. Sharpe. 1982. John Wiley and Sons, New York.

Listening Behavior by Larry L. Barker. 1971. Prentice-Hall, Inc. Englewood Cliffs, NJ.

Principles and Types of Speech Communication by Alan H. Monroe and Douglas Ehninger. 1975. Scott, Foresman & Co., Glenview, IL.

The Interpreter's Handbook by Russell K. Grater. 1976. Southwest Parks Association, Globe, AZ.

9

Communication Techniques—
The Print Media

*Those who write clearly have readers,
those who write obscurely have commentators.*
—Albert Camus

Communication in the form of printed messages is second in importance only to the spoken word. Our printed language is the cement that binds and stabilizes society. It preserves and communicates laws, theories and history, yet it can be as personal as a diary, letter or will. More than every other form of communication, it is also subject to strict rules and the critical scrutiny of others.

Skillfully done, communication in the written form can reach large numbers of people with a minimum of effort and expense. Printed messages also have the advantage of appearing authoritative. "It must be true or it would not have been printed" is the common reaction of many who place confidence in the print media. To the public relations practitioner, other advantages are: the reader can absorb the message when he is ready, and can refer to it as often as needed (it won't disappear like a minute on television or radio); errors can easily be spotted and corrected as material is reviewed prior to publication; and since reading is a habit, specific channels can easily be selected to reach a target audience. Examples of the latter might be the use of the outdoor page in a local newspaper to reach deer hunters, or the *Journal of Forestry* to reach foresters. Depending on the purpose of the communication, one can select from a multitude of magazines, in-house organs, and newspapers including dailies, weeklies, special interests, college papers, religious papers and others. Other print media include brochures, booklets and letters to name a few.

There are disadvantages, too, and some of these have essentially crippled the use of print media as an effective tool of resource managers. One problem with print is that when an error does slip through, it is there to haunt the writer for as long as one copy remains. This may be a grammatical error that merely reflects poorly on the author and his employer, or it may be false information that is in some way actually damaging. Another disadvantage is time lapse. The lapse from sender to receiver in radio or television may be but seconds. With written media the time from sender to receiver may be hours, days or even months. Many things can happen during the interim to change or refute the original story. Even under the best of conditions, another problem with print is that sight is the only sense used in receiving the message. There is no sound, movement or music to make the message more appealing, understandable and memorable. Illustrative materials such as drawings, photographs, cartoons and graphs increase clarity, but still only one sense is used in reception. Therefore, learning and understanding are slower and more difficult, and unaided recall is seriously inhibited.

WRITING TO BE READ

All other disadvantages combined are not as serious as the problem of natural resource managers failing to write in such a way that they will be read by their target public. Crisp, interesting, easy to read copy should be the cardinal rule when writing for public consumption. Instead, the style of most natural resource managers is stiff and formal, full of jargon, and generally written for peers.

Writing for non-technical purposes should be in simple language that relates clear thoughts and definite ideas. Most people do not understand words and phrases such as environmental assessment, sustained yield, silviculture, or juxtaposition. Technical jargon is understandable by those in the profession but not by the average layman. This principle was stressed by John O'Hayre (1966) in one of the wisest booklets ever printed by the government press, *Gobbledygook Has Gotta Go.*

Simplicity is the key to writing an understandable message. Little words such as trees, grass, cows, deer and soil have big "picture value" in that they can be easily visualized by most readers. Personal pronouns, conversation style and short paragraphs all aid "readability." In short, using the level of language and the style that a reader is used to *hearing* will go a long way toward enticing him to make the necessary effort to decode and absorb your written message.

Based on the principle of simplicity in writing, numerous reading ease formulas have been devised for checking copy intended for public use. Few measure a writing sample exactly the same way, and each formula has its strengths and weaknesses. Each also requires somewhat tedious counting and calculating. Now a computer program called Readability Calculations is available from Micro Power & Light Company (12820 Hillcrest Road, Suite 219, Dallas, TX 75230) that yields the results of nine formulas from any sample of your writing. Taken together, this gives you a more accurate picture of the level at which you are writing than any of the formulas by themselves. A sample of the results is illustrated in Figure 9.1.

Two of the most popular formulas are Flesch's (1949, 1974) readability formula and Gunning's (1952, 1962) Fog Index.[1] Both attempt to measure "readability" by computing average sentence length and the number of syllables per word.

To use Gunning's Fog Index, follow these steps:

1. *Select a writing sample of at least 100 words. Find the average number of words per sentence by dividing the total words in your sample by the number of sentences. (Treat independent clauses as separate sentences. For example, "we read; we learned; we improved" would count as three sentences.)*
2. *Count the number of words of three syllables or more per 100 words. Don't count: (a) capitalized words, (b) combinations of short easy words such as "timekeeper," (c) verbs that are made three syllables by adding "ed" or "es"—such as "collected" or "trespasses."*
3. *Add the answers from 1 and 2 above and multiply by 0.4.*

1. Gunning's Fog Index is the property of Gunning-Mueller Clear Writing Institute, Santa Barbara, California, and is used by permission.

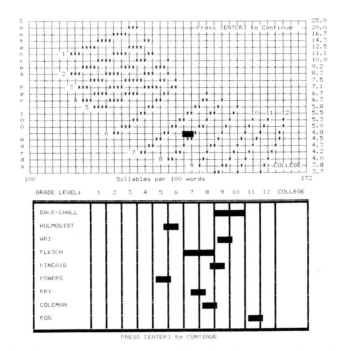

Figure 9.1. Computer analysis of a writing sample removes the tedium from using readability formulas and presents the results using 9 formulas.

The resulting figure is the Fog Index. It corresponds roughly with the number of years of schooling a person would require to read the passage with ease and understanding. Thus, a Fog Index of 13 (college freshman) or above is difficult reading. Most people can figure it out, but will need to make an extra effort to do so. Editors of popular magazines recognize this basic fact and most of them keep the reading level at 12 or below. In fact, the majority of best-selling books and a large number of the classics test between the 6th and 10th grade reading levels (Gunning, 1962).

Flesch's "reading ease" formula may be used in a similar way. Flesch also developed a rough measure of "human interest" that takes into account a personalized, conversational style of writing. The Flesch formulas[2] are summarized on the following page.

2. Specified material from HOW TO TEST READABILITY by Rudolf Flesch. Copyright *1951* by Rudolf Flesch. Reprinted by permission of Harper & Row, Publishers, Inc.

Reading Ease

Randomly or by an unbiased, systematic method select 3 to 5 100–word samples from your manuscript for a magazine article or short publication. Avoid introductory paragraphs and be sure your samples start with the beginning of paragraphs. Count contractions and hyphenated words as one word. Count numbers and letters in the text as words. Use the following formula for each sample, then see Table 9.1 for a description of the resulting scores.

Multiply the average sentence length by 1.015 _____
Multiply the number of syllables per 100 words by .846 _____

Add _____

Subtract this sum from   206.835
Your "reading ease" score is   _____

Human Interest

For each sample, count "personal words."

Personal words are:
   a. all first-, second-, and third-person pronouns except neuter pronouns (it, its, itself) and they, them, their, theirs, themselves—if referring to things rather than people.
   b. words having masculine or feminine natural gender (John Jones, Mary, father, sister, iceman, actress). Do not count common-gender words like teacher, doctor, spouse, etc.
   c. the group words *people* and *folks*.

For 100–word blocks that include the above samples, count "personal sentences."

Personal sentences are:
   a. spoken sentences.
   b. questions, commands, requests, and other sentences directly addressed to the reader, e.g., This is a point to remember.
   c. exclamations, e.g., It's unbelievable!
   d. incomplete sentences whose full meaning has to be inferred, e.g., Well, he wasn't.

Use the following formula for each sample and check Table 9.1 for a description of its human interest score.

Multiply the number of "personal words" per 100 words by 3.635 _____
Multiply the number of "personal sentences" per 100 sentences by .314 _____
The total is your "human interest" score _____

Hunt and Brown (1971) used the Flesch formulas to test 18 publications intended for public use. All 18 were produced by the USDA Forest Service, National Park Service, and Bureau of Land Management. They found 10 of the publications "difficult" to read and another 7 "fairly difficult." Thirteen of them also were "dull" and only two were considered "interesting." Several years later the same tests were applied to 115 pieces of literature intended for wilderness recreationists using land managed by the USDA Forest Service, National Park Service and U.S. Fish and Wildlife Service. The results indicated little improvement. The average score was "fairly difficult," and human interest registered between "dull" and "mildly interesting" (Fazio, 1979). Table 9.2 contains some additional estimates made more recently on a random selection of resource-related literature intended for the agencies' external publics. As can be seen, the problem of complex and dull writing continues to dominate.

Readability formulas are checks on simplicity, and this should be an important consideration in preparing copy for the print media. Another consideration is the principle stressed in preceding chapters—tailor the message to *the* public at which you are aiming. Several versions of the same

Table 9.1.
Description of Flesch Readability Scores (Flesch, 1974).

Formula Score	Description of Style	Estimated Reading Grade or Typical Magazine
Reading Ease		
90-100	Very Easy	5th grade
80-90	Easy	6th grade
70-80	Fairly Easy	7th grade
60-70	Standard	8th and 9th grade
50-60	Fairly Difficult	10th to 12th grade
30-50	Difficult	College
0-30	Very Difficult	College graduate
Human Interest		
60-100	Dramatic	Fiction
40-60	Highly Interesting	*New Yorker*
20-40	Interesting	Digests
10-20	Mildly Interesting	Trade
0-10	Dull	Scientific

Table 9.2.
Examples of Reading Ease and Level of Difficulty[1] in Publications Related to Natural Resource Management.

Publication and Agency	Reading Ease	Human Interest Style
Forests and Water (U.S. Forest Service)	Fairly Difficult	Mildly Interesting
Search for Solitude (U.S. Forest Service)	Standard	Dull
The Corps Cares About Fish (US Army Corps of Engineers)	Difficult	Dull
Shenandoah National Park (National Park Service)	Fairly Difficult	Dull
Promise of the Land (Bureau of Land Management)	Difficult	Dull
All Around You: An Environmental Study Guide (Bureau of Land Management)	Easy	Interesting
Interpreting Our Heritage (Freeman Tilden)	Fairly Easy	Very Interesting

1. Based on Flesch's (1974) formulas using three randomly selected paragraphs of at least 100 words in length.

story may need to be developed to reach a variety of people with the same message. For example, how many different publications could be used to explain the natural role of fire in forests to various publics?

The principles of simplicity and targeting are commonly overlooked, and Robert Wray (1977) added a third problem he discovered in 20 years of helping foresters and scientists improve their writing. This is the lack of a systematic approach. Wray stated that all good writing should be *clear, concise* and *effective* (that is, it should do some job other than entertain its author). To achieve these, and to help potential writers get organized, he offered the following suggestions:

Plan

1. Before starting, be able to state *why* you are writing. What do you want to achieve?
2. Next, jot down answers to the following:
    a. What one main idea should I communicate?
    b. Who exactly is my intended reader?
    c. Why should the reader be interested? How can he use this information?
3. Outline the points you want to include and arrange them in a logical way.

Write

4. Carefully write the introduction. We will see later that its content will differ depending on whether it is a news story or a feature article. Usually, the objective is to "hook" the reader into wanting to know what follows.
5. Keep your words, sentences and story simple, lively, and free of excessive facts and figures.
6. Beware of (and remove):
    a. *Nouns that should be verbs.* Most words ending in -ion, -ism, -ment, -ance, -ence are verbs masquerading as nouns. Verbs make shorter, livelier reading and make it easier to picture what is happening. Instead of: "The forester had to make an adjustment in the land-use plan," why not write "The forester had to adjust the land-use plan."
    b. *Excessive passive voice.* Usually the subject of a sentence is the "actor," not the recipient of the action. Thus, "Man is bitten by dog" should become "Dog bites man."
    c. *Useless words.* All first drafts include these gremlins. For example, the first seven words of the following sentence would be obvious to the reader and can be deleted: "*An examination of the data revealed that* growth of red pine doubled after thinning."
7. Observe the basic rules of grammar, but don't let visions of your old English teacher completely cramp your style. If you want to begin a sentence now and then with "and," toss in a sentence fragment, or occasionally split an infinitive, so be it. And use an exclamation mark—or dashes—for emphasis when needed!
8. Stop when you've accomplished your objectives for the article. A brief summary or restatement of your main point should usually be included in your close.

Check, Trim and Double Check

9. Let it sit for a day or two. Then re-read it and make revisions. Look for clarity, accuracy and brevity. Trim it again if you can.
10. Have someone else review it, and *not* someone you know will be kind to you. An honest review in private can save much embarrassment in public.

DID YOU KNOWED BETTER?

Here is some good advice to writers, taken from *The Quill.*

Don't use no double negative. Make each pronoun agree with their antecedent. Join clauses good, like a conjunction should. About them sentence fragments.

When dangling, watch your participles. Verbs has to agree with their subjects. Just between you and I, case is important too. Don't write runon sentences they are hard to read.

Don't use commas, which aren't necessary. Try to not ever split infinitives. Its important to use your apostrophe's correctly.

Proofread your writing to see if you any words out. Correct spelling is also esential.

NEWSPAPERS

Newspapers are the oldest of the mass media. Julius Caesar is given credit for publishing the first newspaper in 60 B.C. In Colonial America newspapers were a well established and cherished means of communication. Newspapers still are considered to be the leader in the race among newspapers, radio and television for numbers of people contacted. They also lead all media in money spent for advertising. More than 66 percent of all adult Americans, and 58 percent of 18–24 year olds, regularly read newspapers, and these readers are supplied with their news from 1,708 dailies, 7,626 weeklies and 768 Sunday papers (Cutlip et al., 1985). In addition, there are many more special interest tabloids, campus newspapers and others that make news available.

With so many people being reached by such a wide array of publications, it is little wonder that newspapers were rated highest in importance in our 1985 national survey of information and public relations executives (Table 7.1). All resource agencies use newspapers to some extent, mostly for news releases. Table 9.3 shows two other possibilities for using newspapers.

Although newspapers are an indisputably important medium, they should not be relied upon to the exclusion of other media. For example, one of our studies revealed that only 2 percent of the user public in the Selway-Bitterroot Wilderness Area obtained their wilderness-related information from newspapers. Similarly, Rocky Mountain National Park backpackers were not effectively reached by this medium even after a special attempt was made in an experiment (Fazio, 1979). Newspapers also are losing ground in the number of people they reach. One might speculate that in the electronic age people are turning more to media that require less effort to "receive." Whatever the cause, there has been a slow but steady decline in newspaper readership at all age levels over the past two decades. Another limitation is that those people who do read newspapers cover only one-fifth to one-fourth of the editorial content (Cutlip et al., 1985). We stress these problems because so many resource managers believe they are effectively communicating with "the public" simply by putting an article in the newspaper.

Table 9.3.
Use of Newspapers by Resource Agencies to Disseminate Information Through Newsletters and Columns.

Agency	Send Newsletters to News Media (N)	(percent)	Average Frequency To Newspapers (per month)	Have "Regular" Column (N)	(percent)	Average Column Frequency (per month)	Column Authors (Regular Columns Only)		
							Information Staff (N)	Other Agency Personnel (percents)	Free-lancer or Other
State Headquarters									
Fish and Game	27	85	3	27	30	3	8	95	5	0
Forestry	14	14	1	14	21	4	3	30	53	17
Parks and Recreation	10	50	.5	9	0	0	0	0	0	0
Conservation, Lands, Natural Resources	15	33	1.4	15	20	4	3	12	88	0
Federal Units									
Army Corps of Engineers (Divisions)	2	0	0	2	0	0	0	0	0	0
Bureau of Land Management (State offices)	6	50	1	6	0	0	0	0	0	0
Fish and Wildlife Service (Regional offices)	4	25	4	5	40	2.5	2	23	77	0
Forest Service (Supervisor Offices)	81	22	2	80	13	3	10	40	59	1
National Park Service (Superintendent offices)	79	10	1	79	10	2	8	76	3	21

Despite their weaknesses—and *all* media have weaknesses—newspapers are powerful and must be given serious attention by anyone concerned with developing good public relations. Press personnel are an important public that should be won over to the agency side of natural resource management. Newspaper people can be influential friends or formidable enemies when they agree or disagree on an issue. As an unknown writer once stated, "newspapers comfort the unduly afflicted and afflict the unduly comforted."

Developing a Good Working Relationship

One question that immediately arises is who in a natural resource agency should write for newspapers? Should the agency personnel write the newspaper article or story themselves, or should this be done by an employee of the newspaper? A categorical answer cannot be given. Individuals and situations vary. Usually, if it is a "hot" news story—something very important and just happening—news personnel prefer to cover the event themselves. In this case, resource personnel need only to alert local media and provide the requested information. Examples might be a serious accident, fire, dispute, or the visit of a top ranking official. Newspaper articles that are strictly of a publicity nature will usually need to be written by agency personnel and submitted to the press. Either way, good press relations are necessary to avoid being on the outs with the representatives of this important medium.

Good relations with the press do not happen by accident any more than they do with other publics. Here are some guidelines that should help develop a good working relationship:

1. *Know your editors. Before* news happens, stop in and get acquainted. Take a labeled file of background information on your agency, and be sure you leave your name and phone number so the editor will consider you a "contact" when he needs information. Do *not* visit prior to deadlines; and *do* keep your visit brief. You might also invite the editor and other key personnel to a special event or show-me trip.

2. *Treat all newspapers in your area equally.* When submitting news, be sure all receive it simultaneously. If you have both morning and evening newspapers, alternate release times of important information so one time the morning paper will be able to carry it first; the next time, the evening paper will have that opportunity.

3. For each newspaper with which you should work, *make a list of its personnel and their phone numbers* (the editor can help you with this). Be sure to include:

Managing Editor   Farm Editor
City Editor   Outdoor Editor
Regional/State Editor   Columnists/Special Writers
Feature Editor

Also list any local correspondents who may be assigned to regularly cover your agency.

4. *Find out who local "stringers" or correspondents are for statewide or regional newspapers* and treat them as you would the locally-based media. Also find out how to submit copy to wire services in your area. Local media personnel can help you, or write to:

Associated Press, 50 Rockefeller Plaza, New York 10020
Reuters, 1212 Avenue of the Americas, New York 10036
United Press International, 220 E. 42nd St., New York 10017

5. *Know and religiously respect deadlines* if you are asked to submit information. If you hope to get a release in a specific edition, use the following guidelines:

Afternoon papers —File before 10 a.m.; noon at latest
Morning papers   —File before 3 p.m. if possible
Sunday papers   —File by noon Friday, or earlier
Weeklies   —As early in the week as possible

6. *Cooperate fully and cheerfully* in helping media personnel obtain whatever information is requested (within legal bounds, of course).
7. *Never ask to have a news article suppressed.* And don't tell things to an editor or reporter prefaced by "This is off the record. . . ." It is their livelihood with which you are dealing.
8. *Do not ask to review copy* before it is printed.
9. *Be honest, accurate and candid, always.*
10. *Remember to say "thank you"* and be complimentary when the press does a good job for you.

One final word of advice. Most editors are fair and will try to correct inaccuracies when called to their attention. However, the relationship between a source of information and the medium is not equal and two-way. An editor's judgment is absolute regarding what is used, when, and in what form. By all means point out inaccuracies, but don't quibble over word changes made in copy you submit or if something is not used. Above all, don't sulk and refuse to work with a particular newspaper when things go wrong. Editors and reporters are human, so try again. Work hard to create understanding and a good relationship *before* the next news story breaks, or the next publicity piece is submitted.

Writing a News Story

Basically, there are two kinds of newspaper articles. First is the feature story, which is similar to a magazine article and requires a different style than does the second kind, the news story. Although correlation with current happenings is necessary, the feature is not a news story as such and the urgency of timeliness is not present. This type of writing is closely related to magazine writing and is discussed in that section.

In the news story, the first thing to decide is—Is it really *news?* True news is a perishable commodity; old news is history. If your story is timely and of consequence to the readers of a particular newspaper, its chances of being used are good. As a test for news value, your article should meet all or most of the following criteria:

√**Timely**—An event that has just happened or is about to happen. Or, it may have a close tie-in to other events of current interest. An example of the latter would be an item on Christmas tree cutting in mid-December.

√**Human Interest**—(See paragraph below)

√**Proximity**—It should usually relate to the community served by the newspaper at which you are aiming.

√**Prominence**—Are well-known people involved? For example, a minor injury to an "important" person can be a front page story.

√**Consequence**—Something of importance to the readers. Closing a sawmill has consequence for readers of a small town paper, whereas this story usually would not be of consequence to readers of the *Wall Street Journal.*

Human interest is the element of a news story (or feature article) that will attract the attention of readers. Editors are attuned to the interests of their readers, so it is crucial to include the human interest angle. This might be:

an appeal	sex
animals	suspense
conflict	sympathy
old age or youth	unusualness
progress	

On the basis of newsworthiness and human interest, opportunities abound for news articles in the natural resource professions. Even something as generally unappealing as the issuance of an environmental impact statement or the planning of a public involvement session can be made into news by highlighting some feature from the above list. Most activities, however, require little contrivance to make a good news story.

Opinions and conclusions have no place in a news story. They belong in the feature, the editorial column or letters to the editor. An exception might be when the opinion of an expert or high official *is* the news or part of it. Usually, however, news must be *factual,* with most articles including the famous five W's and an H:

$\sqrt{}$*Who*—The person, group, or organization that is the subject of the story. Be accurate with titles and names.

$\sqrt{}$*What*—What happened or is going to happen?

$\sqrt{}$*Where*—Do not assume readers know where the Diamond Mountain livestock exclosure is located, or how to get to the park headquarters. Always orient the reader to the event's location.

$\sqrt{}$*When*—Self-explanatory and essential, but sometimes left out!

$\sqrt{}$*Why*—This is an elaboration on the what and can sometimes be omitted. Sometimes, however, it is an opportunity to interpret the events and meet some of the agency's public relations objectives.

$\sqrt{}$*How*—How it all came about.

News stories usually adhere to a highly structured, standardized format. This is shown as the inverted pyramid in Figure 9.2. The lead is the first paragraph and should feature whichever of the W's and H are most important to that story. After that, increasingly less important material is presented. There are two good reasons why this format should be followed. One is that most editors constantly face the problem of having more editorial content than space to print it. Therefore, many stories get "chopped." If the least important copy is consistently in the last paragraphs, it makes the job easier, faster, and there is less chance of deleting something essential. The other reason also relates to precious time, but in this case the reader's. Newspaper readers quickly scan headlines, then read only the first paragraph or two of most stories. They expect the "meat" of the article to be there, and will read further only if very interested. This, of course, points out the importance of taking care to make the lead not only complete but also compelling. Leads in feature articles are handled differently.

The less work an editor needs to do on an article, the greater its chances of being published. Therefore, all news items submitted should be typed in a way that will be convenient to that person. The life or death of the article may depend on it. A well-designed news release is illustrated in

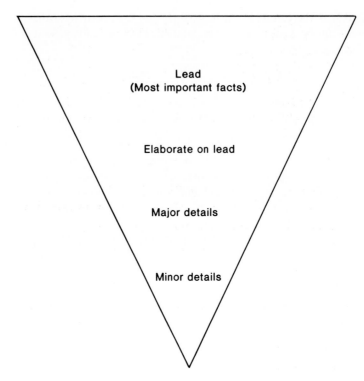

Figure 9.2. Diagram of a news story structure. The purpose of this structure is to aid both the editor and readers.

Figure 9.3. Its important format features are the same as for feature articles and are discussed in the next section. The only major difference is length. The news story should be short, and paragraphs should also be short—20 to 60 words. Accuracy, brevity, and clarity might be thought of as the ABC's of good news writing.

News Photos

Illustrations aid a newspaper story. They make the article more interesting and understandable, and good quality illustrations will be welcomed by the editor. Photographs should be at least 5 by 7 inches (and preferably 8 × 10) with a glossy finish. If a newspaper uses color pictures, original transparencies are preferred. Quality is essential as photographs lose definition in newspaper printing. Composition is also important because most photographs will be reduced in size or cropped to fit a one or two column cut. Also, editors are trained to know good composition, and many will not settle for less.

Photographs should depict their own story and must be able to "stand alone" or be nearly self-explanatory. A caption should be typed on a piece of paper and taped lightly to the photo. If there are people in the picture, written clearance for its use is a good idea but not usually necessary

UTAH

BLM
BUREAU OF LAND MANAGEMENT

FOR RELEASE IMMEDIATELY
CONTACT   JIM KENNA
(801) 637-4584

News Release

UNITED STATES DEPARTMENT OF THE INTERIOR
Moab District Office, 82 East Dogwood, P. O. Box 970, Moab, Utah

BLM CONDUCTING WOOD CUTTING TOUR

Commercial woodcutters interested in purchasing green pinyon and juniper firewood are invited to participate in a tour scheduled for May 21, according to Leon Berggren, Price River Resource Area Manager for the Bureau of Land Management.

BLM will be conducting the tour for prospective bidders of approximately 183 cords of fuelwood located on Cottonwood Ridge in Carbon County, approximately 70 miles northwest of Price. The tour will leave the Price BLM office, 900 North 700 East, at 8 a.m. on May 21. The tour is recommended to bidders because the sale will be based on field inventory. Inventory amounts range from 15 to 69 cords, in 5 separate areas ranging from 1.4 acres to 4.8 acres.

If demand is present, additional cutting units will be made available. For more information about the tour and bidding process, or stipulations, contact BLM's Price River Resource Area Office at (801) 637-4584.

Figure 9.3. Example of a well-designed press release.

if it is used for news rather than profit. Names of people are indicated in the order of first, middle and last name, and the people should be identified from left to right. Pictures with more than six people should be avoided because identification becomes cumbersome. People holding dead fish, pointing, or smiling gamely as they are handed a check should also be avoided, as they are just too trite. Otherwise, the personal flavor introduced by pictures of people involved in any story is an asset. Photographs usually will not be returned, as they will be marked up with editorial instructions.

Figure 9.4. A news photo should tell its own story with a minimum of explanation. (Photo by J. R. Fazio.)

Additional Do's and Don'ts

Before submitting a news article, it is good practice to check with superiors and any unit of the agency involved in the story. It certainly does nothing for internal relations to release a story on a subject someone else planned to cover at a later date. This is especially true of research projects. Many researchers do not wish to have publicity until they have enough results to make defensible conclusions. Release of such stories should be at the researcher's discretion.

A good way to keep all media continually informed of happenings in the agency is to include editors and key reporters on the mailing list to receive newsletters (Table 9.3). The ideal is a separate newsletter for external publics, including a notation that stories and photos are available on any item in the newsletter simply by contacting _____ . When a newsletter is used for this purpose, it should have a neat, colorful, attractive title with the agency's logo always present. Subheads should be used to permit rapid scanning by the potential users.

Keep a file or scrapbook of clippings as a historical record and for future reference. Circulate clippings to everyone in the agency who was involved or should know about the publicity. However, *purchase* newspapers for this purpose, don't ask for free copies.

Finally, get acquainted with newspaper people. Theirs is an exciting world, and our ability to use this segment of the print media will be far greater if we gain a better understanding of it.

Letters To The Editor

The very mention of "letters to the editor" calls forth an array of emotions. Perhaps it is snickers as we recall some of the "dumb" things we have seen in that section of the newspaper (or magazine). Perhaps if you are a resource manager, a flush of anger comes forth as you recall being stung by an irate citizen who took up the pen to make public unfavorable views on your ability! One thing is certain, the letters section is one of the best-read sections of a newspaper. In fact, it is a cherished part that readers look upon as their very own. Kalman Seigel (1972) of the

New York Times called it ". . . the reader's lance as he tilts with City Hall . . . his passport to a community of interest with his fellow man or an arena of controversy in which he can test his thinking with those who differ. It is a town meeting in print, his approach to a purer form of participatory democracy."

The letter section can have important uses in public relations work. For one, it is a good way to monitor public opinion. Not all letters are published (the *New York Times* has space for only about 7 percent of those received), and they cannot be viewed as a *sample*. But the letters reveal a *range* of prevalent opinions on an issue and—importantly—the *reasons* for those opinions. This can be helpful in planning future tactics and informational programs. Monitoring letters in small communities or rural areas also can help identify individuals who are outspoken. This can help in developing mailing lists or seeking out those you believe should be included in public involvement efforts.

Since the letter section is a two-way street, it is also appropriate for an official to respond to inaccurate or unfair charges. This should be done with discretion and never in anger, as the intent should be clarification, not revenge. It should not provide an opening for additional charges. One must weigh the opportunity to respond against the opportunity to select from among the other tools of public relations.

Particularly in small communities, and if not over-used, the letter section of a newspaper can sometimes provide an excellent channel for communicating other types of information. For example, more people would read an announcement (written as a letter to the editor and in the form of an invitation) about an open house at the ranger station or fish hatchery than if it were printed as a news item. Similarly, public involvement meetings or requests for letters would certainly attract more attention as a letter than as a news article. Countering rumors and issuing a "thank you" to the community, a merchant, or some other individual are among the other uses that occasionally can be made of the letter section.

To submit a letter to the editor, Lloyd Sveen, executive editor of the Fargo, North Dakota *Forum* has offered the following suggestions:

1. Keep it short
2. Stick to the point
3. Don't repeat yourself
4. If expressing an opinion, use reasoned logic, not rambling attacks
5. Don't demand publication on a certain day
6. Be accurate in content, grammar and spelling
7. Submit the letter typed, double spaced and on one side of a page only
8. Expect that it may receive some editing like any other article

The Outdoor Column

One of the most rewarding uses of a newspaper is to write a regular column. Those who use this method usually write weekly or twice-a-month columns, sometimes as an official responsibility and sometimes on a freelance basis (Table 9.3).

The advantages are that good columns, like good comic strips, build a devoted readership. People begin to look forward to reading what you write and will read it regularly. And you know that what you write will be used. There is not the anxiety and risk of wasted time that goes with sending in an occasional article or news item, then waiting and hoping it appears. With an accepted column, you can pick your subjects, write with confidence, and know exactly when it will appear.

To start a column, study the papers in your vicinity to see if they already have an outdoor columnist. If not:

1. Decide on a general theme or approach. These include: traditional hunting and fishing; all outdoor sports; nature; things to do, places to go; environmental issues; resource management; agency/company events; or some combination of these.
2. Write 2 or 3 sample columns, giving them your best effort both in content (interesting, helpful, unusual) and format (clearly typed, grammatically correct).
3. Create a title ("Outdoor World," "Woodland Wanderings," "Forest Echoes," "Outdoors in Latah County").
4. If an artist is available, have a distinctive (but small) column heading or logo made in a form easily used by the target newspaper.
5. Make an appointment and visit the managing editor. Propose your idea and offer your samples. If done on a freelance basis, be prepared to accept or reject the amount of pay if offered, which is usually on a per-column-inch basis.

Once accepted, list possible topics for several weeks or months in advance, taking advantage of holidays or other timely topics. Don't miss deadlines. Keep a few columns on hand for weeks you will be away or get too busy to produce the column. Stay ahead or the job will become a nuisance instead of a pleasure, and keep your subjects interesting, informative and varied.

MAGAZINES

Magazines present a channel of communication for natural resource managers equally as impressive as newspapers, if not as timely. There currently are over 10,000 major magazines circulating in the United States and seven out of every 10 people over 15 years old read magazines regularly. Conservation organizations have long been part of the magazine trade and are leaders in quality. *Audubon, American Forests* and *Living Wilderness* are diverse examples that rank among the best. These three alone have approximately one-half million subscribers. *National Wildlife,* with over three and one-half million subscribers, has a companion magazine specifically for young people (*Ranger Rick*) and *International Wildlife* for worldwide concerns. These are but a few from the private press that reach the well-educated, often influential or wealthy conservationists. Each has its own "personality," carefully preserved by editorial policy, consistent quality, and carefully considered standardization of size, format, type style and other features we sometimes take for granted.

Another important group of magazines are those published by state fish, game or conservation departments (Figure 9.5). Nearly all states produce some kind of conservation magazine, with the average annual subscription cost being held to an affordable $5.00. More data on this major communications channel are presented in Table 9.4. These magazines, too, each have a personality. Some, like *Pennsylvania Game News* are strongly oriented to hunting. Others, like *The New York Conservationist* are more general in coverage, ranging from mushroom identification to air pollution control. All are grounded in concern for environmental quality and an understanding of ecological principles.

Magazines present one of the most easily identified channels for reaching specific publics. There are trade journals for everyone from tug boat operators to loggers, and Christmas tree growers to sawmill operators. Dozens of hobby and recreation magazines reach pet owners, hang gliders, joggers, backpackers and climbers. Pilots read magazines like *Plane and Pilot, Private Pilot,* and *Flying;* young western homemakers read *Sunset;* and farmers are reached by no less than 522 magazines that can be classified by state, region or crop. A large number of people in *any* imaginable public can be reached with news, features or advertising carefully geared to publications serving that audience. In Ohio, for example, it was found that the average sportsman received the major amount of his conservation information from outdoor magazines (Belak, 1972). Nationwide, more than 5 million hunters and fishers receive much of their information about nat-

Figure 9.5. Attractive state-sponsored conservation magazines reach millions of readers each month.

Table 9.4.
Publication Frequency of State-Sponsored Conservation Magazines in the United States.[1]

Agency	Number of Respondents	Publish a Public Magazine (Percent)	Annual Frequency					
			Twice/ Year	Quarterly	Every Other Month	Monthly	Other	No Response
			—Percents					
Fish and Game	26	92	0	13	54	29	4	0
Forestry	14	26	0	60	20	20	0	0
Parks and Recreation	10	70	0	43	0	29	14	14
Conservation, Lands, Natural Resources	15	67	10	20	40	20	10	0

1. From an unpublished nationwide survey of natural resource agencies conducted in 1985 by J. Fazio.

ural resources from the Big Three—*Field and Stream, Outdoor Life* and *Sports Afield.* Sometimes magazines are the *only* practical way to reach certain publics; other times they offer one of several techniques in a saturation campaign designed to make certain that information reaches its target.

Several references are available at larger libraries to help free lance writers find outlets for their work. These same references can yield valuable, up-to-date information for use in public relations work. They provide such data as the name of magazines by subject (e.g., Mining, Blacks, Juveniles, Artists, In-flight magazines, Travel Agents), the kind of readers they serve, circulation figures, the kind of material they accept for publication (including style, format, length, acceptance of photos, etc.) and even how much they pay for articles and illustrations. Three of these references are:

> *Literary Market Place* (1180 Avenue of the Americas, New York 10036)
> *Directory of Publication Opportunities in Journals and Periodicals* (Marquis Academic Media, 200 E. Ohio St., Chicago 60611)
> *Writers Market* (Writer's Digest Books, 9933 Alliance Rd., Cincinnati, Ohio 45242)

Writing the Feature Article

After you identify informational needs and target publics in a public relations campaign, magazines can be listed that have the potential of reaching the people in whom you are interested. The next challenge is to produce something the editors of the magazines will use.

If it is advertising copy, no problem. If it is a well done PSA or a news item, it also has a good chance of being used. However, one of the most effective uses of a magazine is through publication of a feature article. And it is here that natural resource professionals consistently pass by golden opportunities. For example, despite some improvement in recent years, most stories in the popular outdoor press are the "How I got a Full Bag Limit" (or the biggest buck), or the "Vicious Killer Meets Death" variety. In comparison, how many do you see about good sportsmanship, low impact camping, sound resource management, or the results of research projects? This problem is not entirely the fault of the publishers. Some blame falls on natural resource managers for not writing the stories. In part, the problem is also in not making these efforts so readable that editors will use them and people will read, understand and be impressed by them. The written conservation story and associated problems must be told so that they come alive, stir feelings, change opinions and result in action. Poor writing is wasted effort; good writing can take natural resource management into the homes and minds of millions.

A magazine article can be considered about the same as a feature story in a newspaper. However, it is quite different from the *news* story. Instead of key information being in the first one or two paragraphs as in a news story, the reader is taken along a gradual, building-up process to the "meat" of the article, then to the climax and finally to a definite end of the article. This process is diagrammed in Figure 9.6 and can be compared with the news story in Figure 9.2.

Plan Your Approach

One of the first steps toward successful publication is to study the magazine in which you hope to publish. Read some of the articles and see what topics have been covered in the past year or two. What is the length of most of the articles? What slant seems to be used most? That is, do they use a "how-to" approach often, or humor? What level of language is used? What kind of illustrations can be included?

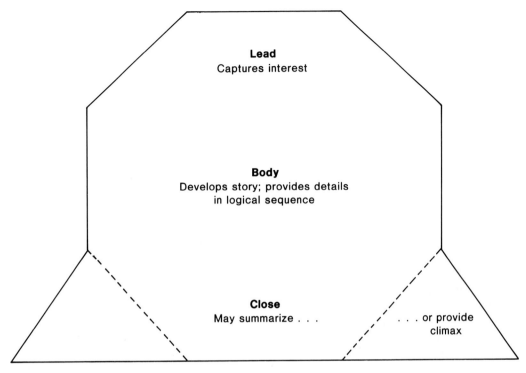

Figure 9.6. Diagram of a feature article.

Next, consider the *kind* of article you want to write that will fit best into the target publication and at the same time meet your objectives. Here are some rhetorical forms that should be considered:

The *narration* is simply telling a story in a straight-forward manner, usually in chronological sequence. The "me and Joe" and similar first and second person stories often are all narrative, although narration frequently includes parts of other forms, such as description or dialogue.

Exposition is to explain something in terms of reason. A story on "How to Survive in the Desert" would probably be presented in exposition form.

Description or Illustration also explains, but in terms of the senses. "Alaska—Land of Contrasts" suggests a descriptive form. Description lacks "forward movement" and can easily become boring if not done well or mixed with other forms.

Dialogue, on the other hand, is a fast-paced form. However, when characters speak it must "sound" natural. The conversations should also have purpose, such as to help characterize the speaker, advance the story and/or inform the reader about something he should know.

Dramatic Action may combine other forms but with the attempt to create scenes and situations that are suspenseful and exciting. This is often a good way to begin a story, and it is the fastest moving kind of story.

Introspection delves into the mind of the main character. The reader and author think with the character, such as might be done in an article on arsonists written for law enforcement officers. This technique is excellent for a change of pace and is much used by the fiction writer.

Analysis is an excellent form for creating opinion change. It is a dissection of the issue or case in point and can easily be structured to subtly persuade. Or, this form can be used to simply dissect a situation in an objective way to bring about better understanding.

Argument is a less subtle attempt to influence opinion or action and may use any of the techniques discussed earlier in the section on persuasive communication.

Comparison and Contrast can be used to help describe, analyze or persuade. "New York's Gateway—New Concept in National Parks" would be a natural for using comparison and contrasts.

Rhetorical form will help determine how to proceed, but regardless of the one or combination of forms selected, many experienced writers next make an outline. This is a working tool, so it need not be anything fancier than notes on a scratch pad. It can also be changed as the writing proceeds. It is simply a way to organize your thoughts in a logical sequence, making sure your objectives will be met and that you will not forget important points. It can be done similar to the outline described for the oral presentation (Chapter 8), or in any way that is helpful. However, it should always include at least three parts—the lead, body and close.

Titles and Leads

Titles and leads have the essential function of attracting and holding the attention of readers. Frequently this is called "hooking" the reader. Developing a good title and lead is often the most difficult part of writing a feature article. However, it is well worth considerable time and thought, because printing a story with a poor title or lead is like seeing the proverbial horse led to water then refusing to drink.

There are at least eight kinds of titles and seven similar kinds of leads. They may or may not be used in the same article, or with the article's rhetorical form of the same name. That is, a descriptive article does not have to have a descriptive title; it could just as well be headed by a startling statement or a question. Having a list of the kinds of titles and leads can be helpful in getting started, so for that reason these are presented below along with examples and brief explanations:

Summary   "Maryland's Indians—Top Conservationists"
                     "Publications *Can* Be Effective"

The main idea or conclusion is presented in the title.

Narrative   "How to Wax Skis"
                     "The Town Rescued the Railroad"

Title reflects a story that follows the narrative form, i.e., a reciting of details, usually in chronological sequence.

Descriptive   "The Forest Products Lab in Madison"
                     "Orlando—Refuge for the Cold Blooded"

Title reflects the descriptive content of the article.

Startling statement "She Shaved the Legs of Spiders"
                     "They Are Trying to Steal Your Land"

These titles are statements that are an all out attempt to attract attention and interest by startling readers who are skimming titles.

Quotation   "We'll Rough It"
                        "I Ate Lizards To Survive"

Usually intended to have the effect of a startling statement, but using a direct quote from the article.

Question   "Can Our Forests Produce A Sustained Crop?"
                        "Is Wilderness Being Loved to Death?"

Asks a question that will pique the curiosity of the target public.

Direct address   "Eastern Dude—You Have A Stake in Western Land"
                        "Mr. Farmer, Erosion Costs You Money"

The target public is addressed in the title.

Alliteration   "Purple Perch With Pink Polka Dots"
                        "Rape of Our Rivers"

Main words in the title begin with the same letters of the alphabet. Alliterations have a pleasing, catchy effect. Or, like the words "rape" and "river," the title juxtapositions two words beginning with the same letter but designed to have shock value.

Titles must not only be catchy, but short. A maximum of 10 words is suggested, but three or four words often make excellent titles. The exception is the technical or scientific article where the title must tell what the article is about. The reading audience, for the most part, will be those already interested in the content for professional reasons. Therefore, catchy titles are not necessary or desirable for technical publications.

If a title succeeds the reader will be tempted into the opening, or *lead paragraphs*. Now the job of "hooking" must be completed. Keeping these important paragraphs short and crisp, you must make the reader want more. There are several ways to do this and, again, a list of examples may be helpful. The categories are almost the same as those used for titles and include:

Summary—"If the proposed irrigation of desert lands continues as planned, an ecological chain of events will occur that spells disaster for birds of prey."

Narrative—"It was a misty November day when my aide and I set out on what was to be the most memorable timber cruise of my career."

Descriptive—"Like a rushing mountain stream suddenly frozen for eternity, the Mendenhall Glacier winds down out of the jagged peaks to the sea."

Startling statement—"Nobody, as far as I have been able to ascertain, seriously wants to quick-freeze an elephant."

Quotation—"We had better stop fooling ourselves and admit that the life-support systems of this planet are in jeopardy," warned a leading scientist from the SUNY College of Environmental Science and Forestry.

Questions—"Is it possible to provide wood for our growing nation and at the same time have adequate areas of wilderness?"

Direct address—"Planner, you had better get acquainted with your boss—all 150,000 of them!"

Contrast—"Twenty years ago I watched racoons frolic by that creek. Today it flows through a concrete straitjacket so people can crowd into fast food joints that line the highway." (Other extremes can be highlighted, such as tragedy with comedy, age with youth, past with present, hopes with failures, etc.)

The Body

The body of the article develops the story by presenting the details in a logical, carefully planned sequence. There is no attempt to present the most important details first; it all depends on what works best given the particular topic.

In the body, examples and specific incidents should be used liberally. Student papers are usually full of generalities, whereas the professional carries the reader along by reinforcing each point with a mental illustration. Anecdotes can be used for humor or entertainment and to increase understanding. Action, adventure and controversy also create and hold interest. Vocabulary should be in keeping with the knowledge level of the audience. For example, technical jargon does not belong in a sportsman's magazine. There is no point in the author trying to show how smart he is. The important thing is to put the message across to the reader. Most authorities agree an 8th or 9th grade reading level is about right for the average magazine story. This can easily be checked by having several freshmen in high school read the story and see if it is readily understood.

Several years ago, The National Wildlife Federation hired a children's writer to "bring down" articles in their magazines to the desired level of comprehension. This, and the liberal use of outstanding photography probably accounts for the immense popularity of the Federation's magazines.

The feature article should be designed so it can be scanned by those who are not interested in reading it word for word. This can be done with the help of such tools as headings and subheadings, boldface type, underlining and italics. The use of colors and illustrative materials, such as tables, charts, photographs, cartoons and caricatures or drawings, also help. But, an illustration should be used only if it will attract interest, increase clarity or add to content.

Photo-stories also can be a good way to get your message before a public. These usually are submitted to the publishers as 8 × 10 inch glossy black and white photos, or 35 mm or larger transparencies. Along with carefully worded captions, these tell the complete story. Normally about 6 to 12 photos and less than one page of manuscript make up the photo-story. Quality again is the key to success.

Data and statistics may be necessary in a technical manuscript, but they should be omitted from a popular or semi-popular story unless absolutely necessary to prove a point. People do not like to mull over a mass of figures when reading for pleasure. They simply will not read the story.

Unlike articles for scientific or scholarly journals, most popular articles do not require documentation with references. Credit must be given where necessary, but this should be done directly in the copy. For example, it is usually enough to make a statement such as, "according to Walter Chapman of NL Industries in Tahawus, New York. . . ." Literature citations and footnotes are not used, nor is a bibliography usually necessary.

A popular article should be as personal as possible. People should be able to identify with the story and have their questions answered. Names, places and conversation help. The author must invite reader participation.

To contribute to good public relations, the writer should never forget that he is trying to influence people's thinking and to change or reinforce public opinion. The ultimate goal is to motivate and bring about action by a specific public.

The Close

The close in a news story contains minor details and is dispensable. In a feature article, the close is essential. The extreme case, indicated by a flare in the base of Figure 9.6, is the climax of a suspense format. Short stories by the immortal O. Henry used this technique. It is a difficult form of writing, but when used well it almost guarantees that a reader will not quit until the article has been read in its entirety.

More commonly, the close is used to repeat the key points of the article, ideally in a fresh, memorable way. In some cases, it is also the place to suggest what action the reader should take. For example, is there some place to obtain more information, send a contribution, or express an opinion? Like the title and lead, the close has a *function* and should be put to work in meeting your objectives.

Other Considerations

Writers work in different ways. Some write fast, others slowly. Some rewrite only once, others have to write a story many times. An effective approach for some is after the first few paragraphs are carefully written, the rest of the article is written as rapidly as possible. The author doesn't worry about minor points of grammar, spelling or punctuation. These are corrected in later editing. The important thing is appropriate sequence and getting the facts down in a logical order. Then the manuscript is put away to "cool off." After several days or weeks, final editing and polishing readies the manuscript for publication.

The length of an article must be fitted to the magazine and the subject. This can be done by making a word count in articles that have been published in your target magazine. Conservation magazine stories average 1,000 to 2,000 words or four to eight double-spaced pages. First efforts usually end up too long rather than too short. Too many authors try to touch on several topics with one effort. It is far better to deal fully with one subject than partially with several.

Submitting the Finished Product

If your name is James Michener or Edward Abbey, you can probably submit your article on a brown paper sack and be reasonably confident it will be published. For the rest of us, how the article *looks* when submitted to an editor is almost as important as how it is written. At first glance, the editor will begin forming an opinion about your article. He is the judge who determines whether or not the article will live or die.

Many writers make the first contact even before the article is started. A query is sent to the editor of the publication for which the article is being planned. This query is a letter which gives the idea, length, a summary and other characteristics of the story, such as number of pictures, special angles and illustrations. Often an outline also is sent. Naturally, the query must be the best effort possible because the article may be accepted or rejected on this basis alone.

The editor will give a positive or a negative reply. With a positive reply, the procedure is under way. It is not unethical to query more than one editor, but after an acceptance or expression of interest has been made, the author has an ethical obligation to work only with that editor.

Most magazine editors like to have articles well in advance of the desired publishing date. A minimum of three months is suggested and six months is better. To illustrate, if an article is written about hunting deer during November, it should be in the publisher's hands by early summer. A planning calendar can help to coordinate this timing.

√ SUBMITTING THE FEATURE ARTICLE

_____ Send manuscript flat (not folded) in a large manila envelope, with a light sheet of cardboard for protection. Use two sheets of heavy cardboard when photos are enclosed.

_____ Enclose a self-addressed envelope with correct postage for return of manuscript if not accepted.

_____ Enclose a business style cover letter briefly stating your qualifications and background relative to the article, and in a sentence or two describing content or intent of article. Address it to the individual who is editor, *not* to Dear Editor!

The Manuscript:

_____ Use good quality white bond. *Never* tissue or erasable paper. (The ink smears, edges curl, and it is annoying to editors' eyes when the page is not opaque.)

_____ If computer-printed, separate the sheets and remove perforated edges.

_____ Always type, using double spacing and one side of a page *only.*

_____ Place your name and address in upper left corner of first page; approximate number of words in upper right.

_____ Start first page ⅓ way down with the title in all caps, followed by author's name in upper and lower case.

_____ Use adequate margins—1″ right edge, 1½″–2″ others (Editors write notes in these spaces).

_____ When story continues to next page, write "More" in parentheses at bottom of page centered two spaces below last line.

_____ After the first page, place author's last name and abbreviate title in upper left corner of each page. Example: Miller—Aerial Logging.

_____ Number pages at top right corner or center. Example -10-

_____ At end, place—The End—two spaces below last line.

_____ Hold manuscript together with paper clip.

_____ Submit the original, not a copy. Keep a copy for your files or future use.

Photographs:

_____ Black and white photos should be 8″ × 10″ glossy prints; 5″ × 7″ at minimum.

_____ Captions for photos should be on regular bond and attached lightly to back of photo by rubber cement or narrow edge of tape. Place paper so that it will fold over photo from bottom and, by unfolding, a viewer can see photo and caption at the same time. Do not use paper clips, staples or write on back of photo.

_____ Color transparencies should be in clear plastic envelopes or in boxes.

_____ The numbered slides should have corresponding captions typed on a separate sheet titled "Color Slide Captions". It is suggested that your name be placed on all slides.

When submitting the article, every effort should be made for it to look like a professional product. This means it will be neat, convenient for the editor to work with, and will conform to the traditional standards of the print media. The checklist in the boxed insert provides a guide to meeting these requirements.

If the article is rejected the first time, it can be submitted elsewhere. Or, the approach can be changed, corrections made in response to editorial comments, and it can be sent again to the same editor. Because of space limitations and the great number of articles received by most magazines, rejections are more the rule than the exception. Therefore, keep trying! Ultimately, success will breed success as you perfect your writing ability and learn what editors are looking for in a feature article.

Style Manuals

For the serious writer, style manuals (or stylebooks) are an important tool of the trade. These are compilations of rules followed by a particular magazine, newspaper or publishing organization. For example, a fraction of 100 can be expressed as per cent, percent or %. The style manual used by the target magazine tells you which one to use. These guides are especially important when writing for technical journals where there are highly standardized methods for citing literature, writing footnotes, constructing tables, ad infinitum. Some manuals contain a wealth of other information ranging from proofreader's marks and type faces to details on the Copyright Law.

Most natural resource journals, including *The Journal of Wildlife Management* and *Journal of Forestry,* adhere mainly to the CBE Style Manual published by the Council of Biology Editors and distributed by the American Institute of Biological Sciences (1401 Wilson Blvd., Arlington, VA 22209). Journals in the social sciences usually follow the popular *A Manual of Style,* published for the past 75 years by The University of Chicago Press. Newspapers may have their own manual or use one that has been developed by the Associated Press or United Press International. Especially for the beginning writer, a set of style manuals can be a helpful way to prepare copy that will please that all-important editor.

IN-HOUSE PUBLICATIONS AND EXTERNAL REPORTS

The House Organ

The house organ, also called the house publication, is the internal newspaper or magazine of an organization. Its target is the internal public. In natural resource agencies and the educational institutions that train their future employees, it is often a mimeographed newsletter bordering on the inane. In industry it is big and serious business, with an estimated 66,000 employee publications (Cutlip et al, 1985). Often there are conflicting demands on what the house organ should do. One school of thought is that the house organ should focus on what the employees will enjoy, such as news of their sport teams, families, awards and similar news. The other is that the publication should be a propaganda device telling its readers only what the employer wants them to know. After all, it's company money.

Properly used, the house organ can be an effective public relations tool for communicating with and among the organization's most valuable public. By mixing the serious messages of business with the more enjoyable news of family life, the house organ can help build morale, prevent problems that stem from lack of accurate information, quell rumors, gather support for causes or events, and generally contribute to the welfare of both employer and employee. It is also an excellent opportunity for conducting employee opinion polls, then publishing and discussing the results. Given these important potentials, it follows that it is worth investing money and time to do the job right. Birth announcements take little time, and frequently that is all that is expected of the editor. However, to examine two sides of a controversy, conduct a survey, or to prepare a well-researched article on *why* the agency plans to take a certain stand in an issue—*that* takes time and talent. Therefore, it seems prudent to select qualified employees for the task and to allow them the time and funds to produce a quality house publication.

The house organ should contain all the quality that goes into an external publication. Sloppy writing, poor grammar and misspelled words will create a poor self-image among employees. At least some copies invariably end up in the hands of external publics, so this makes it doubly important to insist on quality.

Frequency depends on the needs of the organization, but once a month would seem the minimum. Whatever the frequency, regular deadlines and publication dates help stimulate interest. People begin to look forward to it and know they can depend on it to get announcements out on time.

To be successful, the house organ must be accepted, read and contributed to by workers and management at all levels. Assigned "reporters" can gather information for each issue, or collection boxes at different locations can be used for gathering contributions. While co-editing a weekly house organ at Cornell University, we found it was helpful to include a structured contribution sheet in each issue. Different sections of that page asked for information on coming events, professional news, family items, humor and opinion. This page also showed the date of next issue and reminded potential contributors where to deposit the form.

With a mix of the bad news along with the good, management policy along with employee opinion, and the fun with the serious, the house organ offers an unparalleled opportunity to build "oneness" within the natural resource organization. The task should not be taken lightly.

Policy Manuals

Policies should be put in writing. The accepted way is to publish and make available a manual containing all policies. Thus, the rules and regulations of the organization are available for all employees to read and to follow. This manual should be considered the "bible" of the organization. It must be up-to-date and pertinent with the purpose of providing employees with a guide to conduct in all matters.

The policy manual should be simple in organization and must not confuse the employee or create "red tape." A table of contents is necessary with subjects grouped into definite categories. This publication, or a summary of it, is another vehicle to welcome a new employee to the agency. It should be accompanied by a letter from the supervisor or director. The organization structure and history can be given on the first one or two pages. Suggested inclusions, besides policies on specific issues, include employee benefits, working conditions and employee responsibilities. A loose leaf manual offers the opportunity to keep the publication current by adding or subtracting pages as policies change or new ones are added.

All characteristics of good writing are as important here as elsewhere. The material should be short and to the point. Symbols and other illustrations break up the monotony. Art, headings and subheadings aid in rapidly scanning a section or locating a part. The material must be readable and understandable or the whole reason for a policy manual is lost.

Annual Reports

The annual report is both an internal and an external publication, a fact that should make it exceedingly important from the public relations standpoint. Unfortunately, too many agencies consider the annual report a necessary evil instead of an important source of information. It usually ends up dry as the desert, but it shouldn't. This is one publication in which the lay person expects data and statistics; therefore, it offers an opportunity to make such matters known and available. Items such as the financial situation of the agency, problems, personnel changes, summaries of jobs, inventories and predictions can be included. But, it all should be written in an interesting and attractive way. The annual report offers the organization a chance to publicize its expertise, and it should be used to the fullest.

Each annual report should have a keynote issue or theme. This is changed from year to year. Natural resource examples might include an accelerated research program, a particular phase of management, history of the organization, the increasing number of users, or access problems.

As in any other publication for public consumption, the key prerequisites are accuracy, simplicity, attractiveness and brevity. The report should be highly illustrated and written at the high school level of readability. Perhaps half of the content can relate to the year's theme, with the remainder used to describe the general state of the organization, including accomplishments, desires and justifiable budgets. If it is done well, the annual report can serve as an historical record, a working tool and one more means of fostering good internal and external public relations.

Research Reports

Many natural resource managers find themselves in positions involving research, whether its social or biological in nature, and most public relations specialists at one time or another find themselves working with researchers. For these reasons, reporting needs to be addressed.

Reports without purpose are better left unwritten. However, reports *with* a purpose can be an effective tool for public relations in several ways. We contend that no research project is complete until the results have been made available in at *least* three ways. One is for other researchers working on the same or similar problems. This is accomplished through scientific journals, experiment station reports and papers presented at technical meetings. Unfortunately, this is where many studies end. The reason for this may be found in communication theory. People tend to communicate with like others. Therefore, social scientists tend to want to communicate primarily with other social scientists, and biologists with like-minded biologists. The other reason is the reward system. In universities, especially, more weight is given to consideration for promotions and raises when a faculty member has published research results in a prestigious scientific journal.

The second obligation is to extend findings to the managers or other people in the field who can use them. From the word *extend* comes the term *extension,* which is the special communication function of "technology transfer", or making new information available to those who can use it. In land grant institutions, Cooperative Extension usually serves this function. But in any organization and for every scientist it is an obligation of no small importance. Failure to meet this obligation is resulting in resentment and poor pubic relations with those who fund research or cooperate in other ways. An instance is recalled when a Forest Service district ranger was approached for his cooperation in a study of recreationists. It took considerable convincing on the part of the young researcher because several other studies had been conducted in the area and not once did the ranger receive the results.

The third level of report is for interested individuals among the general public or specific user publics. These are the taxpayers, and if they know the merits of a study, they are much less likely to scoff at it when they see it on *Sixty Minutes* or learn of its being given recognition like Senator Proxmire's "Golden Fleece Award." It would also help show that college professors do more than teach and take long vacations, and that the Forest Service, National Park Service, fish and game departments, and other federal and state agencies have more dimensions than commonly believed. Even in the forest industries, it is important to continually share research findings with forest users and the general public so that they know the advertising they see is not simply corporate propaganda. Adequate reporting contributes to good public relations.

BROCHURES AND PAMPHLETS

Ah, the brochure! To many natural resource managers, this *is* public relations. To many it is the panacea for communication with external publics. Actually, it is neither.

Despite enormous popularity with managers, and *sometimes* with the public, every natural resource agency has a closet, garage or storage room someplace piled high with brochures that never did their job. We have seen some—especially on visitor safety—that sit for weeks in an information rack or on a counter without being touched. Others, like those in our experiment at Rocky Mountain National Park, may be thrust into the hands of visitors but are either not read or have no measurable effect on the reader's knowledge of the subject (Fazio, 1979).

The brochure, or pamphlet, should be viewed as just one more channel for reaching a specific public under specific circumstances more efficiently and effectively than any other way. If it does not do that, it should not be used. Following are some of the many uses of brochures, and some observations that may be useful in planning their use in the future.

Public Education. In 1962 Gilbert reported that 36 state conservation agencies published an average of 14 "educational" pamphlets or brochures each year. A check on this in a 1985 survey shows the figure to now be 17 for state fish and game departments. Among 231 state, federal and Canadian agency units responding to our survey, the annual average is 13 titles. Generalizing from our data, it appears that over 4,000 brochures related to natural resources are aimed at citizens each year.

Most of the brochures produced are truly "educational," with little intent for them to directly influence public opinion. With topics ranging from understanding forest planning processes to how game should be dressed in the field, education is probably the greatest use of brochures. Unfortunately, there is little testing of this channel for effectiveness; and the number distributed is almost meaningless except for determining costs.

Safety. Visitor safety is of particular concern to park and recreation managers. In many areas, all incoming visitors receive a brochure about the hazards of bears, traffic, snakes, theft, etc. It is probable that the great majority of these publications are not read. Recreationists, especially young ones, are more interested in having a good time than reading unpleasant warnings. Therefore, to increase effectiveness the messages must be partially disguised in material that indeed will be *fun* to read. One of the best examples of this approach was an Andy Capp comic book the National Park Service distributed several years ago. It was packed with safety messages illustrated by the misadventures of Andy. *Andy Goes to the Parks* was so popular many parks had trouble keeping it in supply! In fact, according to a Park Service official, it died from success— the printing costs became more than the Park Service could afford.

Interpretive Trail Guides. A comparison by Sharpe (1982) showed an advantage of the leaflet and marker medium over signs and audio techniques. However, research indicates the leaflet method is least *effective*. In addition, it has been our experience that more often than not the supply of leaflets is allowed to become exhausted, thereby reducing the trail's interpretive and public relations value to zero. Nevertheless, when kept in supply and written in an interesting, brief and helpful manner, these leaflets can often reach large numbers of people, especially considering their souvenir potential. A good image of the providing agency can be presented in a format that will be retained.

Event Publicity. Our studies of annual continuing education courses consistently show that brochures are the most effective means of recruiting participants. The reason is probably less the brochure *per se* than the fact that the announcement is mailed directly to a well-defined target audience. Regardless, the method seems superior to other media for bringing people together at a conference, workshop or similar gathering.

Activity Information. Most land management agencies are making greater efforts to help people obtain satisfactory recreational experiences. Managers may find that brochures can be a help in this, especially by following the example of the Sawtooth National Recreation Area (Figure 9.7). For each recreation activity there is an easily identified brochure on the literature rack. A person interested in mountain climbing picks up that brochure; another who wants to snowmobile receives a brochure devoted to that topic. Using this approach, more information can be provided, and the chances are enhanced that recipients will be interested enough to read it.

Wilderness Education. For almost three decades wilderness managers have recognized a need to influence their user publics to protect the quality of wilderness resources. This effort has included promoting low impact camping. Various ways have been tried to accomplish this, with brochures and literature sometimes being less than successful (Fazio, 1979). Finally, in 1979 Jim Bradley and others of the Nez Perce National Forest developed a booklet that may have all the elements necessary to be effective (Figure 9.7). It contains the essentials on ethics and low impact practices, but they are cleverly sandwiched between cartoons and illustrated copy on the area's history and folklore, plant and animal life, bird lists, first aid instructions, survival tips, and other information just about any wilderness user would *want*.

Maps. Maps are a kind of brochure, and a kind that most current and future outdoor recreationists *want*. In recent years some agencies have turned their maps into colorful, pictorial masterpieces. One sometimes wonders if there is any objective behind the design other than an outlet for the creative expression of some graphic artist. It would seem that in addition to an accurate and useful map, there would be considerable advantage in selecting no more than six or seven key messages important to agency objectives and including *those* as the copy and illustrations on the map's reverse side. This may have the additional advantage of keeping production costs low enough that distribution of the maps can be free to the public. Charging a fee only reduces dissemination of information to the very people who perhaps need it most.

Checklists. Wildlife refuges sometimes distribute checklists of birds and mammals. For one segment of the visiting public these represent an excellent communication channel. Messages serving public relations objectives should be included someplace on the checklist, but care should be taken to tailor the message to the relatively knowledgeable amateur naturalist public these serve.

Employee Information. Many brochures are designed to impart information to employees. This is sometimes the best method to assure complete coverage and with insured accuracy. "How-to" information, a new policy, background on an issue or just about any other information may be disseminated. For complete dissemination, the brochure may be mailed to each person's home, or inserted with the paycheck. For distribution to selected sub-publics, they can be handed out by a supervisor. Unfortunately, these brochures are often "dry" and read only by the most devoted workers. The one illustrated in Figure 9.7 takes a different approach. In a crisp, modernistic and entertaining style, *Visitor Sense* was developed by the California Region of the USDA Forest Service. Content is *not* sacrificed for the sake of style or brevity. Rather, only the key points are presented and the format almost guarantees that it will be read by a large percentage of the target public.

Figure 9.7. (Top) Different brochures designed for specific publics and which focus on specific topics. This is a better approach than trying to cover too many topics. (Bottom) Modernistic style combining humor with points of important information. This encourages reading and results in effective communication.

Producing the Brochure

Brochure production is the job of an expert, usually a graphic artist. However, ideas must originate with the natural resource manager, public relations specialist or other person who has a communication problem the brochure may be able to solve. The more accurately this person can communicate his ideas to the artist (or printer when no graphic specialist is available), the greater the chances that the final product will be what was wanted.

For best results, the originator of the idea should do two things. First, set objectives for the brochure and prepare the *copy* needed to meet those objectives (See Chapter 4). The copy should carefully follow the principles of simplicity and human interest. Next, you can either tell the artist to use complete license in designing the brochure, or you can provide a *rough* along with the copy

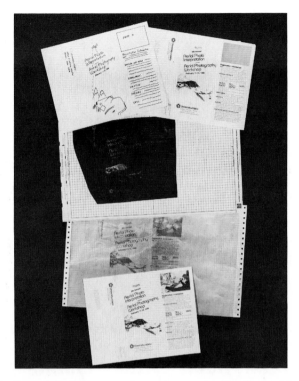

Figure 9.8. From top, left, a rough, pasteup, negative for making an offset plate, the offset plate, and the finished product.

sheets. If you give the artist license, be prepared to accept whatever results. This can sometimes be the best route, but it can also be risky, disappointing and expensive. With a rough of the planned publication, you communicate your ideas to the specialist and can request that they be developed into the finished brochure.

Figure 9.8 illustrates a rough. It should be a sheet of paper cut and folded exactly as you envision the brochure. Headings should be hand lettered or sketched to approximate size. Blocks are drawn to indicate the location of photos, art work and copy. Each block can be labeled "A, B, C," etc. to correspond with the illustration or typewritten copy submitted separately.

Whether you ask a graphic artist to do the entire job, or submit a rough yourself, be prepared to answer questions about the following elements of brochure preparation.

Type—Let It Help

Typography—the style, arrangement or appearance of typeset matter—is a world of its own. It has its own history that predates Gutenberg's Bible, its own classification system almost like binomial nomenclature, a detailed morphology of even the tiniest letters, a peculiar measuring system and a large number of dedicated devotees. Fortunately, just a basic awareness of typography will help the occasional user get by, and even put it to use.

This is 8 point Airport Bold

This is 10 point Stymie Light

This is 10 point Stymie Bold

This is 12 point I. B. M. Typewriter

This is 12 point Caslon

This is 12 point Venus

This is 14 point Weiss Roman

This is 14 point Brush

This is 14 point Czarin

This is 18 point Weiss Italic

This is 18 point Corvinus

This is 18 point Bodoni Italic

This is 24 point Gillies Gothic Bold

This is 24 point Onyx

This is 36 point Brush

This is 48 point

This is 60 po

Figure 9.9. Some of the type and sizes available from one print shop. Type has character and should be carefully selected to help communicate the message.

The most important thing to realize is that type has character, and therefore it can either help or hinder in delivering your message. This should be discussed with the artist or printer. He will have a booklet or chart showing each type face and size available in that shop (Figure 9.9). For example, if you want your message to sound informal, a "script" (like handwriting) or "cursive" (like italics) variety may be appropriate. One family of script type is called "Brush;" another is "Kaufmann." "P.T. Barnum" has the appearance of western "Wanted" posters; "Park Avenue" and "Onyx" are fancy and rich-looking. Consider them carefully, remember your objectives for the brochure, ask advice, and select the type most appropriate to your communication task.

Another useful thing to know about type is how it is measured. The term that indicates its size is called a *point*. Each point is .0138 of an inch. Sizes typically are available from 5½ point to 72 point for any family of type. This book is set in 10 point Times Roman type. Others are shown in Figure 9.9.

Color Can Help Too

Remember, color has meaning. This, too, should be considered when designing a brochure. As with type, color should be selected on the basis of what will help meet the objectives at hand. It can help transmit meaning (red for a safety message, perhaps), create instant recognition (blue and white for cross-country skiers), or function primarily as an attention-getter. For example, a brochure that is bright and highly legible is more likely to be noticed in the in-coming mail or on a bulletin board. In publicizing a short course or other event, this becomes very important.

Color can be obtained in one of several ways. The least expensive is to use colored paper with regular black ink. The second method, the use of colored ink, requires that the printer take time to change the ink, clean the press and stock a supply of something that gets relatively little use. You pay for it. And the more colors you use, the more you pay. Full color is actually a combination of four separate printings (red, yellow, blue and black) after a color photo or painting has been "separated" into those four components to make four different printing plates. This is the most expensive process. Other ways to get a colored effect include using shades of black, or tints of the same colored ink. If either is on colored paper, a 3-color effect can be obtained for the price of one color. Care must be taken to use only colors that harmonize, and shades of the same color should be used with *purpose* (such as highlighting key points of the message with a more solid tone—or a lighter one, depending on the color and which way it would stand out the most). If using a rough, color should be indicated by colored paper, crayon, felt marker or other coloring method.

Paper

Perhaps you never gave much thought to paper, but it is a critical factor in the production of a brochure. It will determine the durability of your publication, and part of the cost. Like type faces and the use of color, it can also help communicate the message. Extremes of paper differences are wedding or other formal invitations vs. newsprint or mimeograph paper. Factors to consider are: how well it takes ink (especially if color is to be used), opacity, whether or not it has texture appropriate to the topic, how well it can hold up when folded and unfolded many times, how durable it is if used outside, and how heavy it is if distribution will be by mail. These are important details, so be sure to ask about them in your first meeting with the printer or graphic artist.

Quantity

Quantity is a detail the printer will need to know before the presses roll. Estimates can usually be based on the use or demand for a similar brochure in the past. When uncertain, it is best to over-estimate. Running out prematurely will cost your agency in lost effectiveness or in considerable additional cash outlay if another press run is necessary. There is an old and truthful saying that the first copy is the expensive one. That one reflects the personnel costs, camera costs, overhead and similar expenses that are part of the printing operation. After the press starts its run, only paper and a small additional amount of labor go into printing a larger quantity. Per copy, the price goes down as quantity goes up. An example is the $8\frac{1}{2} \times 11$ inch 3-fold brochure in Figure 9.8. It may have cost $148 for 500 copies. For twice as many, the cost only went up 5.4 percent, to $156. An additional 2,000 copies took the price to $208. Thus, the cost per copy went from 30¢ to 6¢ as the quantity increased.

The Due Date

The due date is another detail the printer will need to know, and it is probably the one that causes more poor relations between printers and clients than any other matter. To prevent problems, the rule is—and it is one that defies human nature—provide plenty of time. Most printers are artists, not racers. They try to do a good job, but they hate to be rushed. Usually, an extra charge will be assessed for rush jobs, so check well in advance (months, if possible) of when the publication is needed and get your part of the job done early. Printers are human, too. Frequently a promised completion date will not be met. The reasons are myriad, but the only way around this problem is to extend the old rule—leave plenty of time between the due date and when you actually need the publication.

Information Racks

Brochures do little good in a closet or garage. They must be made available to target publics through mailing or personal distribution. Another common means of distribution is the information rack. By its location, the rack and its literature can be directed at selected publics to at least some degree. If the material is for the benefit of internal publics, the cafeteria, lounge, or near the timekeeper's clock provide good locations. A rack beside the office door provides all external visitors a chance to help themselves. Remote locations such as sport shops, garden stores or the local barber shop should not be overlooked as a way to reach publics that may never visit a ranger station or park office.

To prevent waste, it is a good idea to place the most expensive or attractive brochures on the top rack out of the easy reach of children. Children's literature, of course, should be low enough to be reached by its intended recipients. One individual should be accountable for keeping the racks supplied. If that person keeps a record of distribution, it can help in evaluating the kind of information people are seeking, the rate of consumption, and what future quantities may be needed.

Information racks come in many varieties and may be obtained from office suppliers, school and library equipment outlets, store decorator firms and some exhibit contractors. They are also easily constructed, but should be of the same high quality as anything associated with the agency's name.

USING THE MAIL

Direct Mail

When the idea first appeared along with the advent of public relations practice and mass advertising, bulk mailings to selected publics were referred to as using the "sucker lists." Today the technique goes by a more respectable reference—direct mail. Not only is it respectable, it is effective. To some it is considered "junk mail," but to professionals in the advertising industry it is recognized as a multi-million dollar business that offers the channeling of information to almost frighteningly well-defined target groups. For example, *Standard Rate and Data Service* provides annual listings of where you can purchase mailing lists ranging from computer executives to the subscribers of juvenile magazines. Other listings include the source of mailing labels to 9,000 sawmills and logging camps, 39,500 retail lumber dealers and 20,100 chain saw dealers. The cost of these lists are approximately $35 per 1000 names for one-time only or one-year usage.

Another reason that direct mail is effective and ranks as one of the top favorites of advertisers is because it is *personal*. The message reaches the individual in his house and seemingly on a one-to-one basis. Edward N. Mayer, past president of the Direct Mail Advertising Association, adds that you can *". . . address your customer or prospect individually by the most important word he knows—his name. Basically, you seek to create the impression you know who he is and what he is like. In most direct mail copy, you talk to him as you would if you were face to face"* (Sandage and Fryburger, 1971).

In the conservation field, the private organizations are the only groups that have really perfected this technique. Appeals from National Wildlife Federation, The Wilderness Society, American Forestry Association and many others go into the mail by the millions. Most employ advertising agencies, and the products are of professional quality. Some offer the recipient benefits ranging from discounts to the inner glow that comes from doing one's part to save whales. Some send stamps, calendars, free booklets or other tangibles to arouse guilt if a donation or membership is not returned. And *all* attract the eye of the reader. A good example was a brochure received a few years ago with only a colorful photo of Mount Vernon on its cover. Above it were the striking words, "They wanted to make this a resort complex." The message that followed on the inside pages was a membership appeal from The National Trust for Historic Preservation.

Natural resource agencies and related professional societies use direct mail only to a limited extent. When they do, it is usually in the most traditional way, i.e. a letter. There is considerable untapped potential in direct mail campaigns not only in public relations, but also in trying to solicit public involvement from unnatural publics. The innovative communicator should stop thinking in terms of "junk mail," and begin looking at direct mail as one more tool for reaching a target public.

Letters

Letters, like mailed brochures, can be a good tool when it is important that all members of a public receive the exact same message at approximately the same time. Dissemination can be rapid and thorough, but may be more expensive than a meeting. Mass mailed letters can be personalized and made easy to read if wording is used carefully and the Flesch or Fog Formulas are applied. The use of computerized typewriters allows insertion of individual names at the top of each letter, in the salutation, and even within the body of the letter. A small number of letters can (and should) be personally signed, but signature machines usually do the job for mass mailers.

Blue ink will help draw attention to the fact it is personalized. And regardless of what your grammar or typing teacher may have told you—the P.S. *does* have its place. It is an excellent way to highlight an important part of a letter, or to further personalize it.

A disadvantage of letters, brochures and other kinds of publications is the lack of an opportunity for immediate feedback. However, this does not mean the feedback loop of communication should be ignored. Quite to the contrary, every effort should be made to encourage questions or other responses. This can be done through proper wording and a specific name and address for replies. Coupons to clip and mail, or postage paid mail-back cards are also effective. The latter costs the sender nothing, and it costs the agency or organization nothing if it is not mailed. When it *is* mailed back, the Postal Service charges the permitee several cents over first class rates for the service. Usually this comes out to be less expensive than using stamped reply cards in each envelope.

When a personal concern or request for information is received by letter, it provides natural resource personnel with an excellent opportunity for communication. The sender is obviously aware, interested and probably still in a stage of evaluating information prior to adopting an opinion or practice. Just what the public relations person dreams of! So what happens in many offices? The response is entrusted to the lowest level clerk, seasonal employee or even a volunteer. With little instruction and often no supervision, "handouts" are crammed into an envelope and frequently the person's letter also is stuck in, and the package is mailed. In one test of this situation, under the guise of a potential wilderness recreationist, we wrote to offices of three federal land management agencies and asked for information about their areas. Forty-six percent of the replies contained *no* individualized letters (not a single one from 28 National Park Service units.), and 44 percent of the time our letter was returned in the envelope (Fazio, 1979). Is this use of the mail for the kind of effective communication Edward Mayer described? Clearly it is not. In addition, we carefully made no reference to the sex of the sender. The incognito letter was signed *D. M.* Chapman. Regardless, 79 percent of the envelopes from the agencies were addressed to *Mr.* D. M. Chapman—a risky approach at best in these days of sensitivity to sexism.

Response to letters should be made by the appropriate official. Government tradition often requires that the letter be "from" one official (the district ranger, let's say) even though it is written and signed (often without benefit of the signer's name in typed form) by a subordinate. This is a relic of militarism and certainly is not in the spirit of personalized communication. If a forester or biological aide is the appropriate person to respond, *that* person's name and title should be clearly conveyed on the letter. It is a more personal approach to communication and much less confusing to the recipients.

All letters should be answered promptly. In our wilderness information experiment, one of our requests sat for 29 days in someone's office. However, in 51 percent of the cases the ideal turnaround time of one day was achieved. The average was 3 days.

When routine requests are handled by a clerk or other low-level processor, specific instructions should be provided and periodic checks made. Appropriately worded form letters are better than no letter at all. A handwritten note on the form adds an effect that may be both helpful and appreciated. The sender's letter should be discarded or filed for use in developing mailing lists, or for year-end statistical purposes (the boss will be more impressed by the specific number of requests received each year than by a hazy statement about heavy workloads). Literature sent in response to a request should include only *single* copies of each piece (unless more are requested) and should be relevant to the request or specific management objectives or both. Our experiment yielded many wasteful duplicates and large volumes of literature totally unrelated to our request or to the area's management problems. On the other hand, if a problem exists, such as fire danger, then *all* outgoing packets should include information on that topic.

Letters and responses to requests should be viewed as opportunities for high quality, personal and effective communication. The task requires planning, conscientious handling and a means for quality control.

Maintaining Mailing Lists

More and more natural resource agencies are mailing announcements and news releases, public involvement requests, environmental impact statements and smiliar material. The research stations also routinely use mass mailing to make people aware of new publications. To cut expenses and not bother people with literature on subjects in which they have no interest, care of the mailing list becomes important. One way to trim costs is to periodically ask the recipients to return a card by a specific date if they wish to be retained on the list. If the card is not received, the name is purged. Similarly, they may be asked to check only those topics in which they have an interest. Such a list from the Bureau of Land Management follows:

Land Use Planning	_____	If only specific resource areas, please identify _____
		_____
Environmental Impact Statements	_____	If only specific EIS's please identify _____
		_____

Off Road Vehicles	_____	Lands	_____
Wilderness	_____	Soils and Watershed	_____
Rockhounding	_____	Wildlife	_____
Archaeological and Historical	_____	Water and Air Quality	_____
Wild Horses	_____	Regulations and Legislation	_____
Range and Livestock	_____	Contracting	_____
Minerals and Mining	_____	Agricultural Development	_____
Forestry	_____		

The above techniques are suggested if the mailings are purely for educational purposes. Obviously you would not want to eliminate people you are trying to influence and who do not normally seek information on a voluntary basis. Unnatural publics often fit this description. Few would return the card asking to be left on the mailing list, yet to meet certain public relations needs the practitioner must mail to these people.

On any list, duplicates can result in presenting an image of waste and carelessness. Lists should be checked periodically and duplicates should be purged. Similarly, address changes and notifications of persons deceased should be handled promptly. In mailing to agencies or many kinds of organizations, much of this kind of upkeep can be eliminated by using titles instead of personal names. Thus, "*Silviculturalist,* White Mountain National Forest" will not change although many individuals may hold the position over a period of years. Of course, this should not be used if opinion influence and personalization are objectives of the communication.

Most lists today are computerized. This allows rapid recall by alphabetical order of last name, by ZIP code, profession, interest areas or just about anything else coded into the system. This can be an important aid in channeling information to specific audiences for specific purposes.

TRY SOMETHING DIFFERENT

The whole point of using the print media is to place messages in front of selected publics in such a way that they will be read and understood. Why, then, be saddled with tradition? Instead of dire words about safety in the park or the need for habitat protection, why not use a comic book (Figure 9.10)? Adults as well as children will be drawn to such a publication and will *read* it. Another example of the liberal use of illustrations to communicate a complex message is shown in Figure 9.11. Few readers would absorb that amount of information through text alone, or without the appealing caricatures.

Coloring books, games and puzzles provide a prime channel to children. One of the best examples of coloring books is the Discovery Series created by Gary and Sally Machlis for several national parks in the Northwest. The geology of Craters of the Moon National Monument, and the clash of cultures that led to the massacre at what is now Whitman Mission National Historical Site, are presented in coloring books in a way that can achieve understanding among large numbers of young people. Similarly, *Splash!* is a game that uses a simple paper "board" along which players move as they learn about life cycles and the perils of being a salmon. Even more innovative is Jean Bullard's *Let's Go Camping in a National Park* (SIRPOS Press, Box 785-E, Carbondale, CO 81623). This is a "scratch and smell" book, complete with odors of pine, ginger campcakes, and campfire smoke. Messages about fire prevention have been printed on everything from T-shirts to beach balls and are available for distribution through Woodland Enterprises, Box 3524, Moscow, ID 83843.

What else might be used? How about a stunning color poster that most people could not bring themselves to throw away? Posters are popular, especially among teen-agers and college students. The American Forest Council took advantage of this a few years ago and distributed a large poster of a beautiful lake and forest scene with these words tastefully printed near one edge: "Voyageur—How industrial forestry changed a rock pile into a park." On the back was the story.

Other clever ways to distribute the printed word include rulers, bookmarks, calendars, and just about any useful item. And why not on milk cartons or breakfast cereal boxes? With a little persuasion, public service companies or other businesses will even include brochure inserts in monthly messages or bill statements.

The Soil Conservation Society of America developed a way to make their color cartoon booklets easily available to educators, youth group leaders and others. They printed a booklet of tear-out coupon cards. Each page represented a different booklet that was available. It had ordering data, then a perforation, then a descriptive coupon card—its reverse side already addressed to the Society and even postage-paid. The entire booklet, titled *Mailkards*, was mailed to target publics who could then read it and respond with a minimum of effort. In one form or another, this is what communication through print is all about—targeting, attracting readership, persuading or informing, and providing an opportunity for action. The only limit in using these diverse media is your imagination.

Figure 9.10. 'Comic books' present serious messages in a format that attracts readers—and not just children.

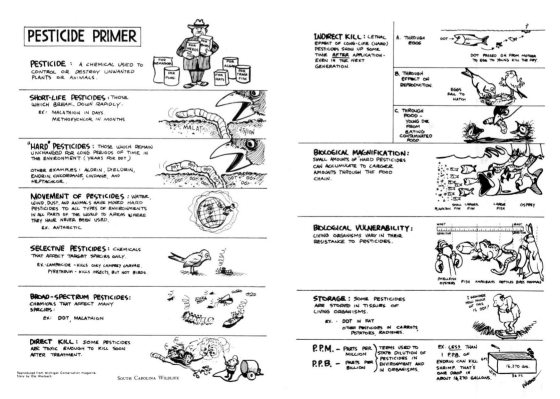

Figure 9.11. Cartoons and caricatures attract interest and increase understanding of complex subjects.

PRINT MEDIA TECHNOLOGY

A working knowledge of the printer's trade is not necessary in order to use the print media skillfully. However, being aware of the basic processes can do no harm, and at times can be quite helpful.

Office Copiers and Duplicators

Office copiers and duplicators need to be mentioned only in passing, as they are more the domain of secretaries. Let them worry about the operation and mechanics, but at least be aware of some basic differences. For example, copiers and Xerox machines are not synonymous. Xerox is the brand name of a copier just as Scotch is only one brand of cellophane tape. Thermo-fax is another brand, this one using a special carbon and heat process to "burn" the image onto another sheet of paper or overhead acetate.

In office processing of printed material, copying is relatively expensive, but rapid and relatively effortless. A less expensive process is the fluid duplicator, better known as the Ditto machine. This produces the familiar blue copies we grew up with in school. However, the process has evolved over the years, eliminating what was once a transfer of copy from a master onto a gelatin slab, then back onto paper. Today the image is transferred from the master by chemical reaction to other sheets of paper without the gelatin slab as an intermediary. Sometimes referred to as a *hectograph*, this word gives a clue to its biggest disadvantage. *Hectare*, from "one hundred," indicates the short runs (usually of no more than a couple hundred sheets) before the master wears out (Arnold, 1972).

Mimeograph is a brand name for a fluid duplicator that works on a different principle. A *stencil* is used, with ink passing through it where typewriter keys or a stylus have cut through an oil-like substance on one surface. Duplicates are in black ink (although color is possible; even photographs if a special photographic process is used). Runs of 3,000–5,000 duplicates are common with the method, and the quality—with care—can be almost as good as actual printing.

Letterpress Printing

Letterpress is the oldest of the major printing methods. Its use stems back to Gutenberg's invention of movable raised letters, or type. From that time on, copy for letterpress was set by hand until Offmar Mergenthaler mechanized the process in 1886. His invention, commonly known as Linotype (another brand name), is still the primary way of setting type for letterpress printing. At the operator's touch of a key on a typewriter-like keyboard, brass letter molds fall into place. When enough are assembled, they are used for casting a "line of type" from a molten lead alloy. This has led to the term "hot type" printing. When the hot lines of type ("slugs") cool, they are laid one after another into a "galley," with galleys then laid into a page form. Next, ink is applied and paper is *pressed* against the raised *letters*, transferring the raised images to the paper and into the familiar columns of print that we read.

Illustrations require special treatment. The negatives of line drawings (no shades of grey) and photos (called "halftones" because they contain a range of grey) are used to expose a photochemically treated metal plate to the image. The image is then chemically etched into the metal plate. Line drawings result in raised lines. Halftones result as a series of raised dots because the negative is made by shooting through a screen, rendering the shades of grey into less dense dots than the blacker areas.

Type set for letterpress is durable for long press runs and it produces very sharp images. However, the "make ready" time is quite slow, especially if illustrations must be added. Except for hobby use and small presses, the venerable letterpress may largely become a thing of the past in this decade.

Offset Printing

Offset is one reason for the demise of letterpress. Instead of using "hot type" or raised letters, a photochemical process is used to place the image of an entire page of copy and line drawings directly onto a thin aluminum plate. Ink adheres only to the chemicals that form the image.

Offset printing, sometimes called offset lithography, is an outgrowth of lithography, a process invented in Germany in 1799. The inventor, Aloys Senefelder, used a flat stone and the principle that oil and water do not mix. He wrote on the stone with grease. Then he applied water which, of course, was repelled from the greasy image. When an ink roller passed over the stone, the ink would stick only to the image, and not on the water-wet areas of the stone.

The only problem with this procedure is that it requires backwards application of the image to the stone so that the mirror image on paper is correct for reading. *Offset* lithography makes this backwards application to the plate unnecessary. It works by taking the image's ink off the plate (which has replaced the stone) and onto a rubber roller. On the roller it is backwards. The roller then presses the ink back on to paper and the image is again correct. It was *off set* onto the roller, then printed onto the paper.

Today the image is placed onto the plate in several very rapid steps. First the copy is made ready by typing, hand lettering or just about any other means. The page is then photographed and a negative made. In the same way a photograph is printed on paper in the darkroom, light is passed through the negative onto a thin metal plate coated with light sensitive chemicals. The plate is developed and is ready for ink. Beyond that point, the chemistry is little different than in Senefelder's day.

Offset printing once had an appearance inferior to letterpress. Today it has won respectability in the printing industry and is the method you will most frequently encounter, especially in producing low quantity runs of brochures and booklets. In some cases you may even make the paste-up from which the printing plate is made (Figure 9.8). The greatest advantages of offset are speed and low cost. Since type need not be cast for each letter, the process is rapid and is therefore the most inexpensive method available. Another advantage is that rubber roller. Since it is soft and pliable, it can be used on special presses to print on wood, metal, book covers or other rough textured surfaces.

Gravure

Gravure is a method most natural resource professionals never encounter except in viewing the results in *Playboy, Fortune,* the Sunday newspaper supplement, or on paper money.

In gravure, the images are etched into a metal plate using a photo-chemical process and finely-screened negatives. Ink is then spread over the plates and goes into the engravings (tiny wells or "graves" of varying depths). The excess is wiped off, paper is pressed onto the surface under tremendous pressure, and the ink is drawn up out of the engraved image (called an "intaglio") and onto the paper. The repeated process is extremely rapid. Also, the plate is very durable, so extremely long runs can be made with no loss of quality. The engraving process, however, is slow and expensive, and few printing jobs in our field require the long runs or extremely fine quality of gravure.

Silk Screening

Silk Screening is not a method of printing articles or publications but is often useful in making exhibit panels and small quantities of signs. The principle is very much like the common stencil. That is, ink is forced through an opening to transfer an image onto some surface, and held back where it is not wanted. In the silk screen process, fabric is drawn tightly over a frame. The image is then hand painted or photo-chemically placed onto the silk in a liquid called tusche. When the tusche dries, the whole screen is covered with a glue. Later it is washed in kerosene and the tusche disappears leaving the silk porous again where the image had been. Paint or ink is then squeegeed across the screen and transferred to the paper, cloth, wood or other material on which the screen is placed. The process can be repeated almost indefinitely and the screen can be saved for future use. This method of printing is available to anyone. Kits may be purchased at hobby shops and art supply stores.

Futuristic Technology

The technology of print is rapidly evolving. The result may bring changes in the Eighties as radically different as today's printing is from Gutenberg's invention. Putting this into perspective, consider that around 1450 it took Gutenberg five years to cast and compose the movable type to print his historic Bible. Today, the entire Bible can be set in type and composed into pages electronically in just over one hour (Lessing, 1969)!

In the late Sixties and early Seventies newspapers and many magazines began converting from letterpress to offset. This drastic conversion to "cold type systems" included typing copy on a key punch that produced a strip of perforated tape. The tape could then be fed through a photocomposing machine which automatically printed neat, "justified" columns (adjusted so both margins are perfectly straight). These could be quickly arranged into page paste-ups and printed by the offset process. Today the process is usually more computerized through the use of visual (or video) display terminals (VDT). A typist—often the reporter or other writer—types the story which is then stored in a computer. It can be displayed at will on a viewing screen for rapid, electronic editing. It can also be stored indefinitely, or called up at any time and arranged into a page, complete with headings of any size—all on a screen. When the page appears satisfactory, the editor presses a button and the whole thing is printed out and is ready for offset processing.

A goal in the printing industry is to develop a system that will carry photos and typed words directly through to the printed page entirely by electronic impulses. In fact, the technology exists and is becoming increasingly feasible to put into practice on a large scale. The method of the future will probably key on *electrostatic printing*, the same principle used in Xerox office copiers. In this process, dry or fluidized pigment particles, called toner instead of ink, place an image on paper not by impact or ink transfer, but by electrical attraction. Using electric charges from cathode ray tubes and needle-like styli, 50,000 characters per second may be imprinted on paper—the equivalent of seven novels a minute (Lessing, 1969). In addition, laser beam scanning combined with video transmission have resulted in the ability to transmit photographs with amazingly fine resolution (sharpness).

Future technology along with today's computer graphics and sophisticated use of telephone lines promise the ability to routinely transmit printed communications instantly to other offices, visitor centers or private houses. Through home computers and television sets, the day is not far off when any citizen will be able to view and call up a printout of the latest stock market report, physician's instructions, reports, novels or desired sections of the evening newspaper.

What does all this mean for natural resources and public relations? The best answer may be that we cannot afford *not* to watch developments; instead we must begin planning how they might be utilized to meet our objectives. It staggers the imagination to think of having access to home printout units. News on road or weather conditions, campground availability, hunting, fishing, and myriad other facets of public information could be flashed to the receiver. Data for public involvement and facts to counter false rumors could also be instantaneously disseminated to any citizen willing to receive the information. There will be possibilities we cannot imagine. Just as computer technology has been a boon in natural resource management, the new print technology will present a whole new array of tools for developing good public relations.

A Word About Computer-Printed Materials

The advent of word processing equipment clearly suggests the need to change and adapt. A writer today without a word processor is like someone sticking with feather and ink after pens were invented. But some things are changing that should not.

For one, the use of our mother tongue requires rules of spelling, grammar and clarity that are as valid now as when taught to us by our grade school teacher.

Another is that computers do not give us license to provide sloppy materials to those who must read it. As a professor I have had students hand me term papers and thesis drafts on continuous printout forms, complete with perforated edges, unintelligible graphics, words and sentences split in a confusing manner, unuseable margins, different size type and the other artifacts of hasty production via the brainless computer. Although computer-generated copy is increasingly accepted by editors (and in some cases even required to be submitted for editing and processing on computer disks), its use should adhere to all the rules of format and presentability that apply to typewritten copy.

Finally, computers should aid better communication, not hinder it. Increasingly, computer-generated letters are received from government offices or small companies printed on sheets of plain computer paper with no letterhead. Sometimes the return address is at least typed on, but often with no telephone number. Frequently the page is completely without the impressive graphics and type styles that lend character to letterhead or memos and help portray that all-important image of an agency or firm.

Earlier predictions that computers would produce a "paper-free" office or even eliminate printed mass communication are proving to be unfounded. In fact, quite the opposite may be true. The printed word is here to stay. Let computers help you compose it and transmit it, but do not be guiled into surrendering control of your work. Pride of workmanship in content, structure and overall appearance is the timeless mark of a professional.

SUGGESTED REFERENCES

Freelance Writing—Advice from the Pros by Curtis Casewit. 1985. Collier Macmillan, New York.

Pictures on a Page: Photojournalism and Picture Editing by H. Evans. 1978. Wadsworth Publishing Co., Belmont, Calif.

Pocket Pal: A Graphic Arts Production Handbook. 1974. International Paper Company, 220 E. 42nd St., New York 10017.

Put an Editor in Your Shoes. National Shooting Sports Foundation, 1075 Post Rd., Riverside, Conn. 06878 (Free booklet).

Telling the Story: A Guide to Better Press Relations. 1978. American Forest Council, 1619 Massachusetts Ave., N.W., Washington, D.C. 20036 (Free booklet).

The Elements of Style by William Strunk, Jr. and E. B. White. 1972. The Macmillan Co., New York.

The Magazine Writer's Handbook by Franklynn Peterson and Judi Kesselman-Turkel. 1982. Prentice-Hall, Englewood Cliffs, NJ.

The Word—An Associated Press Guide to Good News Writing by Rene J. Cappon. 1982. Associated Press, New York.

10

Communication Techniques— The Electronic Media

It is impossible to think of public relations without electronic media to help meet the challenges.

The Twentieth Century dawned with the introduction of Marconi's marvelous invention— the "wireless." At mid-century, black and white television skyrocketed to the fore of public communication, literally changing the life styles of most Americans. Now we can go to the beach and take along a portable television, or a radio the size of a cigarette pack, return home to eat dinner while listening to quadraphonic music broadcast to our living room radio, then retire for the evening to play computerized games, watch our own productions, or view automatically recorded selections from earlier in the day on the giant-sized screen of our color television. Few would disagree that we are all products of the Electronic Age. Is it not strange, then, that most natural resource managers have never had a single hour of training in the use of electronic media? Except for the information specialist, most have not been inside a radio or television station, or put together an automated sound/slide program.

To many, the thought of using electronic media is bewildering and perhaps terrifying. The eerie silence of a sound-proof cubbyhole in a radio station or the single eye of a television camera can make the bravest forester feel like a child going to the dentist! Basically, it is fear of the unfamiliar. But with repeated exposure to the electronic media many resource managers have become caught up in the excitement that only these media can offer. In the 1980's it is impossible to think of public relations without also considering an array of electronic media to help meet the challenges.

Traditionally, the term "electronic media" refers to radio, television and sometimes computerized communication. In this chapter, for the sake of convenience in reviewing useful media, we have taken the liberty of expanding the term to also include motion pictures and automated sound/slide productions.

RADIO

Radio became important as a public communication channel in the early 1920's. By the late 1930's and early 1940's it dominated the field of mass communication. Since that time, with the advent of television, the power of radio has declined but its growth has continued, albeit at a slower rate.

Figure 10.1. Radio is a mass medium that can reach almost any place at any time. Like all media available to help improve public relations, it has many disadvantages as well as advantages. (Photo by Sally Schulze.)

There are approximately 4,880 AM, 3,860 FM, and 1,255 public radio stations in the United States, and the number increases annually. Ninety-nine percent of all homes have radio—a total of over 79 million homes with an average of 5.5 radios per family! Although money spent for radio advertising ranks behind that spent for advertising in newspapers and on television, it still totals $4.7 million per year (Info. Please Almanac, 1985; Stat. Abstracts of the U.S., 1985).

There have been many changes in radio since its zenith four decades ago. In its adjustment to television as the primary entertainment medium, radio changed from its fare of long, dramatic programs to a format of music, news and short features. Network domination also decreased, freeing radio to focus on matters of *local* interest. Both changes have resulted in greater opportunities for natural resource personnel.

Radio offers some distinct advantages as a news medium. In addition to being of high local interest and relatively accessible, it can literally reach everywhere (Figure 10.1). It is in the hunting camp, automobile, waiting room, workshop and the home. It is present while the listener is resting with eyes closed. The homemaker can be ironing or doing some other task where visual concentration is needed and still be listening to the radio. Farmers have radios in their barns and with them in the fields. Cowboys and landowners can put a radio in their shirt pockets while riding or working a fence line. In urban areas, the quality of stereo or quadraphonic music, or the happy chatter of a familiar disc jockey, make radio a tempting companion through large segments of the day. And, of course, there are the masses of teenagers and others in the "youth cult" who seem to make radio a part of their very being.

Considering the large number of people who can be reached—in some cases repeatedly— radio production is relatively low in cost. It is also a *timely* medium that can be used to flash warnings to recreationists, report on-the-spot news, or promptly refute erroneous or damaging information. Radio can also be used to direct news, announcements and features to *specific* publics. Its audiences are not as well defined as a magazine's, but every radio station can provide advertising data that describe its programming (that is, the content of what is aired and the audience it attracts) and the size of its usual listening audience. The descriptions are often given on an hour by hour basis since programming changes throughout the day on many stations. This kind of information, along with names of station personnel, may be obtained through such annual publications as *Standard Rate and Data Service* (5201 Old Orchard Rd., Skokie, IL 60076) or *Broadcasting Yearbook* (1735 De Sales, N.W., Washington, DC 20036).

Problems with the Use of Radio

Perhaps the greatest disadvantage of radio is the passive nature of this form of communication. Although great numbers of people can be *reached*, it is possible that only a few will actually *listen*. For example, the homemaker doing the ironing may be listening to the radio only for musical entertainment. He or she may completely "tune out" any spoken message. Students listening to radio while doing their homework have a natural talent for this mental feat. It points again to the fact that *contact* does not necessarily mean *communication*. It is also questionable whether radio is a very "personal" form of communication. In some cases the messages can be directed to the individual on a seemingly one-to-one basis. In fact, call-in talk shows and record requests can be highly personal in nature. However, the usual fare makes the listener very aware that he is just one small soul out there in Radioland.

Radio is also only one-dimensional because nothing but the sense of hearing is used. The image created is in the listener's mind. There is no picture on paper or on a screen. To be effective this "theater of the mind" must be so vividly portrayed that the audience not only listens but also associates itself with the idea or proposal being broadcast. Talent and the use of many techniques and facilities are necessary to interest, motivate and stimulate a public to action when contacted by radio.

Radio is an immediate medium and the message effectiveness generally depends on a "one shot" effort at contact and understanding. The message can't be folded up and put aside for later digestion or reference. A program once missed is usually gone forever. If it *is* received, and makes an impression, it can not be passed on to others exactly as it was received. This invites distortions.

In some kinds of formats used, the problems of sponsorship and scheduling for a natural resource radio program are acute. The scheduling of many conservation programs is changed repeatedly, and many programs may not be broadcast at all. This problem occurs because most are broadcast on public service time. Perhaps more effort should be made to pay for the time used or to find a sponsor to pay for it. Or, an agreement should be made with the station to schedule the program in one time spot, whether sustaining or not, so a regular listening audience can be established.

Concentration on radio talent and efforts on public information staffs has decreased. Radio now appears to be a stepchild to television. In many natural resource organizations radio receives the time and talent left over after the demands of television, newspapers and magazines are satisfied. It should not be this way. Radio is not a panacea for communication problems, but it can be an important means of communicating with many people.

Use by Natural Resource Agencies

Studies of radio effectiveness in natural resource communication have not been numerous enough to form definite conclusions. However, two studies known to the authors indicate that radio in those cases was either not being used sufficiently by management organizations, or the information was just not being received effectively by the tested publics.

In the one study, only 11 percent of the teachers attending a statewide environmental education workshop in Pennsylvania reported they "often" or "always" used radio as a source of conservation or outdoor recreation information. Sixty-nine percent "seldom" or "never" used this medium for such information (Zimmerman et al., 1978). The other study determined the channels through which Selway-Bitterroot Wilderness users obtained wilderness-related information. The 601 respondents mentioned radio fewer times (less than 1 percent) than any of 14 other communication channels (Fazio, 1979).

In his 1962 survey of I and E in state conservation agencies, Gilbert received conflicting opinions about the effectiveness of radio. Some respondents thought radio very effective. Others believed it is overlooked and should be used more. Still others believed it is the least effective medium and a waste of time and effort. The interest in and enthusiasm for radio seemed to be greater in the more sparsely settled states of the West than in the more densely settled East.

Mindick (1981), in an update of the 1962 survey, found that radio was considered by most executive information specialists to be the least effective of the major media in helping them obtain their goals. In a repeat of this study by the senior author in 1985, but using an expanded list of media, radio came out about midway in perceived effectiveness (Table 7.1). None of these studies, however, suggest that radio should not be used. The logical conclusion is that like any medium, radio's limitations should be recognized and it should be used judiciously and in conjunction with other channels of communication. It is a tool and, like any tool, for the right job it can be used better than any other.

Currently, about 66 percent of all major units of natural resource agencies use radio. Spot announcements are used the most, with 88 percent of radio users reporting little problem in receiving donated air time. Fifteen percent of 268 units responding in a 1985 survey had regularly scheduled radio shows, with state fish and game departments (37 percent) using this format more than most agenices. Five minutes was the most popular length of regular shows.

Formats for Radio

There are many ways to use radio. A few that have been used successfully in the natural resource fields are presented below along with suggestions for making more effective use of this medium.

Public Service Announcements

One of the easiest ways to get some kinds of information on the air is to submit it as a public service announcement (PSA). It can be pre-recorded on tape, or simply typed out for station personnel to read. Either way, following a few simple rules will increase the chances of its being used.

The first rule is *simplicity.* Writing material to be read aloud requires even greater care in this matter than when writing for the print media. If the copy is complex, poorly organized, wordy, or full of jargon, it will probably not be used by the station. If it *is* used, it will probably not be listened to, or understood. According to Gorden Webb, supervisor of the radio center in Cornell

University's College of Agriculture and Life Sciences, all broadcast styles should be *conversational*. As an example, he offered the following news item written two ways. The one on the right, although longer, meets the criterion of being crisp, snappy copy that will read well over the air:

"(SACRAMENTO)—FISCAL WATCHDOGS ON THE LEGISLATURE'S EFFICIENCY COMMITTEE SAID TODAY THEY WILL CONTINUE TO PROBE THE DISCLOSURE THAT THE STATE'S TAXPAYERS WILL HAVE NO CHOICE BUT TO ASSUME RESPONSIBILITY FOR THE 93-MILLION DOLLAR FREEWAY BONDS DESPITE A RULING BY THE ATTORNEY GENERAL'S OFFICE TO THE CONTRARY."

"(SACRAMENTO)—LAWMAKERS WHO WATCH THE WAY CALIFORNIA SPENDS ITS MONEY SAY THEY'RE CONTINUING TO STUDY THE FREEWAY BOND DISPUTE. THE BONDS TOTAL 93-MILLION DOLLARS . . . AND THE QUESTION IS WHETHER CALIFORNIA TAXPAYERS MIGHT HAVE TO PAY FOR THEM. THE ATTORNEY GENERAL HAS RULED THEY WILL NOT . . . BUT FINANCIAL ADVISORS SAY HE IS WRONG . . . THAT THE TAXPAYERS WILL HAVE TO PAY FOR THE BONDS. TODAY . . . THE LEGISLATURE'S EFFICIENCY COMMITTEE ANNOUNCED IT WILL CONTINUE TO INVESTIGATE JUST WHO MUST PAY FOR THE FREEWAY BONDS."

Other suggestions for writing a PSA for radio are:

1. *It must be short and precise.* The preferred lengths are 10 seconds (20–30 words), 30 seconds (approximately 75 words) and 60 seconds (150–200 words). This *must* be indicated on the top of the script, and it *must* be exact.
2. *It must be catchy, clear and motivating.* It is necessary to immediately attract attention, communicate one main idea, and clearly indicate what action should be taken (perhaps a change of opinion, behavior, or some follow-up action like writing for a booklet or attending a meeting).
3. *Punctuation rules can be stretched.* This is to make the announcer's job easier. For example, dashes and dots can be used instead of parentheses or commas. In writing for radio (television or slide scripts, too) the following would be acceptable:

   THE BODY OF A YOUNG MAN—BELIEVED TO BE THE BACKPACKER LOST SINCE LAST SUMMER—HAS BEEN FOUND ON MOUNT WASHINGTON. THE VICTIM WAS FOUND IN A SLEEPING BAG . . . AND THE CONTENTS OF HIS PACK WERE MISSING.

4. *Quotes should be used with care.* Quotes slow the pace of an announcement and can cause confusion. When used, a cue should warn the announcer and the listener that a quote is coming up. An example might be:

THE FOREST SUPERVISOR ATTACKS *WHAT HE CALLS*— "MIS-LEADING AND IRRESPONSIBLE STATEMENTS IN THE OCTOBER ISSUE OF MUDRAKE MAGAZINE."

5. *Avoid symbols.* To assist the announcer, such symbols as ¢, $, %, # should be written out as in 13 cents, 500 dollars, nine percent, number one.

6. *Follow broadcasting style for numbers.* Here are some rules:

Write out numbers from one to nine except for scores, time or dates. Use numerals for 10 to 999.

Write hundreds, thousands, millions and billions: five-hundred, 15-thousand, 12-thousand-500.

Round all figures unless the exact number is absolutely necessary.

When a figure begins a sentence, spell it out. "Fifteen loggers attended the meeting."

Numerals are used in writing dates: January 5th, February 19th.

7. *Use phonetics.* Difficult names and words should be followed with a phonetic version in parentheses.

8. *Avoid most abbreviations.* Spell out names of states, months, days of the week, etc. Exceptions are common titles like Dr., Mrs., Mr. For those things meant to be read as initials only, separate them with hyphens (e.g. Y-C-C, Y-M-C-A). Abbreviations that are to be pronounced as a word should be written without hyphens (e.g. NATO, BIFC).

9. *Make typed lines about 10 words long.* Simply set the typewriter margins to that width. The reason for this is most announcers read about 15 lines per minute. Thus, 150 words equal about one minute of time. This helps the announcers adjust their pace.

Additional information on writing for radio can be obtained in *Broadcast Stylebook* (United Press International, 220 E. 42nd St., New York 10017).

The most effective PSA's include sound effects. An example of a PSA with sound effects that was successful in putting a message across to a hunting public consisted of a shot, a scream and a voice saying, "Don't take sound shots. See your target before you shoot." This took only 15 seconds, but hunters remembered the message. Their attention was obtained, they were given a vivid message, and they were told to *do* something. Another example included sounds of a chainsaw followed by a tree crashing to the ground. The announcer then came on with a message for owners of small woodlots on how to harvest some of their timber while at the same time protecting the aesthetics of their land. The Smokey Bear campaign often uses the sounds of burning forests, or the crackling radio transmissions of fire fighters and lookouts. Calls of ducks and geese may form the background for a message from the department of fish and game urging waterfowl hunters to know species of waterfowl. The chatter of children at play surround safety messages or announcements of summer camp opportunities. Radio *is* sound—and nothing more. Sounds in addition to an announcer's voice can attract attention, hold interest, and aid recall. They provide the color and movement of radio. However, sound effects must be added with care and skill. There is nothing that makes a PSA seem more amateurish than the inappropriate use of background sounds, or music that is not fitting for the message.

There are two ways to add sound effects. One is to produce it yourself; the other is to write a *production script* and have it produced by radio station personnel, specialists in your agency, or a private company. If you produce it yourself, it is necessary to maintain the high technical standards of broadcasting. At minimum this requires the use of a good microphone and other equipment, and recording full track on quality tape at 7½ ips (inches per second). This approach is too difficult for most natural resource personnel.

Production by experts, using *your* script or one developed with the aid of an experienced script writer, is usually the better alternative. In many communities, if good rapport exists with local media personnel, the station will do the production either as a public service or at cost. In some rural or small communities locally-oriented PSA's are so rare the station actually welcomes material aimed at its audience.

For someone else to produce a finished product from your idea, a detailed plan is needed. It is similar to the *rough* in publication work, but in the electronic media it is the *production script*. Parts to be read should follow the suggestions described earlier. In addition, it is necessary to clearly indicate the sounds needed, where they fit in relation to spoken parts, and whether they should be full volume or faded in (sound increased gradually) or out (sound reduced gradually). Most radio stations and production studios have entire records and tape series of recorded sounds; otherwise, they can obtain the sound effects through on-site recording or imitation. Hundreds of sounds, plus all varieties of music, are indexed and may include:

glass breaking	hand saw	ambulance siren passing
gong	chain saw	fire engine
fog horn	babbling brook	traffic on highway
applause	rain	helicopter flying overhead
birds	surf	crickets
rooster	thunder	horse whinny

The information that should go on a radio production script, and a suggested format, is shown in Figure 10.2. Of course, an explanatory cover letter (and/or personal visit) should accompany the script. When it is given to a radio station, the appropriate person to contact is either the "program director," or at large stations, a specialist titled the "public service director."

There is one other kind of public service announcement that does not require scripts or production, but has been highly effective in creating favorable public relations. This is the regularly scheduled emergency announcements to visitors in a park area, people fishing the Great Lakes, or hunters during big game season. An example is the "Buckskin Network" organized by the Colorado Division of Wildlife in cooperation with the Colorado State Highway Patrol to get emergency messages to hunters in the field. Citizen band radio clubs also help with the operation. Commerical stations in the vicinity of the hunting area broadcast messages at prearranged times. Hunters are informed of these broadcast times and frequencies in advance through newspaper and magazine articles, and when they enter the hunting area.

Radio News

As discussed in preceding sections, news can either be engineered in the form of publicity, or it may be "hard" news. Either way, the content must meet the criteria outlined in Chapter 9. Radio news is no different. It should be considered as one of the outlets for the continuous stream of planned publicity, and it is a medium with which you must cooperate when newsworthy events occur that are unplanned.

PSA PRODUCTION SCRIPT FOR RADIO

From: John Doe, Chairman
Friends of Wildlife Committee
110 Marcy Road
Ithaca, N.Y. 14850
(Phone: 885-6668)

Title: Control of Dogs
Audience: Pet owners
For use: Nov. 1 through May 1

Time: 1:00 minutes

Words: 159

SOUNDS: Fade in barking dogs.
Rifle shot.
Barking stops abruptly except one dog yelping in pain (Fade out).

ANNCR:

ALMOST EVERY DAY IN TOMPKINS COUNTY SOMEONE'S PET DOG IS SHOT BY LAW ENFORCEMENT OFFICERS.

NO OFFICER ENJOYS KILLING SOMEONE'S PET . . . BUT UNTIL MAY FIRST THE LAW REQUIRES THAT NO DOG BE PERMITTED TO RUN LOOSE— EITHER DAY *OR* NIGHT.

WHY IS THIS LAW NECESSARY? IF YOU EVER WATCHED A DOG KILL A DEER . . . YOU WOULD *KNOW* WHY.

THE DRAMA TAKES PLACE DAILY RIGHT HERE IN THE WOODLOTS OF TOMPKINS COUNTY. EVEN THE MOST QUIET . . . LOVING PET ANSWERS ONLY TO NATIVE INSTINCTS WHEN ON THE LOOSE IN THE WOODS. UNDER WINTER CONDITIONS . . . DEER ARE EASILY OVERTAKEN. *THEIR* THIN LEGS BREAK THROUGH THE SNOW'S ICY CRUST . . . BUT DOGS MAY RUN SWIFTLY OVER THE SURFACE.

NEXT—THE KILL. AGAIN . . . ANSWERING TO INSTINCT . . . DOGS NIP AND TEAR AT TENDER LEG MUSCLES. THE DEER ARE IMMOBILIZED . . . THEN LITERALLY EATEN ALIVE. THERE IS NO DEATH THAT IS WORSE.

JOIN THE CAMPAIGN FOR HUMANE TREATMENT OF WILDLIFE. KEEP *YOUR* DOG UNDER CONTROL AT ALL TIMES.

Figure 10.2. Sample production script for a one minute public service announcement.

To submit publicity items for news broadcast, they should be typed following the same rules described for the PSA. The same release should *not* be sent to both print media and radio.[1] In addition to shorter length requirements (usually 100 words or less) and format differences, there is an important difference in how the lead should be structured for radio. In radio, if the most important details were placed first, a great many listeners would simply not hear them. Therefore, it is necessary to catch their full attention, then proceed with the essential details. For example, instead of the opening sentence

TOM ROPENTIE WAS APPOINTED TODAY TO REPRESENT RANCHERS ON THE ADVISORY COUNCIL OF THE BUREAU OF LAND MANAGEMENT. . . .

---

1. An exception is to send the fuller newspaper release along with the one written for radio. This provides station personnel with more detail in case they want to follow up and do more with the story.

listeners should first be alerted to this news. A better approach would be:

A PROMINENT UTAH CATTLEMAN WAS APPOINTED TODAY TO REPRESENT RANCHERS ON A GOVERNMENT ADVISORY COUNCIL. TOM ROPENTIE . . . OF MOAB . . . WAS NAMED TO THE ADVISORY COUNCIL OF THE BUREAU OF LAND MANAGEMENT. . . .

Hard news for radio usually can not await the writing and delivery of a release. The electronic media thrives on instantaneous reports of news. Therefore, natural resource personnel at all levels frequently are asked to give telephone or on-site taped interviews. This may be a frightening experience at first, but usually it requires nothing more than answering questions. Statements from this conversation will then be selected and spliced into the newscast. The key to a good performance is to forget the radio aspects and simply answer the questions as though you were talking to a friend on the street. Be natural rather than attempting the carefully planned delivery of a Dan Rather. A good reporter will help by asking questions he knows you can answer straight forwardly. It also helps to discuss the questions with the reporter before the taping begins, but this is not always possible.

Hosted Programs

Having your own regular slot on radio is much like writing a regular column in a newspaper or magazine. The intent is to build an audience—people who will tune in for each show because they like the program and want the information that comes from it. Hosting a show, whether it is five minutes or 15, requires substantial preparation time. However, if the idea is cleared with supervisors, and "sold" to a station's program director, it can become a powerful tool for developing good public relations.

The show can either be aired as a public service, or sponsors can be found. On rare occasions, an agency or organization may even pay for its own sponsorship. Whichever way is decided, a prerequisite to success is *regularity*. The show must be on at the same time on the same days, and it will need to be publicized and promoted. If it is commercially sponsored, a tag line (closing statement) is usually in order to disclaim any endorsement of the sponsor's products or services by the agency. This usually is enough to prevent problems, and using the sponsored approach will help endear you to the station.

The program format can be structured several ways. Unless the host is an extremely dynamic and witty individual with an endless source of fascinating information, the *monologue* usually is boring. Instead, most shows include guests who are interviewed, either singly or in panels. In some cases, a debate may be arranged. For example, parties from both sides of a controversy on nuclear power may be asked to present their views on the same program. Usually a debate is best if limited to two guests. Interviewing a guest on radio requires skill and planning. It doesn't just "happen"— even though that is the impression you'd like to leave with the audience. It should sound informal and conversational, but for this to be done in a professional manner the show must follow a planned outline. Figure 10.3 is an example of such an outline. It could be more elaborate if necessary, even including the specific questions to be asked. However, questions and other material should not be read. An air of informality derived from conversation lends intimacy that does not come from reading. Few people have the ability to read aloud so it cannot be detected as such. A few errors even add life to the desired "air of informality." In the case of panels, so does spontaneous laughter, cutting in to dispute a point, or other actions common in conversation. All guests should receive a copy of the outline or all questions *prior* to the program. Notes and other personal aids can be added as needed, and by everyone going over the outline together before the program, confidence is increased and triteness or redundancy prevented.

PROGRAM OUTLINE FOR ENVIRONMENTAL ROUNDTABLE

Topic:	"Are We Teaching Johnny Conservation?"
Guest:	Dr. Richard B. Fischer Professor of Environmental Education Department of Education College of Agriculture and Life Sciences, Cornell University
Time:	13½ min.

Music:	Up, hold and fade to. . . .
Anncr:	FROM CORNELL UNIVERSITY . . . IT'S ENVIRONMENTAL ROUND-TABLE . . . A PROGRAM TO FOCUS ON THE ISSUES AND ANSWERS OF TODAY'S ENVIRONMENTAL PROBLEMS. AND NOW THE HOST FOR OUR PROGRAM . . . DR. DOUGLAS GILBERT, PROFESSOR OF NATURAL RESOURCES.
Gilbert:	HELLO EVERYONE AND WELCOME TO ENVIRONMENTAL ROUND-TABLE. OUR TOPIC TODAY IS "ARE WE TEACHING JOHNNY CONSERVATION?" WITH US IS (GUEST)
Discussion Items:	1. Dr. Fischer's position at Cornell 　　A. Nature education at Cornell since turn of century 　　B. Environmental Education programs today 2. Ways to develop an ecological conscience in young people 　　A. College courses 　　B. School curricula, K–12 　　C. Community nature centers 3. What needs to be done? 　　A. Environmental education for all student teachers 　　B. Teacher workshops, including sponsorship 　　C. Community action to develop nature centers 4. What individual citizens can do to help with above
Gilbert:	THANK YOU DR. FISCHER. THAT ABOUT WRAPS IT UP FOR TODAY. WE HAVE TALKED ABOUT (GENERAL SUMMARY). BE WITH US AGAIN NEXT WEEK AT THIS SAME TIME WHEN WE WILL DISCUSS (NEXT WEEK'S TOPIC AND GUEST). THIS IS DOUG GILBERT REMINDING YOU THAT THE QUALITY OF OUR ENVIRONMENT DEPENDS ON YOU.
Music:	Up and hold at low level
Anncr:	(Closing statement, again mentioning program and university sponsor)
Music:	Up, then fade out.

Figure 10.3. Sample program outline for a hosted radio program.

A good program host must be multi-talented. In natural resources work or other low budget endeavors, the host usually turns out to be the one who first contacts station personnel and convinces them that the program is worth trying. He must then win and maintain good relations by being as professional as possible, seeking and heeding advice from station personnel, always being on time and always keeping the show on time. Timing is critical, and the electronic media are precise media. This is a difficult lesson for some people to learn, especially students who may be used to showing up late for class or being excused for turning in late assignements! The host may also need to see that the show is adequately publicized, although usually the station will cooperate or handle this important detail. A good host is always alert for program ideas that are interesting and will appeal to the station's particular audience. A file of ideas and possible guests should be developed.

If the host has the right attitude toward the job, and selects guests carefully, a big step toward a successful program has been taken. The idea for the show should be thought through completely and visualized in detail. Enthusiasm and desire are prime requisites for success and make errors or lack of ability and experience less noticeable.

The hosted program can be done in a local community with a single station, or it can be taped and distributed (or made available on request) to many stations. For example, *Colorado Wildlife* is a program taped each week by personnel of the College of Forestry and Natural Resources at Colorado State University in cooperation with the University Audio-Visual Service. These tapes are reproduced, and copies sent to approximately 20 stations throughout the state. This program has been reduced from 15 minutes to 5 minutes in length, but it has been broadcast each week for over 20 years.

Features

There are no definite rules for calling one type of radio program "hosted" and another a "feature," but for convenience the two categories are used here. Like a program with a panel or discussion-type format, a feature may be produced for a single station, but more often it is distributed to several. The feature may take many forms. It may be a one-shot broadcast on a special interest theme or it may be a regular program with a variety of formats.

An example of the one-shot special feature was a 14 minute program produced by a natural resources college on "Bigfoot—Fact or Fraud." The objective was to call attention to unique summer jobs obtained by its students. In this case, a student had joined an expedition to attempt documenting the existence of Bigfoot. The program won a first place award from the Agricultural College Editors Association.

Features on a regular basis may include a five minute broadcast on hunting and fishing conditions, a "roving reporter" interviewing employees and visitors in a national forest, or a series of straight-talk programs on a variety of topics.

In features it is especially important to enrich the program with sound effects, music and interesting, fast-paced information. It is also important that the introduction serves as a "hooker" just as it must in a feature article. A clever opening statement or drama, music, and at least a hint at what follows can help keep the listener's fingers away from the dial.

Sound effects and descriptions turn radio into the "theater of the mind." A recording along a nature trail at a 4-H camp might include the sounds of wind and birds. Supplementary comments also help complete the picture. Along the trail, the broadcaster may say, "We are now making our

INTERVIEW TECHNIQUES FOR RADIO AND TELEVISION

1. In advance of the interview, get all the background that you can on the guest and topic.
2. Be at the studio to welcome your guest well before air time. (In TV, the use of all visuals should be planned in advance. Discuss visuals with director; when to show, how to be used, etc.)
3. Get from the guest key points he wants brought out in the interview.
4. Brief your guest again as to the nature of the audience. (This also needs to be done in initial contact.)
5. Arrange these key points in what seems to you the best possible order.
   For example:
   - Q1: Brings out guest's position in his/her field, why the person is visiting in this area; discovers for audience something about his/her personality; establishes the guest as a real living person, not just a representative of an organization.
   - Q2: Something about the guest's background, personal or professional, that the audience can relate to.
   - Q3: Leads into main topic and why this guest is a good one to tell about it.
   - Q4, 5, 6, etc. Developmental questions to bring out information or guest's point of view on the topic.
   - Q: Last question: Action desired and/or summary of interview.
6. Other patterns of arrangement:
   a. Chronological
   b. Geographical
   c. Divisions of audience: Men, women, children.
7. General procedures:
   a. Plan the area to be covered.
   b. Keep some interesting material for the middle and end.
   c. Keep the spotlight on the person being interviewed.
   d. Make transitions from question to question, if at all possible. Use the preceding answer as a spring board into the next question. At times you may have to clarify something said in an answer.
   e. Keep transitions short.
   f. Ask only one question at a time.
   g. Ask questions requiring comment and interpretation or extending information. Avoid "yes or no" questions.
   h. Seize control of the interview at the end so you don't have to interrupt the interviewee to end show.
8. DON'TS:
   a. "I see" "Uh-huh"
   b. Vocal pause: "er" "uh"
   c. Double barreled questions, or double questions.
   d. Restate interviewee's answers "in other words"
   e. Stalling: "Well, er, what I'd like to ask you is. . . ."
   f. Surprise questions or topics not previously arranged.
   g. Asking potentially embarrassing questions unless you have previously cleared them with the guest.

way through a patch of ripe paw paw bushes that are taller than my head. But I am almost to a wooden footbridge that crosses Raccoon Creek, and there we will be joined by Diane Spott, the person who designed and constructed this unique trail." During many years of broadcasting, Doug Gilbert made tape recordings with excellent results while listening to grouse booming, while counting elk from an airplane, at game check stations, and in duck hunters' blinds. Vividness, reality, and credibility are obtained this way. *Remote* or *on the spot* recordings should be made only on the best portable equipment, again adhering to the specifications for full track recordings at 7½ ips.

In all formats, dialogue should be simple and non-technical. The use of gestures and facial expressions, although unseen, will cause body movement to incite naturalness in the voice. For example, one can count the fingers while counting on the air. Actually counting something usually makes it sound better. Contractions are a natural way of speaking and help a radio message sound natural. However, a person using radio should enunciate distinctly. Words such as get, just, probably, and February should be pronounced the way they are spelled, not "git," "jist," "probly," and "Febuary." Pronunciation can be improved with practice and by making a special effort to use the mouth and lips to form the correct sounds.

Radio is here, there and everywhere. It is an inherent part of our daily lives. It is intimate and flexible. It is depended upon and taken for granted. Again, it is not the sole answer, but it is an important mass medium that should be used in addition to, not instead of, other techniques of communicating. As with other mass media, radio is most effectively used at the interest and awareness stages of adoption. It can also be used as a reminder in the later stages.

Short Range Radio Transmitting

Another way of disseminating information via radio is through use of a short range transmitting system. In this technique, a continuous loop tape is usually connected to a low power transmitter and broadcasts on a pre-set AM frequency. Anyone within range (Usually ¼ to ½ mile in hilly terrain) with a regular AM radio can monitor the message.

The most common use of this system has been in national parks. In Yellowstone, for example, motorists approaching the entrance gates see signs suggesting they turn to 650 on their car radio. They are then advised about entrance fees, safety, important rules, current state of accommodations, and any other information that park rangers record on the tape. Approximately 75 percent of the visitors "tune in" and park officials have found that it speeds the entrance process. The National Park Service also uses the system for roadside interpretation of natural and historical features.

As a tool in public relations, opportunities seem endless. Easing the process of entering a park can certainly contribute to better public relations. Similarly, the system could be used at any point where anxieties or frustrations might be expected to occur. Examples include construction zones, areas with weather or terrain hazards, congested intersections or confusing parking areas, permit-issuing stations, and game check stations. Short range radio can be a permanent fixture, or used for an occasion as temporary as a sports event or the dedication of a new facility.

Message length must be short (2–3 minutes) if cars pass the transmitter at highway speed. At pull-offs or parking areas, message length is limited only by the recording equipment and the length of time people will remain interested. The broadcast may also be done "live" if circumstances warrant.

Equipment usually consists of a recorder-player unit, a transmitter, and either a pole-type or underground cable antenna. A vandal- and weather-proof box houses the equipment out of sight. Power is supplied either by battery or from an AC source.

In theory, these devices seem like an efficient way to disseminate information under certain conditions. In reality, they have been plagued by mechanical problems and a scarcity of technicians to service the units. Suppliers have also been few and in some cases here one day and gone the next. However, the technology is improving and recently an innovation was introduced to remedy the worst problem. The recording tape has been the weakest link in the system. Sometimes it does not stand the stress of temperature change and continuous use for even an hour or two after installation. More often they last about two weeks. Thus, unless the units were regularly monitored and serviced, *poor* public relations frequently resulted from visitors not being able to receive a broadcast after tuning in as directed by the sign. More frustration instead of less! Now a solid state voice storage unit is available that eliminates recording tape. A voice, music or other sounds are digitally stored in integrated circuits. Through electronic scanning, the message is decoded and amplified with just as high quality as that provided by recording tape. At present, cost for these units is relatively high and recording capacity rather limited. For example, a basic unit may cost $650 with a recording capacity of only 2.5 seconds. To increase this to 5.0 seconds, there is an additional charge of $127. For 20 seconds it is $889. Beyond that special orders are required.

More information on short range broadcasting and solid state sound storage is available from: RA Com Products for Communication
    5504 State Road
    Cleveland, OH 44134

TELEVISION

Television! The magic medium, the Pied Piper of our culture, the communication channel so powerful and so alluring it has been called the medium that *is* the message. Many resource managers can remember when there were no televisions, or at least not in people's homes. They can remember, too, the first time they viewed this talking box, perhaps with only a seven inch screen and definitely in black and white. By 1985 there were 831 commercial television stations operating in the United States and 283 non-commercial, or *public television,* stations. In addition, more than 6,200 cable systems enter 43 percent of American homes and satellite discs have given the most remote rural residents access to scores of stations. In fact, over 97 percent of American homes have at least one television receiver, 90 percent have color sets, and 41 percent receive 11 or more channels (World Almanac, 1985; Stat. Abstracts of U.S., 1985). It has been said that more homes in the United States have television sets than indoor plumbing!

Television offers many advantages to anyone concerned with influencing public opinion. This is evidenced by the fact that it is second only to newspapers in the amount of advertising money attracted. High numbers of viewers and their high degree of interest add up to wise expenditures when computed on a cost per person contacted. Another advantage is that, like radio, advertising data are readily available to help pinpoint the size and characteristics of the audiences reached at any hour on any given day. At some times, a broad range of audiences can be reached simultaneously, an advantage not easily obtained with most other media. At other times, it is possible to zero in on nonconsumptive outdoor enthusiasts or sportsmen, intellectuals, young women, middle-aged women, senior citizens, rural folks, city dwellers or just about any public that can be defined.

Figure 10.4. Live shows, such as *Colorado Outdoors* which was hosted by D. L. Gilbert, were common in the early days of television. Today videotape allows greater flexibility and less pressure on the talent. (Courtesy of Colorado State University.)

And television is effective. Through sight, sound and motion it captures attention, excites the imagination and rivets images and ideas firmly into the minds of millions. Moreover, despite its mass appeal, it can be a "warm" and highly personal medium. That is, it allows a speaker or message right into the home and is usually viewed alone or in a small, familiar group setting. To many, the television is a trusted companion, and often the relationship is not too unlike a one-sided conversation with a friend.

Problems With the Use of Television

When television made its debut, the biggest problem was filling a 15- or 30-minute time slot with a flawless performance. If it was not flawless it was embarrassing, as there was no videotape to allow editing out the bloopers. Live broadcasts are still made on some stations, and when they occur, timing and studio arrangements can present challenges. For example, what could be worse than running out of something to say with five minutes of a time slot remaining!? Also, there may be three minutes or less to move equipment and "props" (ranging from aquaria filled with water to live mountain lions) into the studio and to get them arranged. There also is the problem of straightening up before the next show can go on. These obstacles can be overcome with adequate personnel and studio space. Stations with two studios or one very large studio, do not present this problem for live shows. Fortunately, with the exception of news, weather and sports, most local programming we see today has been videotaped in advance of broadcasting. This means that mistakes or other problems can be edited and portions can be retaped. Still, a studio is a busy place and a flawless performance will be very much appreciated by the director and other personnel.

One of the main problems encountered in using television in natural resource work on commercial stations is that of scheduling. Many shows first go on the air as unsponsored public service programs at an agreed upon time. This time soon may be sold to make room for another show, a sponsored one that pays the station for time used. The natural resource program is then given a less desirable time, and that again may be sold. The length of the program may also be cut several times to accommodate commercials. These events are understandable because a commercial station is a business that sells time, and it must make money to stay in operation.

The solution is that the natural resource agency can either buy time or obtain a sponsor. The first possibility is usually prohibited by cost or policies of a public service organization. Fish and game departments use television the most, yet only about 15 percent of their air time is purchased by the agency. The only alternative is to interest an appropriate sponsor—no easy task given the costs of television.

The time required to prepare and present a good television program can be overwhelming. As an individual gains television experience, however, he becomes increasingly confident and needs less time for preparation. The usual time, at the start, will be about 15 hours of preparation for a 15-minute program. This includes everything from the hours of worrying and trying to get ideas for the next show to leg work in assembling props.

It takes a certain kind of personality to succeed in television work. In some, this personality can be cultivated. In others it is never present, while in some cases the personality is present but desire or will is lacking. A natural resource management employee capable of doing good television work is even more rare than one who can speak well over the radio or write acceptably.

Another problem, especially in metropolitan areas, is getting *on* television. Competition for television time is more severe than for any other medium. This problem will be addressed later, but unless a large budget is available, most natural resource programs or messages are aired solely on a public service basis. There is no control on when the material is broadcast (if it is at all). Nor is television a panacea when you do manage to get a program on the air. For example, according to an A. C. Nielsen survey, the average American home has a television set on seven hours and two minutes per day. However, in a study of Selway-Bitterroot Wilderness Users, 82 percent of Bramlette's (1977) respondents watched less than two hours per day. If these users were the target public of some public relations effort, there are more efficient information channels to use than television.

Powerful as it can be, television is still much like any other medium. Its use requires skill, overcoming of obstacles, and a systematic approach to matching a message to a target public to meet pre-established objectives in the most efficient way available.

Use by Natural Resource Agencies

Depending on how one defines "conservation," it can be said that programming of this nature has enjoyed moderate to spectacular success. For example, shows like *The American Sportsman, Wild Kingdom, Lassie* (during its Forest Service period in the Sixties), and many National Geographic specials have achieved superstar status for messages related to the management of natural resources. Most recently, in 1984 *The World of Audubon* premiered on a cable "superstation," gaining access to some 30 million homes. To millions of urban Americans, these and similar programs have been their *only* exposure to resource utilization or management problems.

Natural resource management agencies have considerable room for improvement in using television as a channel of communication. In a 1985 survey we found only 55 percent of our respondents from among major natural resource agencies using television in any way. State agencies (with the exception of state parks) use this medium far more than their federal counterparts. Most use is for news, followed by use for public service spot announcements.

Getting on Television

To someone with no courses or experience in television, this medium at first seems shrouded with an inpenetrable mystic. Also, some claim that television is the medium of inflated egos. Everyone who has dealt with television has encountered station personnel who were less than helpful or cooperative. This image is unfortunate. True, television can be a complicated medium, and workers are under great pressures and time demands. However, with some advance preparation any natural resource manager can usually find an outlet for information on television.

Commerical Television

Commercial television offers the largest audiences and the greatest variety of publics. With sponsorship money in hand, the resource person will have little trouble finding an appropriate time slot and necessary production assistance. Without funding, your cause has a much better chance of reaching the airwaves if you understand the hierarchy of a television station. This varies depending on size, but a typical structure is shown in Figure 10.5. The functions of these personnel and who should be contacted are summarized below:

General Manager	Overall management responsibility, including funding and budgeting. Usually not involved with actual programming.	Contact to discuss contracting or sponsorship ideas.
Program Director	Supervision of all programs at the station. Usually decides what programs are aired and in what time slots.	The best person to approach to discuss ideas for special features, broadcasting a film or beginning a hosted program. Also contact when air time under the Fairness Doctrine is being requested.
Public Service Director	Whoever has responsibility for selecting PSA's and making sure an adequate amount of time is dedicated to local public issues. May be separate position, program director, or "Traffic Manager"—the person who keeps daily log of programming.	Best contact for PSA's. In large stations where seeing the program director is difficult, a good alternative for discussing larger programs that will not be independently sponsored.
News Director	Supervises news programs, including reporters, camera personnel and editors	Contact with all news items and information about impending events of news/publicity value.

Production Director	Responsible for facilitating the actual production of programs.	
Producer/Director	Often the same individual is both producer and director. The producer is responsible for the production of specifically assigned programs, including props, talent, script, etc. The director is in charge during actual filming; directs the talent, camera positions, which shots to use (close-ups, side angles, etc.).	If the station decides to accept your idea or produce a sponsored program, work with the producer/director who is assigned.
Production Personnel	The staff of technicians who run the cameras, lights, sound equipment, graphic production and property management.	These people are experts or they would not hold the positions they are in. Take their advice and cooperate fully.
Talent	This is the term applied to all personnel who appear on camera—announcers, hosts, guests, news people, actors, actresses, etc.	

Public Television

In structure, there is little difference between a commercial television station and a *public television station*. However, there is a very important difference in funding. Commercial stations are profit-motivated and highly competitive. Public television stations are supported primarily by congressional appropriations, foundation grants and donations from local viewers.

Public television has evolved from 47 educational television stations that made their appearance in the 1950's. These early stations were privately supported through gifts, grants and local or state governments. In 1962 Congress amended the Communications Act to provide federal financing, and educational television quickly grew to more than 200 stations. But there was confusion and even a stigma attached to the term "educational." In a report by the Carnegie Commission in 1967, the suggestion was made to call the medium "public television"—the term most widely used today. In public television there is less concern about competition for large audiences and more for providing alternatives to the mass entertainment fare that dominates commercial broadcasting. Personnel at public television stations actively seek to meet local communication needs and to fill the gaps not covered commercially. For example, they may program minority news broadcasts, operas, plays, local political debates and similar important but limited interest material. For the natural resource manager this provides an excellent opportunity to get "on the air." The drawback is the limited viewing audience. However, this audience usually includes the more highly educated, and research indicates it is a good way to reach a variety of opinion leaders.

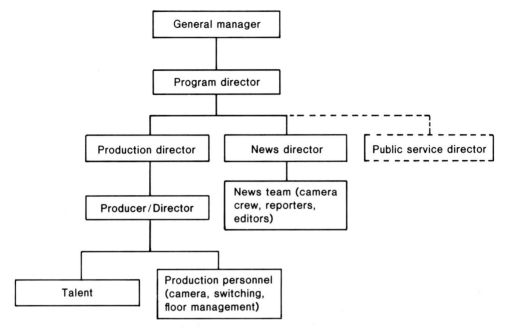

Figure 10.5. Typical hierarchy in a commercial or public television station. In small town stations, one person may fill two or more positions.

Cable Television

Cable television is a concept that at one time promised to wire the entire nation together, not unlike our telephone systems.

Cable was started in 1950 to serve a town that was in the "shadow" of a mountain and unable to receive broadcasts from a nearby city. An enterprising individual erected an antenna on the offending mountaintop, amplified the signal, and relayed it to the town below by "cable" attached to existing utility poles. This service was then sold to subscribers on a monthly basis and was known as *community antenna television* (CATV).

Cable television quickly expanded to "importing" additional broadcast signals from distinct cities. Microwave relay systems were set up for this purpose. To protect and encourage *local* use of the television medium, the FCC eventually developed a series of regulations to keep cable importations from stifling local stations, or local program content. One of these rules, originating in 1969 and reinforced in 1972, required cable television to provide original material "to a significant extent." In other words, it would be like having a studio added to the cable office from which local programs would be transmitted through the wires to subscribers' homes. This and other regulations raised the hopes of some resource managers and environmental educators for bringing their messages to the community via television.

Unfortunately, events in the mid-1970's proved less than encouraging for the use of cable for "significant" local communication. Instead of original programming, many cable companies merely focused a camera on a clock or weather instruments. In addition, financial problems plagued the companies as subscription growth was slower than anticipated.

Finally, FCC regulations were relaxed and the cable industry today continues to be in a period of change and deregulation, and it is facing a brighter financial outlook. It is also facing stiff competition from direct-broadcast satellite (television beamed direct to homes with dish antennae) and multipoint distribution systems (land-based microwave transmitters that cover large areas and boast of being a cable system without cables). Even so, cable is thriving and below are a few current features either mandated or technically feasible in areas served by cable outlets and which may be of use in public relations work.

1. Rules requiring local origination have been largely abandoned. However, some small cable companies will cooperate with local parties wishing to "broadcast" material in the public interest. This is done by providing the company with a ¾″ videotape or other material they agree to use. The company then uses a "public access channel" or preempts their continuous time and weather information to transmit the program. The burden of drumming up an audience for such a broadcast rests heavily upon the party providing the program.

2. A more dependable way to use cable television is to lease a channel. Technologically, a cable may be able to carry 40 or more channels to a house (which can receive these by renting a converter that has an equal number of channels on its dial). The company may make some of these channels available at a profitable fee. For example, a *program* can be put on a cable that has 25,000 customers ("subscribers") at a charge of perhaps 1¢/subscriber/hour. Or, the entire channel can be leased for perhaps 10¢/subscriber/month. These are sometimes called *leased access channels*. Again, it is up to the leasee to publicize the program or channel, a difficult challenge at best.

3. An *educational access channel* is available in some communities, and more can be expected. This channel provides a linkup within a school system, a university, or perhaps between neighboring systems or universities. On this channel a speaker, panel, demonstration, or taped program can be shown to all classes having the appropriate equipment.

Formats for Television

There are many ways to take advantage of television. The skilled public relations person will use the one determining factor that should guide *every* selection of a communication channel—what is the best way to reach a specific public with a specific message?

The PSA

The major difference between PSA's for radio and television is that a visual component is essential in the latter. Otherwise, time lengths, script writing, local interest and similar considerations are no different than those described earlier. The visual component can either be a short 16 mm film (commonly called a *film clip*) with or without pre-recorded narrative, a videotape cartridge (usually 2″ or ¾″), a slide with the message printed on it, or slides with an accompanying script that the announcer reads. Regardless of the format used, one study has shown that 30 second PSA's are much more likely to be used than those of other time lengths (Goulard, 1974).

The film clip and video cartridges should be produced by specialists within the agency, a commercial contractor, or with the assistance of local station personnel. These are convenient for the station to use and can be mailed or delivered to any number of outlets, but they usually require a cash outlay ranging from minimal production costs to sizeable contracts. Also, with technology changing so rapidly it is best to check with stations you hope to use.

PSA FOR TELEVISION
(Narrator script and slides)

From: Paul W. Bradford, Chairman
     Education Committee
     Onondaga Environmental Action
     Assoc.
     7455 Tully Road
     Manlius, N.Y.
     (Phone: 876-4000)

Title: "Use Returnable Containers"
Audience: Housewives
For Use: February 1 through April 30

Time: 30 seconds

Words: 80

Visuals: 4 2 × 2 color slides

Slide No. 1 (Garbage dump with "closed" sign)	ANNCR:	WHERE DO WE PUT IT WHEN WE ARE OUT OF SPACE? SOLID WASTE DISPOSAL IS USING UP PRECIOUS LAND.
Slide No. 2 (Supermarket isle of beverages)		PART OF THE PROBLEM STARTS HERE—THE ONE-WAY BOTTLE AND DISPOSABLE CAN.
Slide No. 3 (Woman loading grocery cart with bottles and cans)		PART OF THE ANSWER IS HERE—THE CONSUMER WHO MAKES THE CHOICES.
Slide No. 4 (Logo and wording: "Ask for Returnable Containers")		YOUR ONONDAGA ENVIRONMENTAL ACTION ASSOCIATION URGES YOU TO ENCOURAGE YOUR GROCER TO STOCK BEVERAGES IN REUSABLE CONTAINERS. THEY WILL COST YOU LESS . . . AND WON'T BECOME PART OF THE SOLID WASTE DISPOSAL PROBLEM IN YOUR COMMUNITY.

Figure 10.6. Sample public service announcement for television using a minimum of visual material. Some messages may be prepared with a very low investment in production.

The method anyone can afford is use of 35 mm slides. One technique is to approach the public service director about using a "shared ID spot." If he likes the idea, he will most likely help with the production. This is simply an appropriate slide used during station breaks and carrying both your short printed message and logo, and the call letters of the station. A slogan on fire prevention, outdoor recreation, littering or a similar topic might be appropriate. If it is attractive and timely, there is a good chance the shared ID spot will be used by a local station many times a day, even during prime time.

Another easy use of slides is the *slide/voice-over* announcement. In this case one slide or a short series is provided to the station along with a script. A suggested format for this kind of PSA is shown as Figure 10.6.

As obvious as it should seem, it is important to stress that when a station uses your PSA, a phone call or note of thanks should occasionally be extended. This not only is a nice gesture, it also provides the station manager with evidence that he is serving the public interest. This is important for renewing his license to operate. One instance is known where a natural resource organization sends an attractive certificate of appreciation to any station after it contributes over $35,000 of free time for PSA's. In the fine art of creating good media relations, remembering to say "thank you" can be the key to future cooperation.

Television News and Features

News is news whether it is for use in a newspaper, radio or television. Hot news should be phoned to the news directors of *all* stations serving the area. If they are interested they will either interview you on the phone or dispatch a news team to cover the story.

In public relations, a continuous stream of favorable publicity stories is usually a primary objective. This effort cannot rely upon hot news, so "news features" become an important way to use television. These are short items that are high in human interest and can be used to spice up newscasts. Ideally they are timely and of local interest. It may be a story on training seasonal fire fighters in June or advice on cutting and preserving Christmas trees in December. Whatever the topic, it must be short (perhaps 45 seconds to 2 or 3 minutes) and *interesting.* It can be supplied on film or videotape if the agency has good equipment, skilled operators, and if the presentation style is similar to others used by the target station. A better approach, however, is to describe the idea, provide background material to the news director, and let the station produce the story. In such a case it is ethical to rotate among all local stations when approaching them with ideas for news features. However, if the station initiates the idea, work only with that station until the program is aired.

An extension of the news feature is used by many larger stations. This is the "magazine" or "news-magazine" program. *Sixty Minutes* is a nationally telecast version of this concept which often stresses the negative or exposé angle of stories. Frequently, however, the magazine format is a series of interesting or light stories about local people and events. Currently at least 60 stations air such programs, usually in the time slot between the evening news and the start of prime time entertainment. Regular hosts—often young and highly energetic—are a part of the popularity. Usually they conduct interviews in the local area. However, a large number of stations belong to "cooperatives" such as that run by Westinghouse Broadcasting's Group W Productions. Each local station makes and contributes at least one story each week. Then a "national reel" is completed and made available to each member of the cooperative to select the portion they want to use. In this way there is a mix of local appeal and the most interesting stories nationwide.

To get a natural resource story on the series, contact the program's producer and outline your idea in detail. Watch the program for several weeks before developing the idea (a good procedure with *any* use of television!). Then be sure to stress the uniqueness of your story. Also suggest how the hosts (who are often the hams of journalism) can actually participate—perhaps by donning spikes and climbing a spar tree in a cable logging system, putting on the bulky equipment of a smokejumper, or helping with a maple syrup operation.

Hosted Programs

Producing a hosted show is extremely time-consuming. Nothing is less appealing on television than two talking faces, so it is necessary to liven up the program with demonstrations, film clips, slides, unusual objects, and other techniques that add action. This takes time and practice. In fact, a good presentation requires about one hour of planning and preparation for every minute of air time (Sandfort and Cone, 1977). The result, however, can be a large and faithful audience.

If your idea for a regular program is cleared by supervisors and a station's program director, many of the considerations discussed for radio shows are also true in developing a good television program. These include program publicity, working compatibly with station personnel, being on time and staying within time limits, pointing a program toward a specific public, developing programs after doing opinion research, striving for local interest, working from an organizational calendar or schedule, using an "attention getting" introduction and covering one topic well rather than covering several halfway.

The outline for a hosted television program can be similar to the one for radio in Figure 10.3. However, an additional column is needed down the left side to indicate what visuals are to be used at each point in the program. This is essential not only for planning the program but for use by the director and switcher (the person who controls which of two or more cameras will be recorded on the videotape). For example, one camera may be shooting a close up while another is focused on a wide angle view of the studio setting. Both are operating and the switcher monitors both scenes on screens in the control room. He continually presses buttons that control which scene is recorded on the master tape (or broadcast if it is a live program). The director is also involved, making suggestions to the switcher and through earphones directing the camera operators to move into different positions. For example, if the director knows the talent will soon be discussing a map, he may order one camera to get prepared by focusing on it for a close-up. The program outline is the essential blueprint that coordinates the dozens of behind-the-scenes workers as well as the proper timing of sound effects and the slides, film clips and superimposed titles that appear on the screen. The following illustrates a segment of a program outline used in a show on overcrowding in wilderness:

Video	*Audio*
Gilbert at desk	GILBERT: THE PROBLEM BEFORE US TODAY IS AN IMPORTANT ONE. WE ARE DEALING WITH A VERY LIMITED AMOUNT OF LAND . . . AND THIS FINITE AREA WILL HAVE TO SERVE OUR RECREATION NEEDS FOREVER.
Slide 1 (Mountain Lake) Wipe to slide 2 (Crowded lakeside)	THE CHALLENGE TO LAND MANAGERS AND CONCERNED CITIZENS IS THIS. HOW DO WE PREVENT AN AREA LIKE THIS LAKE . . . FROM TURNING INTO SOMETHING LIKE THIS?
Gilbert at desk	PERHAPS THAT WAS A RATHER DRASTIC EXAMPLE, BUT THE PROBLEM *IS* A VERY REAL ONE. TODAY OUR PANEL WILL DISCUSS THIS PROBLEM WITH A MAN WHO WORKS WITH IT THE YEAR 'ROUND.
Panel	(Introduce Jim Fazio, Elyse Deffke and Dave Butts, Resource Management Specialist, Rocky Mt. Nat'l. Park)

Gilbert at desk	WHILE WE WERE PREPARING FOR TODAY'S PROGRAM, WE INTERVIEWED SOME OF THE PEOPLE WHO USE THE WILDERNESS FOR RECREATION. WE ASKED THEM IF THEY SEE THE GROWING POPULARITY OF WILDERNESS RECREATION AS A PROBLEM. LET'S LISTEN TO WHAT SOME OF THESE PEOPLE HAVE TO SAY.
Film of interviews (2:25 min.)	(Sound on film)

Most professionals in natural resource management are more likely to be invited as a guest on a hosted show than to have a show of their own. To use the opportunity to advantage, it is important to know what to expect and to have a basic knowledge of a few rules of communicating in front of a camera. It is also important to beware of the slipshod host or one who will not discuss questions ahead of time. It is better to turn down an invitation than to appear on a program that is poorly done or maliciously slanted. Fortunately, most hosts will have your best interests in mind as well as their own and will help you do a good job.

Rehearsals are a help, not as a way to memorize or prepare a rigid format, but simply to help remove the mystery of a studio and learn basic procedures. Two rehearsals before the actual presentation are ideal. A walk-through or "dry-run" rehearsal need not be in the studio and can be done alone if this is not part of the usual station routine. It helps you get your part ready and it is wise to do it in front of a tin can or paper cup that represents the TV camera. This is an aid to becoming accustomed to talking to the camera and getting used to the stare of this single "eye."

A dress rehearsal incorporates the use of all equipment and individuals exactly as it will be on the air. This rehearsal is used to insure accurate timing, tailoring, adding and subtracting. This is the time to detect and correct errors. For example, the door on a deer trap may stick. It is far better to have this happen during a rehearsal than on the air. The dress rehearsal should not be concluded until everything is exactly right.

Many large television shows have a camera rehearsal in addition to the two already mentioned. At the other extreme are the shows that go on with no rehearsals at all. Unfortunately, most associated with natural resource personnel fall into this category. All background props, demonstrations and visual aids should be discussed at the outset with the director. This person is the boss of all station activities relative to the program. Proposed movements should be indicated as nearly as they can be predicted. Time needed for film clips or slides can be decided. Also, if live animals or firearms are to be used, it will be necessary to explore possible conflicts with studio policies.

Despite the best efforts, few shows go exactly as planned. If errors or problems are too drastic, and if it is being videotaped, the segment can be reshot. However, this should not become a crutch, as studio personnel are very busy and prefer a straight run through. On live shows, sometimes the results are better when the unexpected happens. For example, regardless how calm a person thinks he is, if animals are used they can sense nervousness and anxiety. Sometimes tame animals revert to their wild nature. In one instance a docile, descented pet skunk was used. This pet bit the handler's finger to the bone. He calmly pried the skunk's mouth open with his other hand and the skunk bit another finger to the bone! Blood was gushing, but the audience thought the show was excellent. Actually, there are three kinds of television programs: the kind that is planned, the kind that is done, and the kind one wishes had been done after the program is televised.

The following are additional suggestions that can help make a success out of using television either on a regular basis or as an occasional guest:

1. The program should be publicized as much as possible. It is good business to have a large viewing audience. This is usually the station's responsibility but supplementary publicity is often necessary. Moreover, the more audience you can build for a station, the more you and your program will be endeared to station managers.

2. Station staff should be allowed to fully exercise their normal responsibilities. An outsider must not attempt to tell them how to do their jobs.

3. A specific subject is better than a general one. It is better to develop one idea or topic well rather than to skim over a broad subject or to touch lightly on several topics.

4. Clearances and copyrights for all materials used must be checked. This includes photographs, films, maps and music. Some educational films, in addition to requiring special clearance, may not be used on shows which are preceded or followed by programs on which alcoholic beverages or tobacco are advertised. It is impossible to be too careful in checking and avoiding any legal problems.

5. Dress appropriately. For example, if showing how to plant shade trees, a person should not wear a suit and tie. A casual shirt, open at the collar, would go well with such a program.

6. Jewelry can reflect lights and should be used with care.

7. Black and white clothing should be avoided as it can create a "halo." Pastels such as blues, greens and yellows are better television colors than black and white. Colors to wear depend largely on the background; the idea being to contrast with the background. Blue should not be worn if slides are to be electronically placed on the screen behind talent—a procedure called *chroma-keying*. Any blue in front of the camera may disappear when this technique is used. Pinks or corals look like flesh on color TV and can cause embarrassment. Vertical lines give an illusion of slimness horizontal lines make the person look broader.

8. The camera shows the real person. It doesn't lie. All efforts should be made to enhance appearance. Bad points, such as lack of a shave and rumpled clothing seem to be accentuated. Make-up is often used and covers up blemishes. Bald spots can be dusted with powder to stop the shine. A new hair cut should be avoided as the person may appear "scalped."

9. The backdrop or background is important. A scene which suggests the out-of-doors, such as a fireplace and rustic paneling is appropriate for forestry, wildlife and outdoor recreation themes. Something more formal or urban would be necessary for shows dealing with problems of environmental management like industrial pollution, solid waste disposal, urban sprawl and similar issues.

10. Introductions and announcements should be brief.

11. Every program needs an "attention getter" at the start. This may be a film clip or slides of a live animal, some other unusual visual, or an intriguing question. The purpose is to interest viewers enough that they will want to keep watching the whole program.

Figure 10.7. Speaking to a camera should be like speaking to one individual. The red light near the lens is used to indicate which camera is "live." (Courtesy of Cornell University.)

12. Much "show how" and little "tell how" should be used on television. The best type of show is the demonstration where something is shown and explained. A lecturer is deadly to any television program.

13. A good way to relax is to yawn just before the "you're on" cue.

14. Talk slowly. Keep conversation simple, frank and convincing. There is no need to project. Terms too technical for the viewing public should not be used. This especially is important at the start of a program when trying to capture an audience.

15. Do not read a script. It is all right to use an outline or cue sheets, referred to as "idiot sheets" by the professionals, but there is no excuse for obvious reading. The only exception is when a law, policy or someone's written message is to be quoted. In that case, to be shown reading adds credibility to the preciseness.

16. When talking to the camera instead of someone else on the set, speak as though you are addressing only *one* person. Use a phrase like, "I hope you will write today," NOT "I hope all of you out there will write today."

17. Look either at the camera or another individual on the program. The "live" camera, the one sending the picture out over the air or being recorded on the master tape, always will be indicated by a red light being on near the lens. Do not look at a monitor set in the studio even if the camera is not on you; it *may* be at any moment!

18. There should be no reference to last week's program. All of the current audience may not have seen it. Nor should the audience be labeled by a certain classification, such as "you fishermen," or "you ranchers." Some viewers are not fishermen or ranchers, and besides, you want to create the illusion of there just being you and the person watching.

19. All movements, including getting up from a chair, must be slow so that the camera can follow. And, of course, movement on the set should be included in the program outline so the director and camera personnel know of it in advance.

20. A complex object should be shown for at least 30 seconds. This helps the viewers become fully aware of the item and what is being said about it.

21. The number of people in an average scene should be limited to two or three. More than this gives an impression of disorder and diverts attention.

22. Minor accidents or blunders can be glossed over, but obvious ones should be acknowledged gracefully, or perhaps humorously. They may liven up the program and will certainly create informality.

23. Watch the time closely. Know exactly how long the closing remarks will take. This way it is possible to end right on time. Time cues will be given by the floor manager. These should be understood before the program.

24. It is a good idea to have some "cushion material." This can be included or left out, depending on how the time is going.

25. If hosting a show, it is wise to keep one spare, complete program in readiness at all times in case key people do not show up or collapse from fright. It is best to assume nothing. Motion pictures can also be used as substitutes if necessary, but they must be appropriate, the right length, approved or edited for television use, and they should be introduced if being used in lieu of a regularly scheduled program.

Major Features

Although the opportunity to produce a major feature may be relatively rare, there is much to be gained by taking advantage of these opportunities. Many 30 and 60 minute productions have focused on natural resource management—some favorable and some unfavorable to scientific management. Like any other idea for television, the content of a major feature should be outlined

Figure 10.8. The U.S. Forest Service served as the setting for Wrather Corporation's Lassie series in the 1960's. Cooperation with individuals or corporations producing television features provides an opportunity to assure accuracy and enhance the image of natural resource management agencies. (Courtesy of USDA Forest Service.)

in enough detail to clearly communicate why it should be made. After clearing it with superiors, the program manager at different stations should be contacted until one agrees to produce the feature or the idea must be abandoned because of no interest. If sponsors (including foundations) are found or money made available for production, the chances are much greater that the idea will be transferred into a finished product.

Another opportunity arises through cooperating with others who are producing a major feature. The most outstanding example of this was the Forest Service-Lassie series that was produced from 1964 through 1970 by Wrather Corporation. This popular weekly show, which at one point was among the top 10 on television, had such an impact on the Forest Service image that a special position was established to provide a technical adviser to the show. He coordinated the Forest Service's assistance in providing vehicles, uniforms, equipment and ideas. In return for this cooperation, the corporation adhered to a strict code of ethics and portrayed Forest Service procedures with a high degree of reality.

Portable Videotape

In 1956 the first videotape recording equipment weighed over 1,000 pounds and cost $60,000. Today similar equipment weighs 30 pounds and can be purchased for about $1,000. Portable videotape cameras are used by elementary school children as well as by skilled television news teams. The equipment is not only light weight, but also amazingly simple to operate. Some models now even eliminate cables connecting the camera and videocassette recorder and have cameras that fit in one hand.

Use of videotape equipment in natural resource public relations work has been slow in catching on. Many agencies own equipment, and while examples of uses are many, outstanding accomplishments are few. Perhaps this remains a medium of the future in the resource disciplines. Those uses that have been made of videotape include:

1. Training—This use is best for routine procedures such as using equipment or learning a skill like how to letter with a Leroy set. The National Park Service has found it especially effective in teaching living history techniques to new seasonal personnel. Actually seeing and hearing living history interpreters from the previous year is far more effective than reading about it in a report. It is also commonly used for improving oral presentations, practicing for television appearances, or correcting faults in skiing, shooting and similar physical activities. When linked up with a computer, both videotape and videodiscs (which are even better for this purpose, albeit more expensive) also can provide excellent simulation and interactive learning opportunities. Flight simulators work on this principle, but it can just as effectively be applied to fire management and many other topics where the action on the screen is altered by the student's choices. In continuing education efforts, videotape has made lectures and entire workshops available to much wider audiences than more traditional training methods.
2. Public Information—At public involvement workshops, open houses or similar meetings with external publics it is possible to show small groups of people a variety of landscape scenes and management practices with more action than slides allow and without the high costs of motion picture films. In other cases, fire suppression activities have been

taped and shown to politicians, mass media representatives, agency officials and at community meetings to clarify the fire emergency and assure people of efforts being made. Also, tapes can be made using a story format for use in schools and colleges having playback equipment.

3. Exhibits—Anything that can be shown as slides or motion pictures can be shown on videotape. In the case of slides, the images are simply shot by a videotape camera while they are projected on the screen. Or, the slides can be videotape recorded through internal mechanisms and then played back on a monitor built into an exhibit case. Thus, instead of four or five pieces of equipment necessary for rear-screen projection in dissolve, only two are necessary (recorder/playback and monitor) if the program is put on tape. Two additional advantages are cooler operation in confined areas, and the opportunity to link the videotape player to more than one monitoring screen so many groups can view it simultaneously.

4. Documentation—Criminal evidence, the behavior of drunks, the actions of vandals, fires, floods, or accidents are some of the things that can be quickly and easily documented on videotape by anyone who can hold a camera.

5. Security/Research—At museums and large visitor centers cameras are sometimes mounted in hallways that can not be observed from the information desk. Monitors under the desk counter can then be watched for vandalism. The very presence of the cameras seems to be an effective deterrent. If hidden, they can be helpful in research to find out how people react to the various exhibits. However, before using cameras in this way, it is necessary to obtain agency clearance. For example, for making counts or studying behavior, researchers in federal agencies are often required to adjust the lenses so that the subjects' faces can not be identified.

6. Interpersonal Communication—For making a strong impression, a videotaped message can be far superior to a memo or letter. For example, the chief of an agency may want all regional or district supervisors to support a newly issued directive. If equipment is available for replay, the chief's message can be sent to each office as easily as a letter, but with the added force of sound and non-verbal expressions. In another example, a staff officer was on a trip a long way from headquarters. He encountered a local manager facing a touchy public relations problem. Rather than relying on notes and memory to convey the situation back to the chief administrator for a decision, he set up a videotape camera and recorded the discussion with the manager. In this way a clear, accurate version of the problem was later communicated to the decision-maker.

There are probably additional uses of this medium and one might think we have omitted the most important—use of agency-produced videotapes for broadcast on commercial television. Unfortunately, the quality possible through most "home" and "institutional" videotape equipment does not meet the exacting standards of broadcast television. Studios usually use 2 inch videotape, whereas most agencies have ¾ inch equipment. Some may even use ½ inch formats. The latter is to television what the Brownie camera is to photography. Even ¾ inch tape is used by most studios only if it is absolutely essential (like highly unusual news footage) or is of the highest technical quality. Also, special equipment is necessary to convert the ¾ inch tape to a larger size before telecasting it over the airwaves. Some smaller stations do not have such equipment. Still, for most uses other than broadcast television, ¾ inch is the best choice combining satisfactory quality and compatibility with the widest range of equipment.

Figure 10.9. Portable camera and videocassette recorder powered by batteries. (Courtesy of Sony Video Products Company.)

The basic equipment in a videotape ensemble consists of a camera, a videotape recorder (VTR), and a monitor. The camera can be hand-held or mounted on a tripod. The VTR is very much like an audio tape recorder (Fig. 10.9), and the monitor is simply a TV screen. In addition, there must be a power source. This can be either a portable battery pack, or regular AC current that runs through a power adapter. Equipment is also available to adapt power from a 12-volt car battery. Operation of the equipment requires little more than a reasonable amount of practice and following the instructions that come with the equipment. Other suggestions are provided in the checklist insert.

Editing videotape requires two monitors, a VTR, an editing deck and connecting cables. For good results two high quality editing decks are best. This costs money, takes a surprising amount of time and requires a high degree of patience. Unlike film, videotape can not be cut and spliced, it must be electronically edited. Books are available on the techniques and styles of editing, but for the occasional user it will pay to use someone else's facilities. The other way to avoid the expense and time commitment is to shoot in a carefully-planned sequence (following a production script), stopping to erase whenever an error occurs. The results are invariably less satisfactory than if edited, especially because of the "glitches" that appear when the tape starts and stops after triggering the camera. The final use of the tape must determine whether the expense of editing is justified.

Television Graphics

Television is a visual medium. Whether you are a host, guest or producer, every effort should be made to take advantage of visual aids. However, television has three characteristics that must be remembered when considering the use of visuals. One is the standard *shape* of television screens, a rectangle that is 3 units high by 4 wide. This is the *aspect ratio* and must be invariably respected. Fortunately, 35 mm slides closely match this ratio, but only horizontal slides may be used. Artwork for television is usually done on 11″ × 14″ cards. Around the edges of this format there is a

---

√ **CHECKLIST FOR GOOD VIDEOTAPING TECHNIQUE**

Camera Techniques

_____ Plan your production ahead of time. Use a production script.
_____ Shoot in a logical sequence to avoid the need for editing.
_____ Shoot cut-aways for transitions from scene to scene.
_____ Avoid jump cuts (shooting an object at similar angles or distances from the camera).
_____ Make all pans and zooms very *slowly*.
_____ Don't over use the pan and zoom. This is a common error of amateurs.
_____ Hold the camera as still as possible and use a tripod whenever possible.
_____ Keep lenses clean and camera in good working condition. (Avoid shock and rough handling).

Audio

_____ Use separate microphones for the main audio pick-up and background pick-up and route everything through an audio mixer.
_____ Use wind screens (that fit like a glove over the microphone) during windy outdoor productions.
_____ Microphones must be kept in close proximity to talent. Lapel or necklace-type mikes are ideal and cordless ones are now available.

Lighting

_____ Never, never aim the camera directly into the sun or bright lights. This will damage the pick-up tube.
_____ In studio situations, experiment with various lighting angles including key spotlights, back lighting and full lighting.
_____ Try to illuminate your subject as evenly as possible (unless an unusual effect is desired).
_____ Be careful of things that cause glare.
_____ Continually monitor lighting levels and adjust as necessary to the proper aperture

Miscellaneous

_____ Always carry spare cables, microphones, and batteries for all video and audio equipment on remote productions.
_____ Keep all video equipment clean and moisture free.
_____ Avoid exposing equipment to extreme heat or cold.
_____ A periodic maintenance check-up is a good idea.

---

narrow strip that is likely to be "cut off" on home monitors that are not in perfect adjustment. About 10 percent of any slide, photograph, static graphic or other visual should be considered to be in this border. Therefore, all lettering, people's faces, and other important content should fall within the remaining *safe* or *essential area* (Figure 10.10).

Contrast is another important consideration in designing television graphics. The primary rule is that the color of an object on television is influenced by the color surrounding it. Therefore, all color combinations in a graphic must be complementary. A color wheel should be consulted as a guide. Otherwise, hands sometimes turn blue, trees show up black, and other embarrassing freaks reveal that the designer did not do his homework. When using black and white combinations, it is best to substitute grey for white. In any visual, glare must be prevented through use of a dulling spray or, for photographs, a matte finish.

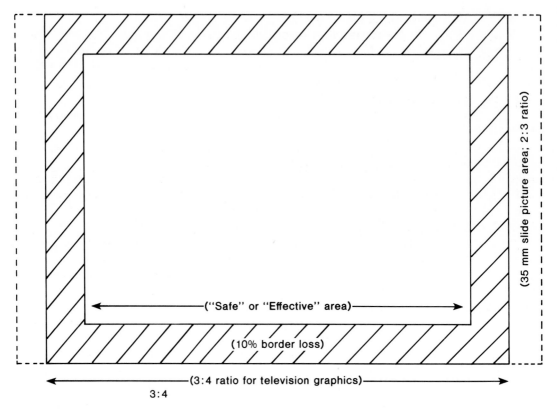

Figure 10.10. The 3:4 aspect ratio and safe area for television graphics. On slides or other graphics, words and essential information must be in the center area.

Resolution (sharpness of the picture) on television is the third consideration. A television picture actually consists of several hundred horizontal lines flashing a rapid succession of scenes across the screen. Because of this, fine horizontal lines and details are often lost. This makes it important to keep all lettering simple, bold and limited to three or four lines. Bold-faced, sans serif letters (the kind without—*sans*—the tiny hooks at their ends) are best and should be at least 1/6 the height of the graphic's safe area.

Many stations have graphic artists who produce the artwork. If not, the above guidelines should help avoid most problems. Other practices include placing slides in glass mounts if they are to be returned. This prevents damage, but it is important to first check on whether the station's equipment can handle the kind of mounts you use. Slides a little on the light or "thin" side are better, as television seems to darken the effect. These are overexposed rather than underexposed. All slides should be previewed before showing. Carelessness is the only explanation for the wrong picture or an inverted image. This may be the responsibility of station personnel, but the natural resource manager is the one who is blamed and looks foolish.

Film clips add motion and take the viewer out of the studio and into the forest, marshland or other resource area. Sound can be on the film or it can be narrated in the studio. Longer films, especially made for television, should be from 12 to 14 minutes or 27 to 29 minutes long. This allows time for commercials or spot announcements. Most studios prefer 16 millimeter film taken at 24 frames per second, which is sound speed. All motion pictures should be checked before use on television. Those found to be scratched or having torn or badly worn sprocket holes should be rejected. Some that were not made for television may present problems with aspect ratio. These, too, should be rejected. Possible legal restrictions should also be checked to make sure the film has been cleared for television use and that no royalties will need to be paid to the film maker.

Looking to the Future

The day is past when good public relations could be achieved by just "spittin' n' whittlin' " with local landowners or by making an annual presentation to the Kiwanis Club. Not only is it essential to analyze issues and plan appropriate strategies, it is important to reach large audiences on a continuous basis. Television is a key to the latter. It appears that the television set in the 80's will get bigger, better and more flexible. It may even begin to incorporate holography or other kinds of projections in three dimensions. In tandem with home computers, it may help people select portions of the daily newspaper to read on the screen or print out, or the latest stock market reports, skiing conditions, or maybe even data about state park conditions, forest planning or fire danger. Cable and satellite are linking the entire nation into a readily accessible audience. In theory, every citizen could watch the same event simultaneously. In reality, there is increasing opportunity to select from scores of channels on cable or from space. The new television provides access to entertainment, education, and special interests ranging from religion to pornography. Combined with two-way capability, television systems will someday also be the setting of gargantuan town meetings or other forums where public opinion can instantly be obtained.

In the house of the future, the television set is likely to be the entertainment and communication center for the family and the nation. Already television is growing toward life-size imagery. Also millions of homes have recording/playback units they can use for recording incoming programs and their own productions, or for reviewing rented or purchased full-length features. Capitalizing on this new medium, some advertisers such as car dealers are beginning to loan tapes to potential customers so they can watch a product in action or receive detailed information from the factory or testing grounds. Travel agents also make good use of videotape in enticing customers to buy cruise tickets or visit some exotic resort. Educators are even catching on and making instructional tapes more available. Economics and perfected technology will eventually make all these innovations as common and widespread as the color television set.

Will the natural resource manager come out of the woods and take advantage of this communication technology? Or will we collectively write it off as too sophisticated? The success of public relations in natural resource management may well depend on the answer. The possibilities are limited only by our imaginations and our willingness to become skilled in this rapidly changing medium. It must be recognized by both managers and public relations specialists as one more opportunity to communicate effectively.

MOTION PICTURES

Motion pictures have many of the same attributes as television. Most importantly, people associate these media with entertainment. Also, attention-holding action can be vividly portrayed. Motion pictures, in addition, have sharper resolution than television, can be shown to larger groups at the same place and time, and require display equipment that is more widely available at locations ranging from schools to sportsmen's clubs. Its format is also unalterable, so the messages are received in the precise order intended by the sender.

Virtually all natural resource agencies have their motion picture libraries. Mindick (1981) found that the average state fish and game agency had 42 different titles, up slightly from 39 reported by Gilbert (1962) and 29 by Kilgore (1953). Forest Service regional offices averaged 206 available titles, more than any other agency. For all agencies combined, however, only 12 percent of the films were produced by the natural resource agency offering the films for loan. The others were acquired from various sources. There are two good reasons for this, and they are the greatest disadvantages of this medium—skill and cost.

To produce a film worthy of public showings, expensive equipment is required as is a high degree of training to plan, shoot, edit, add sound and produce the finished product. This equipment and talent are unavailable to most natural resource managers. To contract the job, a 14-minute film could run from $10,000 to $50,000. Few budgets can fund communication projects at that level very often. Why so expensive? As an example of what can be involved, consider the production of *In Search of Balance,* a 25-minute film produced by Anthony T. Lorch for the National Recreation and Parks Association. It took 10 months to make the film, with a staff of up to 7 travelling some 20,000 miles to seven states. The film used 28 different voices, 12 different people on camera, original music (called the *score*), and required information from more than 110 people. Eventually 15,000 feet of 16 mm film were shot and edited down to 936 feet for the 25-minute and 45-second product (Anon., 1978). Had this not been a gratis contribution to NRPA, the price tag would have been at least $52,000.

Motion pictures may be produced in several sizes (irrespective of length) which have certain characteristics. These are:

8 mm   The original "home movies" size. These are inexpensive to produce, but each frame is so small that projected quality is too poor for most public use. This size is mostly of a by-gone era.

Super 8   This innovation is an exception to the motion picture cost barrier. Although only 8 mm wide, each frame was enlarged by reducing the wasted space on the edge of the film taken up by sprocket holes in regular 8 mm film. The result is a film that can be projected to at least classroom size wlth reasonable quality. Moreover, it is ideal for continuous loop, rear-screen projection in exhibits or auto-tutorial carrels. Cameras and equipment for processing, editing, projecting and even converting to videotape are very affordable.

16 mm   The picture areas, or frames, in 16 mm film are about three times larger than those in super 8. Resolution, even when projected in most auditoriums, is excellent. This is the size of nearly all motion pictures produced for public presentations in the natural resource (or other) professions. It is also the size readily accepted by television stations for use as film clips, PSA's or full length features. Projection equipment for 16 mm is commonly available, easy to use, and affordable.

35 mm   Few of us will ever see anything of this film except the projected image. It is the size used in most commercial entertainment productions shown in theaters and drive-ins. It is the celluloid of which Hollywood is made.

Motion pictures in public relations work are the realm of highly skilled professionals. Amateurs interested in super 8 productions for exhibitry or training purposes should obtain one of Kodak's fine publications on movie-making or seek another source of "how-to" information. Through reading and practice a reasonable product can be created for limited use. Naturally, the basic rules of planning apply, specifically: zeroing in on a particular public, defining objectives, and keeping messages brief, attractive and to the point. A production script like those described earlier will also help immensely.

For production of 16 mm films, there are two advisable alternatives: work through agency motion picture specialists or contract with a reputable film maker. Either way, the first meeting should include a frank discussion of available funds. It is not what you do, but how you do it that can make a lot of difference in cost. Next, the film maker should be given clear guidance regarding the intent and general nature of the film but without crimping his creative abilities. For example, Crawley Films Limited provides clients with a specification outline which states, "This form will help you consolidate your thinking and ensure that everyone is working precisely to your objectives. It is based on Crawley's experience in producing more than 2,000 motion pictures for marketing, information and public relations programs." The questionnaire is then divided into the following headings:

1. **The purpose**—Both primary and secondary.
2. **The audience**—Again, primary and secondary, a checklist of publics.
3. **Distribution**—What system(s) will be used to make the film available to the target public.
4. **The Scope**—The client is asked to provide the key points of the subject which would achieve the stated purpose with the target publics.
5. **Technical elements**—film size, length, color or black and white, existing or original music, suggested locations, professional actors, etc.
6. **Client Information**—The name of the client's representative, what facilities and materials are available, existing film footage, how many years the film should be active (this is an often overlooked detail), due date and budget.

The final product is a team effort, but a very specific contract should spell out such details as: which party is to provide what, when it is to be done (script written/approved, storyboard drawn/approved, first print produced/approved, and final print delivered—and how many), and what degree of quality can be assured by the producer. The best results can then be obtained if the producer is allowed to use his imagination in weaving the story and photography together into a film that meets the stated criteria. Of course, approval of each step should remain the prerogative of the client—and should be made or denied promptly—but the producer usually will have a less biased, more imaginative and more experienced perspective to bring to bear on the project. A state by state list of commercial motion picture producers is contained in Walter Klein's excellent book, *The Sponsored Film.* It is included in the suggested references at the end of this chapter.

Not too long ago, Gilbert (1971) found it necessary to report that "too many natural resource films are the result of splicing haphazard photographic efforts of amateurs. The reception of the public reflects this, and what money is spent is largely wasted." Today natural resource films rank with the best. For example, the Missouri Department of Conservation consistently produces first class films on the lives of foxes, mourning doves and other conservation topics; private individuals have powerfully used emotion in award-winning films such as Bill Snyder's *Cry of the Marsh* and spectacular photography in Marty Stouffer's *Bighorn*! In 1977 student Mike Way made a strong statement against extinction of wildlife in the award-winning *At the Threshold of Eternity*. One reason for the rise in quality may be the annual film contests sponsored by organizations such as the student chapter of The Wildlife Society at the University of Montana, the Outdoor Writers Association of America, and the Society of American Foresters. It may also be due to the rising awareness that this means of communication—if used correctly—can take powerful messages to many key publics time after time.

AUTOMATED SOUND/SLIDE PROGRAMS

In recent years automated sound/slide productions have come to be seen as an inexpensive approximation of the motion picture. The format was initially crude. Some efforts were silent, rear-screen monstrosities used in exhibits in which a large, Viewmaster-like reel holding the slides turned at timed intervals before a projector lamp. Front-screen programs for groups began with a tape recording accompanying a tray of slides, with an audible tone signal beeping, clicking or chiming to alert an attendant to advance the tray at that point in the narration.

Today equipment is available in affordable price ranges that allow quick, easy and totally automatic synchronization of slides to narration and/or music and other sound effects. Procedures and equipment vary, but basically the message and music are recorded on audio tape. At each point where a slide change is desired, an electronic impulse is added to the tape. According to Sam Ham, an interpretive specialist at the University of Idaho, there are now dozens of brands of equipment currently available to do the job (ranging from $50 to $10,000 or more), but all work on one of these principles:

Indiscriminate Noise Signal—The earliest truly automatic system. It requires placing all narration and music on one channel of a stereo tape, and *any* sound (buzz, screech or abruptly spoken word like "now") on the other channel. In playback, the audience hears the one channel, whereas an electronic decoder "hears" the other track and advances the projector each time it "hears" a sound. These are the least expensive and go by such brand names as Kodak's "Sound Synchronizer" and Optisonic's "Sound 'o' Matic."

Frequency-determined Signal—This was developed to provide greater versatility of functions performed by the equipment. Again, the narration is placed on one track of a stereo tape (or two in some equipment, since there actually are four soundtracks when you recall that tapes can be "turned over" and run both ways—two tracks each way on stereo systems). On the unused track(s) go signals of different frequencies to trigger various functions. For example, one frequency may activate or shut off the house lights; another may operate the curtains or place an automatic "black slide" in position to darken the screen; others signal one or more projectors to advance, or various rates of dissolve to occur between slide changes. Examples of equipment that operate on this principle include Spindler & Sauppe's "Dynamic Dissolve" and "Quadra-que," and Audiotronics' "Classette" tape recorder.

Digital Impulses—A problem with frequency-determined signals is that they are occasionally misread by dirty synch mode sensors, or they misfire if similar extraneous "noise" accidentally gets on the tape, or they are not discerned correctly as the equipment gets old. Any misreading can bring disaster to a coordinated program (like having the curtains close instead of a slide tray advance!) Therefore, the most advanced step in the evolution of common sound/slide systems is to use digital impulses to trigger different functions. An example of equipment using this technique is Wollensak's "Digi-cue Pro" series, AVL's "animal series" (Eagle, Dove, Fox, etc.), and Kodak's Programmable Dissolve Control.

Automated sound/slide production, particularly when coupled with dissolve units and/or multiple projectors, adds an exciting and sophisticated dimension to presenting messages. Movement can be portrayed to a limited degree without the expense of film or the viewing limitations of videotape. Messages can be developed and distributed with little danger of their being altered. The medium is fairly easy to use, productions are cost-effective and the finished product can be highly attractive. The greatest disadvantages are the initial expense of stereo recording equipment and the programmer (synchronizer), and the fact that many schools or other organizations do not have playback equipment readily available. It is much easier to ship a 16 mm film and have it shown than it is to package slide trays and a tape and have the receiver assemble the necessary compatible equipment. With so many devices involved, there is a lot of room for foul-up.

Another objection sometimes is the complexity of planning the script and synchronizing the message with music and slide changes—especially if multiple projectors are involved. Certainly this medium is not for the person (perhaps the *typical* natural resource manager!) who throws together some slides, grabs a projector and rushes off to make a presentation. An automated sound/slide production requires the same careful planning and development of a production script as would be necessary for a film or television. The production script needs one column for the narration, one for the accompanying music (what record or piece on a tape and at what point in the narration it should fade in or out), and one for each screen if it is a multiple-image production (i.e. indicating what scenes are on each). With a carefully prepared script, it is easier to "mix in" the appropriate music at the precise moments and at the desired volume. At the same time, or usually later, the electronic impulses can be added at the points indicated in the script. The script is the key to simplifying the most complex sound/slide productions.

In considering this medium for use in public relations work, there is a temptation to think only in terms of super, wham-bang extravaganzas using a dozen projectors and a barn-sized screen. While this may be necessary at a world's fair or other very special occasion, just as much can usually be accomplished with much less equipment. For each projector added, the potential for problems at least quadruples. This risk, along with cost, must be considered in arriving at a reasonable compromise on how far to go with automated slide productions.

For public relations purposes, the other extreme should not be overlooked. This is the self-contained, rear-screen viewing unit such as Singer's "Caramate" or Bell & Howell's "Ring Master." These are the simplest projection devices to program, and they are inexpensive, dependable, easily transported, and available in most schools. Programs can easily be developed and mailed, or units can be placed in ranger stations' waiting rooms, or other points where target publics can be reached.

SUGGESTED REFERENCES

Communicating Effectively on Television by Evan Blythin and Larry A. Samovar. 1985. Wadsworth Publishing Co., Belmont, CA.

Handbook of Interactive Video by Steve and Beth Floyd. 1982. Knowledge Industry Publications, White Plains, NY.

Images, Images, Images by Michael F. Kenny and Raymond F. Schmitt. 1979. Eastman Kodak Corp., Rochester, N.Y.

Radio in the Television Age by Peter Fornatale and Joshua E. Mills. 1980. The Overlook Press, Woodstock, N.Y.

The Art and Science of Radio by Linda Bush and Donald Parker. 1984. Allyn and Bacon, Inc. Boston.

The Sponsored Film by Walter J. Klein. 1976. Communication Arts Books/Hastings House, Publishers, New York.

Understanding Broadcasting by Eugene S. Foster. 1978. Addison-Wesley Publishing Co., Reading, Mass.

UPI Broadcast Stylebook. 1979. United Press International, 360 N. Michigan Ave., Chicago, Ill. 60601.

PART IV

Some Special Considerations

In this final section we review several aspects of public relations that do not fit logically elsewhere in the book. Their placement here does *not* mean they are less important. For example, operating within the world of politics is increasingly a way of life for natural resource and recreation specialists. It is no longer possible to think we can "rise above politics." Natural resources belong to or affect everyone, and citizens are viewing this ownership as important like never before. The political system offers citizens one way to express the degree of their interest and to attempt controlling what is theirs. To help guide actions and to compete in the arena of public opinion, the natural resource manager must have at least a basic understanding of the political side of government and how it is influenced.

Emergency information services are a special form of public relations. Some resource managers are involved with communicating during emergency situations quite frequently, as in the southern California area with its annual brush fires. It was there that the specialty of fire information arose. Others may encounter such situations only rarely. Whatever your situation, Chapter 13 will help you be prepared for what could be one of the most intense experiences of your career.

The closing chapter contains an array of topics that mostly relate to the future of public relations in natural resource management, including the training of men and women to work in this important field.

11

Communication Techniques—Exhibits, Special Events and Photography

In addition to personal appearance programs and mass media methods of communication, there are other ways to contact and influence people that do not fit either of the two categories. There are, in fact, more ways than can possibly be fitted into one book. In this chapter we have selected a few of the techniques that are often used by natural resource personnel for public relations purposes.

EXHIBITS

Exhibits are a time-honored favorite channel of communication with people of all ages. As late as 1977 they were also used more among fish and game agencies than any other nonpersonal channel except news releases (Wildlife Management Institute, 1977). By the time of our 1985 national survey, exhibits did not seem as popular with fish and game personnel or other agency employees (Table 7.1), but their use is still very high.

In the natural resource fields, exhibits range from table-top displays at public meetings and portable exhibits at county fairs to world fair extravaganzas and mobile exhibits such as the Idaho Forest Council's $70,000, 18-wheeler that makes the rounds to schools and communities throughout the Northwest. Some exhibits, like the sawmill in Figure 11.1, have appeal because they miniaturize the giant and put it on a scale people can comprehend. Battlefield dioramas are another good example. Other exhibits, like rare gems or historical objects in a museum, make it possible to see the uncommon or the unique. Still others overwhelm by bringing life-size giants within reach, a technique unequaled by the blue whale in New York's Museum of Natural History.

Regardless of size or purpose, exhibits can be effective channels of communication *if* the designer follows the ABC's of good exhibitry—*attractiveness, brevity* and *clarity.* The following are guidelines toward this end.

Attractiveness

The most powerful message will have no effect unless people are attracted to the exhibit. Given the formidable competition of surrounding exhibits or activities, this challenge must be given careful attention. Some techniques that usually work include:

Giveaways—Rulers, book marks, maps, litter bags and tree seedlings are among the giveaway gimmicks that not only attract attention and make others want to stop, but also can extend the exhibit's message. At fairs, perhaps sun visors or shopping bags printed with the organization's name are best of all as an attractant. They are highly visible, immediately *useful* and will attract large numbers of people who want the item.

Lights—The flash of an emergency vehicle's red light is an attention getter, but may have limited appropriateness. Other blinking or moving lights, or special effect lighting, may be able to be worked into the exhibit.

Movement—Running water, mobiles, motion pictures and scenes with mechanical parts will help draw the interest of passers-by.

Giant Objects—Who has not noticed the oversize Paul Bunyon at a fair, or a parachute held aloft by helium-filled balloons? Similarly, such items as a giant hatchet from a hardware store display, or a six-foot fishhook will not go unnoticed.

Live Animals—These are always among the most popular exhibits. However, great care must be taken not only to protect viewers from the animals, but also to avoid even the suggestion of any abuse of the animals.

Sound—There are often ground rules preventing loud speakers or broadcast sounds. Always check. If permitted, sometimes the repetition of a sound is an attraction, perhaps a recorded crow call or coyote howl. Periodic demonstrations also draw crowds. Sound transmitted in individual earphones or at low volume to small groups watching a slide show is particularly effective.

Participation—Many people like to push buttons, lift flaps, turn knobs or feel strange objects. Any technique that physically involves the exhibit viewer will not only attract others, but will aid recall of those contacted. For example, research has shown that short quizzes arouse more interest, subtly causing the viewer to look more carefully at the exhibit.

Brevity

Exhibits can be cost effective, flexible and easy to use. But one thing they can't be is lengthy. The average exhibit is viewed for less than 60 seconds by most people who see it. Shiner and Shafer, Jr. (1975) conducted an interesting experiment at the Adirondack Museum in Blue Mountain Lake, New York. They timed how long it would take the average person to read all the copy in an exhibit. Then, from a hidden position, they clocked visitors who stopped at the exhibit. After doing this with 14 representative exhibits and dozens of people, they made their conclusions, underscoring the need for brevity in exhibit copy. They found that messages requiring 2 to 4.9 minutes of viewer attention were actually viewed 1.3 minutes—or 45 percent of the time necessary for the entire message to be communicated. Exhibits that required 5 to 28 minutes of attention received proportionally less attention. For example, only 27 percent of the total required time was taken at exhibits where it would be necessary to spend 15 minutes or more. And this was at an extremely attractive place where the visitors had paid good money to get in!

Figure 11.1. A lumber company takes a miniaturized working model of a sawmill to fairs and special events. It is a popular attraction and opens the way to communication. (Photo by J. R. Fazio.)

Anyone planning an exhibit should keep the 60 second time frame in mind. This is not much time to do what all good public relations exhibits should—*attract attention* and *arouse interest, stimulate thought,* and *motivate the viewer to act, or be persuaded (or reinforced) toward a point of view.* But this is possible, despite the short amount of time to do the job. Consider the power of some billboards, despite the fact that they are viewed on the average of only *five* seconds.

Careful design can impart the message rapidly, at least through the third level of detail which will be explained later. Clever exhibitry can also be used to entice the viewer to stay longer, pick up material to read later, or to engage in conversation with an attendant who can then use the powers of interpersonal communication (Figure 11.1).

Clarity

To communicate quickly requires more thought and careful planning than when a larger time period is available. It is also essential that all aspects of the message be crystal clear. To achieve this, it is necessary to begin with an objective—a step most people completely skip. To see if this is true, visit the educational exhibits at a fair or conference and ask the attendant, "What do you hope to achieve with this exhibit?" In the commercial sector, the objective is obvious—to sell a product or service. But among the resource agencies present, more often than not the person you ask will have only the vaguest notion of what exactly the exhibit is to achieve. Before a word of copy is written or the first sketch is made, decide one or two things to be accomplished. Examples might be to: *inform* about fire management policies in wilderness; *persuade* that steel shot is the best shotgun shell load to use; *teach* campers how to survive in grizzly bear country; or *stimulate interest* in a new hobby such as woodworking.

Next, think carefully about your *target* public. It is impossible to design exhibits to reach everyone, so consider the characteristics of those you are aiming at in your objective. Consider their likely age, sex, interests, educational level and position in the adoption sequence. For example, an effective exhibit where one is trying to teach campers to survive in grizzly country needs to be quite different if aimed at car campers stopping at a campground office in Yellowstone National Park than if the target public were experienced backpackers finally "making it" to the Arctic National Wildlife Refuge.

Clarity also results from *simplifying* and *organizing* the message. Simplifying means focusing only on one or two objectives. It also means arranging the wording to speed delivery of the main points. For example, full sentences are not always necessary. Sentence fragments may be quite acceptable, as are listed items next to *attention marks* ($\sqrt{}$ * ● —, etc.) that can replace narration in presenting key points.

Organization refers to arranging the content of an exhibit in some logical order that will help communicate with people having different degrees of interest. The "logic" comes from being aware of four levels of messages. These levels provide the framework on which to build communication that helps make an exhibit truly effective:

Level I—Story Awareness. This level of message is the title on an exhibit, its color, a background silhouette, three-dimensional objects, or some combination of these elements. The function at level I is to initially interest the viewer and foreshadow what can be found in the exhibit. For example, the most rushed visitor should clearly see the title (preferably located at or just above eye level) and either know what the exhibit is about or be enticed to find out. Level I, especially the title or objects, is the "hooker."

Level II—Theme Awareness. Level II should quickly and clearly convey the "so what?" Usually subtitles and subheads serve this function. If the title was "Stay Alive in Grizzly Country," a level II message might be:

Most Victims Have Violated One of Three Simple Rules.

If a person stops for only a few seconds, he should be able to derive some information from this part of the exhibit that helps meet the objective for the exhibit. Ideally, however, it will draw him into the third level message, much like a good lead in a story draws the reader into the body of the text.

Level III—First Order Detail. This is the body of the exhibit's story. It may be copy, photographs, an audio message, or anything else that is used to elaborate on the theme and provide the essential information. It is the "meat" of the communication and provides enough detail to fully meet the objective(s) set for the exhibit.

For the above example, a level III message might be:

Ninety percent of the bear-human accidents in this park's backcountry during the past 10 years could have been prevented by (1) making noise while hiking, (2) camping away from the trail or water's edge, and (3) storing all food away from the camp site.

Level IV—Second Order Detail. This level is for those people who really get hooked. They are the relatively few who want more. Usually this level is communicated through a handout, but it might be in a film, videotape, audio message repeater, or personal communication. The information is related to the topic of the exhibit, but it either goes into more depth on the theme than is necessary to meet objectives, or it goes beyond the theme into other related concepts.

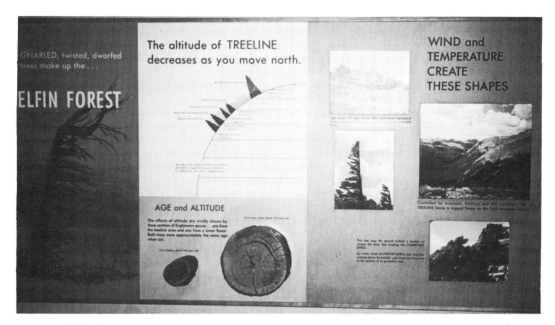

Figure 11.2. Visual flow is a quality of effective exhibits, incorporating design, color, or both to guide the eye through the messages in a planned sequence. Three levels of messages are also evident in this exhibit. (Courtesy of The National Park Service.)

Design Principles

An exhibit has the inherent problem of being a *non-linear* medium. That is, the viewer is not forced to receive the message in the sequence intended by the sender. A film or speech is *linear,* but in an exhibit the viewer can start at the end and read or observe backwards, or even skip critical portions of the message. The only way to overcome this weakness is through careful design. Most design principles are common sense but essential. For example, to take advantage of our cultural trait of reading left to right, the sequence of the exhibit should also follow that order. Other principles include those discussed earlier in the section on visual aids and colors, and on print media. Letter size, type style and color selections should all contribute to legibility and rapid communication. Most importantly, layout and/or color should be used to create *visual flow.* Visual flow is some method of guiding the eye through the exhibit's messages in the sequence that is most effective. This may be something as obvious as arrows, connecting lines, or numbered steps, or it may be more subtle like a progressive change in background color or small to large shapes.

In planning an exhibit, it helps to review some of the considerable volume of literature resulting from research on the design of exhibits. This is found largely in the museum field in publications such as *Curator* and *Museum News.* The USDA Forest Service and several universities have also done useful studies, one of which is listed at the end of this chapter. Another, conducted by Washburne and Wagar (1972), determined several exhibit characteristics that influenced visitor interest. These are briefly summarized in Table 11.1 and provide useful clues to designing effective exhibits.

Table 11.1.
Exhibit Characteristics in Relation to Expressed Visitor Interest
(Based on Washburne and Wagar, 1972).

Exhibit Element	High Interest	Interest Value[1]	Low Interest	Interest Value[1]
Presentation	Motion pictures	2.30	Text	.71
Stimuli	Changing lighting	1.89	Backlighted slides and	
	Music	1.66	transparencies	.69
	Audio sequences	1.65	Black and white	
	Scale objects	1.42	illustrations	.59
	Paints or drawings	1.25	Mounted photographs	.57
	Authentic objects	1.16	Flatwork	.46
Strategies	Cause-effect		Isolated facts and	
	relationships	1.70	identification	.66
	Parts making a story	1.33	Superlatives	.55
	Seating provided	1.30	Participation	.35
			Relating to common	
			knowledge	.32
			Surprise	.21
Subjects	Violence or destruction	1.82	General environment	
	Land-shaping		and scenery	.71
	processes	1.28	Climate and weather	.23
	Aesthetics	1.28		
	Ecological relationships	1.15		
	Mammals and birds	1.14		

1. Ratio of actual choices ÷ expected choices. 1.00 is average. All values shown are significantly (.05 level) above or below the average. See original report for exhibit elements determined to have interest value around 1.00.

Another important aspect of design is durability and the ease with which the exhibit can be transported, set up, and taken down. An exhibit with lights out, audio-visual equipment malfunctioning, or parts torn off by vandals reflects poorly on the sponsor. Rugged, vandal-resistant materials should be used, and construction should be done by skilled workers or commercial designers. A list of contractors, as well as a guide to companies selling exhibit frames and accessories, can be obtained through The Official Museum Directory (National Register Publishing Co., 5201 Old Orchard Rd., Skokie, Illinois 60077).

Exhibit Attendants

When personnel accompany an exhibit, they too are on display. To the thousands who pass by, these individuals are *the* agency or organization. The job they face is extremely important, since the effectiveness of any exhibit is either enhanced or negated by the attendants. Why, then, does it seem to be a tradition among natural resource agencies that exhibit duty is relegated to the low person on the totem pole? In some instances seasonal or new employees are sent out alone with the exhibit to represent the organization to all whose interest is aroused.

√ **CHECKLIST FOR EXHIBIT ATTENDANTS**

_____ During exhibit assembly and take down, follow directions. Store after use, *ready* for next time. Check carefully before leaving for a remote location. One missing bolt or projector cord can spell disaster.

_____ Only knowledgeable personnel should be used. Select this representative *carefully*.

_____ If you don't know an answer, get the visitor's name and address and send the answer to him / her later. This is not only good service, it makes a very favorable impression.

_____ Know the building. Be able to direct people to restrooms, show rings, first aid station, etc.

_____ Be cheerful. This is not easy after a couple of hours on duty.

_____ Arrange for relief. This helps everyone stay cheerful!

_____ Keep surrounding area neat and clean. Continually pick up pop bottles, coffee cups, etc.

_____ Know how to repair possible breakdowns.

_____ Identify yourself with *legible* name tag. This means large letters; preferably with title and agency.

_____ Talk to anyone who looks interested, but don't frighten away the timid

_____ Don't sit in front of the exhibit *or* place chairs there. This commonly violated rule probably negates more good exhibits than any other.

_____ Don't let loose cords lay around.

_____ For your own protection, don't set down purses or other valuables. Remove or lock up valuable parts of an exhibit at night.

We believe that exhibit duty should be taken quite seriously. It presents an excellent chance to receive feedback. It also is an opportunity to influence people who have passed the awareness stage or who are at such a point in the sequence of adopting or rejecting an idea that only convincing, personal communication will be effective. Skilled, credible individuals are needed for this public relations function. Otherwise, it is better to have no one at all with the exhibit. The boxed insert provides guidelines that should help make the most out of exhibits that are accompanied by personnel.

Bulletin Boards

Bulletin boards are to exhibits what newsletters are to the print media—a potential for immediate and effective internal communication, but often relegated to little or no importance. This is unfortunate, because if used correctly, bulletin boards can be a key point for daily communication. For example, if a bulletin board is maintained and used for internal public relations, workers will make it a habit to check that location daily. If this is the case, it can be a reliable communication channel for posting new or changed regulations, coming events, news clippings about employees and the organization, safety alerts and other news. Importantly, it can also be used for stopping rumors.

More often than not, the bulletin board is virtually a wasteland of outdated notices. A cartoon once depicted this nicely. Sad Sack, the cartoon character, was looking at the bulletin board. In a corner under sheaves and sheaves of paper was a notice that read, "All men will fall out at 1400 hours and proceed to cross the Delaware"—signed, G. Washington.

Figure 11.3. Bulletin boards have the potential for rapid and effective internal communication. Unfortunately, they are often neglected and considered of little importance. (Photos by Jim Briggs, top, and Bruce Andersen.)

Like any other technique for creating good public relations, the effective bulletin board does not just happen. First must come the desire to use the tool correctly, followed by the two ingredients for success—organization and currency. Both can easily be achieved if—and this is a big IF—one person is delegated to take a few minutes *each day* to maintain the board. First it is necessary to bring order to chaos. The bulletin board shown in Figure 11.3 is a good example of how this can be done. Once the board is divided into sections to hold the most commonly used items, the next step is to keep it current. This is easily done by checking it daily or placing a removal date on each item, or both, and discarding notices no longer current. Items with no time value (such as a cartoon) should remain posted only a few days. The shorter the time period that things remain on the board, the more frequently viewers will visit it.

It is also good practice to require all posted items to be routed through the board keeper so that inappropriate items can be screened out. If they get posted by someone else, the keeper should remove them. Otherwise, the board loses its focus and becomes cluttered with items that do not meet the objectives set for that communication medium.

The use of color-coded panels is another way to help organize the board and make it attractive and neat. Keeping it interesting can be aided by a continual stream of cartoons and candid or informal photos of employees.

SPECIAL EVENTS

Ceremonies and Similar Staged Events

Staged events are both a form of publicity and an excellent way to create a forum for face-to-face communication. The idea is to create a "happening" that attracts visitors and media attention so that some specific message can be effectively transmitted. Favorable media attention and communication with visitors also help make those essential deposits in the "Bank of Goodwill."

Staged events have long been used in the natural resources field and have taken many forms. Generally they have been successful, effective, and have involved a wide variety of publics. Some, such as fishing derbies or beauty queen contests, are best left in the past. Others are viable as ever. These need to be considered when seeking ways to develop a total public relations program. Examples include: a parade to herald fire prevention week or the opening of a new bridge, fish hatchery, or highway; poster contests for kids; banquets for cooperating organizations or landowners; prominent speakers to "dedicate" a new (or remodeled) building or nature preserve; and ceremonies to "celebrate" the millionth visitor to an interpretive center, the hundredth tree farm in some locale, the anniversary of a mill, company or organization, or just about any other landmark occasion. Awards, too, can be built into staged events, usually centering around a prominent speaker who will make the event more newsworthy.

With imagination and careful planning, a staged event can be developed around almost anything. The key ingredient is to make it something that people will *want* to attend. A review of the elements that make "news" will suggest what attracts media representatives. Techniques that attract others include free prizes, contests, craft sales, free refreshments, rides (helicopters, fire trucks, horses, air boats, etc.) and similar devices.

IN STAGING A CEREMONY, DON'T FORGET. . . .

Preparation Prevents Problems

_____ Plan the agenda in detail (20-30 minutes is a good length for ceremonies)

_____ Schedule speakers and a M.C.; be cognizant of protocol in arranging order of speakers and seating

_____ Announcements in the mass media and to employees

_____ Special invitations to key people or organizations

_____ Prepare press kits and schedules of events for distribution

_____ Make a "contact list" with name, address and phone number of everyone you will be dealing with

_____ Arrange for a band or other music, clergy, color guard or entertainment where appropriate

_____ Visit site and be sure it is cleaned up and ready

_____ Make plans for bad weather

_____ Prepare and distribute a detailed itinerary for entire day (arrival of VIP's, who will meet them, transportation, etc.)

The Ceremony

Set your alarm and allow enough time to get to the ceremony site early. Review your checklist:

_____ Place directional signs if needed

_____ Seating arranged on platform for all speakers (and safely away from edge); reserved section ready for other officials and press

_____ PA system ready and working. Recording or other AV equipment ready

_____ VIP's—Assignments to pick them up, greet them, provide program (some like press kits), show them to seat

_____ Press—Press booth or room ready for passing out kits, badges and providing light refreshments. If VIP has agreed, arrange for news conference following ceremony; allow room for TV people to set up lights and cameras

_____ Audience—Ushers ready, distribution of programs arranged, crowd/traffic control ready (police)

_____ Flags and seals on speakers platform

_____ Photographers ready, band on hand, clergy, color guard

_____ Certificates, awards, plaques, deeds, etc. signed and on hand (in podium or with person to do the presenting)

Post Ceremony

_____ Have a definite ending (such as the M.C. announcing that the ceremony is concluded and thanking everyone for coming)

_____ Allow time for press shots before VIP's depart

_____ Facilitate getting VIP's and news media together if arrangements were made in advance (have room or other location reserved). If none was planned, ask VIP if he/she would like you to try arranging one. Do not play favorites with the media; give each the same opportunity

_____ If appropriate, a tour of the area for VIP's and press (by bus so all can be together)

_____ Luncheon, if appropriate (gratis for news media)

_____ Transportation for VIP's in time to make plane or other connections

_____ Cleanup of area

_____ Collect news clippings and photos; send copies to VIP's

_____ Evaluate what happened, right and wrong

Now you can have that nervous breakdown you've been promising yourself!

—Adapted from De Rocco (1974)

For a staged event to be a success, much advance planning is necessary. It must be done well or it should not be done at all, because negative results are always a possibility. Little things are important, such as adequate parking space and sufficient refreshments. People do not like to wait or be left out. Events must move like clockwork. Also, if the events are outdoors, a suitable rain alternative must be completely planned in advance.

Publicity is necessary before and after the event. All media should be used to attract attention. Special invitations should be sent to particularly important individuals or publics. After the happenings, follow-up pictures and stories will aid in obtaining the greatest value from the occasion. It is important to have your own photographer(s) record the events so that a file is available for future use. For the media representatives present, the best aid to getting good publicity is to furnish *press kits*. These can be specially printed folders or nothing more than manila envelopes. However, the contents must be of highest quality and should include:

- *Texts of any speeches*
- *Biographical sketches of speakers*
- *Black and white photos of speakers, facilities or other special features*
- *Quotable "fact sheet"*

- *Background brochure about the sponsoring organization*
- *Short articles focusing on any particular topic important to the public relations objectives.*
- *Checklist of other materials/services available (plus postage-paid envelope or request card)*

Open House

An open house is a staged event, yet it is different in that the publicity usually is not pointed toward any specific feature or deed of the organization but toward the entire effort. An open house can take place any time, at any natural resource agency facility, and simply gives the public a chance to see at least part of the organization's internal operations. An open house often is used to "show off" a new facility, but just as often it is at a place that is an established part of the community. It provides an "excuse" for people to finally go inside the fire house to get a close-up look, or to find out what takes place in some laboratory, school, mill or office.

An open house also provides an excellent opportunity for employees to show their family and friends where they work and what they do, and perhaps to meet "the boss." By serving as guides, formally or informally, a sense of pride can be established in employees at all levels. Others can demonstrate equipment, be projectionists for film or slide showings, serve refreshments or assist in other ways that involve as many as want to help.

To help get everything done and to spread out the workload, it is best to organize employees into committees. The number and kind of committees will vary, but here are some to consider. The *steering committee* is responsible for overall decisions, including planning times and schedules. The *publicity committee* handles publicity and announcements, within the organization and with external publics, before and after the actual happening. The *preparation committee* is responsible for facility readiness, safety and space coordination. Exhibits, displays, demonstrations, features, decorations and speeches are planned by the *special events committee*. The *tour and guide committee* coordinates the flow of traffic and assignment of guide duties. Refreshments, first aid, child care, playground supervision and greetings are handled by the *hospitality committee.* The last committee, *traffic,* is charged with parking problems, entry and exit of automobiles, and overall control of transportation.

Planning for an open house (and most other special events) should start at least two months ahead of the date. Announcements and advance publicity are suggested at six to seven weeks. Brochures and itineraries must be made ready one month before the event. Letters of invitation are sent to especially important people, including employees and media representatives, about three weeks before the event. Publicity such as posters, picture stories, spot announcements and newscasts are put into use one to two weeks before the open house.

During the open house, visitors should see and learn as much as possible in the time available. A definite itinerary should be developed and each person should receive a copy of it plus other printed material that might help meet the organization's objectives. Interested and capable guides must be present to explain things and answer questions. Tours should be neither too long nor too short. Explanations must be simple and interesting. Groups should be small enough for all persons to see and hear well. It is also a good idea to give some small souvenir, and refreshments usually are appreciated by everyone.

Tours

Through guided and self-guided tours, some organizations essentially host a continuous open house. For example, at Patuxent, Maryland, the U.S. Fish and Wildlife Service has installed continuous-loop recorded messages for visitors to its wildlife research center. Many forest product companies feature free guided tours through their mills and woodlands.

Many consider tours a nuisance and an expense. Others believe them to be a worthwhile investment in fostering good public relations. Often the tour guides are employees who have other duties between tours. They are selected on the basis of personality, knowledge and perhaps training in interpretation. They are the key to a successful tour program.

Tours begin with publicity describing the times and starting locations. Posters or brochures in motels, restaurants, chamber of commerce offices, visitor information centers and the mass media not only make the tours known to interested parties, but also provide one more avenue of continuous exposure in a favorable light. The tour itself must be highly organized, safe and interesting. It should begin on time at a location with adequate parking and with rest rooms available. Following a cheerful welcome and orientation, the tour should follow a logical sequence. Examples would be to follow a log through to lumber or wood chips to paper products. Other procedures are discussed in the section on Public Field Trips in Chapter 8.

At the conclusion of a facility tour, a brochure or other piece of literature will help multiply the benefits of the effort. It can reinforce key messages, help promote a favorable image, and serve as added publicity for the tour program. Another parting gesture is to provide a sample product or other souvenir. This might include a pad of writing paper from a paper mill, a wooden toy or knick-knack from a lumber mill, maple candy from a sugar bush, or a Smokey Bear item from a ranger station.

Evaluation of the tour, or any staged event, can be obtained by distributing postage-paid, mail-back questionnaire cards. To help improve future efforts, the cards might include such questions as:

What part of the tour (or program) was most interesting?
Were operations explained and questions answered to your satisfaction?
Was your guide attentive and courteous?
Was the length of time or distance satisfactory?
How did you learn of this tour (or open house)?
Would you recommend this to others as worthwhile?
Have you any suggestions for improving the tour (or event)?

Hunting and Fishing Day—A Success Story

One of the most successful special events related to natural resources is the annual National Hunting and Fishing Day. Brainchild of The National Shooting Sports Foundation, an industrial association, the event's steering committee includes representatives of a wide variety of conservation groups. These include the National Wildlife Federation, The Wildlife Society, American Forestry Association, the Izaak Walton League and others. The event is actually an impressive package of events put on by sporting groups, scouts, conservation organizations and others from coast to coast. It is a splendid example of what planning and promotion can do to publicize a message if someone believes in it strongly enough. In this case, the message is that hunters and fishers provide millions of dollars for conservation through the purchase of licenses and payment of excise taxes. And, to defuse any charges of propaganda, there is also a focus on the promotion of gun and boat safety, and the need for conservation of natural resources.

National Hunting and Fishing Day was first "celebrated" in 1972. That first year its various events attracted over 4 million people. By 1977 the number had grown to 20 million. By 1985, more than 2,500 programs were featured in communities nationwide and the "day" is considered by many an annual tradition. Earth Day (April 22, 1970), by contrast, was a spectacular flash in the pan. Like Arbor Day, it has not disappeared or been totally forgotten as an annual event, but its use as a special event has been irregular and anemic at best. The difference reflects what is stressed throughout this book—the need for planning and organization for successful public relations. In the case of National Hunting and Fishing Day, a single special interest group organized the support of sister organizations and other allies, then set up the mechanism to promote a nationwide event using "grassroots" assistance. From the sponsor's headquarters (1075 Post Rd., Riverside, Conn. 06878) each year comes a stream of publicity. It begins with the date set for the observance and culminates in an annual report documenting the success of the effort. Moreover, the sponsors provide ideas and materials (free or at cost) for use by any organization interested in helping. Items provided have included:

*"How to" booklets on conducting a wide range of events
*Slide set and script on improving NHF Day programs
*Fact sheets on contributions to conservation by hunters and fishers
*Decals, posters and bumper stickers

*Sample "Proclamation" drafts for state or local officials to sign in recognition of NHF Day
*News releases, photos
*Reproduction proofs for a complete newspaper supplement called "The Outdoor Tradition"

Figure 11.4. National Hunting and Fishing Day is a highly successful staged event that annually involves millions of people. The publicity focus is on how hunters and fishers contribute to conservation. (Courtesy of National Shooting Sports Foundation.)

The National Shooting Sports Foundation makes it easy for local groups to co-sponsor NHF Day. The results have been phenomenal with participation even including the President of the United States (via a national "proclamation"). From it all, improved public relations result for hunting and fishing enthusiasts, the industry they support, and the managers charged with stewardship of the resources involved.

Boise Cascade's Tour Offers

Another case where imagination in the public relations department has brought favorable national attention to natural resource management is a bold combination of open houses and tours offered by Boise Cascade Corporation.

Despite economic problems that troubled the forest product industries in the mid 1980's, Boise Cascade decided that it needed to try something new to promote its image as a responsible land owner and resource manager. As stated by Doug Bartels, Manager of Corporate Public Relations, "We decided to do more than *tell* people we do a good job. We invited them to see for themselves. We wanted to prove we have nothing to hide."

The invitation went out in the form of ads like those shown in Figure 11.5. Placed in national magazines such as *Newsweek,* readers were invited to write for information about mill tours and woods tours they could join while on vacation. In the first six months of the initial campaign in 1984, 5,400 inquiries were received in the headquarters office from throughout the nation!

To meet the demand, mills were made available for public visits and 30 tours were arranged in Boise Cascade's seven timberland regions. The regional communication manager worked in cooperation with local foresters in arranging these ambitious undertakings. Visitors were informed by mail when and where to meet (such as at an easily-located cafe), then they were transported

Figure 11.5. Boise Cascade Corporation's national advertising campaign invited thousands to special woods and mill tours throughout the country.

to the woods on rented buses and treated to a half-day inspection of forestry *a la* Boise Cascade. Snacks and literature were part of the package, of course, and few of the thousands of visitors would ever forget the good time and the new understanding provided by this company.

PHOTOGRAPHY

The old adage "one picture is worth a thousand words" is certainly true in public relations. Photographs are used, and should be used more, to illustrate technical reports, popular articles, news stories, exhibits and various kinds of visual aids. A photo increases interest and lends authenticity, both so important in communicating for public relations purposes.

In natural resources management, photography is a widely used tool. It helps census wildlife, recreationists and timber, documents evidence of criminal activities, provides records of research, and records changes in range, forest and campground vegetation. Infrared films have added new dimensions to aerial inventories, including the detection of diseased or insect damaged plants. Resource managers and scientists are making wide use of photography, often requiring skills in this area to be on par with the use of other tools of modern science. Similarly, the public relations practitioner must understand photography and be able to use it to help influence public opinion.

Figure 11.6. Wolf Point Forest on a Weyerhaeuser tree farm near Longview, Washington. Photo series can provide convincing arguments about the regenerative powers of managed forests. (Courtesy of the National Forest Products Association.)

Photography can be an exacting art. As an artist creates with brush and paint, the photographer creates with camera and film. Color, contrast and composition are all important components of each artist's product. Some even consider it more exacting and more difficult to arrive at a high quality product with camera than with palette and paint. This is because the entire picture is produced as a unit, all at once, and cannot be conceived or produced in parts or at different times. Once the expression is gone, the animal has moved, or the lighting has changed, the shot may be missed and the identical picture probably will never be available again. Thus, the photographer must know his camera so well that its operation becomes second nature. Also, a knowledge of films, lenses, filters and composition is essential to bring together the best of each to produce a picture that effectively communicates. Any book store, photo store or library has an endless array of books to help in this subject, and it is recommended that some of these become part of your personal library. The following sections should also help the uninitiated. However, once the basics are understood, there is no substitute for practice, including keeping careful notes of each shot so the results can be checked against the camera settings or other procedures used to obtain the picture.

Cameras and Their Equipment

A camera really is nothing more than a light-tight box with a lens, shutter and viewing system. A photograph actually can be taken with a light-tight box with a tiny pinhole poked in one end and a piece of unexposed film placed at the end of the box opposite the hole. The hole acts as the lens. A finger or flap over the hole acts as the shutter. A picture can certainly be produced in this way, but it is doubtful it will ever grace the pages of *National Geographic!* On the other hand, an expensive camera with high quality shutter and lens does not necessarily guarantee a good picture. However, quality equipment does increase the likelihood of useable pictures when in the hands of a careful, skilled photographer.

The Lens

The lens is usually the most expensive part of a camera. It determines to a large degree the quality of the image that is recorded on film, controls light entering the camera, and can magnify or reduce image size as well as increase or decrease the *field of view,* or area in the picture.

The *focal length* of a lens governs the image size and is the distance from the lens to the film when the camera is set at infinity. A camera with a 50 mm lens, which is about average for the popular 35 mm cameras, theoretically will produce an image size nearly equal to the way it appears to the human eye. A 135 mm lens on the same camera will produce an image size approximately 2.6 times larger (135 ÷ 50). A 300 mm lens will magnify six times; a 400 mm lens will magnify the image size eight times. Each time the image is magnified, the field of view becomes proportionally smaller.

For most public relations photography, the standard 50 mm lens does nicely. If we had a choice of two other lenses to expand the range of pictures possible, one would be a 25 to 35 mm *wide angle lens.* A wide angle lens decreases the image size but it increases the field of view. The image size with a 35 mm lens will be approximately 3/5 the size of one taken with a 50 mm lens. The wide angle lens is especially useful in photographing broad vistas or large groups. The other lens in our collection would be a *telephoto lens,* not exceeding 180 to 210 mm. So much the better if this is a *zoom lens* that allows instant adjustment from, say, 85 to 210 mm. At ceremonies, or when photographing workers, this is sufficient to obtain close-up pictures without interfering with the activity. For scenery, it allows framing or deleting portions of the scene with a minimum of changing your location.

The quality of a lens can be indicated by its upper limit of light-admitting ability. This is the largest possible size of the lens opening, or *aperture,* and is called an f/value. It is one of two settings important in regulating exposure of the film. To get the f/value of a lens, focal length is divided by the diameter of the largest lens opening possible. For example, with a focal length of four inches and a diameter of the largest possible lens opening being one inch, the f/value of the lens would be f/4 (4 ÷ 1). The lens with the largest opening (smallest f/value) generally is of the best quality when compared with others of equal focal length and from the same manufacturer. To the public relations photographer, this factor can be critical. A larger opening will allow shots in dimmer light, a common condition in forest settings, at fires and in conference halls.

On the barrel of any adjustable camera is an aperture ring with a sequence of f/numbers. When the ring is turned, going up or down the sequence, the amount of light allowed to enter the camera changes accordingly. Each larger number on the ring decreases the f/stop and the amount of light by approximately one-half. For example, an f/16 setting allows about one-half the amount of light to enter as an f/11 setting. Similarly, an f/8 setting allows twice the amount of light to enter as a setting of f/11. Again, f/stop controls the size of the opening, or by analogy, the size of the window to the film.

The f/stop also controls the *depth of field,* a term used to describe the range of distances in which included objects will be in focus. With a large opening (such as f/numbers f/2.8, f/3.5, f/4, etc.) the depth of field is much shorter or smaller than with smaller openings (f/numbers such as f/8, f/11, f/16, etc.).

The Shutter

The second setting necessary to regulate film exposure is shutter speed. This can be likened to the shade on a window and how fast it is opened and closed. More expensive cameras have a wide range of shutter speeds—commonly a second or longer to one thousandth of a second. No camera should be hand-held at a shutter speed slower than 1/30 second. (If a telephoto lens is being used, a tripod is necessary even at faster shutter speeds.) The slower the shutter speed, the more apt camera movement is to produce a blurred picture. This is one error that cannot be corrected in the darkroom.

Shutter speed is calibrated in seconds or fractions of seconds. A shutter speed of 1/25 second is half as fast as 1/50 second and lets in twice as much light. *T* and *B* settings are for time exposures. *T* stands for "Time;" when the shutter is tripped, it will stay open until tripped a second time. *B* stands for "Bulb," (a carryover term from pioneer photography), and when the shutter is tripped it will remain open as long as the release is held down. A *cable release* or rubber air bulb on the end of a thin hose is often used for this purpose to prevent shaking the camera.

Shutter speed is the camera's feature that allows the "freezing" of action. Thus, to photograph sports action or a bird in flight, a fast shutter speed is needed, perhaps 1/500 to 1/1000 second. To admit the same amount of light as would enter at a slower speed, the size of the aperture (lens opening) must be increased as the shutter speed increases. This works in reverse when a slow shutter speed is desired (for example, to intentionally blur part of an action scene).

Table 11.2.
Adjustable Camera Settings Allowing Approximately the Same Amount of Light to Enter, and the Effect on Depth of Field

Aperture	f/stop	Shutter speed in fractions of a second[1]	Depth of Field
Largest	2.8	1/800 (1/1000)	Smallest
↑	3.5	1/400 (1/500)	↑
	4	1/200 (1/250)	
	5.6	1/100 (1/125)	
	8	1/50 (1/60)	
↓	11	1/25 (1/30)	↓
Smallest	16	1/10 (1/15)	Largest

1. The two columns represent two different shutter speed gradations commonly used in cameras.

Frequently, depth of field is one of the most important considerations in composing a picture. For example, if you want a sign in the foreground and distant mountains both to be in focus, a small aperture is necessary. Thus, a slow shutter speed will be needed to allow in adequate light to compensate for the small "window opening." If the sign is to be the only part of the scene in focus, a wide aperture and fast shutter speed will do the job. Learning to manipulate the f/stop and shutter speed to produce the desired results is an important part of photography. In making these adjustments, start with the most critical factor (i.e. motion or depth of field), make the corresponding adjustment, then the remaining adjustment. When freezing motion *and* large depth of field are important, it may be necessary to use an especially light-sensitive film. Table 11.2 may be helpful in visualizing exposure equivalencies in an adjustable camera.

Viewing Systems

Another important part of the camera is the viewing system. An *optical, or second lens,* viewing system consists of a separate window. That is, the photographer sees the scene through one window and the picture is taken through another. The difference between what is seen and what the film records can cause *parallax* problems. This becomes more acute as you take closer pictures. For example, you may want to take a full frame picture of a Christmas tree. In the viewfinder it extends from top to bottom. However, the lens is slightly lower than the viewfinder so that it "sees" from perhaps a foot below the tree to a foot below its tip. In this same way, many heads are cut off people thanks to parallax. The solution is to move the camera slightly up and to the right or left (depending on where the viewfinder is located) to compensate for the difference.

Parallax problems are nonexistent with single lens reflex cameras. These cameras allow the photographer to look through the same lens with which the picture will be taken. This is done with a mirror inside the camera set at a 45° angle. The mirror reflects the image onto ground glass. When the image is sharp, the picture is in focus. When the shutter is tripped, the mirror flips out of the way and the film is exposed. This allows not only the important advantage of seeing exactly what will be taken, but also makes *through-the-lens* light metering possible. This is not

Figure 11.7. From left to right, rear: so-called "press camera," twin lens reflex, auxiliary lenses for a single lens reflex, 35–mm single lens reflex, and 35–mm camera with range finder viewing system. In front is an electronic or "strobe" flash attachment.

only a more accurate way of measuring light that will reach the film, it also means that without moving the eye from the viewfinder, it is possible to compose the picture, focus, and adjust the aperture ring to the right f/stop (by centering a tiny meter needle visible in the view finder).

Many cameras, both with optical and ground glass view finders, have split-image focusing. This is an easy to use aid in accurate focusing. For example, in photographing a tree, if the picture is not in focus, the top of the tree will not be in line with the bottom. When the adjustment is made and the top is in line with the bottom, the picture is in focus.

What Camera Is Best?

There was a day when the only camera any self-respecting public relations person would be seen with was a *press camera*. Speed Graphic was the standard, and it still yields quality pictures that are beyond reproach. These cameras use individual sheets of film ranging in size from 2¼ × 3¼ to 8 × 10″. Single sheets offer an advantage in that you do not need to waste a whole roll of film to take three or four shots. Also, the larger the film size, the greater the resolution (sharpness) of the picture when it is enlarged and printed.

Because of their large size and delicate nature, press cameras outside of studio settings are a rarity today. Perhaps the two types of cameras with the most devotees among natural resource public relations people are the twin-lens and single-lens reflex cameras. The "reflex" refers to the fact that light (the image) enters the lens then is "bent," or bounced off a mirror, toward the viewfinder. In a twin-lens reflex the viewing lens is slightly above the picture lens; in a single-lens reflex the mirror moves out of the way during the instant the picture is taken. The greatest advantage of the twin-lens reflex is that it uses a larger film size (such as 2¼ × 2¼″). Most single-lens reflex cameras use the 35 mm format. For those who can afford it, several cameras are now available that combine the best of both worlds and offer a very fine quality single-lens reflex in 2¼ × 2¼ format.

It would be fair to say that the 35 mm single-lens reflex is the most popular camera for routine news, publicity and slide photography. Despite the small film size, high quality enlargements are possible with today's films and processing. These cameras are also lightweight, compact and rugged, with flexibility that is virtually limitless with their readily interchangeable lenses. Within minutes, it is possible for a photographer to shoot through a microscope, capture a distant eagle and record a stage-full of workers who just received their 10-year service pins. Computer technology has made the job even easier. From virtually full automation to cameras that "talk" to you, photography has become one of the most accessible tools for helping build better public relations.

Accessories

In the way of accessories, one that is necessary is a flash attachment. Flash can come to the rescue in a dark forest or shadowy rock overhang. Or, it can be used indoors or out to reduce squinting and shadows on people's faces, accentuate a foreground, or darken shadows when desired. Indoors, it frees us completely from worrying about available light.

A *guide number* is given for all flash bulbs. This number, in combination with the film speed and the distance of the object to be photographed, will yield the appropriate f/stop to use (Guide No. ÷ Distance = f/stop). Electronic flash units eliminate the need for bulbs and are the most commonly used flash units. With most models, automation has eliminated the need for calculations. Automated electronic flash with a quick recharge is well worth the added cost.

Filters are also useful accessories, and there are many kinds. Some "filter out" certain colors and enhance others. Other filters are used to cut haze in distant shots. Still others make it possible to use indoor film in the outdoors; make clouds appear light and fluffier; decrease effects of glare; darken the blue of sky; and make other effects possible. Some of the more commonly used filters are shown in Table 11.3.

When some filters are used, they cut down on the amount of light entering through the lens. Unless the camera has a through-the-lens meter, this means a correction must be made. In this case, if the stated *filter factor* is 2, it means that the filter will cut the amount of light by half. Thus, the exposure must be doubled by either a change in shutter speed or f/stop. If the filter factor is 1, the filter can be left on the lens at all times. It does not cause a problem by cutting down on light, and by being left on the camera it protects the much more expensive lens from nicks and scratches.

Wide angle and telephoto lenses have already been mentioned as basic for public relations work. Equipment for closeup photography is also useful in any of three ways. A telephoto lens can be used for getting fairly close to large-sized subjects. However, for small objects or taking copy shots of print or small artwork, a closeup lens is necessary. An auxiliary closeup lens fits over the regular lens like a filter and acts as a magnifying glass. If a high quality camera lens is covered by an inferior closeup lens, the overall quality of the system is reduced to the level of its poorest component. To prevent this, high quality must be used for all lenses, or a third technique can be used. In this method, which is less convenient, tubes or bellows are placed between the regular lens and the film, thus increasing the focal length. Closeup photography is achieved and the quality of the regular camera lens is not impaired.

Table 11.3.
Common Filters and Their Uses[1]

Filter Type	Color or Description	Factor		Use
		Daylight	Tungsten	
For All Films				
1A	Skylight	0	0	Eliminates ultra-violet to which film is sensitive, and some visible blue. Gives more precise rendering of color in open shade or on overcast days. Can be left on camera continually for protection.
UV-Haze	Clear	0	0	Eliminates ultra-violet light to which film is sensitive; has no effect on any light visible to the eye. Can be used at all times under all conditions.
Polarizing	Photo Neutral	1½–2	1½–2	Removes or reduces reflection from non-metallic surfaces, darkens blue skies while increasing color saturation, penetrates haze. Simply rotate the filter in its mount until the optimum effect is obtained.
ND–3 ND–6	2X Neutral Density 4X Neutral Density	1 2	1 2	Uniformly reduces amount of light without changing color rendition. With high speed films in bright light, allows use of slower shutter speeds or wider apertures. ND–3 transmits 50%, ND–6 transmits 25%.
Cross Screen	Clear	0	0	Produces dramatic star-shaped flares on highlights in night scenes, seascapes, still lifes, etc.
Soft Focus	Clear	0	0	Produces a delicate soft focus atmosphere especially suitable for portraits, moody landscapes, etc.
For Black and White Films				
No. 8 (K2)	Yellow	1	⅔	Renders an accurate tonal reproduction of daylight scenes as the eye sees them. Natural rendition of contrast between sky and clouds, flowers and foliage.
No. 11 (X1)	Light Green	2	2	In portraiture, renders an exact tonal reproduction of skin as the eyes see it. Increases contrast between blue sky and clouds; lightens foliage and darkens flowers.
No. 15 (G)	Deep Yellow	1-⅔	1	Emphasizes contrast between blue sky and clouds, increases brilliance of sunsets. Special applications in architectural photography.
02	Orange	2-⅓	2	Creates dramatic contrast between blue sky and clouds, flowers and foliage. Special applications in document copying, beach and snow scenes.
No. 25 (A)	Red	3	2-⅓	Darkens blue sky to create spectacular contrast with clouds, simulates moonlight scenes in daytime with slight underexposure, increases contrast between foliage and flowers. Special applications in document copying and with infrared film.

1. As recommended by Vivitar Corporation.

Table 11.3.—*Continued*

Filter Type	Color or Description	Factor		Use
		Daylight	**Tungsten**	
For Color Films				
	Recommended Film Type	**Lighting**	**Factor**	
80A	Daylight	3200° Lamps	2	A cooling filter which converts Daylight color films for use with 3200°K lighting. (3200°K to 5500°K)
80B	Daylight	3400° Lamps	1-⅔	A cooling filter which converts Daylight color films for use with 3400°K photoflood or quartz halogen lighting. (3400°K to 5500°K)
80C	Daylight	Clear Flash Bulbs	1	A cooling filter which converts Daylight color films for use with clear flash bulbs. (3800°K to 5500°K)
81A	Daylight and Type B	Daylight, Electronic Flash, 3400° Lamps	⅓	A warming filter which prevents excessive blue with daylight color films in cloudy weather, shade, or indoors with Electronic Flash. Also corrects Type B films (3200°K) for use with 3400°K photoflood or quartz halogen lighting.
81B	Daylight	Daylight Electronic Flash	⅓	Same applications as 81A, with warmer results.
81C	Type A	Clear Flash Bulbs	⅓	A warming filter which converts Type A films (3400°K) for use with clear flash bulbs.
82A	Daylight and Type A	Daylight, 3200° Lamps	⅓	A cooling filter which reduces excessive warmth of light in early morning or late afternoon. Also corrects Type A films (3400°K) for use with 3200°K lighting.
85	Type A	Daylight	⅔	A warming filter which converts Type A films for use in daylight. (5500°K to 3400°K)
85B	Type B	Daylight	⅔	A warming filter which converts Type B films for use in daylight. (5500°K to 3200°K)
FLD	Daylight	Fluorescent	1	Converts Daylight color films for use with fluorescent lighting. Eliminates blue-green cast which ordinarily results.
FLB	Type B	Fluorescent	1	Converts Type B films (3200°K) for use with fluorescent lighting. Eliminates blue-green cast which ordinarily results.
CC30R	Daylight	Underwater	2-⅓	Compensates color distortion when using daylight color films underwater or when photographing through transparent plastic windows.

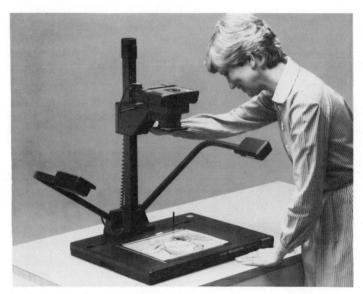

Figure 11.8. KODAK's Instagraphic copy stand can be used by people with no photographic training to copy artwork or 3-dimensional objects up to 2 inches in depth. (Courtesy Eastman Kodak Company.)

Closeup shots often require additional light on the subject, so flash units are commonly used at the same time. Flash also allows "stopping down" to a smaller aperture, thus increasing the depth of field. Without this extra light source, the depth of field will usually be quite small—a condition that can be either an advantage or a problem, depending on what is to be shown in the photograph.

Other accessories that are "must" items include whatever is necessary to protect the basic equipment. Cameras and lenses are expensive, precision instruments and must be treated accordingly. Dust caps should be in place at all times when the camera or auxiliary lenses are not in use. Lenses should be cleaned regularly with a combination camel-hair brush and air bulb available at photography stores. (They are also useful for dusting off slides and negatives.) For storage and transport, a 50 caliber machine gun ammunition box is a good example of the kind of light-proof, dust-resistant box that keeps equipment in top working order. These are available in Army surplus stores and can be padded with foam rubber cut to fit around the equipment. Not only are they more crush-proof than more expensive leather cases, they are also more likely to foil thieves.

Other equipment for the public relations operation might include a tripod, copy stand (Figure 11.8) and a storage file for photographs *and* negatives. Often the latter are filed in separate places, keyed together by a number on the back of the print and on the cellophane envelope containing negatives. Slide storage systems are discussed in Chapter 8 (Figure 8.13). Unfortunately, most natural resource photography is done in the slide format. Few offices also have a systematized, up-to-date collection of black and white prints. One of the first steps in developing a public relations program should be to have complete, orderly sets of slides, prints and negatives on all aspects of the agency's operations.

The Darkroom

Fortunate indeed is the publc relations person who has access to his own darkroom. More commonly, because of the expense, skills, and short-lived chemicals involved, specialists will operate a centralized darkroom, or the photo work will be sent out.

In the darkroom, film is *developed* by processing it for specific intervals of time through a series of chemicals kept at exact temperatures. Either a slide transparency or a negative results, depending on the film used. In the case of slides, they are dried, mounted and ready for use. When the film is for color or black and white *prints,* the negative requires an additional series of steps. In the dimness of a special *safe light,* the black and white (b & w) negative is placed in an *enlarger* between a light bulb and a sheet of unexposed photographic printing paper. The enlarger light is then turned on for a specific number of seconds and the paper is exposed. Then in what certainly must be the most exciting moment in photography, the paper is emersed in a tray of liquid developer and an image slowly appears. When the contrast of blacks and whites appears as desired, the paper is thrust into a second tray of chemical solution to *stop* the development action. A bath in *fixer* then preserves the image—possibly forever—before it is washed in water and placed in a drier. Color printing is more complex, much more expensive, but all the more fascinating.

Many faults of a picture can be corrected in part in the darkroom. Parts of the negative can be enlarged or *cropped* (deleted). Segments can be darkened or made lighter by covering part of the paper under the enlarger. Underexposed negatives can be timed accordingly in enlarging or printing to give a usable picture. Contrast can be increased by using appropriate filters on the enlarger or by using "hard," contrasty, white papers (photographic paper numbers F3 or F4, for example). By the same token, contrast can be decreased by using a soft, off-white paper (F1 or F2). Glossy papers and pictures should be used for reproductive purposes. Matte, dull papers and pictures generally are best for framing and for television.

Film

Light is reflected as radiant energy in varying amounts from objects. Because of color and tonal differences, the reflected light has different wave lengths and intensities. This light is focused by the lens onto the film. In b & w photography, the film is coated with light-sensitive silver salts. With chemical processing, the silver salts are changed in proportion to the amount of light energy that struck them when the picture was "taken." Thus, an image is produced. In color films, there are several layers of emulsion, each one sensitive to a different primary color. When printed or projected, the recorded images on each layer are recombined to produce what appears as the original colors of the objects that were photographed.

Film speed is the film's sensitivity to light. The higher the speed of the film, the less the exposure needed. Film speed was once shown as an ASA (American Standards Association) number. Now these numerical references have been adopted worldwide by the International Standards Organization and the old ASA numbers are noted as ISO numbers. DIN is a similar reference used mostly in Europe and expressed with a degree symbol (e.g. 21°). These numbers usually appear on or in the film container and may be seen in Table 11.4.

The higher the ISO number, the "faster" the film. Some films are so fast that a fairly high quality, printable negative may result if the picture is taken by the light given off by one candle. The faster the film, however, the coarser the grain. A print made from fast films often will show this peppery quality. A fine grain film with slow speed usually is better to use if enlargements are

Table 11.4.
Speeds and Important Characteristics of Selected KODAK Films[1]

Film Name	Speed (ISO)	Characteristics
Black and White		
PANATOMIC-X	32	Extremely fine grained. Excellent for enlargements. With special processing, the 135-size will produce positive b & w slides.
VERICHROME Pan	125	A good general film with extremely fine grain. A good balance between speed and resolving power. Not available in 35 mm.
PLUS-X Pan	125	Similar to above except this one is for 35 mm cameras.
TRI-X Pan	400	Excellent for shots in dim light inside without a flash. Fast action and great depth of field. Combines very high speed with reasonably fine grain and excellent sharpness. A highly flexible film for the PR person.
Recording 2475	1000	When highest speed is required, such as to stop action using existing light source. Coarse grained, 35 mm film.
ROYAL-X Pan	1250	Similar to above but in 120-size.
Technical Pan 2415	—	An extremely fine-grain, high-resolution emulsion with extended-red sensitivity. Useful for high quality enlargements of 25× and greater. Very slow speed. Consult technical guide to determine. Moderate to high contrast, controllable by type of developer used.
Color—for Slides[2]		
EKTACHROME Slide Duplicating Film (tungsten balanced)	4	A film for making color duplicates from color slides.
Photomicrography Color	10	High contrast and extremely fine grain. For shooting through microscope. Also good for copying original art and color line drawings.
KODACHROME 25 (Daylight)	25	Favorite for color slides. Excellent color quality, high sharpness and extremely fine grain.
KODACHROME 40 (Type A)	40	For indoor use with 3400K photo flood lights. Excellent color quality, fine grain and high resolving power. Good choice for portraits and copy stand work.

1. Adapted from *KODAK Black-and-White Films for General Picture-Taking* (1984), *KODAK Color Films for Still Cameras* (1984), *KODAK Professional Black-and-White Films* (1984), and various *Film Information from KODAK* leaflets.
2. In color films, the suffix "-chrome" indicates slide film. However, with some loss of quality, it is possible to have color prints or b & w prints made from slides.

Table 11.4—*Continued*

Film Name	Speed (ISO)	Characteristics
KODACHROME 64 (Daylight)	64	About twice as fast as Kodachrome 25 film with little sacrifice in resolution. Excellent color rendition, remarkable sharpness and freedom from graininess.
EKTACHROME 64 (Daylight)	64	For general picture-taking to yield color slides. For home-processing or "overnight" commercial processing service. In development it is tolerant to "pushing" to higher speed to compensate for dimly lighted scenes. (Available in 110 and 126 sizes. For 135, 120 or 220, ask for KODAK EKTACHROME 64 Professional)
KODAK EKTACHROME 100 (Daylight)	100	Medium speed, very high sharpness, very find grain and resolving power. Improved flesh tone quality. Good all-around choice for PR purposes. Available in 135 size.
EKTACHROME 160	160	High speed for use with 3200K tungsten lamps. Excellent with household lighting, stage lighting, outdoor night spectacles, and spotlighted buildings, monuments and fountains. Also used with tungsten lights for portraits.
EKTACHROME 200 (Daylight)	200	High-speed color-slide film with good color rendition, grain and sharpness. Tolerant to "pushing" to ASA 400, but with some loss of quality. Good for available-light portraits.
EKTACHROME 400 (Daylight)	400	Very high speed. Excellent in variety of light sources, and for dim lighting, fast action, extending the distance range for flash pictures, and when both depth of field and high shutter speeds are required.
Color—For Prints		
VERICOLOR II Professional, Type S	100	A color-negative film for portraits, commercial and industrial photography. Slightly lower contrast and less saturated colors than Kodacolor II film. Should be kept under refrigeration until shortly before use.
KODACOLOR VR 100	100	KODAK's sharpest color-negative film. Excellent general use film with good enlargement results, excellent color and contrast.
KODACOLOR VR 200	200	Similar to above but with twice the speed.
KODACOLOR VR 400	400	For use when high speed is important. Satisfactory prints possible with moderate enlargement.
KODACOLOR VR 1000	1000	KODAK's fastest color-negative film. Useful when very high speed is essential, such as taking pictures with a telephoto lens with a small maximum aperture.

needed, adequate light is available, and the subject is stationary. The skilled photographer will learn the characteristics of each film and use them to advantage in producing the desired effect in the finished product. Table 11.4 may help by describing important characteristics of some commonly used films.

SOME FILM QUALITY DEFINITIONS

Graininess— Sandlike or granular appearance in a film, slide or print. Graininess tends to increase with film speed and increases by overexposure or overdevelopment of black-and-white films or underexposure or overdevelopment of color negative films.

Resolving Power—The ability of a film or print to record fine detail.

Sharpness—The visual impression of good edge sharpness between details in a photograph.

Degree of Enlargement Allowed—The effect of one or more of the above on a photographic negative determines the *ultimate* definition that can be realized in a photograph when starting with a good quality negative. Based on this, each film can be rated extremely high to low depending on its capability to be used for enlargement.

—Adapted from *KODAK Films,* KODAK
Publication No. AF-1, 1985.

Composition

Regardless of how expensive the camera and how much knowledge one has of its mechanical operation, and regardless of the amount of care in choosing and processing the film, the composition of a picture is the most crucial part of the final product. True, if enough film is exposed, sooner or later a good picture may result. In fact, it is not uncommon for a *National Geographic* photographer or other professional to shoot 100 pictures to obtain the *one* that is just right. Still, with each shot the good photographer uses light, shadows and visual balance to compose and create the finished product he desires.

The first step in composition of a photograph is to have a definite purpose or objective in mind. Of course, some efforts must be opportunistic. However, a picture is an aid to communication—a way to help tell a story or make a message clearer and more meaningful. With nearly every shot, the public relations person should have a *reason* for taking that particular picture.

The next step is to be aware of every element of the scene. It helps to remember that the human eye is selective whereas the camera's eye is not. Figure 11.9 offers a good example. If we were actually present when that photograph was taken, our eyes and thoughts would have been on the farmer and the burned fence post. When the scene is recorded on film, however, the poles in the background become much more noticeable, especially with one "sprouting" from the man's head! By changing the angle of the shot, the objectionable background could have been deleted from the scene.

Backgrounds and foregrounds should be used to advantage. For example, an object in focus in the foreground may give *perspective,* or the illusion of three dimensional depth, to an object or scenes such as a mountain range or valley that is also in focus in the distance (Figure 11.10). Other times it may be advantageous to throw the background and foreground out of focus. This may be true if the object, such as a bird or mammal, will nearly fill the entire frame or if objects in the foreground and background are undesirable. Recall that depth of field is primarily controlled by the f/stop.

Figure 11.9. All elements of the scene must be considered by a photographer. A "sprout" from the man's head reveals that the background was forgotten. (Used by permission of The Wildlife Society.)

The kind of background used depends entirely on the purpose of the picture. Fluffy clouds in an azure sky can help create a pleasant scene if a shelterwood cut is being portrayed as a beneficial silvicultural treatment. On the other hand, charred snags beneath a gray sky will help communicate the evils of wild fire in a commercial forest. To focus attention on a flower, arrowhead, pine cone or other small item photographed close up, a piece of plain cloth (black velvet is especially good for white objects) held or laid behind the object eliminates all distractions. Usually, however, the background should be carefully used to help portray feeling or a sense of place.

Good composition also includes purposeful or pleasing location of objects in the picture. There are many rules of thumb to guide you in composing a scene, but there is a danger that such "rules" can inhibit creative photography. Nonetheless, most people agree that asymmetrical design is usually more pleasing than having the focal point dead center or the scene abruptly bisected by a vertical or horizontal line. In action shots, it is usually best to have the movement entering the scene. A canoe heading into the picture in the left one third of the scene is an example of this principle. *Framing,* like the conscious use of background, can help "tell the story" in a photograph as well as presenting a more aesthetically pleasing picture. Shots from doorways or windows, branches or grass stalks on two or more sides of the scene, or something contrived like a camping

Figure 11.10. Foreground used to advantage for framing and in giving perspective to the scene. A small aperture also helped by rendering both foreground and background in focus. (Courtesy of National Park Service.)

scene between crossed skis in the snow, are examples of framing. Like any technique of composition, framing should not be overused, but it definitely should be considered when trying to find the best way to meet the objective for any particular picture.

Scale is another important consideration. The size of large trees, glaciers or similar natural giants can not be accurately communicated without a person or other familiar object included in the photograph for comparison. Similarly, very small objects like a leaf bud or alpine flower need a pencil, ruler or other means of putting it into true perspective. If done tastefully and creatively, the comparison object can be made an unobjectionable part of the scene.

In natural resources work, there seem to be three main weaknesses in the average person's photography. This can be seen time and again at conferences, in slide talks, or in the mass media and illustrated reports. The first is that people are often missing from the picture. Whether the subject is wildflowers or picnic tables, people add interest and help hold the viewer's attention. Second, when people are included, too often they appear stilted and unnatural. Part of a photographer's job is to learn to direct his subjects so that they allow themselves to be a natural part of the scene or event. If the shots are taken while the person is working or participating in a ceremony or recreational activity, so much the better. Otherwise, compose the scene and have the individuals assist in making it as natural-appearing as possible. This might include a new district ranger in

Apex Forest Consultants
1049 Colt Road
Somewhere, Maine 03441

MODEL RELEASE

I hereby grant to Apex Forest Consultants the right to reproduce and publish my photograph or likeness in brochures and other advertising media. This permission extends indefinitely and for which I agree to no compensation.

Name _____
(If under 18, parent or legal guardian must sign)

Address _____

_____

Date _____

Figure 11.11. A *model release* should be used to protect against later claims for compensation or damages when someone is photographed in a non-news situation. Wording should be modified to meet particular circumstances.

his office or talking with visitors, a close-up of a biologist marking a research animal, or an award recipient with something in the background related to the particular award. Whatever the situation, avoid at all costs the "line up" shot of people staring blankly at the camera; the "faked check" scene of someone handing another person a check or piece of paper; the "dead fish" shot of someone holding their catch; the "great white hunter" scene of a man or woman kneeling beside a carcass, gun draped across the quarry; and similar shots that are the photographic equivalent of a trite statement. Finally, whether it is people or something else, *move in close*. By getting closer—and perhaps even filling all or most of the entire frame—unnecessary background clutter often can be eliminated, a more striking picture obtained, and the viewer's attention more easily focused on what you want to show. Each time a picture is composed, don't snap the shutter until asking yourself, "Will it improve this shot if I move closer?" Usually the answer is yes.

Photography, like other skills necessary for public relations work, improves only with practice. Approached with the right attitude, it offers the opportunity to combine a personal creative activity with the more practical demands of the job. Study, practice, and invited criticism can result in consistently fine photos that are both personally rewarding and useful for improved communication.

SUGGESTED REFERENCES

Exhibits

Evaluation Techniques for Interpretation: Study Results from an Exhibition on Energy by J. Alan Wagar, Gregory W. Lovelady and Harlan Falkin. 1976. USDA Forest Service, Pacific Northwest Forest and Range Experiment Station, Portland, OR.

Exhibits for the Small Museum: A Handbook by Arminta Neel. 1976. American Association for State and Local History, Nashville, TN.

Handbook of Museum Technology. 1982. Research and Education Association, New York.

The Best in Exhibit Design by Edward K. Carpenter (annual). RC Publications, Bethesda, MD.

Photography

Introduction to Photography: a Self-directing Approach by M. J. Rosen. 1976. Houghton-Mifflin Co., Boston, MA.

Natural History Photography edited by D. M. Turner Ettlinger. 1974. Academic Press, New York.

Photojournalism—Principles and Practices by Clifton C. Edom. 1980. Wm. C. Brown Company Publishers, Dubuque, Iowa.

The Joy of Photography by Martin L. Taylor. 1983. Eastman Kodak Co., Rochester, NY.

12

Biopolitics

Natural resources, their management, and politics are inseparable.

Biopolitics is a term used to highlight the integral relationship between the human institution of politics and the natural elements of our environment. Natural resource managers are charged with stewardship of the latter, but no matter how scientifically sound or technically correct, all actions are confined within the guidelines established through out political system.

To a large degree the ultimate payoff from the practice of public relations is favorable political action at the local, state and federal levels. Reflecting what they believe to be public opinion, legislators allocate funds to manage natural resources; enact laws to allow or prohibit certain forestry practices; establish game seasons, license fees, penalties for violations, and other regulations; create parks; authorize dams; alter land uses; and establish all manner of policy that directly affects the natural resources of our nation. According to the USDA Forest Service, between 800 and 900 bills are introduced during a typical session of Congress that affect this agency alone! Some 200 of these proceed far enough through the legislative channels to require the Forest Service to formally adopt a position toward the proposed law. At the state and local level as well, not a year passes without natural resource management becoming the focus of proposed ordinances or legislation.

Public opinion usually guides the votes in these matters, for ultimately it is public opinion that elects the political figure who does the voting. Clearly, public relations is inextricably related to politics, and politics to natural resources.

For natural resource managers, public relations can work in the political arena two ways: first—and most commonly—by influencing a variety of publics to in turn influence elected officials; secondly, in some cases and usually at the higher echelons of management or administration, through direct interaction with political figures. For whatever purpose the circumstances allow, a clearer understanding of politics will help the practitioner of public relations work more effectively toward adequate funding and policies favorable to the sound management of natural resources.

THE STRUCTURE OF GOVERNMENT

One of the weaknesses of most natural resource curricula is the lack of course work in political science. We are so busy with the science of the physical resources that most graduates have little knowledge of the political structure that governs these resources. For the practice of effective public relations, it is essential to know what elected or appointed positions can affect resource management, then how to work with the individuals in these positions.

Local Government

Local government can affect resource management in a number of ways, but particularly in recreation management and urban forestry.

The grassroots of political organization in most cities stems from *precincts,* which in larger cities are grouped into *wards.* These are usually delineated according to a set limitation on the number of voters (for example, 400–600 to a precinct in Chicago). Political parties elect or appoint ward committee persons and precinct *leaders* or *captains* to run party affairs and promote candidates. Because of their importance in the political campaign, these largely unknown individuals sometimes have direct access to successful candidates from their party and considerable influence in appointments or issues.

The structure of city government varies depending on state law and preferences of the residents. However, the following are the most commonly used.

Cities with Mayor-Councils

Most large cities and about half of those with a population of 5,000 use this form of government (Cummings, Jr. and Wise, 1971). However the power of the mayor varies from being a mere figurehead to holding strong control over all administrative branches (such as departments of parks and recreation, personnel, police, etc.).

In what may be termed the weak mayor system, administrative department heads and board members are either elected directly or selected by the council. In the strong mayor system, the mayor makes these appointments, subject to council approval. In either case, the council is a powerful body in that it performs legislative functions such as enacting ordinances, setting policy and tax rates, and appropriating money. It sometimes also has limited judicial powers, as in the hearing of zoning protests.

Cities With Council-Manager

A form of government that is intended to make the operation of a city[1] less political is that in which an elected council hires a trained, professional manager. The manager, in turn, hires and fires department officials and in theory is free to run the city's daily affairs without interference from the council. However, the manager reports to the council, keeping it informed of city affairs, and performs other duties as prescribed by the council. Obviously he will not remain long if his management does not meet the satisfaction of council members. About half of all cities under 500,000 use this form of government (Cummings, Jr. and Wise, 1971).

Towns and Townships

The term "town" means different things in different locales. In New England, the famous town meeting is an annual event where citizens of village and countryside gather to act on budgets and ordinances or to air opinions before their local board representatives, called *selectmen.* In the Midwest and some areas of the middle Atlantic states, town-like units—usually called *townships*—are often 36 square miles and stem from the original surveys of the post-Revolution public domain. As urban pressures expand into the once rural areas of towns and townships, the roles of selectmen and township *commissioners* become increasingly important in land use planning and environmental protection.

1. Municipalities are variously termed cities, villages, incorporated towns, or boroughs, depending on the region of the country.

Counties

There are more than 3,000 counties in the United States (called *parishes* in Louisiana and *boroughs* in Alaska). The power within their governments ranges widely from almost non-existent in New England where they are subordinate in importance to towns, to being the principal form of local government in sparsely settled areas, especially in the West. One of the functions of counties is to carry out *state* responsibilities locally. For the natural resource manager, this has important implications because of the many agencies that deal with farmers and rural landowners. Roads, deed registration, weed control, rural law enforcement (the sheriff), extension education, rural parks, and land use planning are but a few of the functions of most county governments. Tax assessment is another important function that can often make the difference between long-term resource management or financial pressure to convert the land to building lots. The elected officials that govern the majority of counties are called either the *board of supervisors* or the *county commissioners*. The number runs from 3 to 80, but in most cases is made up of from three to seven of these rather powerful officials. Other elected officials usually include a county clerk, auditor, treasurer, sheriff, assessor, coronor and prosecuting attorney.

Special Districts

When problems of local government cut across boundary lines, or residents using a service are inequitably taxed, a special district is often created. Under state law, such a district may be for fire protection, parks and recreation, sewage, water, schools, mass transit, air pollution control, mosquito abatement or similar purposes. Usually from three to five elected or appointed citizens sit on these boards. These individuals usually have a special interest or knowledge related to the district's purpose.

State Government

For many natural resource managers, states are the most important unit of government. One reason for this is that American tradition gives states the ownership of non-migratory wildlife. States also regulate many forestry practices and manage extensive acreages of their own forests which in most areas are the result of grants from the federal government at the inception of statehood. Another federal act, the Land and Water Conservation Fund Act of 1964, has given state park and recreation departments considerable incentive to plan and develop recreation resources. This is accomplished through using the states (those that have comprehensive outdoor recreation plans) to disperse annual funds for the purpose of acquiring and developing recreation areas and facilities. Many other state powers and responsibilities impinge on natural resource management. In fact, states have the authority to pass any laws not forbidden to them by the U.S. Constitution or their state constitution.

The Executive Branch

The structure and procedures of state governments vary widely. All have a governor, whose power varies dramatically depending on such factors as: (1) the number of other elected *executive officials* sharing power (usually eight), (2) extent of the governor's power to appoint department heads and other officials, (3) veto power, (4) term of office (the longer the stronger), and (5) authority related to the budget.

The executive branch includes the governor and staff, and a variable number of elected executives such as the lieutenant governor, attorney general, treasurer, superintendent of education and others. It also includes agencies such as fish and game, parks and recreation, forestry, and other natural resource departments. The heads of these departments, like most governors, are *administrators,* not policy-makers. That is, they primarily carry out laws and policies established by others. The governor's real control over an agency depends largely on his control over budget, but it also depends on who he appoints to the board or commission established by law to formulate policies and regulations for the particular agency. These individuals have considerable power in most states, and this is a hard pill to swallow for many professional resource managers.

The political influence on the policies of a natural resource agency and its director varies considerably between states, but the theory is that resources belong to the people and the people will set the guidelines for their use and management. Within these guidelines, the professional is charged with exercising expertise to manage the resources accordingly. Ideally there is a two-way exchange, with the skillful department head being able to facilitate both the wishes of the board or commissioners and the best judgements of his professional staff. One thing is certain, the influences of politics should *not* extend into the managerial ranks where the technical judgements are made.

In its review of state fish and wildlife agencies, the Wildlife Management Institute (1977) developed the following suggestions for "an ideal commission or board." The ideas seem equally appropriate for parks and recreation, water, mineral, forest and other commissions or boards:

> An ideal commission or board consists of a relatively small number of nonpartisan members serving staggered terms and appointed by the governor on a statewide, as opposed to district, basis. The commission should adopt a set of policy statements defining its functions, the responsibilities of its individual members, and the functions and responsibilities delegated to the chief administrative officer of the division or department. Commission or board policies should insure that the board's attention and actions are confined to policy, budgetary, and regulatory matters (p. 5).

The Legislative and Judicial Branches

In all states except Nebraska, the state legislative branch consists of two houses that are usually referred to collectively as the *legislature, general assembly, legislative assembly,* or in New Hampshire, the *general court.* State *senators* attend the upper house, with *representatives* serving in the lower house. Their numbers vary widely. For example, Nebraska utilizes only 49 members in its one house system, whereas 424 members in both houses crowd the chambers in New Hampshire. Obviously, the greater the number the more diffuse the power and influence, for even debate becomes awkward beyond a point. In two-thirds of the states, senators are elected to four-year terms, and most members of the houses of representatives serve for two years. In most states the legislators assemble annually, usually in January and usually for a set time limit such as 60 days. In a few states, the legislature meets only every other year.

Legislatures serve the primary function of making laws or removing them. However, in light of the tremendous effect that California's now-famous Proposition 13 had on park management and other state services beginning in 1978, two other methods of law-making need to be understood. Proposition 13 was an *initiative* which limited the amount of property taxes that could be assessed against landowners. In some states, any citizen can use the initiative procedure to propose a law (or in the case of Proposition 13, a constitutional amendment) outside the usual channels of the legislature. This requires that a certain number of signatures be obtained on a petition supporting the proposed law or consitutional change. The number of signatures needed usually ranges from five to ten percent of the state's registered voters. Once obtained, the proposal is either placed on the next ballot or goes before the legislature, depending on the state. Such a process in reverse, called a *referendum,* requires that a law that was passed in the legislature by placed on the ballot for direct approval by the voters. Usually, less signatures on a petition are needed for this action, and for some kinds of legislation a referendum is automatic. As special interest groups become better organized and more skillful in organizational tactics, the initiative and referendum are likely to play a greater role in government.

In both the state and federal governments, the three major units are the executive, legislative and judicial branches. The judicial branch is not included here because it is—and should be—generally removed from the potential influences of public relations practice.

Federal Government

To a seemingly ever-increasing degree, the actions of federal government permeate the management of all natural resources. Few managers can avoid the requirements of environmental impact statements, archeological inventories, public involvement, affirmative action, and the plethora of other laws and regulations created to protect the well-being of society and our environment. The federal government is also a major landowner, controlling more than two-thirds of the land in some western states, and a major employer of natural resource managers. This unit of government is also the prime target of nearly every special interest group and competitive users of natural resources. To a large degree, action at the federal level affects how well the resources of our nation can be managed by the individuals technically trained for the task.

The Executive Branch

The president and his cabinet are the best known figures in the executive branch, with the Secretaries of Agriculture and Interior being the two giants related to natural resources. Unlike the organization of most state governments, the president's cabinet (department heads) works with the president as an advisory team and political ally as well as being responsible for overall administration and some policy formulation of the departments. The secretaries also oversee appointments to key positions, including agency heads such as the chief of the USDA Forest Service or director of the National Park Service. They also can propose legislation and testify with a strong voice for or against proposed legislation. Obviously, with hundreds of responsibilities and tens of thousands of employees, each secretary must rely heavily on several assistants, deputy undersecretaries, and undersecretaries, and dozens of agency chiefs, division heads, regional directors and the lineage of officers that eventually ends with the field manager.

In addition to the 13 federal departments, there are a number of agencies in the Executive Office of the President that answer directly to the President and assist or advise him. One of these is the White House staff itself, members of The Office of the President. White House "staffers" as they are called, are frequently former members of the President's election team, but in specialized areas they may be scholars, business people, or other individuals of great expertise. In what they do, they range from highly paid errand boys to intimate advisors of the President. None should be underestimated in their ability to provide access to the nation's key decision-makers. Of the President's councils, the best known is the National Security Council, but the units most closely related to natural resources include:

National Council on Marine Resources and Engineering Development
Office of Science and Technology
Office of Intergovernmental Relations
Council on Environmental Quality

Probably the least glamorous but most powerful unit of the executive branch outside the White House itself is the *Office of Management and Budget* (OMB). OMB, in its present role, was created in 1970 and charged by the President with these crucial functions: (1) preparing the federal budget, and (2) serving as the management arm of the Chief Executive. OMB officials review all proposed legislation and often hold life or death sway over its outcome. With great influence they recommend how much money each agency will receive and where cuts will be made. They pass judgement on how well federal agencies are achieving their intended purposes, suggest internal changes in structure, and develop reporting and management systems. As federal researchers and public relations persons soon come to realize, they also screen and approve all questionnaires or other devices used in federally-funded projects to gather information from private citizens.

The Legislative Branch

It has been called "the most exclusive club in the world." Nevertheless, in many areas of the country few people take more interest in local natural resources than members of the U.S. Congress. The most prestigious of these are United States *senators,* for there are only two from each

Figure 12.1. To a large degree the ultimate payoff from the practice of public relations is favorable political action. (Courtesy of National Park Service.)

state, and they are elected for six-year terms. *Representatives* (members of the House of Representatives, addressed as Congressman . . . or Congresswoman . . .) are more numerous and are elected for two-year terms.[2] The total number of representatives is up to Congress, but prevailing wisdom has limited it to 435 members. The number from each state depends on its population, with at least one member guaranteed from the less populated states. At present, California has the most representatives, with 45. As each 10–year census is completed, the number of representatives from a state may increase or decrease. Since representatives are elected in each state from *districts* of approximately equal population, major changes in population and numbers of representatives require adjustments in the district boundaries, a process called *reapportionment.*

Any citizen with a cause, or a professional desiring to provide information for federal, legislative decision-making, should know his congressional delegation. The key people, then, are the two senators from that person's state, and the representative from his district. Most also have local staffs and permanent offices around the state as well as in Washington. These staffs are the "ears" of the elected officials and are relied upon heavily to stay in tune with the voters "back home."

All proposed legislation is funneled through a committee in each house of Congress. It is in committee that most of the legislative work of Congress is done. Here the *pros* and *cons* are hashed out in fine detail, expert testimony is heard, political bargaining takes place, and the compromises are made that are the heart of the democratic process. Some committees are more important and prestigious than others, and each member of Congress must apply for membership in specific committees. Appointments are then based on experience, interest, geographical location and successful political maneuvering. Most delegates try to get appointed to committees that deal with laws important to their particular constituents. Thus, a senator from Oregon is more likely to want a seat on the Agriculture and Forestry Committee than is one from Rhode Island. Committees, in turn, are broken into subcommittees to help handle the flood of bills each session. Key people related to this part of the legislative branch are, again, staff members. These individuals are full-time employees serving the committee or subcommittee. Frequently they possess great expertise in the subject dealt with by that committee. They also shepherd the bills through, manage public hearings held by the committee, advise the delegates, and otherwise wield considerable influence. Some of the committees of special importance in natural resource management are shown in Table 12.1.

FROM BILL TO LAW

Someone once said there are two things we would be better off not seeing being made—sausage and laws! Perhaps this is true, but to influence law makers it is essential to first have a knowledge of the process a *bill* (proposed law) goes through before being rejected or passed (an *act*). Unfortunately, this process is extremely complex, and a detailed treatment is beyond the scope of this book. The process also varies between federal and state legislatures and between states. However, the following outline should provide a basic understanding of the process at the federal level. It is structured to especially provide an understanding of points during the process

2. The term "a Congress" or "the 98th Congress" refers to a two-year period that coincides with the two-year term of office. Thus, a senator serves through three Congresses, a representative through one, unless re-elected. A Congress has a first and second "session" with the new Congress convening January 3 of odd-numbered years. This numbering system began in 1789.

Table 12.1.

Standing Congressional Committees and Subcommittees Especially Important in Natural Resource Management[1]

Senate	House of Representatives

Agriculture, Nutrition & Forestry
  Agricultural Research & General Legislation
  Environment, Soil Conservation & Forestry
Appropriations
  Agriculture & Related Agencies
  Interior
  Energy & Water Development
Commerce, Science & Transportation
  Communications
  Merchant Marine & Tourism
  Science, Technology & Space
  Surface Transportation
Energy & Natural Resources
  Energy Research & Development
  Energy Regulation
  Energy Conservation & Supply
  Energy Resources & Materials Production
  Parks, Recreation & Renewable Resources
Environment & Public Works
  Environmental Pollution
  Water Resources
  Transportation
  Regional & Community Development
  Resource Protection
  Nuclear Regulation
Governmental Affairs
  Intergovernmental Relations
  Governmental Efficiency & the District of Columbia
  Federal Spending Practices & Open Government
  Energy, Nuclear Proliferation & Federal Services
  Civil Service & General Services
  Oversight of Government Management
	Agriculture
	  Forests
	  Conservation & Credit
	  Department Investigations, Oversight & Research
	Appropriations
	  Agriculture, Rural Development & Related Agencies
	  Energy & Water Development
	  Interior
	  Legislative
	Education & Labor
	  Labor-Management Relations
	  Employment Opportunities
	  Post-Secondary Education
	  Select Education
	Government Operations
	  Intergovernmental Relations & Human Resources
	  Government Activities & Transportation
	  Environment, Energy & Natural Resources
	Interior & Insular Affairs
	  Energy & the Environment
	  Water & Power Resources
	  Public Lands
	  National Parks & Insular Affairs
	  Oversight/Special Investigations
	Interstate & Foreign Commerce
	  Energy & Power
	  Communications
	  Health & the Environment
	  Transportation & Commerce
	Merchant Marine & Fisheries
	  Fisheries & Wildlife Conservation & the Environment
	  Oceanography
	Public Works & Transportation
	  Public Buildings & Grounds
	  Water Resources
	Science & Technology
	  Energy Research & Production
	  Science, Research & Technology
	  Energy Development & Applications
	  Transportation, Aviation & Communication
	  Natural Resources & Environment

1. *Special, select* and *joint* committees are also appointed as the need arises. Conference committees are appointed to iron out differences in a bill that has passed in both houses or when two versions have been introduced simultaneously.

at which legislation is most vulnerable to public pressure. Generally, it is easier to stop poor legislation than it is to successfully sponsor favorable legislation, but knowing the pressure points helps in either case.

1. Bills can be drafted by anyone, but most originate from members of Congress. Many are initiated in the White House or by agencies in the executive branch. Also, citizen groups and lobbyists sometimes provide a pet bill to their legislators and request its introduction. To curry political support, the wise legislator usually will do this, knowing full well that its chances of making it through the legislative pipeline are slim without laying considerable groundwork and providing constant shepherding.

2. A bill can be introduced into either the House or Senate by the member (or members) of Congress who agrees to sponsor it. Bills with more than one sponsor obviously have a better chance of being successful, especially if the sponsorship is *bipartisan;* that is, sponsored by members of both political parties. Frequently, similar bills will be introduced into both houses simultaneously. The bill is assigned a number in the chronological order of its introduction, preceded by H.R. if introduced in the House of Representatives and S. if introduced in the Senate.

3. The bill is then "read", which usually means it is simply published. *The Congressional Record* is the official organ for this. Therefore, this is the place to look when you want the details on the content of a bill that has been introduced.

4. Next, the bill is assigned to the appropriate committee, which then usually assigns it to a subcommittee. Most never move beyond this point. Since all committees receive more bills than they can possibly cover in a session, the powerful chairperson can select those to be considered and *pigeonhole* the rest. If the committee is thinking about considering a bill, the staff will usually seek comments from established contacts with a known interest in the subject. For example, a forest practice bill might be sent to the National Forest Products Association and the Society of American Foresters for comments. It will also go to the potentially affected department where it is funneled from, say, the Secretary of Agriculture down to a *legislative analyst* in the chief's office of the USDA Forest Service. The bill, an analysis of its provisions, and a statement in favor or opposed (recommended position) then goes to department attorneys for a legal check, then to other agencies if more than one is affected. Next it goes to OMB for their review and approval of the position, and then to the Secretary who signs the report. Finally, the report goes back to the Congressional committee or subcommittee that sought the comments. Unfavorable pieces of legislation are often "sat on" at various points in this maze, and the session ends before they emerge. If the sponsor introduced the bill only as a favor, he knows this will happen and lets it die a natural death. Otherwise, staffers will do all they can to see that the bill gets pushed along.

   A proposed or draft bill originating from the White House or elsewhere in the administrative branch may clear the above hurdles *before* it is introduced by a member of Congress. "Touching bases" in advance or "laying a foundation" for a bill pays off in speedier passage and less embarrassment. But, rare is the bill that does not befall opposition from somewhere.

5. If a bill makes it through preliminary reviews, the next step is for hearings to be conducted in committee or subcommittee. Testimony can be given orally or in writing, and often some real influence on the outcome can be exerted at this point. Agency officials can testify at this time if invited, and "expert" testimony from outside the government is usually requested, with the individual receiving a trip to Washington at government expense to provide information. This is also the time for letters to flood the mailboxes of the committee members. The contents are more carefully noted if the letter comes from a constituent of that committee member.

6. Following the hearings, the members deliberate. They may decide to approve the bill as it was written (an unlikely event); do nothing, thereby killing it; or make revisions. The latter consists of a *mark-up,* which means each point in the bill is discussed and amendments considered. This sometimes excruciating process is the give and take of our political system. The trade-offs are made, some improvements added, some strong points weakened, and eventually a compromise is reached.

7. If the bill was considered in a subcommittee (the usual procedure), and if it is not sidetracked there, it is eventually reported to the full committee. There it may be approved as received, or the whole cycle of hearings and mark-ups may be repeated. If agreement is reached by the full committee, then the bill is "reported out' for a vote by the entire house of Congress where it originated.

8. First, it is placed on the *calendar.* There it can languish, proceed normally in due time, or be pushed ahead by Senate majority leaders or the House Rules Committee, depending on which house it is in.

9. One way or another, the bill may eventually be ready for *floor consideration.* This takes place before the full Senate or House of Representatives (although seldom are the chambers really full for this). The bill is read, section by section, and debate and amendments are allowed. It may even be remanded back to committee for amendments. The floor often provides more show than work and is a very poor place to hope for anything but a last ditch effort for or against a measure.

10. If the bill is not rejected at this point, it is "read" for the third time (this time, its title only), and voted upon. For the actual vote, delegates are called from their other duties or pleasures by bell signals that ring throughout the capital building. Many do not show up. Anyone with an interest in the particular bill will do what he can at this critical point to muster sympathetic delegates. Otherwise, previous lip service amounts to exactly nothing!

11. If the bill passes, it goes to the other house where the whole exhausting process begins again. Of course, unless it has been severely modified the analysis by OMB and affected departments won't be repeated.

12. If it passes the second house but in a modified form, a *conference* committee is appointed. Members from each house then iron out the differences.

13. Finally, it goes to the President for approval or veto. If vetoed, the bill must receive a ⅔ majority vote in both houses to pass without the President's approval, a somewhat unlikely event. Once a bill passes and is approved by the President, it is referred to as an *act, law,* or *statute.* It can be altered only by additional legislation *or* a judgement of the judicial system that it is unconstitutional.

PERSUASION IN THE POLITICAL ARENA

Ever since the time of Gifford Pinchot and Stephen Mather, natural resource management has been very much a part of the political scene. But something happened between then and now. H. R. Glascock, Jr., former executive vice president of the Society of American Foresters, believes "that we got too busy." He has stated:

"We had to develop forestry education. We had to develop the science of forestry as a priority. We had to put into practice what we had learned. And, as we proceeded to accomplish these goals with unusual dedication and vigor, we largely withdrew from the public scene. Other professionals and non-professionals have since occupied the scene and asked: Why forestry, and why foresters?"

Others have indeed reached a level of sophistication in the political arena that is far ahead of most natural resource professionals. An example is the degree of action that resulted in 1977 when Representative Morris Udall introduced legislation that would decide the future of public lands in Alaska. What followed was the beginning of an historic coalition that eventually joined the forces of approximately 40 environmental groups. At the height of its activities, here is how one writer described part of the action:

"Phone banks are set up so organizers can summon a needed response from almost any part of the country. Ten lobbyists prowl the Senate corridors. A recorded phone message is changed daily to record the latest development in the Alaska struggle. Away from Washington, grassroots organizers visit members of Congress in their home districts, ask sporting goods stores to sponsor "Alaska nights" and lobby newspapers for favorable coverage. And they write letters and mail-grams and telegrams. Coalition leaders boast of how astounded members of Congress have been by the mail—more than they've received on any one issue since the civil rights bills of the early 60's." Robinson, 1978; p.10)

Other results included unprecedented contributions and enough personnel to allow the effective luxury of lobbying 10 senators apiece rather than 100.

Admittedly, few natural resource managers have the latitude to openly lobby for or against legislation. At the local, state or federal level, the professional must be extremely careful in working within the political system. In fact, no blanket advice can be offered in this matter, for each situation is different. In some positions, adept political maneuvering is expected. In others, personnel may be strictly forbidden to make contact with political figures. For example, the anti-public relations legislation of 1913 and 1919 that was discussed in preceding chapters was largely intended to prevent employees of the executive branch (including Pinchot's Forest Service) from pressuring Congress. However, the laws have proven largely unenforceable, due in part to loopholes that allow members of the executive branch to contact legislators through "proper official channels" and when requested by a member of Congress (Guide to the Congress, 1976). On the other hand, federal employees in the executive branch (other than top officials who are confirmed by Congress) are strictly prohibited from being active in actual political campaigns. Under terms of the *Hatch Act,* federal employees cannot run for political office, distribute campaign literature, organize or speak at political meetings, circulate petitions, solicit funds, or publish anything soliciting votes.

Keeping Current

With hundreds or thousands of new state laws and as many as 26,000 federal bills dropped in the hoppers during each legislative session, how is it possible to stay abreast? This is important to resource managers and public relations practitioners for two reasons. First, being up to date and well versed is essential to planning strategies and possessing credibility. Second, the most political involvement most of us will ever experience is in supporting or opposing legislation proposed by others. To do this we must know what is being proposed and when to voice our opinion.

Fortunately, especially at the federal level, there are many ways to stay current. For example, the broad scope of legislative action is reported weekly by *Congressional Quarterly, Inc.* (1414 22nd St. N.W., Washington, D.C. 20037). It also offers a summary report after each session of Congress that describes accomplishments and trends. This is conveniently categorized under headings (such as Energy/Environment) and is based on authoritative viewpoints. Another source of broad, but highly respected, coverage is the weekly *National Journal,* published by Government Research Corporation (1730 M St., N.W. Washington, D.C. 20036). In addition, just about every professional society and large special interest group keeps its members informed of pertinent actions. Many even issue "alerts" as important legislation is introduced or approaches a critical stage. Whether or not you agree with the viewpoint of a special interest group, receiving their mailings is an excellent way to help understand their motives and strategies. In the "environmental" arena, some of the more active groups include the Sierra Club, Audubon, National Parks and Conservation Association, Friends of the Earth, and the Wilderness Society. State chapters sometimes also monitor and report on legislation at that level. Other periodical reports include:

Conservation Report
National Wildlife Federation
1412 16th St., N.W.
Washington, D.C. 20036

A weekly report, free to members; primarily on the status of pertinent bills, composition of committees, how members voted, and editorial opinion.

Forest Industry Affairs Letter
213 SW Ash St.
Portland, OR 97204

Biweekly newsletter covering the entire Washington scene. In addition to legislation, changes and rumored changes in agencies, actions of opponent groups, business trends and similar fact and opinion directly oriented to forest industry leaders.

Forest Industries Newsletter
National Forest Products Assoc.
1619 Massachusetts Ave., N.W.
Washington, D.C. 20036

Weekly report to forest industry personnel on legislation and events from around the nation affecting the business sector of forestry.

Public Land News
Resources Publishing Co.
1010 Vermont Ave., N.W.
Suite 708
Washington, D.C. 20005

Issued 24 times a year, this newsletter is an update on legislative and administrative actions primarily affecting lands and resources managed by the Bureau of Land Management.

The cost of these information services is usually high, ranging up to several hundred dollars a year. This alone speaks to the value of being informed and current on political matters. For those not able to afford their own subscription, the best alternative is a group or agency subscription that is then routed (quickly) to appropriate staff. Many university and large public libraries are also potential sources of these and other newsletters.

To help members of Congress determine the current status of bills, a computerized storage and retrieval system was created in 1973. It is best to work through your congressional office, but the operators will usually assist anyone who calls. The Legislative Information and Status System (LEGIS) is available by phoning 202/225–1772 or writing: House of Representatives Legislative Information Status Office, Room 696 House Annex II, Third and D Streets SW, Washington, D.C. 20515. To find out at what point in the maze of legislative channels a bill is located, the inquirer needs to provide LEGIS with one or more of the following retrieval "keys" to the system:

Bill number—The best key to use, assuring an instantaneous response (e.g. H.R. 377).
Sponsor or co-sponsor—This or date of introduction *and* subject matter will locate the bill.
Date of introduction—The day it was introduced by its sponsor.
Subject matter—Since there may be as many as 1,000 bills on one topic ("energy," perhaps) this alone won't help much unless you are interested in all of them or you have additional information to narrow the search.

The capabilities of LEGIS are expanding, but answers that the system can *not* provide include:

—an individual member's vote
—committee amendments on full text of legislative items
—evaluation of content or predictions of legislative action

Some states have similar systems or at least manually retrievable records at a central information desk.

Working With Political Figures

Foss (1960) observed that for any particular problem or issue, elected officials can be divided into two groups: (1) those who have a strong ideological commitment to some values which impinge on the problem, and (2) those who do not. The actions of politicians in the first category can be predicted with reasonable accuracy if it is assumed that they understand the problem. However, they often do not understand it. Nevertheless, this first group of politicians can be expected to react in terms of their ideological commitments.

The politician without strong ideological commitments may want to know many things about the issue at hand and the feelings of the people in his home district—his voters—relative to that issue. First, he may try to find out who is behind the policy or proposal and how intense is their commitment. In other words, how hard will they fight or how much will they spend? How much influence does the group backing the issues have with other persons and groups? How will various alternatives be accepted by the sponsoring group and by constituents? How will the anticipated effects on his constituents and the public affect their voting behavior?

In either case, the natural resource specialist often has excellent opportunities to provide information. Informally, voluntarily, at a hearing or at the personal request of the legislator, being viewed and used as a credible source of information is the most important way of influencing legislation available to most natural resource personnel.

Personal Contact—Keeping in Touch

The ideal situation is to develop enough rapport with members of your Congressional or statehouse delegation that they will either call on you when a natural resource issue occurs, or at least seriously listen when you call. This is quite possible, and two ways for achieving this status

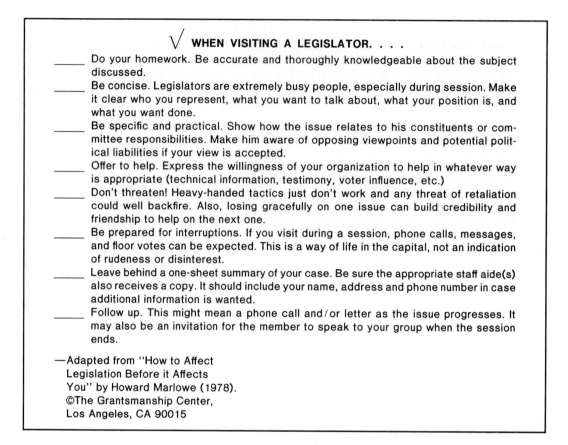

√ **WHEN VISITING A LEGISLATOR. . . .**

_____ Do your homework. Be accurate and thoroughly knowledgeable about the subject discussed.

_____ Be concise. Legislators are extremely busy people, especially during session. Make it clear who you represent, what you want to talk about, what your position is, and what you want done.

_____ Be specific and practical. Show how the issue relates to his constituents or committee responsibilities. Make him aware of opposing viewpoints and potential political liabilities if your view is accepted.

_____ Offer to help. Express the willingness of your organization to help in whatever way is appropriate (technical information, testimony, voter influence, etc.)

_____ Don't threaten! Heavy-handed tactics just don't work and any threat of retaliation could well backfire. Also, losing gracefully on one issue can build credibility and friendship to help on the next one.

_____ Be prepared for interruptions. If you visit during a session, phone calls, messages, and floor votes can be expected. This is a way of life in the capital, not an indication of rudeness or disinterest.

_____ Leave behind a one-sheet summary of your case. Be sure the appropriate staff aide(s) also receives a copy. It should include your name, address and phone number in case additional information is wanted.

_____ Follow up. This might mean a phone call and/or letter as the issue progresses. It may also be an invitation for the member to speak to your group when the session ends.

—Adapted from "How to Affect
Legislation Before it Affects
You" by Howard Marlowe (1978).
©The Grantsmanship Center,
Los Angeles, CA 90015

are suggested. One is to become acquainted with potentially successful candidates and offer advice on campaign issues. This should be done quietly, or behind the scenes. Once elected, politicians usually remember their supporters and utilize them to the degree possible in staff positions, on committees, or for advice and other assistance. Another more common way of developing rapport with legislators is in the "off season." When the session is over a legislator returns home to take the pulse of his constituents. Not only is he trying to find out how the people who elected him feel about how well he did his job in the last session, he is also trying to get some idea how they feel about measures that will come up in the next session. While the lawmaker's time is in great demand during the legislative season, he is usually available and ready to listen when at home.

Regardless of the approach, it helps if you are known by the officials who represent you. This is easier than it may seem, for rare (and probably short-lived) is the politician who will not take time to meet with a constituent and listen. Even in Washington or the state capital during the busy season, there will usually be time for you, especially if you make an appointment in advance. You represent a tie with the home folks—something crucially important to the politician.

Although this is *not* the time to conduct complicated business, it does help to reinforce your interest and position, or to remind the individual of a promise or bit of information just before a vote.

For achieving action at the federal level, the best approach is to work with staffers of Congressmen. The place to begin is the staff representative at the local level. This individual is the Washington office's eyes and ears. He also has a direct line to the legislator or to the most appropriate staff person in Washington. The local representative can also help you plan strategy by suggesting committee members to contact, timing, compromises that may be needed to gain support, and other valuable information.

It is also a good idea to keep the key staffers of your Washington delegates and statehouse representatives constantly informed of potentially volatile issues in their area. This *is* appreciated. Information is power, and politicians thrive on power. Information also helps the politician appear to be on top of matters and to handle new conflicts more intelligently. This can be of particular benefit to the management of natural resources. Here is an example of how one natural resource manager in the Corps of Engineers suggests that information can be used to help maintain good public relations:

> " 'Congressional' is the agency term describing any inquiry by a national or state legislator. We are supposed to respond to a congressional within 48 hours of receipt.
>
> "The district dislikes congressionals. Usually we receive them after we have done something controversial or at least to the irritation of a public. Since the legislator is usually inquiring due to a complaint from a constituent, the district is immediately placed on the defensive, an often weak and always uncomfortable position. An agency's cold, bureaucratic response to a legislator nearly always appears oppressive when compared to the emotion-packed letter of a constituent. Congressionals often misrepresent the district position. But the misleading information is very difficult to effectively counter once stated.
>
> "The district often knows when an action will elicit a congressional. So, it occurred to me. . .that we should anticipate congressionals by writing our letter to the legislator *before* he receives the constituent's letter. We may still suffer from a cold, bureaucratic style, but we will be on the offensive—a positive change, I think. And we will have been able to fill the legislator's information void on the subject before the constituent can misrepresent the district's position. This can only strengthen the district's stand" (personal correspondence).

Testimony

Committee and subcommittee hearings offer an opportunity to influence the outcome of specific legislation. Through a member or staff person, an invitation may be received to provide expert opinion on a bill or proposed amendments. Not many except administration officials receive such invitations, but any citizen has the right to testify at most hearings. Then it becomes only a matter of knowing the status of a bill and the date scheduled for testimony.

In addition to hearings on specific bills, *oversight hearings* are sometimes called by Congress. These are used by legislators to monitor and review government programs or study the need for new programs. Frequently they are a check on whether or not an agency or program is living up to an intended purpose. These are often important hearings, since dissatisfaction can result in abolishment, modification, regulation or other legislative changes. At the federal level, hearing dates are announced in the *Congressional Record* and nearly always picked up by the media related to the topics to be considered. Another way of not missing these dates is to request that the committee staff add you to their mailing list to receive announcements. Rules for presenting testimony vary. In any case, techniques of good personal presentation should be followed and printed material should be provided (often in advance) to highlight your points and aid the members in preparing questions.

Letters

Letters are the most common means of attempting to influence legislation. This can be done two ways. One is the mass campaign by citizens hoping to flood a member's mail in an attempt to show how much support or opposition there is to a proposal. This should not be underestimated, as frequently the letters are viewed like ballots (or ignored if they are merely forms saying the same thing but signed by different people). Incidentally, most letter writers receive a reply—automatically typed and signed after a clerk decides which form letter to send.

A more effective letter is one that is intended to provide information, expert testimony, or the position of some affected group. Even these, however, are often answered by a clerk-activated typing machine and the senator or representative never sees them. The way around this is to address it to the staff aide responsible for natural resources. A directory or phone call will provide the name. This little change in procedure reveals a degree of sophistication that does not go unnoticed. The staffer will take your message seriously, probably relaying it on in a summary to the boss. The aide is also a more accessible individual to pursue as part of the follow-up. Other letter-writing suggestions offered by Marlowe (1978) include:

1. Do your homework and know what you are talking about. (This goes for personal visits and hearing testimony as well!)
2. When referring to a bill, demonstrate sophistication by using the legislation's number and mentioning where it is in the legislative pipeline.
3. Have the 'biggest name' in the group sign the letter. Titles do carry weight, especially in a politician's mailbox.
4. Time your letters to arrive on Tuesday, Wednesday or Thursday. Mondays and Fridays are heavy mail days, and a mid-week letter stands a better chance of receiving attention.
5. Be brief and concise (See point 2 in the box about visiting legislators).
6. Be specific and practical (See point 3 in the box).
7. Send a copy of the letter to appropriate individuals (co-sponsors of a bill in question, other committee members, other staffers, etc.)

Books such as *The Grass Roots Primer* (1975; Sierra Club Books) and *Earth Tool Kit* (1971; Environmental Action, Inc.) have provided environmental activists with a wide range of additional tactics. Many would be inappropriate for professional resource managers, but some good ideas can be gleaned from such sources and used or passed on to groups that support your cause. One thing is certain, regardless of what action is planned, organization is a must. Competition on the political front is fierce and sophisticated, and the politically active natural resource professional cannot afford to be less. One of the first steps toward organized influence is to know *who* to influence. Many suggestions have been offered about when and how to provide input at critical points along the legislative pipeline. To complete these recommendations the following references are suggested to help with making the necessary contacts. Perhaps more in politics than in any other area of public relations, knowing a person's name and responsibilities is essential to opening the door to further opportunities.

Congressional Staff Directory
P.O. Box 62
Mount Vernon, VA 22121

Published annually by C. B. Brownson, this popular directory lists all top members of the three federal branches and their staffs. Committees and subcommittees are also listed. Includes addresses, phone numbers, biographical data, and more. Color-coded for quick reference.

The Congressional Directory
U.S. Government Printing Office
Washington, D.C. 20402

Published annually by the government to provide names, addresses and phone numbers and some biographical data of key officials and staff in all three branches of government. Also lists media representatives.

The Almanac of American Politics
c/o National Journal
1730 M St. NW
Washington, D.C. 25036

Produced by M. Barone and G. Ujifusa, provides a political description of each state and congressional district. Political biography of all members of Congress, including voting record on key issues.

U.S. Government Manual
U.S. Government Printing Office
Washington, D.C. 20402

The official guide to the three branches of government including descriptions of their purpose and structure.

Washington Information Directory
Congressional Quarterly, Inc.
1414 22nd St., NW
Washington, D.C. 20037

Annual directory of executive branch agencies, Congress (including committees and subcommittees) *and* non-governmental organizations headquartered in Washington.

The Book of the States
Council of State Governments
P.O. Box 11910
Lexington, KY 40578

Annual guide to top personnel in each state, and a wealth of other facts and statistics.

Finally, remember to say "thank you." All politicians thrive on approval; their careers depend on it. Therefore, when your efforts at influencing in the political arena are successful, pave the way for success in the next issue through praise, recognition and expressions of appreciation.

A Word About Lobbying

Much of what has been discussed falls under the term *lobbying*. Despite its sometimes evil connotations, lobbying is nothing more than "activities aimed at influencing public officials and especially members of a legislative body on legislation" (Webster's New Collegiate Dictionary, 1973). Clearly, this is within the province of public relations.

The problem natural resource managers have with lobbying—some have been heard to utter, "Please! Don't ever mention that word in my office"—is twofold. One is the tactics used by some lobbyists, and the other is the plethora of legal restrictions surrounding these activities.

Like any form of persuasion, techniques vary greatly with the circumstances and the ethics of the people involved. Except for the forest industries, few in the renewable resources sector have the funds to make large contributions to political campaigns. Yet, as long as disclosure laws are adhered to, this is an accepted practice of many lobbyists. Each year, corporations and other special interests give millions of dollars to congressional campaign funds—an unabashed bid to buy future influence. Also, much of the wining and dining, favor-trading and compromise that is a traditional part of lobbying is repugnant to natural resource professionals. Their emotional and morally intense dedication to natural resources is often out of step with the more mercenary political and economic perspectives of many other lobbyists.

Another reason the word lobbying is largely taboo among our disciplines is that the act itself is prohibited or tightly controlled within most government agencies. Also, in a private non-profit conservation organization, excessive lobbying can lead to loss of its tax-exempt, non-profit status.

Most of the federal agency paranoia stems from Congress' concern that tax dollars not be used to mold public opinion to in turn influence legislation. A Justice Department attorney explained that Congress fears that "the executive branch might become self-perpetuating, using its vast resources . . ." (Moore, 1979). Various laws have been passed over the years to keep the lid on executive branch lobbying, but few if any attempts have been made to enforce them. Still, they make government employees leery, especially when it comes to seeking grass-roots support for appropriations or other legislation. On the other hand, freedom of speech makes prohibitions against lobbying questionable. Also, executive branch agencies are clearly allowed to provide information to private groups about pending legislation, to request legislation or appropriations from Congress, and to supply opinions when requested by Congress. Where these legitimate functions end and lobbying begins is the thin line government professionals must learn to walk continuously. Similar philosophies prevail at the state level in most areas.

Nonprofit organizations have more clearly defined guidelines. In 1976, the Tax Reform Act liberalized the rules and allowed any nonprofit organization (except churches and private foundations) to spend a certain percent of their annual expenditures on lobbying. For example, a nonprofit conservation organization with annual expenditures of $500,000 may spend up to 20 percent of this amount to influence legislative action without losing its tax-exempt status. The Internal Revenue Service should be consulted for specific details and other limitations. There are also allowances made for "educational" activities (that is, not taking sides on a specific bill), "self-defense" lobbying, communication with members of the organization, and other potentially persuasive activities that do not count against an organization's expenditures for lobbying. There is now even legal basis for forming PACs (political action committees) that can unabashedly raise money for the election or defeat of candidates who are for or against the committee's particular cause (See the section on propaganda in Chapter 7.)

Aside from the limitations described above, the key legislative control on Washington's more than 15,000 registered lobbyists is the Federal Regulation of Lobbying Act. Passed in 1946, the law is aimed at those individuals whose "principal purpose" is lobbying. It requires them to register, report their sources of income and account for their expenditures. Many state governments now have similar requirements.

Certainly, anyone considering political action as part of their public relations program should consult legal counsel during the planning stage. But the natural resource management professions should not be intimidated by the problems or competition in lobbying.

Biopolitics. Natural resources, their management, and politics. They are inseparable, as well they should be in a democracy. A better understanding of this important aspect of public relations will go a long way toward facilitating scientific management of our resources.

SUGGESTED REFERENCES

Democracy Under Pressure: An Introduction to the American Political System by Milton C. Cummings, Jr. and David Wise. 1981. Harcourt Brace Jovanovich, Inc. New York.

Guide to the Congress. 1982. Congressional Quarterly, Inc., Washington, D.C.

How Our Laws are Made by Charles J. Zinn and Edward F. Willett, Jr. 1978. U.S. Government Printing Office, Washington, D.C.

How You Can Influence Congress by George Alderson and Everett Sentman. 1979. E. P. Dutton, New York.

Lobbying for the People: The Political Behavior of Public Interest Groups by Jeffrey M. Berry. 1977. Princeton University Press, Princeton, N.J.

13

Emergency Information Services

*No other area of public relations tests the mettle
of the professional as does emergency information service.*

Many in the natural resource professions believe that when an emergency strikes, the niceties of public relations must be suspended until the situation is under control. "Keep people out and tend to business" has been the philosophy of many fire bosses. Worse yet, when an accident has occurred, some have attempted to divert public attention by casting a veil of secrecy over the incident. What usually results from such well-intentioned but misguided procedures is inaccurate information and a public reaction to the resource agency that is neutral at best and negative at worst. In short, ignoring publics in a time of emergency is a sure guarantee of poor public relations. Moreover, the impact of the poor relations is accentuated because at no other time is so much attention focused on natural resource organizations and their management problems.

When fire breaks out in the chaparral forests of southern California, it is not uncommon for ten million people to see the smoke column as it billows high above one of the most populous regions of the country. Millions more will see the flames on television sets across America. When an aircraft goes down in a forested region, or a child is lost in the woods, the entire news-hungry nation is interested. When an avalanche strikes, a mill burns or a drowning occurs, local people immediately demand the details. There is no escaping human curiosity and concern. In fact, citizens have the *right* to know what is happening, and news media representatives will provide that information with or without the assistance and cooperation of resource professionals. If ignored by the resource organization, news people will promptly turn to the victims, to firefighters, neighboring landowners and to anyone else who has something to say. The victim or other landowners may blame the situation on the agency and the crew person may be speaking with complete ignorance of fact or policy, but news *will* go out.

Information service in emergency situations is a necessity and an opportunity. For an entire year, personnel with public relations responsibilities may struggle to gain the attention of news media and the general public, then suddenly a fire or other emergency strikes and there is more attention from the "outside" world than most resource managers know how to handle. In this chapter, some methods are discussed which should help cope with emergency information needs and convert them into productive efforts for improving public relations.

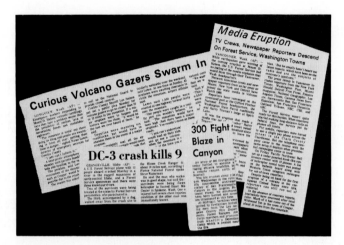

Figure 13.1. A wide array of emergency situations focuses the attention of the nation or the world on natural resource management.

Wildfire is the most common emergency faced by resource personnel, and it was wildfire that gave birth to the concept of fire information officers (FIO's). Until the establishment of this position in the USDA Forest Service, it was common practice for news media personnel to phone the forest dispatcher for information about a fire. Quite naturally this interfered with the other duties of this key person and tied up phone lines that were needed for emergency use. On the Angeles National Forest during the 1950's the situation grew so severe that it was finally proposed to establish a separate position during fire emergencies for the performance of all public information duties. I & E specialists Don K. Porter and Richard F. Johnson were the first to serve as FIO's, and both have contributed much to the procedures suggested below. Another former Forest Service public information officer, John Marker, suggested broadening the concept to include all large-scale emergencies—floods, storms, volcanic eruptions, searches, chemical spills, or plane crashes. Essentially the traditional fire information officer would become an *emergency information officer* (EIO). Marker also proposed creating a pool of trained and certified individuals to serve the information function during emergencies just as qualified supervisory personnel are dispatched to fire fighting duties wherever and whenever needed. This is now linked into the "red card" system used by many agencies to identify personnel who are qualified by training and experience to fill various positions on large "campaign fires."

An Attempt to Coordinate

Today's responses to all kinds of large-scale emergencies are often complex and expensive. In the early 1980's, an interagency National Wildfire Coordinating Group recognized the need for some kind of a shared system that would allow states, local communities and the many agencies of the federal government to work as a team in times of emergency. The National Interagency Incident Management System (NIIMS) was developed to meet this need.

The idea behind NIIMS is to have common terminology, common training standards, shared rather than duplicated resources, and a ready-made organizational structure that is understood in advance by all agencies and ready to implement regardless of where or what emergency strikes.

Already about half the fire and other major emergency organizations in the United States participate in NIIMS. Information officers are an integral part of this team approach to emergency management.

FUNCTIONS OF THE EIO

Despite attempts to standardize and to upgrade the role of the information staff in emergency organizations, there is no single term for the person in such a role. Emergency information officer is a generic term we use here for convenience, but in actual practice the terms information officer (IO) or fire information officer (FIO) are more commonly used.

In whatever situation, the role of the EIO is to provide accurate, current information to external publics, usually (but not always) via news reporters. It is also to provide a service to internal publics through disseminating news and accurate information to emergency workers, and service to managers of the emergency by shielding them from the constant pressure of public inquiries. Finally, the EIO has an important liaison function, making certain that elected officials, media representatives, and citizens with emergency-related problems have safe and prompt access to the appropriate officials at times that will not interfere with emergency operations. This is no minor role. As Porter and Johnson (1961) stated, this work "is not the frosting on top of the cake, it is part of the cake." It is not the easy, luxury job on a fire or other emergency. It is tense, difficult and constant work during, and long after, the emergency. To meet the challenge, adequate staffing is necessary, and the staff must have previous training to do the job right.

To fulfill these functions, personnel assigned to information duty must first win the confidence of the fire boss or others who must cope with the emergency. This comes with repeated, high quality performance and through building rapport *before* an emergency strikes. Emergency managers must know in advance how the EIO fits into the overall flow chart of the emergency organization, be convinced of the advantages and importance of this service, and know that the EIO knows what *not* to say as well as what should be reported. The support of the managers is essential, and only through cooperation can emergency information services be adequately provided.

The EIO must also win the confidence of media personnel. Usually, reporters are happy to have "a contact" at the scene of an emergency. Again, work *prior* to the emergency is necessary, not only in building rapport with key media personnel, but also in making certain that all stations and newspapers know of the services you will provide in an emergency and how they can reach you (for example, through an appropriate phone number that is *not* used for emergency calls). Next, confidence is built through professional performance. The media will happily cooperate and use your information if they consistently receive prompt, accurate information and fair treatment.

Workers at an emergency have information needs, too. When a fire goes on for more than two or three days, crews begin wondering what is going on in the outside world. The military-like regimen particularly necessary at fires creates a situation of isolation for the men and women involved. In addition to food and rest, news of the fire and from the outside makes an important contribution to the worker morale. Sometimes a camp "newspaper" is mimeographed and distributed to all personnel to report the latest fire size and conditions, weather predictions, where the crews are from and similar information that is usually made available only to the "top brass." This is an especially good way to prevent or stop rumors.

Other services can sometimes be provided to emergency workers. For example, a fire in California was beginning to turn into a major conflagration and an FIO staff was dispatched to assist. The location of the fire made it necessary to establish the camp in the fairgrounds of a small, rural town. The staff sensed that social problems could occur from the impact of 3,000 firefighters descending on the town which was not used to crowds of any kind, to say nothing of the young, ethnic mix that makes up a typical fire camp. Immediately the staff began contacting key people and groups in the community to explain what was about to happen, what to expect, and what problems were faced by the firefighters. The newspaper editor, mayor, police, and service club officers were among those who listened. The result was that not only were there no clashes, but townspeople began showing up at the fire camp with games, old books and magazines to provide entertainment for off-duty crews!

The liaison function is particularly important and requires the advance consent of all concerned if it is to work successfully. This role casts the EIO as middle person. It includes not only getting out the news, but also making sure that the media receive direct quotes from those in charge. It may mean obtaining information from the fire boss or weather analyst, or it may mean arranging interviews for media personnel with such individuals. It means playing the role of host to a senator, governor, or other nonagency official who drops in to "investigate" the emergency first hand. Sometimes "town folks" or local recreationists show up for information or out of curiosity. Once, when a fire camp was located next to a state park, scores of onlookers were seen around the boundaries of the camp. An alert FIO soon converted the situation into good public relations. She simply arranged for guided tours through the camp. This satisfied the curious, provided an excellent stage for explaining efficient fire management, and undoubtedly the off-duty firefighters enjoyed the prestige of being the center of attention for awhile.

Another liaison function is in working with individuals holding equivalent positions in agencies that are cooperating in the emergency. It is essential that the EIO staffs work together. Interagency competition will result unless the EIO's get together immediately, share facilities, share information, pool staff members, and agree that all releases and responses to news media will mention or credit all cooperators. Again, advance preparation and training helps smooth the way for a joint operation. At times this can be one of the most difficult problems faced in providing emergency information services, and it is one reason NIIMS is being developed.

PREPLANNING FOR EFFICIENT OPERATIONS

In a lecture on coping with stress, a psychologist listed such means as learning to relax with the aid of biofeedback mechanisms, removing the roots of the cause, or transferring emotional buildups to harmless outlets such as a good game of handball. None would be practical in the sudden emergencies that occur in the natural resource fields. He then added another to the list, and it is perhaps the key to success in emergency information services. He called it "anticipatory coping." And that is exactly what is done in preplanning. To preplan is to attempt imagining all the various situations you could expect to face in a particular area. In a sawmill, it could be a fire, a worker being caught in machinery, a strike, the breakdown of pollution control equipment and similar occurrences. In a park a serious crime, riot or other civil disturbance is always a possibility. If there is water, drownings are almost inevitable; where there are cliffs and climbers, a fall will eventually happen. While no one enjoys anticipating such emergencies, and all efforts should be made to prevent them, the wise public relations person will have a plan ready just the same.

Preplanning can anticipate not only the *kind* of emergency that may be faced, but it can also include the roles of specific personnel, the location of operations, what equipment will be needed, and the general procedures that will be followed.

Personnel

The roles of personnel depend largely on the structure of the organization. Usually, the emergency information function falls to the information or interpretive personnel. Appointments to emergency duties should be made in advance by appropriate authorities, and training specifically for the EIO role should be provided. Seasonal personnel should be included when possible as assistants or trainees. The job of the emergency *managers* must also be made clear, for they are not entirely free of information responsibilities. They are a key element in providing the EIO with information for further dissemination. In special situations, such as deaths or serious accidents, the manager has other important public relations responsibilities as well.

For fire emergencies, roles of FIO personnel and the flow of information are shown in Figure 13.2. The number of information officers may range from one on a small fire (or other emergency) to at least two in the information center and one field person per division per shift on a campaign fire. Thus, on a two-division fire, or two separate but local fires, at least eight FIO's are necessary. Additional assistants could provide relief and gain valuable experience by helping with the myriad details and unexpected problems that arise and require attention.

The personnel structure for emergencies of various kinds and magnitudes can and should be preplanned. The plan should be updated annually, inserting the names and phone numbers of current personnel (including alternates) who would fill each position. The plan should contain personnel in adjoining areas who will be called when a larger number is needed than the local district can supply. Where land ownerships are intermingled, it is also necessary to indicate who will be in charge under various circumstances. For example, in the Angeles National Forest, a fire burning mostly on county land will have an incident commander from the Los Angeles County Fire Department. The FIO in charge will then also be from the county. If it is mostly on the national forest, Forest Service personnel are in the top positions.

Locations

An important part of preplanning is knowing *where* the emergency information center will be located. Of course, this depends largely on the nature of the emergency. In the case of floods, drownings, lost persons, downed aircraft and similar incidents, the local office will usually serve as command post and information center. In the case of large fires, the center will probably be located near the scene. For fires, here is a rule of thumb to help in determining where to locate the center:

Small fires (100 acres or less)	Main office of the area involved, or near dispatcher's office.
Large fires (100 to 1,000 acres)	Nearest guard station, ranger station, fire house or motel.
Campaign fires or multiple fires	In or near general headquarters.

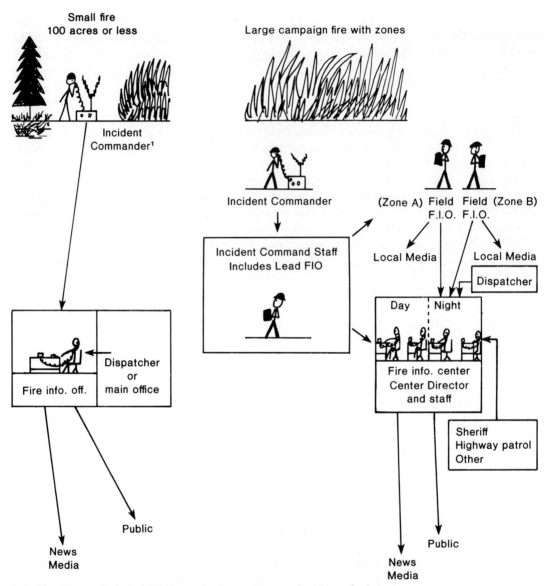

1. Incident commander is the NIIMS term for the person once referred to as fire boss.

Figure 13.2. The typical structure of emergency information services for the two size extremes of wildfires. The large fire structure illustrates an organization that has adopted NIIMS.

Selecting a location depends largely on three main factors. Most important is the availability of commercial phone lines that are *separate* from those used by emergency personnel. This is the main link with the mass media. Ideally at least two lines should be used, even on smaller fires. One will be the number given to the media. The other will then always be open for placing outgoing calls. Frequently, arrangements must be made in advance with the phone company to have phones installed for emergency use. Once the technical details are checked and approved, it is important to have the number of someone to call—day or night—to have the phones installed.

The other consideration is that the center should be accessible to media personnel and the general public. These are the people to be served, so it is important that they be able to reach the center easily. They should also be able to *find* it, so a large temporary identification sign and directional signs en route should be put up right away.

Finally, the center should be out of the way of emergency personnel and equipment. If it is in a fire camp, the edge of camp nearest the entrance or parking area is best. So much the better if it is away from camp but not too distant.

When motels are considered, they should have rooms large enough for four people to work, and the telephone system should not go through an operator. The owner should be contacted for advance approval and briefed on what to expect. Any building with a party line should be rejected.

Selection of a location can make or break the success of an emergency information center. It should be thought out in advance, and once selected for actual use, it should be changed only under dire circumstances. Once the media has been informed of the phone number and location, a change causes confusion and hard feelings.

Equipment

The fire cache with shovels, pulaskis, saws and other tools is as old as the forestry profession. Today it is just as important to have prepackaged EIO kits. This way, when an emergency strikes, no time and effort need be lost in trying to find necessary equipment. It also assures that when the center is set up everything will be there.

The best arrangement is to use large crates that when emptied can double as tables or desks. The kit should contain the following items:

Easel and newsprint pads—This is for listing the name of the fire, current acreage, crew members, weather reports, current news items and similar details. Include two pads of newsprint paper (or pad of preprinted fact sheet outlines as shown in Fig. 13.3) and several felt tip pens.

Maps—Include topographic quadrangles that cover the entire area for which your agency is responsible. Several copies of each will be useful. They will be used for showing the fire boundaries, direction of spread, crew locations, etc. Field persons and some media personnel will need copies. Agency maps of a smaller scale for public distribution will also be helpful.

Radio monitor(s)—This should be capable of monitoring the fire frequency, ideally for all agencies involved. Caution: Information received via the monitor should always be checked for accuracy with appropriate field personnel before using it.

AM/FM radio—One way to check on the amount and accuracy of information being broadcast about the fire. It should *not* be allowed to become a source of musical entertainment or distraction. Include extra batteries for portables.

Copier—The need to make duplicate copies is always a problem. If it is not possible to keep one in the kit, have prior clearance to remove one from an office when leaving for an emergency operation.

Typewriter—Useful in preparing legible statements, keeping records, and making stencils for the camp newspaper or bulletin board announcements. It should be a manual typewriter to avoid relying on an electrical outlet.

Clock—It should be large and have a sweep second hand. The second hand helps keep on time when recording tapes for radio.

Clipboards—One for each FIO.

Flashlights and batteries—Emergency operations go on 24 hours a day. Equipment for field work at night and if electric failures occur is essential.

Hard hats—Extra hard hats can be loaned to media personnel or other on-site visitors.

Signs—One or two to identify the center. Five to ten more for directional signs. By using both sides, arrows pointing either direction can be selected as the circumstances require.

Office supplies—Include paper, pencils, magic markers of several colors, carbon paper, set of colored pencils, paper clips, thumb tacks, two rolls of masking tape, stapler and staples, ruler.

Information notebooks—Two or more loose leaf notebooks should be included. They should contain current phone numbers, names and other data (like call letters) for all media. Political figures might also be included, as well as agency information, personnel, and anything else that will help information specialists working under stress.

Other reference material—Have a small, portable library and include the *Fireline Handbook,* relevant agency manuals or directories, terminology guides and similar references.

Forms—Travel expenses, aircraft liability waiver forms, and others that may be relevant.

Tables and chairs—These won't fit in a crate, but they should be stored with it as part of the kit. Two tables and six chairs is the minimum; all should be sturdy and collapsible.

Identification pins—Plastic pins, imprinted with "Information Officer" are helpful. Addition of the person's name is even more useful.

EMERGENCY INFORMATION PROCEDURES

When word first arrives of an emergency situation, the flow of adrenalin is quick to follow. Voices crack, details are forgotten, judgement sometimes fails. However, the experienced EIO, like the veteran fire boss, learns to suppress emotion and fall into a routine to do the job at hand. The result can be one of the best opportunities available to serve your organization through assuring good public relations.

The Fact Sheet

To bring order to chaos, the very first step is to develop an incident *fact sheet*. This can not be overemphasized. A good fact sheet calms information officers, helps reporters, serves the public and assures that the truth is told and that all parties receive the same information. The fact sheet can be a neatly printed newsprint pad or chalk board. It is displayed in the information center and updated regularly. By having it face the desk where phones are located, personnel can refer to it while under the stress of phone interviews or even while facing a television camera.

The fact sheet will vary depending on the type of emergency, but the fire fact sheet is the most common one. In this case, the following items should be entered as soon as the decision is made to set up the center:

1. **Name of fire**—The official name is usually established by the dispatcher and/or fire boss. It will probably be a creek, mountain or other landmark near where the fire started.
2. **Location**—This is a description of where the fire is burning. Use some reference point that people will understand, such as number of miles and direction from a town.
3. **When it started**—Also include current updates of how long it has been burning.
4. **Responsibility**—Provide agency identity. What kind of land is it on and who is responsible for control? For example, the fire is on public land with control efforts led by the Bureau of Land Management.
5. **Incident commander**—Like naming a general in a war situation, the name of the person in charge adds human interest. In most cases, he should be quoted when providing facts and statistics about the fire.
6. **Cooperators**—Naming all organizations and their lead people in a multi-agency fire is essential to good public relations with these important publics.
7. **How it started**—This should be specified only when the cause is well established, such as an observed lightning strike or a car wreck. Be extremely cautious in blaming anyone. If the cause was incendiary, or someone's campfire, it is best to say only that "the cause is under investigation." If formal charges are brought against the party responsible, this can then be specified. The term "alleged" must always be included until a person is found guilty in a court of law.
8. **Statistics**—These might include the number of fire fighters, tank trucks, engines, bulldozers, airplanes, etc.
9. **Costs**—Try to obtain accurate suppression costs and damage to date.
10. **Control time**—An estimate of when control is expected. Know and use correct terminology when referring to "containment" (scratch line around perimeter), "control" (secure firelines around fire) and being "out" (mop-up completed and no hot spots remaining).

Additional information can be added as appropriate. This might include the latest weather forecast, type of terrain or cover, accidents, or other relevant information.

Whenever possible retain, date and initial all fact sheets and maps of the fire. The information will prove valuable after the emergency for preparing reports and analysis of suppression actions.

Gathering information for the fact sheet begins with the first alarm. The FIO must be alert to radio traffic, and obtain facts from the dispatcher or other individual who received the initial report. Once a fire camp is set up, the FIO should establish contact with the people in command. This will be difficult at best unless earlier relationships have been established and the emergency managers understand the role of the FIO. Assuming that to be the case, then the entire hierarchy contributes information that is channeled to the fact sheet and thence to the mass media and the people.

Figure 13.3. The fact sheet is an essential part of any well organized emergency information center. Whether on a preprinted form (as pictured) or written on a newsprint pad, it should be completed immediately when an emergency strikes and updated regularly. (Courtesy of USDA Forest Service.)

Media Relations

Calm, organized, facts in hand—this should be the first goal of any emergency information officer. Next, using a prepared list of media representatives, all should be notified of the center's location, phone number and hours of operation. Then, be ready to assist. Emergency information services will call forth many of the skills discussed in previous chapters. Radio and television interviews are particularly common, as well as providing both hard news and *side bar* stories—short features or highlights on some aspect of the news—to the print media.

Cooperation and service are the guides to dealing with the media. A recent case is recalled where the opposite was true, at least in the early stages of a fire. During an unusually hot, dry summer, the log deck of a large sawmill caught fire. The flames shot hundreds of feet into the night sky. Reporters from throughout the region began showing up. Unfortunately, they were

Figure 13.4. A news team has been given access to a safe point on the perimeter of a wildfire. One function of emergency information services is to help media representatives obtain the news stories they want. (Courtesy of USDA Forest Service.)

stopped by the company at the farthest gate from the fire. A major news event was unfolding and they were barred from witnessing the action! The reaction was shrill, and the company's loss of image was as bad as the loss of its huge log supply.

The EIO has a responsibility to help the media get their stories—quickly and safely. In the case of the mill fire, reporters could have been conducted to a safe viewing area (and there were some) and been provided with a briefing on what had happened, what exactly was on fire, and how it might affect operations and the community. When a forest fire is involved, the FIO must try to provide media representatives with whatever they request (within reason, of course). Usually it is nothing more than facts or an interview. Sometimes, however, the request may be for an interview with the top boss or a plans chief or the weather specialist. Fire personnel need to know this is part of their responsibilities. The FIO will shield them from constant bombardment, but at times they should be willing to talk with the media people. When a request is received (or sometimes initiated by the FIO), the FIO should arrange a time convenient to both parties. Other requests might include a visit to the fire line, or aerial observation. Agency policies differ on these matters, but whenever allowable and relatively safe, the FIO should try to comply. If it is not possible to accommodate all reporters, a commonly used compromise is to draw straws to see who goes. That reporter is then expected to share his notes and photographs with others in the "pool."

Frequently, as a fire campaign drags on into several days or a week, the media representatives want fresh story angles. Here is a real opportunity for good public relations. The imaginative FIO can suggest stories that feed the curiosity and interests of the public and at the same time promote understanding of the agency's problems and build support for its management actions. This may include a tour of fire camp and the chance to talk with and photograph off-duty firefighters. The integration of women into the firefighting organization is still enough of a novelty to be of interest to the media and the public. The massive food operation is also always of interest.

TEN STANDARDS FOR THE EMERGENCY INFORMATION OFFICER

Any forest fire fighter is well aware of the Ten Standard Fire Fighting Orders. Here is a summary of suggestions for the EIO from Richard Johnson, one of the first fire information officers on the Angeles National Forest.

1. **Preplan**—Anticipate as many kinds of emergencies as possible and how the information needs for each can be handled. Have equipment, procedures and personnel assignments ready.
2. **Be calm**—Don't panic—you're supposed to prevent panic! Assess the situation and set the preplanning into motion—calmly.
3. **Get organized**—Obtain the facts first. Never begin operating from unconfirmed information. Make sure your equipment and personnel are ready and an efficient information center has been established.
4. **Verify**—Check every item of information to be sure it is factual and current. No incident is too small to verify.
5. **Be honest**—Remember this basic principle of public relations at all times. There is no such thing as a "little white lie." If you don't know, can't say, or don't want to say—be honest with people and tell them so.
6. **Be helpful**—Look for opportunities to make life easier for the media representatives, emergency workers, and fellow information officers. Be sensitive to the strain they are under—it will often affect their actions and attitudes.
7. **Manage your time**—Tremendous fatigue builds up in handling an active emergency information assignment. Recognize this and don't overextend yourself or others. Arrange shifts, alternate assignments, and get away from the center every couple of hours.
8. **Be responsive**—Stay alert to current and potential situations. Build up or reduce the EIO staff as the situation warrants.
9. **Be neat**—You are the agency to perhaps millions of viewers. Dress appropriately for the situation, but be neat. Also, maintain the information center in a neat and orderly manner at *all* times.
10. **Evaluate**—When it is all over, critique the entire operation and preplan for improvements.

Perhaps the media can share a camp meal as part of the story. One alert FIO in southern California realized that a campaign fire was going to extend into Thanksgiving. He made arrangements for turkey and all the trimmings to be served that day—and the event became national news that generated immeasurable goodwill toward the agency. Other interesting angles include where the crews are from, what they do when not fighting fires, how aerial operations are conducted, and so forth.

If emergency information services are to effectively work toward good public relations, goals and objectives once again play an important role. Certainly, major goal statements might be:

1. *To facilitate the gathering and release of accurate news story material and other emergency-related public information.*
2. *To relieve fire control personnel and dispatchers from the pressure imposed by news media and other external publics.*
3. *To provide workers with news of the fire and news from the 'outside.'*
4. *To foster good public relations between the agency and its external publics, including the media, political figures, other agencies or cooperators, and the local community.*

In addition, specific information objectives can be determined before or early in most emergency situations, and certainly for all wildfires. These guide the information efforts so they effectively capitalize on the unusual media attention. By recalling annual public relations plans (by whatever name) it is possible to disseminate many of the messages that were deemed priority items on a year-round basis. An obvious example is to have all external publics understand the multiple-use mission of the USDA Forest Service. With this as a guide, news stories should include mention of how the fire is affecting recreation, wildlife, grazing and watershed management. Perhaps a specific objective might be "to have all livestock producers in the area be aware of plans for immediate reseeding operations that will allow limited grazing opportunities the following summer." Local media can then be used to help meet this objective while the whole subject is still news.

Today one of the needs is to have lay people understand the natural role of fire in the forest. The antithesis of this objective occurred in the summer of 1979 during a fire in the Idaho Primative Area, at that time a candidate for the National Wilderness Preservation System. In many of the news reports monitored by the authors, we heard references to the amount of *timber destroyed*, with no attempt to explain that timber production is *not* part of the management in a wilderness area. Careful distinctions need to be made in explaining the broadened concept of fire management. Decades of publicity against the evils of forest fires must be mitigated to bring awareness and understanding that wildfire, controlled burns, and fires in a wilderness or natural area must be viewed differently. Simultaneously there can be no let-up on publicity aimed at preventing human-caused wildfires. This is a challenge for the FIO. Specific informational objectives can help guide the efforts at a time when excellent media coverage is almost guaranteed.

Internal Relations

In the management of emergencies, the officials in charge sometimes lose sight of the need for internal public relations. It is a time of stress for everyone, there is a job to get done, and there are tremendous pressures on those in positions of responsibility. Unfortunately, forgetting the basic principle of good internal public relations can be quite counterproductive to the overall effort. Tempers flare, rumors spread, anxieties rise. The result can be low morale, increased fatigue, a drop in productivity and even a greater tendency for accidents.

Although the EIO cannot correct all these problems, there are a few procedures this person should implement that will make a solid contribution to the team effort. Most of this involves nothing more than providing information. It makes no sense at all to keep workers in the dark about the events that for days or weeks are affecting every aspect of their lives.

One of the best and easiest ways to keep workers abreast of the news is to erect a large bulletin board near some point where they congregate. In a fire camp this is usually near the food line, sleeping area or clean-up area. The board need only be a sheet of plywood nailed to uprights or trees. Some things it should include are:

* Current map of the general fire area (or search area if that is the emergency)
* Current situation (perhaps a copy of the fact sheet or a news release)
* The weather forecast
* Safety news and alerts, including details of any serious accidents
* News clippings about the fire and other large fires in progress
* The sports page, comics and front page of a major daily newspaper

It can readily be seen that this kind of information can dispel rumors, remove the clouds of uncertainty, and give workers the feeling that they are part of a large and important event. It can also keep them in touch with the outside world. In short, it can build morale.

When a campaign fire lasts four days or more and control is not in sight, an FIO should consider daily publication of *Fireline News.* This is a 1–2 page mineograph that includes the same kind of information summary as the bulletin board. It might also carry a message of encouragement from the fire boss or other high official and editorial content on safety or similar subjects. Copies are distributed in the food line which assures that every member of the team receives a copy. Using a camp newspaper increases the chances that the information gets out to everyone, and it has some positive souvenir value that can last beyond the fire.

Another internal function of the EIO is to keep home districts informed of progress. A list should be maintained of where units are from. An occasional phone call to the office clerk or receptionist can provide welcome information to families, supervisors and friends of those assigned to the fire or other emergency. This is especially important after an accident to assure relatives of workers who were *not* involved.

Depending on the circumstances, there are many other small things the EIO can do to be helpful and to build morale. This might be relaying a personal message from a family to a worker (such as a birth announcement) or providing games and reading material for the off-shift. Importantly, it might also include an occasional kindness to help out the top brass. Although the EIO should not be viewed as an errand-runner, it can do wonders for building rapport by bringing current newspapers to the command post, or stopping by with coffee, doughnuts or other items that might be appreciated.

Personnel Management

Without individuals identified and properly trained for duty during an emergency, the information service has little chance of success. It is essential that workshops, an annual meeting and correspondence are used to prepare the information team just as fire or rescue teams are trained and organized before their services are actually needed.

Despite careful preplanning, the individuals who show up for duty will have various skills and levels of previous experience. The officer in charge will usually be determined by what organization is responsible for the emergency. It is then his responsibility to organize the others into an efficient, compatible team.

Whenever there is more than one person assigned to emergency information service, the following responsibilities must be clearly delineated:

1. Who is in charge? Even if more than one agency is working cooperatively, the old maxim applies that there can be only one boss. This responsibility must be delegated when more than one shift is used. This person's responsibilities include planning, scheduling, supervision, management decisions and keeping the fire boss informed of emergency issues and recommended solutions.
2. Who will gather information? This function is sometimes called *intelligence,* or the person is referred to as a *field information officer.* Sources include the fireline workers, dispatchers, plans chief, weather specialists, other agencies and others as necessary.
3. Who will answer phone inquiries while the others work with on-site media representatives? The latter might include arranging interviews, press conferences, helping with feature stories, suggesting side bar stories and generally helping the media.

4. Who will keep records and update the fact sheet?
5. Who will do photography for post-fire use or for distribution to the media if the emergency managers decide to bar news people from the scene?

Other assignments might include contacting local residents or organizations, editing *Fireline News,* or serving as a "floater," assisting where needed.

The EIO in charge should capitalize on special talents of the team. For example, one member may have a good radio voice and experience in broadcasting. That individual should be the one to do radio interviews. Another may be particularly cool in front of cameras. That person is the obvious choice for television interviews. The least experienced can be a general assistant or record-keeper; the most experienced might be assigned to handle complaints or work with politicians who phone or show up at the scene. When possible, duties should rotate occasionally to provide diversity and experience. It is particularly important to make sure individuals dealing with the media have frequent opportunities to get out and observe the action first hand. This adds credibility and makes it easier to answer questions or suggest news angles.

Whether a one-person operation at the scene of a drowning or a staff of dozens at a major conflagration, the keys to a smooth operation are training, preplanning, organization and careful management of talents and characteristics of the individuals who make up the information team.

SPECIAL SITUATIONS

No one can predict the circumstances under which you might serve as an EIO, or the kind of problems you will face. Consider the 65,000-acre Mortar Creek Fire that raged in central Idaho during the summer of 1979. During the three weeks of that emergency—which was complicated by the nearby crash of a private aircraft that killed all six occupants—the information team made over 1,500 telephone contacts with the news media, 350 personal visits with media representatives, and responded to delicate political inquiries and charges from the governor's office, Idaho's congressional delegation, and the White House.

No other area of public relations tests the mettle of the professional as does emergency information service. It is not a duty for the nervous, the bashful or the inexperienced. It is a difficult duty, often unpleasant and always requiring careful judgement. At times it also calls on the best of one's imagination to smooth over a nasty incident or to take advantage of an opportunity to favorably influence large numbers of people. The following are some of the special situations that inevitably will be encountered during emergencies related to natural resource management, and some examples that illustrate how quick thinking met the challenge of unique situations.

Injuries and Fatalities

Of any special situation, the most difficult to handle is an accident where a worker or recreationist is injured or killed. There are dual pressures of communicating with the victim's family and at the same time responding to demands of the news media.

There are two inviolable rules in this case. The first is that no names of victims are released until the next of kin are notified. Second, no information is provided until positively verified as being accurate. Most agencies have policies about who notifies next of kin in the case of an accident. Usually it is the top official responsible for the location in which the incident occurred. This might be the superintendent of a national park, a supervisor or district ranger in a national forest, a state park manager, or similar line officer. Ideally the contact is made in person and by or with someone close to the family. Sometimes none of this is possible because of long distances, unavailable personnel or the need for expediency before an information leak reaches the family. In these cases, notification becomes the proper duty of the information officer. When distance prevents personal notification, it is suggested that local police are called to assure that a neighbor, friend or someone else is with the next of kin soon after the phone call is made. The police should also be given the phone number of whoever should be contacted for details. If the victim is a firefighter or worker from another area, the home unit should be contacted to make the notification.

If notification is made by someone else, it is essential they be instructed to call the information center when it has been completed. Then and only then can names of victims be released.

No word spreads faster than when a serious accident occurs. Any delay in providing factual information leads to rumors, false accusations, anxieties and bitterness. Therefore, a prompt statement is required. A written release is best in this case and should include the essential facts of what, where and when. "Why" should not be included unless no fault is involved and the cause is absolutely clear. An example might be, "the victims drowned when their boat capsized during a sudden thunderstorm." "Who," as explained above, must wait. However, the number of injuries or fatalities can be provided. All releases pertaining to accidents should be approved in advance by the official in charge.

Media personnel are usually helpful and understanding when it is explained that names and details are being temporarily withheld. In fact, if the victims' names are inadvertently mentioned in radio traffic, it can be assumed that local media have monitored the information. This is the one and only time when it is proper to ask an editor or other news person to withhold information. Usually they will cooperate. However, they are *not* understanding about delays in providing reasonable information or acknowledgement that the incident occurred. A lot of poor public relations can be stopped before it occurs simply by applying the principle of "offense" when an accident happens. Get as much information to the media as the situation allows, and as quickly as you can.

In some emergency situations, an office or information center will be invaded by family and friends of victims, and by reporters. When this occurs, information officers should put into action a preplanned method of separating the two groups. Perhaps relatives and friends can be taken to a part of the building or accident scene where media persons are barred. This is not only a simple act of compassion, it prevents unfounded information or emotional quotes from being picked up by the media. Similarly, when nonfatal accidents occur, reporters often converge on the hospital. If this might happen, an EIO (in uniform, of course) should be dispatched to the hospital to help provide accurate details and perhaps screen out falsehoods.

The Irate Citizen

Citizen complaints are a common companion to many emergency situations. These range from the inconveniences of a temporary road closure to serious charges of unwarranted trespass, broken fences or the abusive language of an official. Handling complaints is discussed in Chapter 8 and should be reviewed for application during emergencies as well as in routine operations. Basically, it is a matter of: (1) being polite and listening carefully, (2) obtaining the facts or determining the real issue, (3) finding out what action will satisfy the person, (4) assuring him that you will seek a solution, then (5) following up as appropriate and reporting back to the complainer.

Figure 13.5. Major accidents and natural disasters attract political figures. Pictured is Washington's former governor Dixie Lee Ray during the eruption of Mount St. Helens. With care, emergency information officers can use this as an opportunity for developing good public relations. (Courtesy of USDA Forest Service.)

Frequently, complaints arise from misunderstandings. These are the easiest to correct and can often be converted to goodwill. To illustrate, homes were threatened during a wildfire in southern California. Rumors spread that aircraft were available to help fight the fire but instead were sitting on the ground idle. The problem was agitated when someone phoned the airport to find out the reason. They happened to reach an army officer who replied, "It beats me." The misunderstanding surfaced on a radio talk show and was brought to the attention of the FIO. Since the reason for the grounded planes was high and irregular winds, he promptly made this known in news releases. But he also countered the talk show quickly and effectively. He contacted a friend who was a pilot and asked *her* to phone in to the show. She identified herself as an experienced pilot, explained the wind situation, and assured the audience that no way would *she* attempt flying in such conditions and certainly the firefighters would be crazy to try it.

Many times a misunderstanding can be anticipated and prevented. When homes are near a fire scene, it is a good idea to have one or more uniformed FIO's walk through the affected neighborhoods and talk with as many people as possible. Businesses and resorts should also be visited to personally provide people with information about the efforts being made, weather and terrain problems and similar assurances or pleas for understanding. As with any public relations situation all potentially offended parties should also be sought out and briefed when possible. If the emergency involves a nature preserve, a local conservation leader may be the one. If a valuable hunting area or a fishing area (a chemical spill, perhaps) is involved, a sports club leader might be appropriate.

Politically Sensitive Issues

Among the potentially offended is always the politician. Therefore, his staff or the official, in person, should be kept abreast of any major emergencies. Unfortunately, even this may not help. Many elected officials cannot resist the opportunity for widespread publicity and media exposure that is inherent to emergencies.

The EIO can do four things in an attempt to control the situation. First, find out immediately if the emergency is likely to involve a politically sensitive issue. If it does, an understanding of previous debates can help guide steps to take in the current situation. The prohibition of machinery in wilderness, lack of access roads or fire escaped from a controlled burn are common examples. Second, alert emergency managers to potential issues and help predict outcomes of decisions when alternative courses of action are possible. Third, get the *facts* to all parties involved and to the general public. Try to head off any falsehoods that were brought out in the past relative to the issue. This might mean pointing out that machinery can or is legally being used in a wilderness under emergency conditions, or that efforts are being made *not* to use machinery (depending on the management decision and political climate in the particular case). Finally, when political figures show up or ask to be taken to the scene, every effort should be made to personally conduct them. This way, their request is granted, explanations can be given, and interviews with the right officers can be arranged. It might also assure the safety or comfort of political figures and their assistants. Naturally, equal treatment should be afforded to all.

The Teachable Moment

Any interpretive naturalist knows that there are times to forget the script, so to speak, and take advantage of some unexpected opportunity. This might be a noisy squirrel encountered while on a bird walk, or a distant lightning storm during an evening campfire program on park history. Unexpected opportunities happen in emergency information services as well, and the alert EIO will not miss the chance to garner goodwill for his agency.

One example of this occurred on the Los Padres National Forest. While a large fire was burning in the coastal mountains, someone noticed crowds of up to 600 people gathering each day near the end of the runway at the Santa Barbara Airport. An imaginative FIO with an interest in aircraft went to the runway, set up an easel with flip charts, and began providing information about the scout and retardant planes coming and going from the field. He started with data about the planes but soon worked his way into explaining the role of aircraft in fighting forest fires. His goals were to dispel the myth that planes alone can stop the fires, and to point out the danger of their mission and the need for fire prevention.

Another example was during the early eruption of Mount St. Helens in 1980. At first all the news and information was on a negative tone full of danger and potential danger. But this did not keep thousands of tourists from flooding into the area for a look at the magnificent spectacle of an erupting volcano. Finally, information specialists began directing the sightseers to safe viewing points and even erected informative signs about the mountain's geology and what effects might result from the eruption.

Fire camp tours, meetings with civic groups, suggesting feature articles and countless other opportunities should help the EIO convert an unfortunate situation into positive public relations.

Offensive Action Pays Off

It has been stressed that whether a routine operation or an emergency situation, being on the offense is the guide to good public relations. Consider this case that occurred in the spring of 1978.

USDA Forest Service personnel were cooperating with a local highway department in the control of avalanche hazards. The procedure in such a case is to fire a 75-mm shell into the snow-laden mountain slope to create an avalanche at a safe time and of controlled size. On the snowy morning of March 3, something went wrong. The shell missed the ridge and landed in a residential neighborhood, totally destroying a half-built home and narrowly missing others. Miraculously, no one was injured or killed.

Such an incident has all the makings not only of extremely poor public relations at the local level, but of national publicity sure to cause embarrassment and political damage to the agency. The exploded shell would be expected to seem quiet in comparison with the outrage that would follow. But this did not happen. In what must be a classic example of deft handling of an emergency situation, the Forest Service took the offensive and defused a highly explosive public relations situation.

First, the regional forester was promptly notified and made a rapid and correct management decision. He instructed that the Forest Service would admit that an error had been made and the fault was entirely theirs. Moreover, he insisted that whatever red tape would need cutting, the parties suffering losses from the incident would be fairly compensated and within 30 days. The second outstanding move was that information specialists immediately contacted the mass media to inform them that the accident took place and to provide the details. Third, the district ranger promptly went to the neighborhood, visited door-to-door and explained what had happened and what actions the Forest Service planned to take. Later he also apologized before the city council. There were no delays and no attempts at cover-up, but instead there was swift, positive action and full disclosure of the facts. The result was no lingering law suits, no opportunity for a media exposé, and only the briefest publicity, most limited to the local area and of minor importance compared to how it might have been.

Emergency information service is a relatively new specialization, but one of extreme importance. Its potential should not be ignored by any resource management agency. From the highest level to the smallest field unit, proper handling of information during an emergency can make the difference between the image of professionalism and the image of bungling bureaucrats or industrialists. The benefits of emergency information service are myriad and successful performance is the very embodiment of good public relations practice.

SUGGESTED REFERENCE

Fire Information Officers' Guide. 1982. National Wildfire Coordinating Group (USDA, USDI and National Association of State Foresters), Washington, DC.

14

A Look
Toward the Future

The future belongs to those who prepare.

The mid-Eighties is a difficult time to seek guidance from a crystal ball. In the past five years, the natural resource professions have been shaken by drastic changes that no one could have predicted even six years ago. A decade of growth ended with the triple impact of federal employment freezes, a general rebellion against increased taxes, and a recession in the timber industry. Whether because of these or other factors, such as the allure of the so-called high tech and business fields, another event has been a dramatic decline in the enrollment in natural resource schools across the nation.

During the past five years, declines have been balanced by growth in the area of resource-based tourism. An aging, more affluent population has resulted in use of the outdoors in unprecedented numbers. Visits to areas administered by the National Park Service rose from approximately 220 million in 1980 to almost 250 million in 1984 (NPS, 1984). Sales of recreational vehicles rose despite gas prices and the recession that plagued many American industries during the same period, and the travel and tourism industry is said to now be the nation's third largest retail or service industry.

Certainly interest in resources and the pressures on resources are intensifying. We can also say with certainty that good public relations is needed as never before to balance these pressures with the need for wise, long-term management and support for the management agencies. The needs for public relations in industry are equally strong, not only to help promote the use of products and services, but to gain favorable legislation and to ward off undesirable regulations.

Today's general trends suggest the need for more dollars and more personnel to work on the public relations side of resource and recreation management. Whether or not this is happening is difficult to determine. To measure trends accurately, comparable data must be collected at a minimum of two points in time. This kind of study, called *longitudinal* research, has rarely been done. None are known to exist in the private sector, and in government natural resources work perhaps the best studies have been of fish and wildlife agencies, particularly those conducted in 1948, 1968 and 1976 by the Wildlife Management Institute (1977). In the last report to date, it was found that employment in information and education (I & E) had increased from 544 in 1968 to 606 specialists in 1976, an increase of 11 percent. In 1985, a repeat of this study is needed to obtain comparable data. In a different survey by the senior author in 1985, 27 state fish and wildlife departments reported only 223 permanent professionals in information and education, and just over 300 when considering environmental education and other related callings. Budgets for the information units in these agencies were reported to be about five percent of the agencies' total, down slightly from when Gilbert did a similar survey in 1962, but up 60 percent from figures reported in 1980 by Mindick.

In our survey data shown in Table 2.3, we report at least 1,537 permanent professionals in the communication side of resource management in the agencies that responded to our survey. This does not include many field units such as state parks or national wildlife refuges. However, the survey method, sample and response were approximately the same as Mindick's 1980 survey that showed a total of 2,448. If these and the 1985 budget figures are to be believed, it appears that there may be fewer employees but that they have more money to work with or—and this is more likely—higher costs for fixed expenses such as printing.

Aside from trying to measure changes in budgets and personnel, there is no practical way to measure the emphasis given to public relations functions as a part of *every* employee's duties. National Park Service policies, USDA Forest Service's Host program, Bureau of Land Management's Good Neighbor Program, and the Corps of Engineers' interest in "visitor perceptions" are indicators that there is a growing awareness of the need to integrate good public relations into *everyone's* job.

During the preparation of this book, interviews and the review of literature indicated several trends that may be of far greater importance than statistics in considering the future of public relations practice. One thing is the changing communication technology. As discussed in preceding chapters, new delivery systems in both the electronic and print media open new opportunities for communicating with more people, a wider array of publics, and in more effective ways. The new developments also present the very real danger of natural resource professionals being surpassed by others if we fail to respond to change. As publics become accustomed to sophisticated communications in other areas of their lives, they will expect the same from personnel involved in natural resource management.

Another change is the growing awareness of citizens that they have a voice and a vital interest in the management of natural resources. Backed by a multitude of legal mandates, the citizen enlightenment and involvement of the 1970's will continue to grow in the 1980's. This alone will require greater skill, sensitivity and understanding of people on the part of all resource managers and professional public relations persons.

The role of professionals related to public relations may also be changing, or put another way—coming of age. Managers seem to be relying more on professional communications and public relations specialists for advice and assistance in predicting and solving problems. Public relations is also becoming a popular subject in American journalism schools. Whereas public relations specialists were once ex-newspaper types or retread foresters and wildlife managers, today students are specializing in public relations. There are 5,000 students in college chapters of the Public Relations Society of America, up from 96 students when the society started college chapters in 1968! Most, of course, are headed toward non-resource industries and services, but it definitely shows that the field is maturing.

In the natural resource area, one of the greatest changes we see is the need for an interdisciplinary approach to public relations. Gone are the days when the best writer could be given a title and a typewriter and be expected to achieve good public relations for the employing organization. In communication media alone it is becoming impossible to master the skills necessary for proficiency in each. An exciting, imaginative magazine writer may be a complete bore when creating television programs. The person with an ear for the highest quality in taped sound may be completely blind to balance in an exhibit or the effectiveness of color in a brochure. Moreover, in the area of understanding the psychology and sociology of persuasive communication, the modern public relations person is faced with a virtual explosion of new facts, theories and sophisticated research techniques. Similarly, resource management is becoming increasingly complex. The sum of this is that the future public relations specialist—or part time practitioner—will need to be the *manager* of a team effort for preventing and solving social problems. Like the best managers in any field, these individuals should not try to be jack-of-all-trades. Instead, they will have some understanding of each speciality and a healthy appreciation of each, including knowing their own limitations in each. Then, and only then, are they in a position to plan an effective route of action, seek competent assistance and orchestrate the whole. The result of such an interdisciplinary approach, purposefully guided, will be improved public relations.

THE PUBLIC RELATIONS PERSON

What makes a good public relations practitioner? This is extremely difficult to answer. For one thing, as mentioned above, there are so many facets to modern public relations it is doubtful that any one person could be competent in all. Second, we have known outstanding public relations people from every background. Some have had not a day of college work. Others have been excellent biologists with a natural inclination for communications and public relations work. Some have been journalists or graduates with an English degree who have developed a knowledge of natural resources.

More important than any particular college degree are certain characteristics that seem inherent in some people and lacking in others. In his classic discourse on "the priceless ingredient" necessary for good environmental interpretation, Freeman Tilden (1977) provided the key characteristic—love. He hastened to explain he was not referring to any romantic view of humankind, but rather to the kind of love that draws forth an understanding of other people. This desire to know and understand all kinds of people is indeed essential for public relations work. First and foremost, to be successful in public relations, a person must like working with people and have a driving desire to build bridges of understanding.

Tilden gave us a second characteristic that is as important in public relations practice as it is in interpretation. That is the love of subject. Of three key traits, this is the one most likely to be possessed, for this is what attracts most of us into the field of natural resource management. Unfortunately, for many natural resource managers it is the *only* thing that attracts them to their profession. This has given rise to many of the problems we face after decades of ignoring the human element while honing our skills in the technical aspects of the resource. But neither can the resource be ignored, for it is inconceivable that a good public relations person would have no feelings toward natural resources or would be ignorant of their management needs.

Finally, we must add a third love—love of communication techniques. In many years of teaching we have seen numerous students interested in public relations who possess the first two characteristics. But to be effective and successful as a professional, there must also be an insatiable desire to learn about improving communication. Half in jest, half in earnest, we often ask aspiring students, "Does the smell of printer's ink turn you on? Do you like touching fine quality paper or looking at the different textures of cover stock?" Of course, not everyone will fall in love with the print media! Still, it provides a good self-analysis to think about how you feel toward writing, making oral presentations, taking pictures, building exhibits and working with the many other tools of public relations.

Before looking at what educational preparation might help make "the perfect PR person," let us look at how management sometimes views the less-than-perfect individual. Painful as it may be, it can help improve your image and service by trying to determine how you are perceived by others. Here are the findings of Eugene Miller, a former manager of *Business Week* magazine.[1] They reflect common criticisms among managers who have public relations specialists on their staffs.

1. *The "yes man."* Compared to other staff members, the public relations specialist is often so anxious to please that he loses sight of the need to counsel management on the basis of the best factual information available.

2. *Staff meeting shyness.* Managers have noticed that a certain shyness often sets in when the public relations person is elbow to elbow with other specialists. A confidence in one's own specialization should offset this and help bring out the assertiveness necessary to be heard.

3. *Technical ignorance.* This is the lack of technical knowledge about the business or mission of the employing organization. More than anyone else, the public relations person must be able to understand the technical side of the organization in order to be able to answer questions and communicate effectively with diverse publics. This includes knowing the basics of silviculture, logging economics, wildlife management, range production, fire management or the other matters important to the employer.

4. *Tunnel vision.* This complaint concerns an insensitivity to the employer's immediate headaches. Miller quoted one company vice-president as saying, "My public relations man is talking about some sort of super-duper . . . open house, when my immediate problem is upcoming labor negotiations. Why doesn't he give me a super-duper plan to help solve them?"

5. *Prima donnas.* Another manager called his public relations department "the opera house. . . . It has more prima donnas than the Metropolitan!"

6. *Oversensitivity.* Quite often the public relations person becomes so involved in a project or a point of view that he takes it as a personal affront when it is rejected by the boss. It is important to remember that public relations counsel is but one of many pieces of advice and information the manager must consider in making a decision or investment of funds.

Assuming the public relations person possesses our three loves and guards against committing the above six sins, what other traits might be helpful and should be mentioned? Gilbert (1971) suggested the following:

Curiosity	Thoroughness	Imagination
Honesty	Tact	Patience
Good judgment	Pleasant personality	Ability in administration
Courage	Sense of humor	

1. From *Lesly's Public Relations Handbook* by Philip Lesly. © 1971 by Prentice-Hall, Inc. Published by Prentice-Hall, Inc., Englewood Cliffs, N.J. Reprinted with permission.

Figure 14.1. Regardless of educational background, the public relations specialist must possess a love of people, communication media, and natural resources. (Photos, clockwise: National Shooting Sports Foundation, University of Idaho, National Park Service.)

Educational Background

Some of the necessary qualities for public relations work are impossible to acquire in the classroom. Others, however, must come through formal education if the degree of competency that is necessary in today's world is to be attained. Specifically, knowledge of natural resource management and the tools of public relations are best learned through a college education. But what is the best curriculum to follow to gain this background? Either competency area could require full-time application for at least four years. Which one, then, should receive the academic emphasis, and which should be the minor or left to on-the-job training? There is absolutely no agreement on this important point, yet it is a key factor in the future of public relations in natural resource management.

We have long suspected that a person's opinion on this subject is closely related to his own educational background. If so, extreme caution is necessary in polling "experts" to help create a new curriculum or to help select one's own educational route to a career. Data on this question were collected by Fazio (1971) and Mindick (1981), with both studies arriving at the same conclusion. Most people with degrees in natural resource management or the related sciences believed the emphasis should be there. Those with journalism or communication degrees believed their educational background was best suited to I & E or public relations work in the natural resource fields. Respondents with neither degree tended to support the contention that education in communications is paramount, but their numbers in the two studies were too few to be reliable.

A 1976–77 survey of 1,384 public relations departments and counseling firms highlighted the *diversity* of degrees held by public relations practitioners. Results from that study, conducted by Cutlip and Center (1978), are shown in Table 14.1. It can probably be assumed that many in the "Others" category held degrees in the speciality of the particular employing organization.

For positions most closely associated with public relations work in the natural resource agencies, Mindick (1981) also found diverse educational backgrounds. He found little consistency in the backgrounds of people filling communication positions. As shown in Table 13.2 of our first

Table 14.1.
Baccalaureate Degrees Held by 1,384 Public
Relations Practitioners, 1976–1977[1]

Degree	Percent
Journalism	40
Others	24
Social Science	11
Public Relations	10
Economics/Business Administration	9
Advertising	3
Marketing	3

1. Scott M. Cutlip and Allen H. Center, EFFECTIVE PUBLIC RELATIONS, 5th ed., © 1978, p. 27. Reprinted by permission of Prentice-Hall, Inc., Englewood Cliffs, N.J.

edition of this book, about half the agencies tended to favor people with natural resource backgrounds, and half had more graduates of communication schools. In a 1985 re-survey, fewer agencies responded with data, with fewer personnel included. It is therefore difficult to establish any trends. However, the data in Table 14.2 again shows the extreme diversity of backgrounds, and with caution, comparison of the percent changes from Mindick's study may be indicative that communication functions are being performed increasingly by people with degrees in neither resource management or communication.

Looking at what should be expected of a graduate who will practice public relations may be of more help in deciding the best academic preparation. For the individual who seeks a full-time career combining natural resources and public relations, three areas of study impress us as being about equal in importance. These include a wide sampling of courses in communication techniques—radio, television, writing, public speaking and graphics to mention a few. Second, the basics of the biological sciences and natural resource management must be mastered. Third, to understand publics and how to work with them, it is necessary to study the social sciences, particularly social psychology, cognitive psychology, their more basic prerequisites, and at least one course in related research methodology. The area that is considered the major seems less important than making certain the other two areas of study are not neglected or minimized. In the end, the result should be what Philip Lesly (1983) stated is needed for the future—true scientists of public opinion, not merely information producers, ballyhoo artists, or other narrowly specialized technicians.

One way to meet the three areas of minimum competency is to pursue a graduate degree. For example, the student could focus on natural resource management and the social sciences at the undergraduate level, then seek an advanced degree in the communications field. At some universities, the faculties in these separate disciplines cooperate to produce students who are specifically prepared for careers in the natural resource professions. Financial support for such an interdisciplinary approach has been provided to hundreds of students through the scholarship programs of organizations such as The National Wildlife Federation, Resources for the Future, and The Outdoor Writers Association of America.

Now, for the more common situation—the individual who will have public relations as only part of his responsibilities as a natural resource manager. This kind of student faces a four-year curriculum packed tightly with the courses necessary for competency in managing the resource. Few elective courses remain after the required forestry, wildlife, range or fisheries courses. Worse, few curricula specify more than a basic writing or speaking course to help prepare the student for the overwhelming task of successfully working with diverse publics. This situation must change if public relations is to be improved. It seems doubtful that change will come from the traditionally-trained natural resource faculty. Instead it will take direction from alumni who recognize the deficiency in their education (and there are many), administrators who are expected to take a broader view than a specialist, and the professional organizations—especially if they have accrediting authority, such as the Society of American Foresters.

To perform well in the general functions of public relations, the natural resource manager needs at least one general course in public relations. It must be highly applied and should at least introduce the student to the basic competencies needed in public relations practice. It should stress

Table 14.2.
Reported Educational Background of Personnel in Communication Positions
in Natural Resource Management Agencies, 1985.

Agency	Agencies Responding	Natural Resource Mgt.				Life or Earth Sciences			
		Assoc.	BS/A	MS/A	Doc.	Assoc.	BS/A	MS/A	Doc.
Army Corps of Engineers									
Washington Office	0								
Divisions	2								
Bureau of Land Management									
Washington Office	1		1						1
States	6		3						
U.S. Fish & Wildlife Service									
Washington Office	1			1			1		
Regions	5		3				2	2	
USDA Forest Service									
Washington Office	1		2						
Regional Offices	7		11	1		1	1		
National Forests	83	2	44	6		1	15	1	1
U.S. National Park Service									
Washington Office	0								
Regional Offices	6		3	1			5		
National Parks & Monuments									
(Natural areas only)	81	1	19	3		1	86	13	
Soil Conservation Service	0								
Tennessee Valley Authority	1		1	1	1		6	3	
State Fish and Game Depts.	27	1	47	25		1	15	6	
State Conservation, Natural									
Resources & Lands Depts.	16	3	21	1	1		5	2	
State Forestry Depts.	14		12	3		1	1	1	
State Parks & Recreation Depts.	10						4	1	
Canadian Forestry Agencies	5		1	1			4		
Other Canadian Agencies	2						1		
TOTALS	268	7	167	43	2	5	146	30	1
Percent Change from Mindick's (1981) Survey	−14	−50	−35	−22	−33	+150	−8	−23	−50

communication techniques to the point that the most common ones can be used or requested on a routine basis. An example of such a course is also the first one ever offered. It was initiated at Colorado State University in 1959. It is taught in the College of Forestry and Natural Resources and is required of all majors in forest resources, fishery and wildlife biology, and recreation resource management. Ideally, additional course work will be taken in some of the public relations "tools" of particular interest, and a solid course in social-psychology is highly recommended.

Whether preparing for a career in public relations or trying to obtain a working knowledge to use along with resource management, coursework in personnel management and political science is also worthwhile but usually missing from curricula in natural resource colleges.

Recreation Resource Mgt.				Communication				Others				No Degree
Assoc.	BS/A	MS/A	Doc.	Assoc.	BS/A	MS/A	Doc.	Assoc.	BS/A	MS/A	Doc.	
						1			4	1		
					4	1			2			5
	1			1	15	5		1	7	2		6
						1				1	2	
	8	2		1	1				4			
					6	1			6	1	1	5
		1			10	3		1	9	4		7
1	10	1			20	4		3	32	11		40
	2				3	1			7	1	1	
	41	5	1		5			4	33	6	2	14
	2	4			11	3		1	7	7	1	5
	1	2		6	63	13		6	24	8	1	65
	4	3		3	53	8		8	21	11	2	21
					7	3		1	3			
	3	1		1	7	1		1	7			
	1				2				3			16
				1				2	1			6
1	73	19	1	13	207	45	0	28	170	53	10	190
0	−26	−37	0	−41	−25	+28	−100	+154	+16	−5	+100	+19

Continuing Education

There is an ever increasing awareness of the need for continuing education in all areas of professional endeavor. This is particularly true in public relations. For a great many natural resource managers, workshops and short courses provide their first exposure to the theories and practice of public relations, and to using the many tools to favorably influence public opinion. This kind of brief training is at best an introduction, but helps fill the void made by their being no such courses in the curricula required for most foresters, wildlife managers and other natural resource managers. For information specialists and public relations practitioners, continuing education is an opportunity for upgrading skills and learning of new equipment or techniques. To *any* professional, continuing education should be considered an essential part of growth and the only sure deterrent to mental stagnation.

Continuing education takes many shapes, but is usually considered any kind of nonformal educational activity for individuals who are not actively persuing college degrees. It ranges from in-service sessions conducted by the employing organization for an hour or a day or more, to short courses or workshops[2] conducted externally for varying periods of time by professional societies, universities, or private firms. Continuing education can also include correspondence courses, sabbatical leaves, noncredit evening courses, and staying current through reading professional publications. Because of the variety of "delivery methods" available and the increased motivation for learning that follows post-college entrance into the working world, continuing education offers one of our best opportunities to provide the necessary skills for overcoming public relations deficiencies in the natural resource management professions.

The integration of public relations into natural resource continuing education has been underway for some time, but activity seems to be increasing and the potential is unlimited. Past efforts have included presentations and sessions at annual meetings of such professional organizations as the Society of American Foresters or Association of Interpretive Naturalists; in-service schools in nearly every agency; orientation programs for new employees, especially the well-organized system used for all new professionals in the USDA Forest Service and National Park Service; and workshops at a number of universities, most focusing on various communication skills. Correspondence courses in some of the communication skills are offered by many universities, the Armed Forces Institute and the USDA Graduate School. A successful correspondence course in interpretive methods has been initiated in the College of Forest Resources at the University of Washington, and a course based on this text is available through the University of Idaho.

For many years the authors conducted week-long short courses at two universities that included the following topics:

*The theory (definitions and principles) of public relations.
*Identifying and applying the tools of public relations.
*Improving oral presentations through the use of visual aids, including the more effective use of slide graphics, multiple projectors and presentation mannerisms.
*Improving photography and writing skills.
*Working with the mass media, both print and electronic.
*Understanding children and young people as a special public.
*Familiarization with videotape equipment and the production of automated sound/slide shows.

These were intensive courses, but the post-course evaluations invariably emphasized that the content met a real need. By being held on a campus and being open to any agency, these courses had the added benefit of providing the opportunity for participants to meet people with similar problems and interests. This, in turn, stimulated a rich exchange of ideas. Importantly, despite nationwide annual publicity, the courses rarely attracted participants from beyond an area roughly equivalent to a quarter of the United States. This is convincing evidence that similar short courses are needed to serve professionals in every region. The benefits are many, and the courses can easily become self-sufficient through registration fees.

As travel costs rise, it will be imperative to offer educational opportunities closer to home. This may include more courses to serve smaller geographical areas, or it may require new, innovative approaches. The latter are likely to include a course where instructors and their equipment

2. The term workshop usually implies more of a hands-on experience than a solely lecture format.

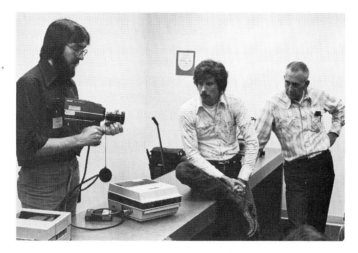

Figure 14.2. Learning is a life-long experience. Short courses and workshops provide opportunities for updating or learning new skills. (Photo by J. R. Fazio.)

travel a circuit to locations where professionals from several agencies can easily gather. It may also mean videotaped courses, or in the more populated areas of the country, the use of public access channels on cable television.

Most people desire some kind of recognition for their participation in continuing education. When a college or university is involved in the program, there are two ways to achieve this, both offering tangible incentives beyond the satisfaction of self-improvement. One is college credit if the criteria for this are met and participants qualify to receive credit from the sponsoring institution. These credits are recorded on a transcript and may be applied toward college degrees, again depending on the rules of the specific institutions. However, most continuing education is offered on a noncredit basis. There is now a way for these kinds of offerings to also be recorded on a "transcript" and made available upon request to use with job applications or for other verification purposes. (For example, the SAF provides certification of accomplishment to members who complete 150 hours of continuing education over a three year period.) The system for recording participation in continuing education involves the CEU (Continuing Education Unit). This may be awarded on a basis of 1 CEU for each 10 hours of attendance. While it is not applicable to any degree and can not be transformed into college credits, neither does it require testing or other work other than attendance and normal participation in the short course, workshop, or even a conference. A record of CEU's will then be maintained by the sponsor and made available on request. To help centralize records, there is now a National Registry for Continuing Education maintained by the American College Testing Program (P.O. Box 168, Iowa City, IA 52240). These developments offer considerable potential for helping to stimulate public relations education among natural resource managers who never had this as part of their formal degree program.

Societies and Publications

Anyone with a sincere interest in public relations will seek ways for self-improvement. One of the best methods is through membership in appropriate professional organizations. This provides access to annual conferences, a regular supply of current reading material, interaction and exchange with others having similar interests, and news such as notification of job openings or continuing education programs. There are many organizations from which to select, some being more appropriate than others, depending on an individual's position. Some of these are listed below:

Association of Interpretive Naturalists
6700 Needwood Rd.
Derwood, MD 20855

Interpretation Canada

Western Interpreter's Association
P.O. Box 28366
Sacramento, CA 95828

These first three organizations represent over 2,000 individuals with a high degree of interest and specialization in communication. Although interpretation is usually considered a special use of communication and is by no means synonymous with public relations practice, the two fields share much in common. A public relations practitioner could learn much from interpreters, and interpreters have much to learn about public relations.

Society of American Foresters
5400 Grosvenor Lane
Bethesda, MD 20814

Of its more than 21,000 members, those with an interest in the broad area of communications and public relations have joined together in an "Education and Communication" working group. The primary activities are a meeting at the annual convention, assuring representation on the program, and input into other SAF activities. SAF was also a cooperator in the production of this book.

The Wildlife Society
5410 Grosvenor Lane
Bethesda, MD 20814

Co-sponsors of the North American Wildlife and Natural Resources Conference, a major annual event where public relations is nearly always a topic.

American Association of Conservation Information
(no permanent address. Contact state fish and game departments)

Made up of I & E specialists primarily in state fish and game departments. They publish a quarterly, *Balance Wheel.*

Outdoor Writers Association of America
2017 Cato Ave.
Suite 101
State College, PA 16801

An organization of professional communicators that uses all media. Membership is open to anyone meeting specific criteria for the regular output of information (so many articles per year, etc.). The annual workshop and monthly publication, *Outdoors Unlimited,* are highly informative and pertinent to public relations.

National Association of Government
 Communicators
  P.O. Box 7127
  Alexandria, VA 22307

Created in 1976 and made up of more than 1,000 government employees, it sponsors continuing education programs, strives to gain professional recognition for information officers, works with the U.S. Office of Personnel Management to upgrade job standards, and is attempting to have laws repealed that limit public relations functions in government.

Public Relations Society of America
  845 Third Avenue
  New York, NY 10022

The principal organization of public relations professionals in all fields. Publishes the monthly *Public Relations Journal,* strives to uphold high ethics in public relations practice, and offers a wide variety of important services to its approximately 9,000 members.

Public Affairs Council
  1220 Sixteenth St., NW
  Washington, DC 20036

An organization of corporate public affairs executives. Through publications, conferences and numerous short courses, this organization attempts to increase the effectiveness of personnel from its approximately 300 corporate members. Strongly oriented toward the political arena.

In addition to publications that come through membership in the above organizations, numerous others are available that contribute to improving public relations practice. Many have been listed in other chapters; several additional ones are listed below. Mailing addresses and subscription information are available at most libraries:

Advertising Age
A-V Communications Review
Broadcasting
Columbia Journalism Review
Human Relations
Jack O'Dwyer's Newsletter
Journal of Advertising
Journal of Applied Psychology
Journal of Broadcasting
Journal of Communications
Journal of Environmental Education

Journal of Marketing
Journal of Personality and Social Psychology
Journalism Quarterly
Marketing/Communications
PR Reporter
Practical Public Relations
Public Opinion Quarterly
Public Relations News
Public Relations Quarterly
Public Relations Review
Quill
Television Quarterly

PEOPLE AND NATURAL RESOURCE MANAGEMENT

The past is prologue, wrote Shakespeare. So, in closing, let us take one more look backwards.

Warning that history could repeat itself, Henry Vaux (1980) pointed out an interesting episode from the very dawn of modern democracy. He explained that some of the first natural resource managers were game keepers—called *foresters*—on the hunting estates of the English nobility. Most management was for the king's hunting pleasures, as well as for the production of wood supplies for the almost constant warfare of the Middle Ages. It so happened there was very little understanding among the king's subjects about how the foresters were in any way serving the needs of the nation. Thus, in the 13th century when the English noblemen confronted King John with the *Magna Carta*, there was an entire section devoted to forests and abating "the evil customs of the king's foresters."

Some might see an analogy with the many laws and regulations of the past decades that have given lawyers and courts so much control of land management. Vaux made the point that unless foresters become more sensitive and responsive to the values of the people who are to be served, especially *urban* people, we could see the entire practice of forestry legislated out of existence. In that we are rapidly becoming an urban nation, the point should not be lost on *any* natural resource manager.

A great many people still view the manipulation of resources as "evil." Their views have been heard, and the result is that not a resource manager in this nation can any longer operate in a vacuum, or surrounded only by like-minded colleagues. By legal mandate as well as by moral obligation, communicating with people from all walks of life must now be considered standard operating procedure. Those who ignore this fact risk their own reputations as well as their employer's. Those who accept it may see it as we do—an unprecedented opportunity for good public relations. With planning, practice and skill, public interest in natural resource management can be parlayed into support. And with public support, few things can fail; without it little can succeed. As pointed out long ago by Abraham Lincoln, "He who molds opinion is greater than he who enacts laws."

Public relations is the essential business of gaining support. Sound technical performance in natural resource management is the foundation, but upon this must be open, honest, two-way communication with people inside and external to the organization. This is the greatest part of natural resource management, and the most challenging. Fortunately, natural resource managers have come a long way in recognizing that people are part of the woods, fields and waters of our nation. Still, as professionals, we have a long way to go before our relationships with those people are harmonious and strong. This is the job of public relations practice, and good public relations is an essential part of good natural resource management.

Bibliography

Albig, W. 1956. Modern public opinion. McGraw-Hill Co. New York.

Anderson, Jack. 1978a. Energy education. Moscow (Idaho) Idahonian Aug. 9.

———. 1978b. Engineers shine own light: congressmen left in dark. Washington Merry-Go-Round, United Feature Syndicate. Washington, D.C. Aug. 21.

Anonymous. 1968. Superchief of information. Time. 92(23): 30–31

———. 1976. Smokey Bear dies: buried in own park. Science News. 110(21): 327.

———. 1977. So long, Smokey. American Forests. 83(1): cover.

———. 1978. Producing 'In Search of Balance.' Parks & Recreation. 13(9): 56–60, 72–73.

Archibald, Samuel J. 1967. Public relations, politics and government. Public Relations Journal. 23(6): 38–40.

Arndt, Johan. 1968. A test of the two step flow in diffusion of a new product. Journalism Quarterly. 45: 457–465.

Arnold, Edmund C. 1972. Ink on paper 2: a handbook of the graphic arts. Harper & Row, Publishers, New York.

Arnstein, Sherry R. 1969. A ladder of citizen participation. American Institute of Planners Journal. 35(4): 216–224.

Audiovisual Notes from Kodak. 1982. Computer generated slides offer wide range of capabilities and prices. T-91-2-1, Eastman Kodak Co., Rochester, NY.

Baertsch, Blaine. 1977. State government PR grows. Idaho Communication Review. 2(1): 5, 11.

Balsley, Gene and Peter Moore. 1980. How to file and store slides. Modern Photography. 44(1): 104–107.

Barker, Larry L. 1971. Listening behavior. Prentice-Hall, Inc. Englewood Cliffs, N.J.

Belak, Edmund R., Jr. 1972. The outdoor magazines revisited. Journal of Environmental Education. 4(1): 15–19.

Bell, Ray L. 1970. The true story of Smokey Bear. (Mimeo).

Benneth, John E. 1967. The engines of public opinion. American Forest Products Industries. Washington, DC.

Billington, Ray Allen. 1974. Westward expansion: a history of the American frontier. The Macmillan Co. New York.

Bird, Donald E. 1953. Teaching listening comprehension. Journal of Communication. Nov. pp. 127–130.

———. 1954. Have you tried listening? Journal of the American Dietetic Association. March. pp. 225–230.

Bramlette, W. W. 1977. Communication characteristics and knowledge levels of Selway-Bitterroot Wilderness users. Master's thesis. University of Idaho. Moscow.

Breiter, L. 1957. Research in listening and its importance to literature. Master's thesis. Brookly College. Brooklyn, NY.

Brion, J. P. 1967. How to build good will from a "hole in the ground." Public Relations Journal. 23(3): 20–22.

Bromley, A. W. 1945. Evaluation of the New York state experimental cooperative landowner-sportsman controlled public hunting grounds program, 1939–1943. Trans. N. Am. Wildl. Conf. 10: 9–29.

Bryan, Hobson and John C. Hendee. 1983. Social impact analysis in the U.S. Forest Service: background and proposed principles. Proceedings of the Interagency Symposium on Social Impact Analysis. Rural Sociology Society, San Francisco.

Cantor, B. and C. Burger (eds.). 1984. Experts in Action: Inside Public Relations. Longman Inc., New York.

Carter, Betsy, Cynthia H. Wilson and Lucy Howard. 1979. No to 'advertorials.' Newsweek 94(1):57.

Center, Allen H. 1975. Public relations practices. Prentice-Hall, Inc. Englewood Cliffs, NJ.

Chalk, J. D., D. I. Rasmussen, F. C. Edminster, C. M. Reed, A. Nicholson, and J. P. Miller. 1940. Is the farmer-sportsman council the answer? Trans. N. Am. Wildl. Conf. 5:54–72.

Cobb, Tom. 1975. So long, Smokey. American Forests 81(8): 30–31.

Cockrell, Patsy. 1985. 1985 Forest Fire Prevention Campaign. Fire Management Notes 46(2):16–17.

Cohen, Wilbur J. 1967. Public information in a democratic society. Public Relations Journal 23(12):6–8.

Communications Act Amendments. 1960. Public Law 86–752, 74 Stat. 889 (Amending Communications Act of 1934, Public Law 73–416, 48 Stat. 1064).

Cook, William W. 1978. Fact-finding for public relations. *In* Lesly, Philip (ed.). Lesly's public relations handbook. Prentice-Hall, Inc. Englewood Cliffs, NJ.

Culbreath, J. C. 1949. Phase of public relations and their effect upon game management. Proc. W. Assoc. State Game and Fish Comm. 29: 45–51.

Cummings, Jr., Milton C. and David Wise. 1971. Democracy under pressure: an introduction to the American political system. Harcourt Brace Jovanovich, Inc. New York.

Cutlip, Scott M. and Allen H. Center. 1978. Effective public relations. Prentice-Hall, Inc. Englewood Cliffs, NJ.

Cutlip, Scott M., Allen H. Center and Glen M. Broom. 1985. Effective public relations. Prentice-Hall, Inc. Englewood Cliffs, NJ.

Dana, S. T. (ed.). 1953. History of activities in the field of natural resources, University of Michigan. University of Michigan Press, Ann Arbor.

Decker, Daniel J. 1985. Agency image: a key to successful natural resource management. Trans. 41st Northeast Sec. Wildlife Society, Hartford, CT.

Delbecq, Andre L., Andrew H. Van de ven and David H. Gustafson. 1975. Group techniques for program planning: a guide to nominal group and Delphi processes. Scott, Foresman and Co. Glenview, Il.

DeRocco, Tom. 1974. Preparation for public ceremonies. Outdoor Recreation Action. Bureau of Outdoor Recreation Report 33, Fall.

Dick, Ronald E., David T. McKee and J. Alan Wagar. 1974. A summary and annotated bibliography of communications principles. Journal of Environmental Education 5(4): 8–13.

Dickson, A. 1970. Receptivity of absentee forest owners to extension forestry. Ph.D. dissertation. SUNY, Syracuse.

Dillman, Don A. 1978. Mail and telephone surveys. John Wiley and Sons, New York.

Eastman Kodak Co. 1967. Audiovisual projection. Kodak Pamphlet No. 5–3. Rochester, NY.

Editor and Publisher International Yearbook. 1980. Editor and Publisher, New York.

Fairfax, Sally K. 1975. Public involvement and the Forest Service. Journal of Forestry 73(10): 657–659.

Fazio, James R. 1967. The image builders. The Northern Logger and Timber Processer 16(6): 12–13, 52–53.

———. 1971. A description and evaluation of a communications short course for natural resources personnel. Master's paper. Cornell University, Ithaca, NY.

———. 1975. Liberty Hyde Bailey and Enos A. Mills, pioneers in environmental interpretation. Nature Study 29: 1–3, 12.

———, and Lawrence A. Belli. 1977. Characteristics of nonconsumptive wildlife users in Idaho. Trans. N. Am. Wildl. and Nat. Resources Conf. 42: 117–128.

———. 1979. Communicating with the wilderness user. University of Idaho Forest, Wildlife and Range Exper. Sta. Bull. No. 29. Moscow, ID.

———. 1983. Fulfilling the needs of forestry students in developing communication skills. *In* Proceedings 1983 Society of American Foresters, Portland, Oregon. Society of American Foresters, Washington, D.C.

Federal Communications Commission. 1974. Broadcast application. U.S. Government Printing Office, Washington, DC.

Festinger, L. 1957. A Theory of cognitive dissonance. Row, Peterson Co. Evanston, IL.

Fishbein, Martin and Icek Ajzen. 1975. Belief, attitude, intention and behavior: an introduction to theory and research. Addison-Wesley Publishing Co. Reading, MA.

5 United States Code 54 (1913 ed.).

Flesch, Rudolf. 1949 and 1951. How to test readability. Harper & Row, New York.

———. 1974. The art of readable writing. Harper & Row, New York.

Foss, P. O. 1960. Politics and grass. University of Washington Press. Seattle.

———. 1971. Recreation: conservation in the United States, a documentary history. Chelsea House Publishers. New York.

Foster, Eugene S. 1978. Understanding broadcasting. Addison-Wesley Publishing Co. Reading, MA.

Gilbert, Douglas L. 1962. Public relations and communications in wildlife management. Doctorate dissertation, University of Michigan.

———. 1967. A short course for game and fish commissioners. Trans. N. Am. Wildl. and Nat. Resc. Conf. 32: 174–177.

———. 1971. Natural resources and public relations. The Wildlife Society, Washington, DC.

———, and R. R. Hill. 1964. The professional looks at sportsmen's organizations. Colorado Outdoors 13(6): 33–39.

Goulard, Cary Joe. 1974. The development of an analysis technique for determining the potential effectiveness of televised environmental public service announcements to cause effective change in urban adults. Ph.D. dissertation, State University of New York, College of Environmental Science and Forestry, Syracuse.

Guide to the Congress of the United States: origins, history and procedure. 1976. Congressional Quarterly Service. Washington, DC.

Gunning, R. 1952. The technique of clear writing. McGraw-Hill. New York.

———. 1962. More effective writing in business and industry. Industrial Education Institute. Boston, MA.

Ham, Sam H. 1980. Slides and sound in synch. The Interpreter 11(2): 8–10, 19.

Hardy, Mal. 1970. Smokey Bear—a biography. U.S. Forest Service. Washington, DC (Mimeo).

Harlow, Rex F. 1957. Social science in public relations. Harper & Brothers, Publishers. New York.

Hawver, Carl F. 1978. The public relations of government. *In* Lesley, Philip (ed.). Lesly's public relations handbook. Prentice-Hall, Inc. Englewood Cliffs, NJ.

Hays, Samuel P. 1960. Conservation and the gospel of efficiency: the progressive conservation movement, 1890–1920. Harvard University Press. Cambridge, MA.

Heberlein, Thomas A. 1976. Principles of public involvement. (Staff paper in Rural and Community Development). Cooperative Extension Programs. University of Wisconsin. Madison.

Herzberg, Frederick. 1976. One more time: how do you motivate employees? Pages 17–32 *in* M. M. Gruneberg (ed.). Job satisfaction—a reader. The Macmillan Press Ltd. London.

Hiebert, Ray Eldon. 1966. Courtier to the crowd: the story of Ivy Lee and the development of public relations. Iowa State University Press. Ames.

High Country News. Can the Forest Service be reformed? March 19, 1984, p. 15.

Hofstede, Geert H. 1972. The color of collars. Columbia Journal of World Business 7(5).

Hollen, C. C. 1972. Value change, perceived instrumentality, and attitude change. Ph.D. dissertation, Michigan State University.

Hovland, Carl I., Irving L. Janis and Harold H. Kelley. 1953. Communication and persuasion. Yale University Press. New Haven, CT.

Hunt, John and Perry J. Brown. 1971. Who can read our writing? Journal of Environmental Education 2(4): 27–29.

Information Please Almanac. 1985. Houghton Mifflin Co., Boston.

Johnson, David. 1978. Hearing fails to yank 2, 4, 5, -T issue from mire of confusion. Daily (Moscow) Idahonian 85(65): 1.

Keerdoja, Eileen. 1977. The twin logos. Newsweek 89(7): 9.

Kent, James A., Richard J. Greiwe, James E. Freeman and John J. Ryon. 1979. An approach to social resource management. Foundation for Urban and Neighborhood Development, Inc., and the John Ryon Co. Denver, CO.

Kiesler, C. A. and S. B. Kiesler. 1969. Conformity. Addison-Wesley Publishing Co. Reading, MA.

Kilgore, B. M. 1953. A survey of the use of motion pictures by state game and fish conservation departments. Masters Thesis. University of Oklahoma. Norman.

Klapper, Joseph T. 1960. The effects of mass communication. Free Press. Glencoe, IL.

Kodak Films. 1985. KODAK Publication No. AF-1. Rochester, NY

Leopold, Aldo. 1921. The wilderness and its place in forest recreational policy. Journal of Forestry 19:718–721.

Leopold, A., G. W. Wood, J. H. Baker, W. P. Taylor, and L. G. MacNamara. 1939. Farmer-sportsman, a partnership for wildlife restoration. Trans. N. Am. Wildl. Conf. 4: 144–146.

Lesly, Philip (ed.). 1983. Lesly's public relations handbook. Prentice-Hall, Inc. Englewood Cliffs, NJ.

Lessing, Lawrence. 1969. The printed word goes electronic. Fortune. 80(4): 116–119, 188–190.

Lionberger, Herbert F. 1960. Adoption of new ideas and practices. Iowa State University Press. Ames.

Machlis, Gary and Maureen McDonough. 1978. Children's interpretation: a discovery book for interpreters. National Park Service. U.S. Government Printing Office. Washington, DC.

Mager, Robert F. 1975. Preparing instructional objectives. Fearon Publishers. Palo Alto, CA.

Marlowe, Howard. 1978. How to affect legislation before it affects you. The Grantsmanship Center News 4(1): 23–30, 47–54.

Marsh, George Perkins. 1864. Man and nature; or, physical geography as modified by human action. Charles Scribner's Sons, New York.

Mater, Jean. 1977. Citizens involved: handle with care. Timber Press, Forest Grove, Oregon.

Miles, Thomas A. 1979. An evaluative comparison of single and dissolve slide projection techniques. Master's thesis. University of Idaho. Moscow.

Mindick, Robert. 1981. A survey of the current use of information and education in natural resource management agencies. Master's thesis. University of Idaho. Moscow.

Monroe, Alan H. and Douglas Ehninger. 1974. Principles and types of speech communication. Scott, Foresman and Co. Glenview, IL.

Moore, John L. (ed.). 1979. The Washington lobby. Congressional Quarterly, Inc. Washington, DC.

Mooty, J. J. 1967. License agents as an internal public of the Colorado Department of Game, Fish, and Parks. Master's thesis. Colorado State University.

Nash, Roderick. 1976. The American environment: readings in the history of conservation. Addison-Wesley Publishing Co. Reading, MA.

National Park Service. 1984. National park statistical abstract 1984. USDI National Park Service, Denver Service Center.

Nelson, Roy Paul. 1977. The design of advertising: an exploration of current practices and techniques. Wm. C. Brown Company Publishers, Dubuque, IA.

Nichols, R. and L. Stevens. 1957. Are you listening? McGraw-Hill Book Co. New York.

Norris, Roger A., Michael Heikkinen and Terry Armstrong. 1975. Alternatives for individualizing biology: the importance of cognitive style and conceptual complexity. The American Biology Teacher 37(5): 291–297.

O'Hayre, J. 1966. Gobbledygook has gotta go. Bureau of Land Mgmt. U.S. Government Printing Office. Washington, DC.

Olmsted, Frederick Law, Jr. and Theodora Kimbal (eds.). 1970. Frederick Law Olmsted—landscape architect, 1822–1903 (Vol. II). Benjamin Blom, Inc., New York.

Paletz, David L., Roberta E. Pearson and Donald L. Willis. 1977. Politics in public service advertising on television. Praeger Publishers, New York.

Pearce, J. Kenneth and George Stenzel. 1972. Logging and pulpwood production. The Ronald Press Co. New York.

Pengelly, W. L. 1959. Why conservation education for adults? Proc. W. Assoc. State Game and Fish Comm. 39:335–343.

Popovich, Luke. 1978. Forestry and the fading consensus. Journal of Forestry 76(10): 674–676.

Porter, Don K. and Richard F. Johnson. 1961. The public information officer's handbook. U.S. Forest Service, Southern Zone, California Region. (Mimeo.)

Presbrey, Frank. 1929. The history and development of advertising. Doubleday, Doran & Company, Inc. Garden City, NY.

Public Issues Research Bureau, Inc. 1976. Media analysis research: forest issues. In Research Recap. American Forest Institute. Washington, DC.

Putney, Allen D. and J. Alan Wagar. 1973. Objectives and evaluation in interpretive planning. Journal of Environmental Education 5(1): 43–44.

Rankin, P. 1929. Listening ability. Proceedings of the Ohio State Educational Conference's Ninth Annual Session. The Ohio State University. Columbus.

Robinson, Gail. 1978. The lessons of the Alaska coalition. Environmental Action 9(47): 10–11.

Rodgers III, Andrew Denny. 1951. Bernard Eduard Fernow: a story of North American forestry. Princeton University Press. Princeton, NJ.

Rogers, E. M. and F. F. Shoemaker. 1971. Communication of innovations. The Free Press. New York.

Rokeach, Milton. 1968a. Beliefs, attitudes and values. Jossey-Bass Inc. San Francisco, CA.

———. 1968b. The role of values in public opinion research. Public Opinion Quarterly 32(4): 547–559.

———. 1971. Long-range experimental modification of values, attitudes and behavior. American Psychologist 26(5): 453–459.

———. 1973. The nature of human values. The Free Press. New York.

Rosenthal, H. C. 1967. Create maximum value from your annual report. Public Relations Journal 23(11): 37.

Sandage, C. H., and V. Fryburger. 1971. Advertising theory and practice. Richard D. Irwin, Inc. Homewood, IL.

Sandfort, Steve and John F. Cone. 1977. Using television effectively. Journal of Forestry 75(2): 80–83.

Schneider, David J. 1976. Social psychology. Addison-Wesley Publishing Co. Reading, MA.

Schoenfeld, C. A. 1957. Public relations aspects of wildlife management. Journal of Wildlife Management 21(1): 70–74.

———. 1972. Irruption in environmental communications. American Forests 78(10): 20–22, 52–55.

Seigel, Kalman. 1972. Talking back to the New York Times: letters to the editor, 1851–1971. Quadrangle/The New York Times Book Co. New York.

Shadduck, Louise. 1977. PR can soften 'future shock.' Idaho Communication Review 2(1): 4,12.

Sharpe, Grant W. (Ed.). 1982. Interpreting the environment. John Wiley & Sons. New York.

———, Clare W. Hendee and Shirley W. Allen. 1976. Introduction to forestry. McGraw-Hill Book Co., New York.

Shaw, D. L. and D. L. Gilbert. 1974. Attitudes of college students toward hunting. Trans. of the 39th N. Am. Wildl. and Nat. Res. Conf. 39: 157–162.

Shaw, William W. and William R. Mangun. 1984. Nonconsumptive Use of Wildlife in the United States. U.S. Fish and Wildlife Service Res. Publ. 154. U.S. Government Printing Office, Washington, DC.

Shick, C. No Date. Farmer-hunter relations. Mich. Cons. Dept., Michigan State University. Coop. Ext. Serv. Unpubl. Rept. (Mimeo).

Shiner, James William and Elwood L. Shafer, Jr. 1975. How long do people look at and listen to forest-oriented exhibits? USDA For. Serv. Res. Pap. NE–325. NE For. Exp. Stn. Upper Darby, PA.

Shomon, J. J. 1952. Education in resource use: our most challenging task in human relations. Trans. N. Am. Wildl. Conf. 17: 525–533.

Smits, L. J. 1937. Publicity in wildlife restoration. Trans. N. Am. Wildl. Conf. 20: 603–609.

Solo, Robert A. and Everett M. Rogers (Eds.). 1972. Inducing technological change for economic growth and development. Michigan State University Press.

Statistical Abstract of the United States. 1985. U.S. Dept. of Commerce. Bureau of the Census. Washington, DC.

Steen, Harold K. 1976. The U.S. Forest Service—a history. University of Washington Press. Seattle.

Strong, Douglas H. 1971. The conservationists. Addison-Wesley Publishing Co. Menlo Park, CA.

Tilden, Freeman. 1977. Interpreting our heritage. The Univ. of North Carolina Press, Chapel Hill.

Titus, H., G. W. Bradt, J. H. Cline, and W. F. Kirk. 1939. Farmer-sportsman, a partnership for wildlife restoration. Trans. N. Am. Wildl. Conf. 4: 176–200.

Trefethen, James B. 1975. An American crusade for wildlife. Winchester Press and the Boone and Crockett Club. New York.

Trudeau, Richard C. 1978. The changing role of public information—after Jarvis-Gann. Parks & Recreation 76(13): 23.

U.S. Department of Labor. 1984. Occupational outlook handbook. U.S. Government Printing Office. Washington, DC.

U.S. Office of Personnel Management. 1983. Occupations of federal white-collar and blue-collar workers. U.S. Government Printing Office. Washington, D.C.

U.S. Senate, Subcommittee on Administrative Practice and Procedure of the Committee on the Judiciary. 1974. Freedom of Information Act source book: legislative materials, cases, articles. U.S. Government Printing Office. Washington, DC.

VanLeuven, James K. 1980. Measuring values through public participation. Public Relations Review 6(1): 51–56.

Vaux, Henry J. 1980. Urban forestry: bridge to the profession's future. Journal of Forestry 78(5): 260–262.

Wagar, J. V. K. 1958. Can weak-kneed public education retain rare wildlife values? Trans. N. Am. Wildl. Conf. 23: 526–532.

Wagar, Alan J., Gregory W. Lovelady, and Harlan Falkin. 1976. Evaluation techniques for interpretation: study results from an exhibition on energy. USDA For. Serv. Res. Pap. PNW-211. Pacific NW For. and Range Exp. Sta. Portland, OR.

Walters, L. and G. Seiben. 1974. Cognitive style and learning science in elementary schools. Science Education 58: 65–74.

Washburne, Randel F. and J. Alan Wagar. 1972. Evaluating visitor response to exhibit content. Curator 15(3): 248–254.

Waters, Harry F., Lucy Howard and Synthia Wilson. 1979. TV's local magazines. Newsweek 94(27): 50–51.

Webb, E. J., D. T. Campbell, R. D. Schwartz and L. Sechrest. 1966. Unobtrusive measure: non-reactive research in the social sciences. Rand-McNally. Chicago, IL.

Webster's New Collegiate Dictionary. 1973. G. & C. Merriam Co., Springfield, MA.

Wessel, Milton R. 1976. The rule of reason: a new approach to corporate litigation. Addison-Wesley Publishing Co. Reading, MA.

White, Daniel L. 1979. Electronic media in natural resources communication: what is available and what is being used in the field. *In* Curt J. Berklund Undergraduate Research. College of Forestry, Wildlife and Range Sciences. University of Idaho. Moscow.

Wild, Peter. 1979. Pioneer conservationists of western America. Mountain Press Publishing Co., Missoula, MT.

Wildlife Management Institute. 1968. Organization, authority, and programs of state fish and wildlife agencies. Washington, DC.

———. 1977. Organization, authority, and programs of state fish and wildlife agencies. Washington, DC.

Wilt, M. 1949. A study of teacher awareness of listening as a factor in elementary education. Ph.D. dissertation. Pennsylvania State University. State College.

World Almanac, The. 1985. Newspaper Enterprise Association, New York.

Wray, Robert D. 1977. Foresters can write. Journal of Forestry 75(2): 77–79.

Zelko, H. P. 1970. What's wrong with public speaking? Public Relations Journal 26(1): 23–24.

Zeller, Tom. 1984. Indiana activists blaze forest management trails. Audubon Action, October.

Zimbardo, Philip G., Ebbe B. Ebbesen and Christina Maslach. 1977. Influencing attitudes and changing behavior. Addison-Wesley Publishing Co. Reading, MA.

Zimmerman, Donald E., Clifford Scherer and Mark Larson. 1978. The use of conservation and environmental mass media by Pennsylvania educators. Journal of Environmental Education 10(2): 43–48.

Index